Frank Adloff, Katharina Gerund, David Kaldewey (eds.)
Revealing Tacit Knowledge

Presence and Tacit Knowledge | Volume 2

Frank Adloff, Katharina Gerund, David Kaldewey (eds.)
Revealing Tacit Knowledge
Embodiment and Explication

[transcript]

Funded by the DFG (German Research Foundation)

Bibliographic information published by the Deutsche Nationalbibliothek
The Deutsche Nationalbibliothek lists this publication in the Deutsche Nationalbibliografie; detailed bibliographic data are available in the Internet at http://dnb.d-nb.de

© **2015 transcript Verlag, Bielefeld**

All rights reserved. No part of this book may be reprinted or reproduced or utilized in any form or by any electronic, mechanical, or other means, now known or hereafter invented, including photocopying and recording, or in any information storage or retrieval system, without permission in writing from the publisher.

Cover concept: Angela Nentwig
Typeset by Mark-Sebastian Schneider, Bielefeld
Printed in Germany
Print-ISBN 978-3-8376-2516-5
PDF-ISBN 978-3-8394-2516-9

Content

Locations, Translations, and Presentifications of Tacit Knowledge
An Introduction
Frank Adloff, Katharina Gerund, and David Kaldewey | 7

PART I: LOCATIONS

Tacit Knowledge: Shared and Embodied
Jens Loenhoff | 21

Embodiment of Tacit Knowledge
Practices between Dispositifs and Interaction
Michael Hubrich | 41

The Background of Moods and Atmospheres
Sociological Observations
Rainer Schützeichel | 61

Tacit Knowledge in a Differentiated Society
David Kaldewey | 87

Questions to Theodore R. Schatzki
David Kaldewey and Theodore R. Schatzki | 113

PART II: TRANSLATIONS

First- and Second-Order Tacit Knowledge
Sociological Consequences of Consequent Pragmatism
Joachim Renn | 121

Tacit Knowledge and Analytic Autoethnography
Methodological Reflections on the Sociological Translation
of Self-Experience
Alexander Antony | 139

Racial Formation, Implicit Understanding, and Problems with Implicit Association Tests
Alexis Shotwell | 169

For a Sociology of Flesh and Blood
Questions to Loïc Wacquant
Frank Adloff and Loïc Wacquant | 185

PART III: PRESENTIFICATIONS

Tacit Knowledge, Public Feeling, and the Pursuits of (Un-)Happiness
Heike Paul | 197

The End of Life and the Limits of Explication
Metaphors and Time in *Everyman* and *Tinkers*
Stephen Koetzing | 223

Moving Images of Thought
Notes on the Diagrammatic Dimension of Film Metaphor
Christoph Ernst | 245

Improvising Faith
An Essay on Implicit Knowledge and Living within God's Story
Wolfgang Schoberth | 279

Questions to Mark Johnson
Katharina Gerund and Mark L. Johnson | 299

List of Contributors | 307

Locations, Translations, and Presentifications of Tacit Knowledge
An Introduction

Frank Adloff, Katharina Gerund, and David Kaldewey

The concept of 'tacit knowledge' points to a set of theoretical and methodological questions in a wide range of academic disciplines (including philosophy, sociology, pedagogy, business administration, linguistics, psychology, cognitive science, and cultural studies). In addition, it refers to diverse practical problems (for example knowledge management in organizations, creative practices in the arts, religious rituals, intercultural communication, or racism). It is not easy to give a precise definition of tacit knowledge: The term may denote the skills we need for bodily performances such as bicycling, playing a musical instrument, or conducting experiments in the laboratory, but it may also point to culture-specific intuitions and pre-reflexive assumptions that determine the way we interact with the world and with society. Any approach to tacit knowledge is characterized by a basic paradox: If this kind of embodied and pre-reflexive knowledge underlies all of our actions and all knowledge production, then how is it possible for us to access it – let alone describe it in the propositional language of scholarly discourse? If this knowledge is in fact tacit, then how (and to which degree) can we transform it into explicit knowledge? One could argue that as soon as tacit knowledge is explicated, it no longer is 'tacit,' and has thus been lost in the act of translation. Following this reasoning, academic discourse may run the risk of viewing tacit knowledge as both ubiquitous and elusive, and surrounding the realm of the tacit with an aura of obscurity.

But is tacit knowledge really that mysterious? If one claims that it is everywhere, that it underlies all explicit knowledge and informs all of our actions, then tacit knowledge actually seems to be neither mystical nor exceptional but rather quite ordinary and maybe even trivial. As Harry Collins (2010: 7-8) puts it:

What the individual human body and human brain do is not so different from what cats, dogs, and, for that matter, trees and clouds have always done. While humans encounter bodily abilities as strange and difficult because we continually fail in our attempts to explicate them, there is nothing mysterious about the knowledge itself.

Yet, if it is in fact everywhere, then it must at least be possible in one way or another to reconstruct, describe, and analyze the manifold processes by which the tacit reveals itself (or is revealed). The contributions to the present volume demonstrate the wide range of current research on tacit knowledge but also probe the limits of accessing and explicating the tacit dimension by employing diverse analytical strategies from different disciplines. Basically, we distinguish three such analytical strategies, which correspond to the three sections of this volume and serve as its organizing principle: The first approach aims at locating tacit knowledge in different sociological and philosophical frameworks (I); the second strategy revolves around the methodological problems of translating tacit knowledge (II); the third approach builds on the concepts of presence and presentification, and is based on the premise that tacit knowledge reveals itself and becomes tangible in manifold forms, for example, in metaphors, feelings, visualizations, or creative practices such as musical improvisation (III).

A survey of the research on tacit knowledge shows that it has long been dominated by philosophical and epistemological studies. Here, the main interest has been to define tacit knowledge in contrast to explicit, discursive, or propositional forms of knowledge and to explain how the two are interrelated. Although the term 'tacit knowledge' was introduced and popularized only in the mid-twentieth century by Michael Polanyi (cf. 1958, 1966), the idea that we have to distinguish systematically between different forms of knowledge is much older: Greek philosophers such as Plato and the Neoplatonists already held that propositional knowledge was complemented by practical skills, experience, and intuitive vision (cf. Wieland 1982: 224ff.), and Aristotle's distinction between theoretical (*epistêmê, nous, sophia*), practical (*phronêsis*), and productive (*technê*) virtues can be understood as a first systematic classification of tacit and explicit forms of knowledge. Nevertheless, in the history of Western philosophy knowledge has mostly been conceived of as propositional knowledge, not least because only this form of knowledge can be methodologically secured and codified in truth-apt sentences. This bias toward propositional knowledge led to a preoccupation with validity claims: Is tacit knowledge 'real' knowledge, although it cannot be verified? Apparently, it becomes 'true' not through valid propositions but through practical success (cf. Renn's contribution to this volume).

This rationalist tradition was prominently challenged by pragmatism, which points to the habitual practices and routines that enable and guide human action. William James for example distinguished between "knowledge of acquaintance" and "knowledge about" (1950 [1890]: 221ff.), anticipating Gilbert Ryle's famous distinction between "knowing how" and "knowing that"

(1945/46). John Dewey also dealt with the relationship between these forms of knowledge and stressed that our experience of the world must not be reduced to its cognitive aspects. For Dewey, our interaction with the world is grounded in pre-reflexive forms of "primary experiences" that underlie the "secondary experiences," such as thinking, knowing, or reflective imagination (cf. Antony's paper in this volume). The idea that non-explicit forms of knowledge are actually the privileged mode of our being-in-the-world can also be found in Ludwig Wittgenstein's philosophy of language and in Martin Heidegger's fundamental ontology (cf. Loenhoff 2012a). Thus, several important philosophical currents of the 20th century have dealt systematically with the problem of tacit knowledge. However, this does not mean that they have developed a common understanding or even a commonly accepted definition of tacit knowledge.[1]

In the last decades, research on tacit knowledge has taken different trajectories and developed along diverse lines of inquiry. One development that can be reconstructed moved from the philosophical discourse on tacit knowledge that had dominated discussions up into the 1960s to a more complex and varied debate which started to take off in the 1970s when other disciplines entered the discursive arena. For example, in the emerging field of science studies, the ideas of authors such as Ludwig Wittgenstein, Michael Polanyi, and Thomas Kuhn were used to challenge the traditional claim that scientific knowledge is rational and objective by showing that it is embedded in social contexts and thus also depends on the tacit knowledge of social actors (cf. Barnes 1974; Bloor 1973, 1976; Collins 1974). This approach integrated philosophical accounts of tacit knowledge into the sociology of knowledge. An important rediscovery in this context had been the work of Karl Mannheim, whose contribution to the problem of tacit knowledge seems to have been neglected until today. Following Mannheim, knowledge is always rooted in a certain "conjunctive experiential space" (*konjunktiver Erfahrungsraum*). The knowledge acquired in such a social space is "a-theoretical" and has to be distinguished from "theoretical" or "communicative" forms of knowledge (cf. Mannheim 1964, 1980; Bohnsack 2006).

One of the most influential sociological perspectives on tacit knowledge has been inspired by Pierre Bourdieu. With the notion of habitus Bourdieu aimed at an empirical reconstruction of the embodiment of tacit knowledge and thereby stressed that social structures are implicitly present in the bodies of individuals, which at the same time unconsciously reproduce these very structures through their practical behavior. Against the background of Bourdieu's "theory of practice" (1977) on the one hand and the philosophical conceptualizations of tacit knowledge on the other, the sociological perspective gained momentum in the 1990s in the form of the so-called "practice turn"

---

1 | For an overview of the current debate on tacit knowledge see Gascoigne/Thornton (2013) and the edited volume by Loenhoff (2012b).

(cf. Turner 1994; Schatzki 1996; Schatzki/Knorr Cetina/von Savigny 2001; cf. also the interview with Schatzki in this volume). By focusing on the relevance of tacit knowledge as a resource for the creative handling of all kinds of situations, practice theory can be understood as drawing on pragmatism while at the same time integrating insights from contemporary social theories (cf. Hubrich's paper in this volume). Building, among others, on Bourdieu's theory of practice, Loïc Wacquant proposes a "sociology of flesh and blood" that acknowledges the entanglement of "body, mind, activity, and world" (cf. his contribution to the present volume).

The short overview of the history of the concept demonstrates that tacit knowledge is not only an epistemological problem but also points to basic aspects of social reality. It is therefore not surprising that starting in the 1980s and 1990s the issue has – sometimes implicitly, sometimes explicitly – been taken up by ever more disciplines: In anthropology, Clifford Geertz (cf. 1983, 1992) introduced the concept of "local knowledge" to criticize the search for a universal and generalizable knowledge about "all societies" (1992: 131);[2] in performance studies, Diana Taylor has introduced the terms "archive" and "repertoire" to differentiate between "supposedly enduring materials" and "embodied practice/knowledge," and has argued for taking the latter seriously as a form of valid knowledge (2003: 16); in cognitive linguistics, George Lakoff and Mark Johnson developed a theory of metaphor that reveals the tacit dimension of language and communication (cf. Lakoff/Johnson 1980, 1999; Johnson 1987; cf. also the interview with Johnson and the contributions by Ernst and Koetzing in this volume); in psychology, Arthur S. Reber (cf. 1989, 1993) proposed a theory of "implicit learning" that takes into account the problem of unconscious cognition and explains how learning processes produce tacit knowledge; furthermore, the relevance of tacit knowledge for learning processes is also of interest for pedagogy (cf. Neuweg 1999) as well as organizational behavior and management studies (cf. Sternberg/Horvath 1999).

Actually it is the latter field that has drawn most attention in the discourse on tacit knowledge for quite some time now. In the 1990s, the organizational theorist Ikujiro Nonaka presented a "dynamic theory of organizational knowledge creation" (1994), and, together with the business administration scholar Hirotaka Takeuchi, published a book about the "knowledge-creating company" (1995) which explained the global success of Japanese companies basically by their ability to transform certain forms of tacit knowledge into explicit knowledge. The theoretical core of these studies is the so-called SECI-Model, which identifies four modes of "knowledge conversion:" 1. Socialization (tacit to tacit),

---

2 | The idea that all knowledge is local also points to the problem of intercultural communication, an issue that is systematically related to the problem of tacit knowledge (cf. Loenhoff 2011).

2. Externalization (tacit to explicit), 3. Combination (explicit to explicit), and 4. Internalization (explicit to tacit). This model – even if it does not adequately reflect the complexities of tacit knowledge as laid out by Polanyi and others – triggered a whole field of academic research (cf. Argyris 1999; von Krogh/Ichijo/Nonaka 2000; Lam 2000; Nonaka/von Krogh 2009) as well as applications in organizational practice, which shows that the study of tacit knowledge can also be quite application oriented.

The intuition that tacit knowledge is not only of theoretical but also of practical relevance is not restricted to the fields of education, professionalization, business, and knowledge management. In her recent book Knowing Otherwise (2011), Alexis Shotwell also conceives of "implicit understanding," as she calls it, as a political and emancipatory resource:

> I argue that the implicit is central to the project of creating political consciousness in a transformative mode. Without being able to think and talk, to feel and move through various forms of implicit understanding, we are not able to work explicitly with and on our implicit, affective, tacit, and embodied experience of the world. If such work is central to the political transformations individuals experience, it is equally central to broader political change. (xxi)

Drawing attention to the political dimension of the tacit, Shotwell reminds us not only that tacit knowledge can stabilize oppressive forces and normative orders (including stereotypes, prejudices, etc.) but that it also has the potential to further emancipatory agendas and social change. She points us to the political dimension of the (academic) discourse on tacit knowledge – what is at stake in labeling some forms of knowledge explicit and others tacit or implicit? How are the boundaries negotiated between those forms of knowledge that are considered to be 'scholarly' and those that are delegitimized, excluded, or dismissed? Her contribution to this volume zooms in on Implicit Association Tests to discuss issues of race, racism, racial formation, and implicit understanding. In a recent article titled "'Race,' Racism, and Tacit Knowing," Heike Paul (2014) argues that several recent publications in African American studies and critical race studies have dealt with the effects of tacit knowledge and attempted to move beyond the representational logic of race/racism without explicitly using the term/concept of tacit knowledge. She not only proposes to connect these fields of inquiry but also points toward the cultural specificity of tacit knowledge. Her essay in this volume further links the research on tacit knowledge with the recent scholarship on 'public feeling' and examines US-American discourses on (un-)happiness.

Such interventions serve as a reminder that intellectual traditions that do not explicitly refer to tacit knowledge may nevertheless examine corresponding phenomena and that, furthermore, we have to pay close attention to the heterogeneous forms of individual and collective tacit knowledge, which of course are not mutually exclusive. To locate the 'tacit' in human subjects and their bodies does not mean to deny its social and cultural character: Tacit knowledge can be "embodied" and "socially shared" at the same time (cf. Loenhoff in this volume). Furthermore, we can assume that the tacit plays a crucial role in the affective dimension of the social. Moods and atmospheres affectively ground personal as well as social approaches to the world (cf. Schützeichel in this volume). Finally, since most authors agree upon the fact that tacit knowledge is 'collective' and thus at least co-determined by social structures, the question arises of how to deal with tacit knowledge in a differentiated society (cf. Kaldewey in this volume). In a complex society, tacit knowledge does not simply mirror a diffuse ultimate category of 'culture' or of 'knowledge-power' but rather is itself differentiated, that is, unequally distributed among cultural milieus in regard to class, race, gender, age, etc., as well as among its functional subsystems like politics, the economy, science, religion, or the arts.

To summarize: In the last decades, the discourse on tacit knowledge has become more interdisciplinary, more heterogeneous, and more practical. The wealth of concepts and analytical approaches that have been proposed no longer allow using the same definition of tacit knowledge in each and every context. This need not be a problem; however, it is important to keep in mind that the 'tacit' points to a wide semantic field of meanings rather than to a concept with a widely agreed-upon, unequivocal definition. Today, tacit knowledge does not function primarily as an analytical term but rather as a boundary object, that is, "an analytic object of those scientific objects which both inhabit several intersecting social worlds [...] and satisfy the informational requirements of each of them" (Star/Griesemer 1989: 393). Such boundary objects "are both plastic enough to adapt to local needs and the constraints of the several parties employing them, yet robust enough to maintain a common identity across sites;" although they have "different meanings in different social worlds," their structure remains "recognizable," and they may serve as "a means of translation" (ibid.). In other words, if we renounce the philosophical ideal of exact and universalist definitions, we are able to conceive of tacit knowledge as something that transgresses disciplinary boundaries as well as the boundaries between the academe and everyday life.

Even as the contributions in this volume acknowledge and build on the long tradition of philosophical and epistemological approaches to tacit knowledge, they are more concerned with recent and new developments in the research on the 'tacit' in different disciplines. Consequently they do not rely on a unifying definition of 'tacit knowledge' but instead showcase a range of possible understandings that can help explore a diverse spectrum of topics. They reflect theoretical debates (Part I: Loenhoff, Hubrich, Schützeichel, Kaldewey) and methodological challenges (Part II: Renn, Antony, Shotwell), but also demonstrate how 'tacit knowledge' can be used in fields such as cultural studies, literary studies, media studies, or theology in order to open up new venues of inquiry in these disciplines (Part III: Paul, Koetzing, Ernst, Schoberth). Each part moreover is complemented by an interview with a well-known expert in the respective field (Part I: Theodore Schatzki, Part II: Loïc Wacquant, Part III: Mark Johnson).

Instead of a neat working definition of 'tacit knowledge' we would like to offer at this point some basic premises which inform most of the essays collected here, as well as additional information on the institutional context of this publication which might be useful for the reader to navigate through the individual chapters.

Tacit knowledge or implicit understanding can very generally be differentiated into 'weak' and 'strong' forms, depending on the degree of accessibility and explicability. Whereas weak forms of tacit knowledge can, at least principally, be articulated explicitly, strong versions of tacit knowledge cannot. However, strong tacit knowledge becomes visible and thus explicates itself in bodily acts. But even a weak notion of tacit knowledge rests on a paradox: If we translate a 'knowing how' into a propositional 'knowing that,' the 'knowing how' is no longer what it used to be: a practical ability or a doing, operating in the background. By being translated into explicit knowledge, tacit knowledge is transformed; a one-to-one representation of tacit knowledge is never possible. To put it differently: There is a difference between knowing how it is to have know-how and giving a description of know-how. This is the reason why many authors assume that there cannot be any explicit knowledge without tacit knowledge. A related problem is discussed by Polanyi (1966): To analyze perception (e.g., recognizing a face), he argues, we have to distinguish between focal awareness (the face) and subsidiary awareness (the nose, the eyes, the chin, etc.). Without subsidiary awareness focal awareness is impossible, and vice versa. Ultimately, every perception and action relies on this 'From-To' structure of knowledge. However, the distinction between focal and subsidiary elements of perception does not correspond to the distinction between strong and weak forms of tacit knowledge. The subsidiary may or may not be articulated – in either case, it is always present. Charles Taylor (1995: 170) put it this way: "Rather than representations being the primary locus of understanding, they are only islands in the sea of our unformulated practical grasp of the world."

It is this spectrum that we want to draw attention to in the subtitle of our volume: The contributions not only locate tacit knowledge somewhere between explication and embodiment but also critically interrogate this spectrum and inquire into the specific forms that the explication and/or embodiment of knowledge take. In addition to this general differentiation, two typologies in particular inform many of the essays collected here and have proven to be helpful to systematize the 'tacit.' Both take recourse to Polanyi's work and both account for strong as well as weak forms of tacit knowledge. Harry Collins (2010) proposes a distinction between three types:

1. "relational tacit knowledge," i.e. a weak form of tacit knowledge which "is tacit because of the contingencies of human relationships, history, tradition and logistics" (98),
2. "somatic tacit knowledge," i.e. an intermediate form of tacit knowledge which is embodied and tacit due to our "bodily limits" (101), and
3. "collective tacit knowledge," i.e. a strong form of tacit knowledge which is "located in society" (138).

While Collins claims that in order to approach tacit knowledge and the reasons for its 'tacitness' systematically, we first have to develop an understanding of the 'explicit' (cf. 2010: 1), Alexis Shotwell, in contrast, tries to shift the focus away from the "inadequate" dichotomies between explicit and tacit or propositional and non-propositional knowledge (2011: xi). Instead, she differentiates between four types of "implicit understanding" (ibid. xi-xii), which are nonetheless intricately intertwined (cf. also her contribution to this volume):

1. "practical, skill-based knowledge," i.e. "'know-how' developed through practice [...] like [...] being able to swim,"
2. "somatic or bodily knowing," i.e. "knowledge people have at the intersection of their bodily and conceptual systems," which is "bodily and social, and thus [...] always political,"
3. "potentially propositional but currently implicit knowledge," i.e. knowledge that can be made explicit and "put into words but is not, now, in that form," and
4. "affective or emotional understanding" that refers to a kind of knowledge which is "not fully or generally propositional or considered a kind of knowledge," i.e. "non-propositional but energetic and moving feelings that texture and tone our experience."

What all these examples have in common is that tacit knowledge, be it explicated or not, makes something else possible: an immediate presence. The program of the Erlangen research group "Presence and Tacit Knowledge" follows the assumption that there is an intrinsic connection between tacit knowledge and phenomena of presence, i.e. situations of spatial and temporal conspicuousness which are perceived non-reflexively (cf. Ernst/Paul 2013). Presence can either be perceived as extra-ordinary (e.g., in the realm of the arts, media events, festivals, performances, etc.) or remain largely unnoticed due to its ordinary and everyday character. In both cases, presence is not based on propositions or explicit knowledge, and thus necessarily has an implicit dimension. Presence presupposes tacit knowledge, and tacit knowledge shows itself through presence/phenomena of presence. Polanyi's argument that tacit knowledge is embedded in a 'From-To' structure is of help here: presence comes into our focal perception from subsidiary tacit knowledge that, in most cases, remains unnoticed and unobserved. Thus, tacit knowledge explicates itself in situations of presence. This explication is normally non-propositional and based on performances and translations rather than on representations. Most dimensions of tacit knowledge are socially acquired and shared and hence are culturally specific. This is the reason why this volume assembles a range of analyses of culturally specific practices where tacit knowledge constitutes phenomena of presence: in Christian faith (Schoberth), in film metaphors (Ernst), in literature's use of figurative speech (Koetzing), or in public feelings (Paul).

Taken together, the essays in this volume cover a range of crucial aspects of the 'tacit' and shed new light on the presentifications of tacit knowledge, the processes and methods by which it is translated into explicit knowledge, and its various appearances in theories, cultural practices, and social interactions.

WORKS CITED

Argyris, Chris (1999): On Organizational Learning, 2nd ed., Oxford: Blackwell.
Barnes, Barry (1974): Scientific Knowledge and Sociological Theory, London: Routledge and Kegan Paul.
Bloor, David (1973): "Wittgenstein and Mannheim on the Sociology of Mathematics," in: Studies in History and Philosophy of Science Part A 4.2, 173-191.
—. (1976): Knowledge and Social Imagery, London: Routledge and Kegan Paul.
Bohnsack, Ralf (2006): "Mannheims Wissenssoziologie als Methode," in: Dirk Tänzler/Hubert Knoblauch/Hans-Georg Soeffner (eds.), Neue Perspektiven der Wissenssoziologie, Konstanz: UVK, 271-291.
Bourdieu, Pierre (1977): Outline of a Theory of Practice, Cambridge: Cambridge UP.
Collins, Harry M. (1974): "The TEA Set. Tacit Knowledge and Scientific Networks," in: Science Studies 4, 165-186.
—. (2010): Tacit and Explicit Knowledge, Chicago: U of Chicago P.
Ernst, Christoph/Paul, Heike (eds.) (2013): Präsenz und implizites Wissen. Zur Interdependenz zweier Schlüsselbegriffe der Kultur- und Sozialwissenschaften, Bielefeld: transcript.
Gascoigne, Neil/Thornton, Tim (2013): Tacit Knowledge, Durham: Acumen.
Geertz, Clifford (1983): Local Knowledge. Further Essays in Interpretive Anthropology, New York: Basic.
—. (1992): "'Local Knowledge' and Its Limits. Some Obiter Dicta," in: The Yale Journal of Criticism 5.2, 129-135.

James, William (1950 [1890]): The Principles of Psychology, Vol. 1, New York: Dover.
Johnson, Mark (1987): The Body in the Mind. The Bodily Basis of Meaning, Imagination, and Reason, Chicago: U of Chicago P.
Lakoff, George/Johnson, Mark (1980): Metaphors We Live By, Chicago: U of Chicago P.
—. (1999): Philosophy in the Flesh. The Embodied Mind and Its Challenges to Western Thought, New York: Basic.
Lam, Alice (2000): "Tacit Knowledge, Organizational Learning and Societal Institutions. An Integrated Framework," in: Organization Studies 21.3, 487-513.
Loenhoff, Jens (2011): "Tacit Knowledge in Intercultural Communication," in: Intercultural Communication Studies 20.1, 57-64.
—. (2012a): "Implizites Wissen zwischen sozialphänomenologischer und pragmatistischer Bestimmung," in: Joachim Renn/Gerd Sebald/Jan Weyand (eds.), Lebenswelt und Lebensform. Zum Verhältnis zwischen Phänomenologie und Pragmatismus, Weilerswist: Velbrück, 294-316.
— (ed.) (2012b): Implizites Wissen. Epistemologische und handlungstheoretische Perspektiven, Weilerswist: Velbrück.
Mannheim, Karl (1964): "Beiträge zur Theorie der Weltanschauungs-Interpretation," in: Wissenssoziologie, Neuwied: Luchterhand, 91-154.
—, (1980): "Eine soziologische Theorie der Kultur und ihrer Erkennbarkeit (Konjunktives und kommunikatives Denken)," in: David Kettler/Volker Meja/Nico Stehr (eds.), Strukturen des Denkens, Frankfurt/Main: Suhrkamp, 155-322.
Neuweg, Georg Hans (1999): Könnerschaft und implizites Wissen. Zur lehr-lerntheoretischen Bedeutung der Erkenntnis- und Wissenstheorie Michael Polanyis, Internationale Hochschulschriften 311, Münster: Waxmann.
Nonaka, Ikujiro (1994): "A Dynamic Theory of Organizational Knowledge Creation," in: Organization Science 5.1, 14-37.
Nonaka, Ikujiro/Takeuchi, Hirotaka (1995): The Knowledge-Creating Company. How Japanese Companies Create the Dynamics of Innovation, Oxford: Oxford UP.
Nonaka, Ikujiro/von Krogh, Georg (2009): "Tacit Knowledge and Knowledge Conversion. Controversy and Advancement in Organizational Knowledge Creation Theory," in: Organization Science 20.3, 635-652.
Paul, Heike (2014): "'Race,' Racism, and Tacit Knowing," in: Winfried Fluck/Erik Redling/Sabine Sielke/Hubert Zapf (eds.), American Studies Today, Heidelberg: Winter, 265-289.
Polanyi, Michael (1958): Personal Knowledge. Towards a Post-Critical Philosophy, London: Routledge and Kegan Paul.
—. (1966): The Tacit Dimension, Garden City: Doubleday.

Reber, Arthur S. (1989): "Implicit Learning and Tacit Knowledge," in: Journal of Experimental Psychology 118.3, 219-235.
—. (1993): Implicit Learning and Tacit Knowledge. An Essay on the Cognitive Unconscious, Oxford Psychology Series 19, Oxford: Oxford UP.
Ryle, Gilbert (1945/46): "Knowing How and Knowing That," in: Proceedings of the Aristotelian Society 46, 1-16.
Schatzki, Theodore R. (1996): Social Practice. A Wittgensteinian Approach to Human Activity and the Social, Cambridge: Cambridge UP.
Schatzki, Theodore R./Knorr Cetina, Karin/von Savigny, Eike (eds.) (2001): The Practice Turn in Contemporary Theory, London: Routledge.
Shotwell, Alexis (2011): Knowing Otherwise. Race, Gender, and Implicit Understanding, University Park: Pennsylvania State UP.
Star, Susan Leigh/Griesemer James R. (1989): "Institutional Ecology, 'Translations' and Boundary Objects: Amateurs and Professionals in Berkeley's Museum of Vertebrate Zoology, 1907-39," in: Social Studies of Science 19.3, 387-420.
Sternberg, Robert J./Horvath, Joseph A. (eds.) (1999): Tacit Knowledge in Professional Practice. Researcher and Practitioner Perspectives, Mahwah: Lawrence Erlbaum Associates.
Taylor, Charles (1995): "To Follow a Rule," in: Charles Taylor, Philosophical Arguments, Cambridge: Harvard UP, 165-180.
Taylor, Diana (2003): The Archive and the Repertoire. Performing Cultural Memory in the Americas, Durham: Duke UP.
Turner, Stephen (1994): The Social Theory of Practices. Tradition, Tacit Knowledge, and Presuppositions, Chicago: U of Chicago P.
von Krogh, Georg/Ichijo, Kazuo Ichijo/Nonaka, Ikujiro (2000): Enabling Knowledge Creation. How to Unlock the Mystery of Tacit Knowledge, Oxford: Oxford UP.
Wieland, Wolfgang (1982): Platon und die Formen des Wissens, Göttingen: Vandenhoeck und Ruprecht.

**Part I
Locations**

Tacit Knowledge: Shared and Embodied

Jens Loenhoff

> It is humiliating to have to appear like an empty tube which is simply inflated by a mind.
> Ludwig Wittgenstein, *Culture and Value*

I. Introduction

The body is omnipresent in the social sciences and in cultural studies these days. Underlying this preoccupation is the suspicion that the body and its social conditions of existence hold a key position in explanations of social action and that human communication cannot be understood without consideration of the symbolic function of the body. New approaches which center on forms of embodiment and incorporation aim to recalibrate theories of action and society in order to more fully tap into their epistemological potential (cf. e.g. Clark 1997, 2008; Malafouris 2013; Morganti/Carassa/Riva 2008; Noë 2004, 2009; Stewart/Gapenne/Di Paolo 2010; Thompson 2007; Ziemke/Zlatev/Frank 2007). In branches of philosophy like ethics and aesthetics, the body also receives much attention, for instance in the context of a soma-aesthetic inspired pragmatism geared towards a melioristic transformation of the quality of life through the improvement of techniques of the body and sensation.[1] At the intersection of all of these considerations is the question of the quality of the body as a bearer of knowledge, as a recipient of the disciplinary power of society, or as the repository of a social praxis beyond language and discourse. The suggestion that a body might be an entity or an active dimension alongside other relevant actors such as the mind – which purportedly lies within, designs, or controls the body – has made a simple analogy seem attractive, namely to ascribe to the body that type of knowledge which had previously been regarded as a natural property of consciousness. This conviction is especially pronounced in the discourse about tacit knowledge. Yet the attempt to relocate the interpretive activities of subjects

---

1 | This goal is pursued, for example, by Richard Shusterman (cf. 2008; 2012), who takes up positions of classical pragmatism as well as of phenomenology.

in the body, and to conceptualize them as incorporated competencies underlying the practical logics of action, runs the risk of inadvertently objectifying the body and hence reiterating the aporias of the very same dualistic models that rightfully emerged as critiques of mentalism. In order to more clearly specify the corresponding problems, the contours of a theory of tacit knowledge will be sketched next, on the basis of which the question as to which concepts of the body, embodiment, and incorporation can be identified in the discourse on tacit knowledge will then be explored. Finally, a pragmatist theory of experience will be taken into account in order to point to several ways in which the conceptual problems of this discourse could be overcome.

II. On the Theory of Tacit Knowledge

Knowledge, according to the consensus within the human sciences, counts as a key concept of human praxis. What one does seems to be based on knowledge, and whoever can do something has knowledge at his or her disposal which is not accessible to someone who cannot do something (i.e. whose action does not succeed) – at least not right at the moment of acting/failing. Since antiquity, the Western concept of knowledge has had a notoriously epistemic character, for what counts as knowledge is not an intuition or unexamined assertion, but only a secured, methodically acquired and communicable insight. Inadmissible for this epistemic concept of knowledge, of course, are those moments when we encounter successful practices that are not so properly identifiable and verifiable as knowledge thus defined. However, a strong concept of tacit knowledge insists that a transdiscursive ability is also a *form* of knowledge, even when it is not linguistically representable. The ability to grasp the structures of meaning in a given situation and to perform appropriate practices demonstrates just as well as orientation in space and the interpretation of expressions, taste, or corporeal shapes how an incorporated and habitualized power of judgment might be imagined. Even when the acquisition of such an aesthetic judgment is supported and structured by verbal expressions, the necessary linguistic competency and creativity relies upon tacit knowledge as its enabling condition.

The concept of tacit knowledge is related to a line of thinking which seeks to deconstruct subject-object relations on the assumption that agents do not stand in opposition to an objective world which first has to be conceptually ascertained. The validity claims of inventories of knowledge in general are called into question when greater attention is paid to the performative dimension of practices and to the tacit backgrounds and inexplicable pre-configurations of all perception and action; at stake in the reconstruction of tacit knowledge and the related antimentalist critique thus is the traditional subject-centered concept of knowledge and the specific qualities of cognitive content, convictions, etc. concomitant with it. For if epistemic practices rely upon communication and hence are ultimately practices whose success cannot be uncoupled from the basis of practical intersubjectivity, then the question of the relationship between tacit knowledge and an explicit knowledge validating propositional claims becomes all the more urgent. This problem becomes apparent not only in the highly ambivalent status of the concept of tacit knowledge in analytic philosophy, but also in theories that adhere to the project of a detranscendentalized communicative rationality (cf. Habermas 1996 [1992]).

Skepticism as to whether and to what extent there can be explicit knowledge unqualified by pre-predicative routines, or whether a type of knowledge is even conceivable that could be regarded as completely explicit, has motivated attempts to salvage *knowing-how* as a variation of propositional knowledge (cf. Stanley/Williamson 2001; Snowdon 2003). According to the hypothesis that tacit and explicit knowledge are structurally analogous, tacit knowledge is merely a (sub)type of explicit knowledge about specific types of actions if the additional criterion of verifiability can be successfully applied (cf. Hawley 2003; Hetherington 2008; Rosenfeld 2004). A strong concept of tacit knowledge that proceeds from the categorical limits of the explicability of non-propositional knowledge is thus confronted with the suspicion that it aims to designate something as knowledge which strictly speaking may not be a type of knowledge at all because it lacks the necessary epistemic quality of discursive availability. Much more pertinent to tacit knowledge, it is argued, is an immunity to falsifiability, which is why it is discarded as a diffuse background of determinate practices from the realm of rational and verifiable knowledge altogether (cf. Habermas 2003 [1999]). In contrast to these positions, in what follows I will systematize the characteristics of tacit knowledge in order to show the extent to which tacit knowledge is a type of full-fledged and inexplicable knowledge and in so doing will defend the position of a strong concept of tacit knowledge.

Tacit knowledge is *fundamental*, because it is both constitutive of and presupposed by propositional knowledge. Such knowledge is acquired not through explicative discourses but through direct exposure to other agents. This pragmatist assertion of the priority of tacit knowledge maintains that explicit convictions always rely on a background set of practical skills which remain implicit. Factual knowledge derives from the ability to participate in practices, and that means: to know *how* to do something. In contrast to these pre-conceptual primary experiences, reflexive stances have an epiphenomenal status. To address, consider, explain or penetrate something scientifically always already presupposes the capacity of agents to adequately define situations and engage in elementary communicative practices. Our primary access to the world occurs in the mode of "handiness" ("Zuhandenheit") (Heidegger 1996: 65) and has the character of a practical ability. It lies beyond conscious goal setting, for even before we have plans, define objectives, or consider options, we are already enmeshed in this world. Authors as diverse as Dewey (1925; 1960), Wittgenstein (1969; 1989), Merleau-Ponty (1962 [1945]), and Bourdieu (1990 [1980]) are in agreement that the structure, connectedness and comprehensibility of social action cannot be attributed to cognitively manifest convictions, the complementarity of interests and values, or a discursively achieved consensus about validity claims, because we always already move within a lifeworld with an open horizon of meaning (cf. Heidegger 1996: 70). The pre-intentional and pre-predicative embeddedness of agents in an intersubjective social praxis is hence based not on explicit knowledge and determinate views with respect to their truth claims, but on pre-reflexive, practical certainties taken for granted within a lifeworld that can be referred to as "tacit knowledge."

Tacit knowledge is *holistic*, because the practices it enables are neither singular nor isolable. They are, rather, inextricably entangled with other contexts of action and their horizons of reference, which, due to their totality, are not representable.[2] Accompanying the argument that tacit knowledge is holistic is a critique of theories of hermeneutics and truth which hold that elementary unities or distinguishable conditions can be said to emerge as knowledge independent of other knowledge and practice in a ramified context of reference. If single actions and acts of predication can only be comprehended in connection with social practices and their entanglement with a cultural way of life, then it becomes clear that an always selective thematization and the resulting explicit knowledge cannot have a primary function for the situated coordination of action. Only knowledge which refuses exhaustive explication can fulfill such a pragmatic function.

Tacit knowledge is *collective* knowledge. It is socially shared, because it is the result of agents' successfully coordinated and co-produced action. That a type of knowledge effective in the coordination of action has to be collective knowledge becomes apparent in the interaction of agents with the indexicality of the communicative situation. Were such knowledge not to emerge out of the context-specific forms of coordinated behavior, it would not be functional for the coordination of action. Explicit knowledge does not have to be collectively shared, because the practical intersubjectivity of speech and action does not depend on it (cf. Wittgenstein 1969). References in the discourse on tacit knowledge to practices such as bicycling, swimming, playing the violin, etc., ignore this collective character, because these activities tend to be understood monologically and individualistically. Riding a bicycle in traffic, playing a team sport, or playing music with others are thus the more appropriate analogies (cf.

---

2 | Heidegger programmatically conceptualized this way of "being-in-the-world" as "[...] the unthematic, circumspect absorption in the references constitutive for the handiness of the totality of useful things" (1996: 71). On the consequences for a theory of meaning, see Dreyfus (1980).

Collins 2010). Tacit knowledge is not solely a matter of physical skills or pre-reflexive interpretive competencies, but includes above all what Bourdieu termed "sens du jeu social" (1980: 46).

Because tacit knowledge is socially shared knowledge, it has a *normative* structure. The ability to behave in a manner suitable to specific contexts – and to be able to expect the same of others – does not presuppose a reflexive stance. The implicit expectations structuring everyday action do not derive their social validity from discourses but from settled and positively sanctioned practices. Their execution does not rely on any explicit justification or problematization, but on socially shared and unexpressed criteria for their appropriate realization. Sanctions thus do not require a discursive expression regarding actions or speech acts but may reveal normativity implicitly. The refusal or denial of a follow-up action suffices to call attention to the failure of an action and to make the expectation noticeable *as* an expectation. The implicit normativity of the kind of tacit knowledge that ensures successive action thus emerges above all in the expectation of those expectations by which social action is structured.

If tacit knowledge is a *form* of knowledge and its fallibility is accepted as a feature of all knowledge, then tacit knowledge has also a rational quality (cf. Renn 2012). The counterintuitive thesis that practical ability designates a form of knowledge is based on the fact that the success and failure of social practices cannot be uncoupled from the specific quality of tacit knowledge. Therefore, the failure of practices can be interpreted as the ineffectiveness of tacit knowledge and hence as its lack of rationality. The primary distinction between the rationality of tacit and explicit knowledge derives from this feature. Entirely different criteria of validity underlie the rationality of explicit knowledge, because it must be justified with reference to articulable, often formal standards, and with respect to the rules of public discourses of rationality. Tacit knowledge, on the other hand, is rational within cultural ways of life to the extent that it enables members of a group to undertake practices with desired effects.

In complex societies, tacit knowledge is *differentiated*, because it is unequally distributed among social and cultural milieus. In modern and especially in multicultural societies, the observable differentiation of tacit knowledge is noticeable as a reduction in shared conventions and general assumptions. One of its consequences for the practical coordination of action is the increasing contingency of an unconstrained stabilization of behavioral expectations. As a result, the differentiation of tacit knowledge through breaches of rules becomes striking on the performative level, for instance in the form of non-identical definitions of situations, different practices of attribution, or diverging standards of suitability (cf. Renn 2013).

One of the most important features often mentioned with regard to tacit knowledge is its incorporatedness, with which I will deal in the next section.

III. Body, Embodiment, Incorporation

Discourses about tacit knowledge focus on the body and its senso-motoric faculties because they break with intellectualist or mentalist positions and oppose the dogma of the Cartesian cogito. The emphasis on the role of the body as generator, medium, or pathway of tacit knowledge can be interpreted as a search for an alternative starting point and guaranty of ultimate certainty that hopes to overcome the aporias of dualism in a convincing way. As is well-known, Western philosophy has been concerned with the body since Aristotle, whose conception of the body underscores its instrumental character and has remained influential into the twenty-first century (cf. Aristotle 1907: II, 1; 412a 27-41b 1). The instrumental character of the body as a means of perceptive orientation continued into Husserlian phenomenology (cf. Husserl 1982: II, §18).[3] Merleau-Ponty is the first to overcome this one-sided perspective by radically transforming Heidegger's thesis that we are always already understanding in the world into a theory of corporeal-sensory anchoring in the world. His attempt to resolve the aporias of transcendental phenomenology ultimately understands primary sociality as inter-corporeality. Not consciousness or language but the body operates as the constitutive moment of practical intersubjectivity, for acts of meaning are first enacted in corporeal intentionality and become manifest contents of consciousness only secondly. "My body has its world, or understands its world, without having to make use of my 'symbolic' or 'objectifying function'" (Merleau-Ponty 1962: 140). In practical action there is always already a pre-reflexive relationship to the world that is structured by bodily dispositions before such a relationship can even be conceptualized. The constitution of meaning does not take place through reflexive acts of consciousness, but already through acts of perception and movement that constitute specific relations to objects.

Yet other approaches, for instance, Gehlen's (1988 [1940]) sensorimotor-informed theory of unburdening, Polanyi's (1966) critique of scientific knowledge, or Bourdieu's (1990 [1980]) concept of habitus, identify in their own ways the body as a site of the construction of habits, of the pre-structuration of all action, and as the executive organ of social practices. Even Wittgenstein, who, in light of his devastating critique of sensation, is not usually considered a philosopher of the body, can hardly avoid kinesthetic and somatic perceptions as a source of evidence in his reflections on certainty.[4] And yet the question of what it means for tacit knowledge to be embodied and, moreover, socially shared, has been insufficiently answered. Gehlen's philosophical anthropology ultimately

---

3 | There is of course another history of the philosophy of the body, which runs from Schopenhauer through Feuerbach and Marx to Nietzsche and Bataille. Yet in this history the body is not a generator but an addressee of social forces.

4 | See, for instance §§ 125, 510 in On Certainty (Wittgenstein 1969).

remains to a certain extent monological, Merleau-Ponty's somatic phenomenology suffers from a deficit of the sociality of the body, and Polanyi's definition of tacit knowledge remains strongly tied to the perception of things and Gestalt theory. If according to the grammar of the concept of 'knowledge' such knowledge must be socially shared in order to be knowledge at all, how can embodied, tacit knowledge have the quality of collective knowledge? How to theorize participation outside of claims of theories of propositional knowledge that subjects mean the same thing, acknowledge a truth content by bringing sentences into agreement with one another, or have the same convictions about facts? In order to approach this blind spot of a theory of tacit knowledge, we must first consider a few common assumptions found in the social sciences.

When a person who intends to perform a transaction at an automated teller machine cannot recall the personal identification number of his or her ATM card, he or she tries to remember the movements of fingers over the keypad, which only works by actually moving his or her fingers because the habitual sequence of movements forms a kinesthetic, proprioceptive Gestalt. Something similar is experienced by a person who focuses on speaking itself and the unplanned articulation of phonetic forms, because he or she has to relinquish all efforts to anticipate what is being said in its entirety and in its parts. And whether someone who took piano lessons many years ago can still play the first prelude of Bach's *Das Wohltemperierte Klavier* can only be ascertained by actually trying to play it again.[5] Such experiences suggest that it is the body which knows something that a wide-awake mind may not be able to recall, and support the assertion of the body as memory of praxis. Meanwhile, some contemporary cognitive sciences scholars have adopted this approach to 'embodiment.' With reference to Husserl and Merleau-Ponty and supported by contributions to cognitive linguistics (cf. Johnson 1987; Lakoff 1987; Lakoff/Johnson 1999) as well as research on expressions in evolutionary biology (cf. Frith/Frith 2001; Johnson/Morton 1991; Thompson 2007; Tomasello 2008), cognitive operations are now regarded as situated and embodied, and the physical dependence of cognitive achievements is emphasized. Cognitive psychology's previously limited interest in the body and its function for communication and action, along with the fixation on input-output models of information theory in research on artificial intelligence, had consolidated over time an understanding of cognitive processes dominated by model subjects whose mental conditions were primarily determined by propositional forms of knowledge. Descriptions from the third-person perspective have thus led to an approach in the classic

---

5 | As Merleau-Ponty aptly phrases it, this is knowledge of the body, or knowledge which is located "in" the body: "It is knowledge in the hands, which is forthcoming only when bodily effort is made, and cannot be formulated in detachment from that effort" (1962: 144).

cognitive sciences that Dewey (1960: 196) rightfully criticized as a spectator theory of knowledge.[6] Only the shifting of attention in recent years to the accomplishments of consciousness under conditions of real-time interaction, and thus to the related pragmatic requirements of cognition, has made possible research into what has been termed "situated cognition" and "embodied cognition" (cf. Hutchins 1995, 2006; Clark 1997, 2008). In this context experiments with interruptions of sensorimotor processes of circulation, rubber hands, and deafferented patients pursue the questions as to how the body enables agents to be in the world and how they are able to identify a body as their own. What is regarded as the condition of a pre-reflexive awareness of the body, then, is the coherency of action and perception in the form of a multisensorial and multimodal integration of heterogeneous sensory systems, including the invariance of corresponding correlations. Investigations into contextualized processes of orientation and coordination very clearly demonstrate that cognitive processes are intertwined with features of the external world, with the corporeal dispositions of the participants, and with the actions of partners in interaction. For earlier Cartesian and internalist theories, these dimensions were insignificant. The departure from the dogma of a self-referential and supposedly autonomous cognition of isolated individuals corrected these epistemological positions by paying greater attention to the interactive relevance of the body and its related sensorimotor functions (cf. Froese/Fuchs 2012; Fuchs/De Jaeger 2009; Lindblom/Ziemke 2008; Wilson 2002). Approaches to a theory of embodied intersubjectivity no longer interpret the understanding of other agents as a representationally conceived process of theory and model construction or of mind reading, but explain it instead without recourse to mental conditions and representations. Cognition and intentionality thus no longer appear as a condition but as a consequence of processes of social interaction, which should be treated above all as an entanglement of sensorimotor activity and inter-bodily functions (cf. Morganti/Carassa/Riva 2008; Fuchs/De Jaeger 2009; Froese/Fuchs 2012).[7] And yet only in exceptional cases has research on embodied cog-

---

6 | This critique is leveled at the view "[...] that the true and valid object of knowledge is that which has being prior to and independent of the operations of knowing. They spring from the doctrine that knowledge is a grasp or beholding of reality without anything being done to modify its antecedent state – the doctrine which is the source of the separation of knowledge from practical activity. If we see that knowing is not the act of an outside spectator but of a participator inside the natural and social scene, then the true object of knowledge resides in the consequences of directed action" (Dewey 1960: 196).

7 | In the words of Froese and Fuchs (2012: 211): "The guiding hypothesis is that through our mutual interactions with others our living and lived bodies become inextricably intertwined in a dynamical whole, thus forming an 'extended body' by which we

nition really been able to shed the representationalism and Cartesian dualism for which it has been criticized. Despite its attack on the modularization of the mind, this notion of embodiment does not really overcome its cognitivist prejudice because it regards only the mental representations of bodily conditions[8] or the cognitive ordering of linguistically objectified relations of bodies as "embodiment" (cf. Gallese/Lakoff 2005). In fixating on the single individual, the mind-body distinction is maintained as an omnipresent organizing principle because it either implies that consciousness operates in the interest of bodily requirements or that the body operates in the interest of consciousness and its demands for representation and orientation. The predominant focus on objective perception in experiments reveals a deficit of sociality in cognitive research, insofar as agents are considered to have a relation to their environments prior to developing relations to other agents.[9] Although research on embodied cognition grants the importance of the body and its achievements, the corresponding conceptualizations remain ambivalent and diffuse.

Others doing research on embodiment hope to explain the relationship between tacit knowledge and the body as bearer of this knowledge by drawing on neuroscience (cf. e.g. Turner 2012). The notion of the body which underlies cognitive science and neuroscience depends, however, on whether it is constituted as an object of study for either the natural or social sciences. References can thus be found to sensomotoric functional cycles, or to the entanglement of perception and movement in real interaction alongside objectivist concepts of sensory and motoric knowledge which understand the body as a physiologically describable sensorimotor system. The treatment of the function of mirror neurons as a form of embodiment in parts of the neurosciences and some kinds of neurophenomenology is an epistemologically problematic assumption, because the pre-reflective intentionality of the body and the related perspective of the participants represent not a *causal* level that can be described by external observation but a *constitutive* one. Yet the body is neither an instrument utilized by the brain, nor does consciousness arise in the brain, as is repeatedly asserted by neurophilosophers (cf. e.g. Churchland 2002; Crick 1995). The assertion that sociality has a neurophysiological foundation is aporetical not only because it contains a categorical mistake; the normativity of social practices that char-

---

enact and encounter the world together." The processes to which the authors refer here were already well described by Bühler (1927: 91ff.) in his model of contact understanding. See also Loenhoff (2001: 182ff.).

8 | This is expressed, for example, in the following statement by Legrand (2006: 89): "The *embodied self* [...] is a mental self (i.e. a self characterized mentally) 'put into' a body, that is, for instance, a self whose mental states would be correlated with bodily (notably brain) states."

9 | Exemplary counter-positions are offered by Dewey (1925) and Mead (1934).

acterizes all sociality cannot at all be integrated into a neurological paradigm due to its fixation on the single organism, or single brain. Normativity cannot be reduced to physiology because it is a result of practical intersubjectivity in the context of coordinated action between persons and not neurons. Neurological explanations cannot account for the question as to how tacit knowledge is incorporated because they do not have a concept of experience, of knowledge, of action, or even of consciousness. Consciousness presupposes participation in a recognized life-form of social practices whose normativity is systematically ignored by neuroscience's notorious internalism.[10] Experiences do not occur within agents but through the world's interference with their actions and situations. The liminal relations constituted by such experiences of the organism are also highly variable, because not only the brain but also the entire body takes part in them (cf. Noë 2009).

Yet also attempts to base social cognition research on an empirically informed, i.e., an experimentally based theory of intersubjectivity in order to circumvent the difficulties of transcendental phenomenology remain partly enmeshed in the old problems of Husserlian phenomenology, and – owing to their Cartesian inheritance – retain unquestioned contradictions between phenomenological and (at least according to their claim) externalist positions. Here, facts have recently been discovered which for a long time have been treated as common knowledge within larger parts of sociological theory from Mead and Dewey to Gehlen and Bourdieu. The same is true for antireductionist and anti-intentionalist positions in pragmatic and analytic philosophy that have turned to the co-production of meaning and the emergence of the social vis-à-vis an unfettered mentalism. Ultimately based on these externalist convictions is the familiar argument that meanings are not contained in the head, but in linguistic praxis and the community of language users. In what follows, I would like to find a way out of the above-described problems with reference to Dewey's concept of habit.

---

10 | This can be seen very clearly in the so-called "enactive approach" and its conception of embodied social interaction. The conception of mutual incorporation as coordination and the interlocking of gestures, mimicry, bodily movements, and expression raise the questions of how and why participants have at their disposal everyday concepts of the body which grasp this dyad as two separate, individual bodies. At least at this point the need for a supplementary perspective of social theory becomes obvious that defines the body in the processes of cultural and social differentiation as a "fait social" in Durkheim's sense.

IV. "Embodiment" in the Context of a Theory of Experience

Dewey's outline of a theory of experience in his early critique of behaviorism (1896) and his notion of the continuum of experience decidedly render two conditions plausible: on the one hand, that there can be no prior determination of or distinction between ends and means and stimulus and response; on the other hand, that the separation of body and reflexive consciousness represents an abstraction that is always experienced as a unity in the originally goal-oriented action and the successful coordination of movements that attends it. If the question of the embodiment of tacit knowledge is situated in the context of such a pragmatic concept of experience, which does not regard the constitution of sense and meaning as contemplative and reflexive acts but as the result of practical action and an active confrontation with a resistant and unpredictable world, then options arise for the resolution of the aporias and inconsistencies mentioned above. Dewey's critique of what can perhaps be referred to as 'multiple isolationism' – in other words, his critique of the separation of organism and environment, body and consciousness, knowledge and situation, and, last but not least, of agents from one another – provides an alternative access to the phenomenon of embodiment.[11] Embodiment, incorporation, etc., can only properly be comprehended as anti-isolationist and anti-dualistic counter-notions if they are grasped as the result of a relationship to the social world and to co-actors immersed in a concrete situation that has become habitual through repetition. The resulting concept of habit – which Dewey critically distinguishes from both Bergson's intellectualistic concept of habit and James's understanding of habit as a product of fantasy (which ultimately also pertains to Gehlen's and Merleau-Ponty's theories of habit) – explains how practices can be completed and mastered without having to pass through objectifying reflection, as well as how the motoric and perceptively active body operates both as an organ of understanding and as a 'point of passage' of movements oriented towards the world without objectifying the body in the process.[12]

---

11 | Dewey's concept of experience shows that all knowledge is interwoven with social practices: "Knowing is, for philosophical theory, a case of specially directed activity instead of something isolated from practice" (1960: 204). Despite his sympathy for pragmatism, Rorty (1982) objected to Dewey's fundamental concept of experience and emphasized instead the primacy of language. Limitations of space do not permit me to take up this discussion (cf. also Shusterman 1999).

12 | Merleau-Ponty similarly interprets the concept of habit as the motoric acquisition of new meanings in order to thereby abandon an intellectual concept of understanding: "As has often been said, it is the body which 'catches' and 'comprehends' movement.

In *Human Nature and Conduct* (1922), Dewey already emphasizes the significance of socially acquired habits for the relationship of an organism to its environment by conceptualizing these habits as a specific mode of the organization of action. In *Experience and Nature* (1925), Dewey then develops a notion of habit that includes the creative self-transformation of action. Habits are hence not understood as monotone regularities within a successful integration of organism and environment, but as implementations which are already formed and organized in relation to possible future transformations. Because habitual practices always collide with conditions of their realization that are only partially foreseeable and hence cannot be completely controlled, only the variation of actions and the ability to master different routines guarantee an action's successful continuation:

> By a seeming paradox, increased power of forming habits means increased susceptibility, sensitiveness, responsiveness. Thus even if we think of habits as so many grooves, the power to acquire many and varied grooves denotes high sensitivity, explosiveness. Thereby an old habit, a fixed groove if one wishes to exaggerate, gets in the way of the process of forming a new habit while the tendency to form a new one cuts across some old habit. Hence instability, novelty, emergence of unexpected and unpredictable combinations. (Dewey 1925: 229f.)[13]

Motoric habitualization through physical virtuosity makes evident yet another connection to the effect that habit formation alters not only the body schema but concomitantly also the perception of the world. This is why, for instance, an experiment can easily show that the perceived size of a baseball depends upon how often and how successfully the ball is hit by a test subject's bat. The ball is perceived by an experienced baseball player as significantly larger than by a beginner. If it is the practical interaction with an object in the world that produces an image of that object which would not exist without the experience of dealing with the object, then knowledge cannot have cognitive independence, because it cannot be separated from the world. The perception of the baseball and its movement constitute a unified experience because its quality would not exist outside of this situation. Here it becomes clear why a concept of tacit knowledge corresponds to an externalist rather than an internalist epistemology. Namely, if habits change in problematic situations, whatever the particular

---

The cultivation of habit is indeed the grasping of a significance, but it is the motor grasping of a motor significance" (1962: 143).

13 | Gehlen later described this schematization as "resistant to critique and immune to objection." This resistance to critique is "a general feature of all habituation, and it appears on the lowest level in the realm of motoric habits, as the strong resistance to which the latter oppose their dissolution and recombination" (1986: 105).

social and material events may be that effect these changes, then they cannot be explained by an internalism which ignores the relation to the world that is constitutive of those habits. Habits embody aspects of the external world and its characteristics; they are thus neither mental nor autonomous. The answer to the question of what enables the body to embody something hence primarily is habit formation as a reaction to the human-specific plasticity of motor behavior and the concomitant contingency of the sensorimotor "comportment" (cf. Heidegger) in relation to the world.

If, however, the practical sense of this comportment is not based on monological techniques of the body but on the more or less felicitous determination of behavior that is always tied to a recognized language game within a shared way of life, then we come even closer to answering the question as to why tacit knowledge is a collective knowledge even if it passes through the single body and articulates itself in techniques of the body. For agents to acquire tacit knowledge, they must be integrated into social practices. Such participation is always tied to the coordination of action, or is even, as in the case of specific forms of communicative action, identical to it. When coping with the indexicality of concrete situations of interaction it quickly becomes apparent how the coordination of action depends upon the scope of this tacit knowledge. If tacit knowledge ensures participation in social practices, then it does so only because it is a shared and situationally adequate knowledge. These properties and the implicit normativity they entail also make clear why this form of knowledge can neither be understood as an idiosyncratic proficiency or individual talent nor be reduced to a subjectively evident physical ability. This is also why the determination and concretization of tacit knowledge by reference to the isolated handling of objects and the familiar examples of bicycling, swimming, etc., fall short. Not the balancing on a bicycle but its use in street traffic among other bicyclists or drivers of automobiles is the poignant metaphor, as is the playing of a musical instrument with an ensemble, or the throwing of a ball while participating in a team sport.[14] It is in this sense that knowledge is embodied in social praxis, because specific activities can only be executed in concert with others through such interactive calibration of action as the mutual sawing of a board, which is experienced as an uninterrupted circular movement; to use a rather labored analogy from Max Weber as another example, bicyclists can easily swerve out of each other's way by coordinating their bicycles, bodies, distance, and speed. Practices of this sort require something that can only be gained *through* practicing and that must be mastered together with others. It is impossible to apply such tacit knowledge outside of a particular praxis; this is especially true of communicative practices, which can never succeed without shared tacit knowl-

---

14 | Collins (2010) clearly distinguishes this type of tacit knowledge from other forms, and ascribes only to it the feature of inexplicability.

edge of the meaning and function of linguistic and non-linguistic expressions. These considerations not only make clear that tacit knowledge is not a matter of content already constituted by a consciousness and embodied only subsequently, as in the surface/substrate-model of phenomenological and other internalist approaches, but they also counteract the danger of objectifying the body into a container of meaning.

V. Consequences

It is one of the fundamental intuitions of modern notions of knowledge that consciousness can only know something insofar as knowledge has something to do with the symbolic relation of the human being to the world. And if the relationship of the human being to its world is exclusively thought to be one of explicit knowledge *about* that world, then the body as a sub-symbolic bearer of knowledge gets discarded from the start. If, however, the concept of experience is elevated to a fundamental category of this relationship to the world because knowledge and its articulation in the medium of social forms first arises through experiences, then there emerges another understanding of the relationship of knowledge, the objects of this knowledge, and the body as medium of having a world. For only beings with the possibility to enter into contact with the world can have experiences, that is to say, can receive effects from this world and can themselves have effects on this world. In other words: only corporeal beings are capable of experience, because one has experiences first and foremost with the senses, with one's entire possibilities of perception and movement. Even if the body is always already the central point of passage for all worldly relations – and Merleau-Ponty demonstrated this most impressively – the argument that it is the body and not consciousness which pre-reflectively 'knows' something is just as much of a lapse of abstraction as the mentalist claim that consciousness is the lynchpin of the world, and resides in the head (or the brain). While the genesis of cognitive structures arises from a sensorimotor practice, this practice, and the related experiences of resistance without which there would be nothing to supply the content of consciousness (cf. Noë 2009), were never the sole product of a single active body, but of its relationship to the world and other agents.

Thus, it is not an isolated body that does something, but an unavoidable relationship of embodied agents and situations that requires corporeal abilities, and functions as tacit knowledge. If the most fundamental level of relationships between agents and situations is the coordination of action, then the basic forms of tacit knowledge do not pertain to a relation to the world of things but to social action and communication. One has to be able to engage in such social praxis in order to know the meanings of action and to perpetuate it. The acquisition of tacit knowledge is thus only possible from the perspective of the participant. If participation, however, is a presupposition of sharing tacit knowledge, then an individualistic epistemology that fails to understand the collective character of this knowledge cannot offer a sufficient account of it. If the body, moreover, is the addressee of discourses by which it is formed and conditioned in order to reproduce these relationships through conditioned techniques of the body, habits, and styles of perception, then the faculties of the body are not to be understood as independent from the cultural ways of life in which they are formed and recognized. Even the naturalist description of the body is itself an effect of a specific cultural development that corresponds to a distancing movement away from the acting and sensing body. Because the question of the body and its characteristics cannot be answered independent of culturally contingent discourses, the conception of the body as an individual entity is an exaggeration indebted to modern societies. Agents do not rule autonomously over their bodies – the body is at least from a sociological perspective not private property, even if it is regarded as such by modern legal systems. Foucault's (1975 [1963]; 1973 [1966]) reconstruction of the genesis of the modern subject, the study of Vernant (1986) of the ancient description of the body, or Butler's (1993) analysis of the social practices that produce gender difference show that the single body can hardly serve as a presuppositionless point of departure for a theory of the social, because a 'collective biomass' must first transform into individual bodies of a certain type through social processes. But it would be just as equally a constructivist exaggeration to treat the body as an altogether passive variable and exclusive effect of discourses. Without its sensorimotor structure enabling the implementation of symbolic practices, there would be no dialectic between incorporation, the production of tacit knowledge, and the perpetuation of specific logics of systems, power relations, or forms of regulation. The mediation, however, of sensorimotor a priori and social structure takes place in the "creativity of action" (cf. Joas 1992) and within the emergent unity of the coordination of action.[15] If the body is conceptualized as a "transactional body" (Shusterman 2008: 214), then the danger of its objectification as well as its uncontrollable deconstruction into a pure effect of discourse can be avoided.

Anti-Cartesian positions, which have good arguments on their side, must resist the temptation to put the body in the same place that was previously occu-

---

15 | Numerous approaches in the first half of the twentieth century have already coined different terms to describe this phenomenon: for instance, as the "sensorimotor a priori" (Buytendijk 1930: 53), the steering of behavior dependent upon signals (Bühler 1927; 1990 [1934]), the founding of intentionality in the experience of movement (Grünbaum 1932; Gehlen 1988 [1940]; Merleau-Ponty 1962 [1945]), the idea of *Gestaltkreis* (v. Weizsäcker 1973 [1940]), or the entanglement of bodily acts in a unity of movement (Christian/Haas 1949).

pied by consciousness or the mind. A look at the history of philosophy and science shows that detours taken into terminological and conceptual marshaling yards have a long tradition. One thinks of Schopenhauer's theory of the will, or of Nietzsche's overreaching somatism with its anti-intellectualist reversal of the mind-body hierarchy, which quickly make the body, instead of the mind, the carrier of all will; or of idealist and materialist all-or-nothing stances up to contemporary neuro-reductionisms, which indeed like to speak of thinking and acting yet disregard the most essential feature of fundamental normativity. The unbroken epistemological attraction of sharp reversals (antirealism, anticonstructivism, antimentalism) is, to be sure, an understandable reaction to persistent problems of explanation, but leads, as is well known, to throwing out with the need for ontological and epistemological reassurance the baby with the bathwater – from the retreat into the head to the retreat into the body, from the psychologization of social practices to their corporealization.

The popular thesis that tacit knowledge is incorporated is only substantial if what is to be understood by such incorporation and its connection to social objectification can be explained. The surprising abilities of the body, such as the ones I have described, warrant the elevation of the body to an agent. Yet one reverts in the process to a variation of precisely that dualism which one had hoped to overcome and according to whose logic either the mind is active, or the body takes over the action. A careful reconstruction of primary experience, on the other hand, reveals that such a distinction is already a product of reflection and the result of an objectification of the body owing to the reassurance of its faculties from the perspective of the observer. For if repetitions go astray, are disturbed, or must be modified during their implementation, they are, as it were, de-routinized and de-schematized; or rather, they become obvious as routines, as kinesthetic forms or patterns of expectation, and their failure triggers a need for ascertainment and reassurance from which such objectification derives. That we ascribe knowledge to the body because we believe to be able to identify a type of agency in it can obviously be traced back to this praxis of reassurance. A theory of tacit knowledge, if it wants to take into account empirical reality, should thus be mindful not to pit pre-reflective practices against symbolically clotted re-codings and objectifications of bodily praxis.[16]

---

16 | Richard Shusterman (2012) has thus rightfully pointed out that Merleau-Ponty's "somatic phenomenology" greatly underestimated the function of reflexive acts for the transformation of practices. I have tried to show elsewhere (cf. Loenhoff 2012b) the extent to which Heidegger's reflections on understanding, exegesis, and thematic statement reveal an interpretive continuum that avoids the radical break between pre-reflexive and thematizing practices of reference without thereby relinquishing or relativizing the fundamentality of a practical engagement.

Works Cited

Aristotle (1907): De Anima, transl. and introd. Robert D. Hicks, Cambridge: Cambridge UP.
Bourdieu, Pierre (1980): Le sens pratique, Paris: Les éditions de Minuit.
—. (1990): The Logic of Practice, transl. Richard Nice, Stanford: Stanford UP.
Bühler, Karl (1927): Die Krise der Psychologie, Jena: Fischer.
—. (1990 [1934]): Theory of Language. The Representational Function of Language, transl. Donald F. Goodwin, Amsterdam: John Benjamins.
Butler, Judith (1993): Bodies That Matter. On the Discursive Limits of "Sex," New York: Routledge.
Buytendijk, Frederik J.J. (1930): "Les Différences essentielles des fonctions psychiques de l'homme et des animaux," in: Cahiers de Philosophie de la Nature 4, 35-94.
Christian, Paul/Haas, Renate (1949): Wesen und Formen der Bipersonalität. Grundlagen für eine medizinische Soziologie, Stuttgart: Enke.
Churchland, Patricia (2002): Brain-Wise. Studies in Neurophilosophy, Boston: MIT P.
Clark, Andy (1997): Being There. Putting Brain, Body, and World Together Again, Cambridge: MIT P.
—. (2008): Supersizing the Mind. Embodiment, Action, and Cognitive Extension, Oxford: Oxford UP.
Collins, Harry M. (2010): Tacit and Explicit Knowledge, Chicago: U of Chicago P.
Crick, Francis (1995): The Astonishing Hypothesis. The Scientific Search for the Soul, New York: Scribner.
Dewey, John (1896): "The Reflex Arc Concept in Psychology," in: Psychological Review 3, 357-370.
—. (1922): Human Nature and Conduct. An Introduction to Social Psychology, New York: Holt.
—. (1925): Experience and Nature, La Salle: Open Court.
—. (1960 [1929]): The Quest for Certainty. A Study of the Relation of Knowledge and Action, New York: Putnam's.
Dreyfus, Hubert L. (1980): "Holism and Hermeneutics," in: Review of Metaphysics 34, 3-23.
Frith, Uta/Frith, Chris (2001): "The Biological Basis of Social Interaction," in: Current Directions in Psychological Science 10, 151-155.
Foucault, Michel (1973 [1966]): The Order of Things. An Archeology of the Human Sciences, New York: Vintage.
—. (1975 [1963]): The Birth of the Clinic. An Archaeology of Medical Perception, transl. Alan M. Sheridan-Smith, New York: Vintage.

Froese, Tom/Fuchs, Thomas (2012): "The Extended Body. A Case Study in the Neurophenomenology of Social Interaction," in: Phenomenology and the Cognitive Sciences 11, 205-235.

Fuchs, Thomas/De Jaeger, Hanne (2009): "Enactive Intersubjectivity. Participatory Sense-Making and Mutual Incorporation," in: Phenomenology and the Cognitive Sciences 8, 465-486.

Gallese, Vittorio/Lakoff, George (2005): "The Brain's Concepts. The Role of the Sensory-Motor System in Conceptual Knowledge," in: Cognitive Neuropsychology 22.3/4, 455-479.

Gehlen, Arnold (1986 [1956]): Urmensch und Spätkultur. Philosophische Ergebnisse und Aussagen, Wiesbaden: Aula.

—. (1988 [1940]): Man, His Nature and Place in the World, transl. Clare McMillan/Karl Pillemer, introd. Karl-Siegbert Rehberg, New York: Columbia UP.

Grünbaum, Abraham A. (1932): "Sprache als Handlung," in: Gustav Kafka (ed.), Bericht über den XII. Kongress der Deutschen Gesellschaft für Psychologie in Hamburg 1931, Jena: Fischer, 164-176.

Habermas, Jürgen (1996 [1992]): Between Facts and Norms. Contributions to a Discourse Theory of Law and Democracy, transl. William Regh, Cambridge: MIT P.

—. (2003 [1999]): Truth and Justification, transl. Barbara Fultner, Cambridge: MIT P.

Hawley, Katherine (2003): "Success and Knowledge How," in: American Philosophical Quarterly 40.1, 19-31.

Heidegger, Martin (1996 [1927]): Being and Time, transl. Joan Stambough, Albany: State U of New York P.

Hetherington, Stephen (2008): "Knowledge-That, Knowledge-How, and Knowing Philosophically," in: Grazer Philosophische Studien 77.1, 307-24.

Husserl, Edmund (1982 [1913]): Ideas Pertaining to a Pure Phenomenology and to a Phenomenological Philosophy. First Book: General Introduction to a Pure Phenomenology, transl. F. Kersten, The Hague: Nijhoff.

Hutchins, Edwin (1995): Cognition in the Wild, Cambridge: MIT P.

—. (2006): "The Distributed Cognition Perspective on Human Interaction," in: Nick J. Enfield/Stephen C. Levinson (eds.), Roots of Human Sociality, London: Berg, 375-398.

Joas, Hans (1996 [1992]): The Creativity of Action, transl. Jeremy Gaines/Paul Keast, Chicago: U of Chicago P.

Johnson, Mark H. (1987): The Body in the Mind. The Bodily Basis of Meaning, Imagination and Reason, Chicago: U of Chicago P.

Johnson, Mark H./Morton, John (1991): Biology and Cognitive Development. The Case of Face Recognition, Oxford: Blackwell.

Lakoff, George (1987): Women, Fire, and Dangerous Things. What Categories Reveal About the Mind, Chicago: U of Chicago P.

Lakoff, George/Johnson, Mark (1999): Philosophy in the Flesh. The Embodied Mind and Its Challenge to Western Thought, New York: Basic.

Legrand, Dorothée (2006): "The Bodily Self. The Sensori-Motor Roots of Pre-Reflective Self-Consciousness," in: Phenomenology and the Cognitive Sciences 5, 89-118.

Lindblom, Jessica/Ziemke, Tom (2008): "Interacting Socially Through Embodied Action," in: Morganti/Carassa/Riva, Enacting Intersubjectivity, 49-63.

Loenhoff, Jens (2001): Die kommunikative Funktion der Sinne. Theoretische Studien zum Verhältnis von Kommunikation, Wahrnehmung und Bewegung, Konstanz: UVK.

—. (ed.) (2012a): Implizites Wissen. Epistemologische und handlungstheoretische Perspektiven, Weilerswist: Velbrück.

—. (2012b): "Zur Reichweite von Heideggers Verständnis impliziten Wissens," in: Loenhoff, Implizites Wissen, 49-66.

Malafouris, Lambros (2013): How Things Shape the Mind. A Theory of Material Engagement, Cambridge: MIT P.

Mead, George H. (1934): Mind, Self, and Society from the Standpoint of a Social Behaviorist, ed. and introd. Charles W. Morris, Chicago: U of Chicago P.

Merleau-Ponty, Maurice (1962 [1945]): Phenomenology of Perception, transl. Colin Smith, London: Routledge and Kegan Paul.

Morganti, Francesca/Carassa, Antonella/Riva, Giuseppe (eds.) (2008): Enacting Intersubjectivity. A Cognitive and Social Perspective to the Study of Interactions, Amsterdam: IOS.

Noë, Alva (2004): Action in Perception, Cambridge: MIT P.

—. (2009): Out of Our Heads. Why You Are Not Your Brain, and Other Lessons from the Biology of Consciousness, New York: Hill and Wang.

Polanyi, Michael (1966): The Tacit Dimension, Chicago: U of Chicago P.

Renn, Joachim (2012): "Was ist rational am impliziten Wissen? Zum theoretischen Status der praktischen Gewissheit zwischen Handlungs- und Gesellschaftstheorie," in: Loenhoff, Implizites Wissen, 150-176.

—. (2013): "Praktische Gewissheit und die Rationalität zweiter Ordnung – zur gesellschaftstheoretischen Analyse des impliziten Wissens," in: ZTS – Zeitschrift für Theoretische Soziologie 2, 56-82.

Rorty, Richard (1982): Consequences of Pragmatism, Minneapolis: U of Minnesota P.

Rosenfeld, Tobias (2004): "Is Knowing-how Simply a Case of Knowing-that?" in: Philosophical Investigations 27.4, 370–79.

Shusterman, Richard (1999): "Dewey on Experience: Foundation or Reconstruction?" in: Casey Haskins/David I. Seiple (eds.), Dewey Reconfigured. Essays on Deweyan Pragmatism, Albany: State U of New York P, 193-219.

—. (2008): Body Consciousness. A Philosophy of Mindfulness and Somaesthetics, New York: Cambridge UP.

—. (2012): Thinking Through the Body. Essays in Somaesthetics, New York: Cambridge UP.

Snowdon, Paul (2003): "Knowing How and Knowing That. A Distinction Reconsidered," in: Proceedings of the Aristotelian Society 104.1, 1-29.

Stanley, Jason/Williamson, Timothy (2001): "Knowing How," in: The Journal of Philosophy 98.8, 411-44.

Stewart, John/Gapenne, Oscar/Di Paolo, Ezequiel A. (eds.) (2010): Enaction. Towards a New Paradigm for Cognitive Science, Cambridge: MIT P.

Thompson, Evan (2007): Mind in Life. Biology, Phenomenology, and the Sciences of Mind, Cambridge: Harvard UP.

Tomasello, Michael (2008): Origins of Human Communication, Cambridge: MIT P.

Turner, Stephen (2012): "Implizites Wissen und das System der Spiegelneuronen," in: Loenhoff, Implizites Wissen, 215-243.

Vernant, Jean-Pierre (1986): "Corps obscur, corps éclatant," in: Charles Malamoud/Jean-Pierre Vernant (eds.), Corps des dieux, Paris: Gallimard, 19-46.

Weizsäcker, Victor v. (1973 [1940]): Der Gestaltkreis. Theorie der Einheit von Wahrnehmen und Bewegen, introd. Rolf Denker, Frankfurt/Main: Suhrkamp.

Wilson, Margret (2002): "Six Views of Embodied Cognition," in: Psychonomic Bulletin and Review 9, 625-636.

Wittgenstein, Ludwig (1969): On Certainty, ed. Gertrude E. M. Anscombe/Georg Henrik von Wright, transl. Denis Paul/Gertrude E. M. Anscombe, Oxford: Blackwell.

—. (1980 [1977]): Culture and Value, ed. Georg H. von Wright, transl. Peter Winch, Oxford: Blackwell.

—. (1989 [1953]): Philosophical Investigations, 3rd ed., reprint, Oxford: Blackwell.

Ziemke, Tom/Zlatev, Jordan/Frank, Rosalyn M. (eds.) (2007): Body, Language and Mind. Volume 1: Embodiment, Berlin: de Gruyter.

Embodiment of Tacit Knowledge

Practices between Dispositifs and Interaction[1]

Michael Hubrich

I. INTRODUCTION

In his famous study "Techniques of the Body," Marcel Mauss depicts the case of a young girl in the following words:

> A little girl did not know how to spit and this made every cold she had much worse. I made inquiries. In her father's village and in her father's family in particular, in Berry, people do not know how to spit. I taught her to spit. I gave her four sous per spit. As she was saving up for a bicycle she learnt to spit. She is the first person in her family who knows how to spit. (1992 [1934]: 472)

In this passage, Mauss implicitly conceptualizes the body not so much as a biological entity or a mere manifestation of genetic predispositions but rather as in relation to sociality. Following Mauss, not only spitting, but all practices assumed to be 'natural,' e.g. eating, drinking, standing, walking, sleeping, sitting, as well as more complex activities like swimming, writing, dancing, or bicycling are culture-specific and become intelligible only if their social dimension is taken into account (cf. Gugutzer 2010).

While the body for a long time had been an "absent presence" (Shilling 1993: 19) in sociology, it has become a focus of sociological enquiry in the last ten to twenty years. For social theory, the 'return' of the body has posed a basic theoretical problem which can also be outlined in Maussian terms. On the one hand, 'body techniques' as the incorporation of a certain type of knowledge are always historical: "There is no technique and no transmission in the absence of tradition" (Mauss 1992 [1934]: 461). In the Berry region visited by Mauss, the technique of spitting was not part of the local tradition, and sociocultural

---

[1] | This article builds on my previous work on embodiment and adds more recent reflections on the topic of tacit knowledge (cf. Hubrich 2013).

knowledge of how to spit thus was not transmitted. On the other hand, that Mauss was able to teach the girl how to spit shows that bodily practices can be learned and therefore that bodily know-how can be modified and transformed in situations of social interaction. In this vein, a practice like spitting can be grasped as a bodily performance which displays a type of bodily knowledge. In sum, Mauss gives a hint to a relational conceptualization of corporeality: While the body is an "ensemble of [...] social relations," social reality is also constantly materially structured by "sensous human activit[ies]:" "it is men who change circumstances" (Marx 1975: 421f.). Social theories of bodily praxis need to take into account those relational an anti-dichotomous implications in order to avoid false binaries. As Nick Crossley states, it seems that "[w]e are being asked to choose. Should we study 'the body' as 'lived' and active or as acted upon, as historically 'inscribed' from without?" (1996: 99). Such a binary approach to the body is problematic, because it reflects common dichotomous figures of structure and agency (cf. Walsh 1998) and results in a dualistic and substantialistic ontology in which the body is either a product of sociality, or the sole producer of sociality.

As already suggested by Mauss's example of knowing how to spit, a sociology of the body cannot avoid thinking about the connection between the body and knowledge. Mauss conceives of the body as "man's first and most natural instrument" and as "man's first and most natural technical object" (1992 [1934]: 461). This also entails that the "body is the ultimate instrument of all our external knowledge" of the world (Polanyi 2009: 15). Following Michael Polanyi, embodied knowledge should not be conceived of as propositional knowledge, but rather as prereflexive 'tacit knowledge,' i.e. as a bodily competence to act and as a skill of perception. The basic assumption is that this kind of knowledge is 'tacit' because it is anchored in the body. In light of this assumption, a theory of tacit knowledge has to deal with the problem of a general sociological theory of the body as outlined above. When theorizing the embodiment of tacit knowledge in dichotomous terms, one has to either theorize embodied tacit knowledge top-down as supra-subjective, i.e. cultural and collective knowledge which materializes in the body, or bottom-up, i.e. as knowledge of how to interact bodily. In regard to the first perspective, it could be objected that the body is reduced to its mere materiality because tacit knowledge can never be possessed or changed by a subject. However, in the latter approach, the body appears as a black box; it cannot explain how knowledge is tacitly embodied and how bodies are socialized, and in some cases may not even theorize tacit knowledge at all, but instead conceptualize the body as tacit. Following this line of reasoning, action and interaction always seem to originate from a continuously reflective actor who acts on the basis of presuppositionless propositional knowledge.

In order to be able to answer the question of whether a sociological theory of embodied tacit knowledge really has to choose between these apparently incompatible points of view, they need to be examined systematically in light of their respective theoretical paradigms. As many sociological studies theorize the body with recourse to the writings of either Michel Foucault or Erving Goffman (cf. Gugutzer 2006; Meuser 2004), two authors who can be read as examples of diametrically opposed sociological theories of the body and of knowledge, I will use them as examples to explicate the problems of the two theoretical positions. First, I will cursorily reconstruct Foucault's genealogical method, which traces the materialization of dispositifs, i.e., certain historical, supra-individual power-knowledge complexes and non-discursive practices. I will discuss his conceptualization of the linkage between knowledge and the body in order to show to which extent his approach can be read as a theory of the embodiment of tacit knowledge. Foucauldian thought will thus serve as an example of an objectivistic historical genealogy which posits the embodiment of tacit knowledge as a mere effect of sociality. Second, I will discuss in the same cursory fashion the role knowledge and the body play in Goffman's interactional theory, which is a good example of approaches that theorize the relation between knowledge and bodily action as a subjectivist orchestration and performance of context-sensitive forms of know-how. In this theory, the embodiment of tacit knowledge is limited to the interactive production of social situations. Finally, I will take into account a general practice theory and connect it to the previously discussed positions in order to outline a relational understanding of the embodiment of tacit knowledge. I will suggest a rereading of both positions to support my thesis that a theoretical shift towards a notion of the embodiment of tacit knowledge as praxis can provide a non-dichotomous understanding of its impact on sociality.

II. Embodiment as Materialization of Power-Knowledge

Foucauldian thinking about corporeal materiality in the context of a "history of bodies" investigates bodies and "the manner in which what is most material and most vital in them has been invested" (Foucault 1978: 152). Methodically, Foucault's genealogy is antithetical to traditional historicism, intellectual history, and the history of ideas. Foucault rejects the concept of 'grande histoire' (cf. Ruoff 2009) and instead traces the genealogy of specific complexes of power-knowledge, defined as structures of power and discursive formations of knowledge which emerge in local and temporal contexts as materialized non-discursive practices. Thus, Foucault is interested in both discursive and non-discursive practices, which constitute specific forms of materialized dispositifs (cf. Dreyfus/Rabinow 1982).

Employing this epistemological strategy for theorizing the embodiment of tacit knowledge, Foucault emphasizes that the body is always interwoven with a locus, or, to use a Nietzschean term, 'Herkunft.' Thus, the body is "totally imprinted by history" and constitutes an "inscribed surface of events." This locus is always a "locus of a dissociated self" that tries to maintain the "illusion of a substantial unity" (Foucault 1984: 83). On the one hand, these theoretical assumptions point to a strong connection between the body and history, and therefore to a certain kind of sociocultural knowledge; on the other hand, they allow one to enquire into the contingent historical power structures which shape and engender the body in social-historical contexts (cf. Siebenpfeiffer 2008). The Foucauldian notion of power implies the deconstruction of the traditional western philosophical concept of reason, instead of which the genealogical perspective posits balances of power which reveal themselves in historical developments and events. Foucault's notion of power is not reducible to something individuals possess or acquire presocially. Even resistance does not undermine power but rather is an indispensable requirement for spreading balances of power. For Foucault, power consists of "maneuvers, tactics, techniques, functionings" and "a network of relations, constantly in tension, in activity" (1977: 26). Therefore, no power relation is conceivable "without the correlative constitution of a field of knowledge" (ibid. 27). Furthermore, Foucault states:

[W]e should abandon a whole tradition that allows us to imagine that knowledge can exist only where the power relations are suspended and that knowledge can develop only outside its injunctions [...]. We should admit rather that power produces knowledge. (Ibid.)

Discursively constructed knowledge is closely linked to power relations through an 'archive' that structures what can be thought or said. The body as an object that is constructed in discourse thus is entangled in power-knowledge complexes. Thus, at the center of Foucault's attention are not interaction orders but rather all-pervasive balances of power which are closely linked to knowledge orders. Foucauldian theory replaces the intentionally and deliberately acting subject with structural patterns of power-knowledge (cf. Bublitz 1999), and revolves around a supra-subjective archive of knowledge that can be said to constitute a form of tacit knowledge.[2]

---

[2] | Foucault's interest in tacit forms of knowledge becomes evident in the following quote: "In a society, different bodies of learning, philosophical ideas, everyday options, but also institutions, commercial practices and police activities, mores – all refer to a certain *implicit knowledge* (savoir) special to this society. This knowledge is profoundly different from the bodies of learning that one can find in scientific books, philosophical theories, and religious justifications [...], and it's this knowledge that I wanted to investigate, as the condition of possibility of knowledge (connaissance), of institutions, of practices" (1996: 13; emphasis added).

This becomes clear when looking at *Discipline and Punish: The Birth of the Prison* (1977), in which Foucault examines the complexes (or better: regimes) of power-knowledge and their 'technologies' that visibly materialize when individuals are subjected to punitive treatment such as torture. In the course of the 18th century, this brutal materialization of "physico-penal knowledge" (ibid. 34) was replaced by the "submission of bodies through the control of ideas" (ibid. 102), which, following Foucault, can be understood as a subtle and tacit "politics of bodies" which works with "semio-techniques of punishment" (ibid.). For example, the public display of convicts' maimed bodies had the implicit function of encouraging panoptic habits of self-discipline. Here, Foucault develops his central theoretical figure of the disciplined body. The body is the physical substratum of the knowledge of disciplining; it comes into being and is normalized via an 'apparatus' of perception and disciplinary codes (cf. Bublitz 2003: 75). Foucault shows how in modernity an anonymous 'micro-physic' of power and knowledge establishes itself in the form of total institutions, which through the distribution of bodies in space, the regulation of bodily activity, and the organization of time produce the 'docile body.' These functions and techniques, understood as practical functions of power-knowledge complexes, produce the docile body in institutions like hospitals, schools, and the military, from where it spreads into society at large. The docile body is also important in Foucault's analysis of the history of sexuality; the normalization of certain sexual practices and the pathologization of others "are linked in a common bond of knowledge, power, and the materiality of the body" (Dreyfus/Rabinow 1982: 171). In other words, it is not the body which carries out practices but rather praxis which governs the body (cf. Gehring 2008).

The significance of Foucault's work on prisons, criminal trials, and sexuality lies in its dissection of specific mechanisms of dispositifs. For Foucault, the body is a contingent material product of cultural transformations. Especially with regard to his diagnosis of the 'disciplinary society,' one can identify parallels to Mauss's remarks on conditioning: It is, the latter writes, "like the assembly of a machine, is the search for, the acquisition of an efficiency. Here it is a human efficiency. These techniques are thus human norms of human training" (1992 [1934]: 464). Applying Mauss's technical terms to Foucault indicates that the impact of dispositifs is an immediately material one. Like a machine, dispositifs literally carve out bodies in a strategic manner. This perspective is in contradistinction to the notion that the body is driven by some sort of vital energy (cf. Gehring 2004: 120ff.). Dispositifs and their regimes of power-knowledge thus have non-discursive effects as they materialize in bodies. For Foucault, discourses and anonymous balances of power and knowledge construct bodies and bodily practices in both tangible as well as tacit ways (cf. Bublitz 2003: 51f.). Hence, from a Foucauldian point of view, the embodiment of tacit knowledge can be understood as the tacit production of bodily practices through supra-subjective knowledge. Discursive power-knowledge, when materialized in praxis, is thus bound up with bodily practices. That kind of knowledge is tacit because of its embodiment. Following Foucault, behaviors are in fact materialized 'knowing how.' Materialization in the sense of embodiment thus necessitates shifting attention from propositional knowledge, which is explicable via an examination of the archive, to practical and embodied 'knowing how' (cf. Ryle 2000). Therefore, Foucault's genealogic studies show how to conceive of embodied tacit knowledge as completely produced top-down by sociality.

In light of this theorization of the embodiment of tacit knowledge, we can speak of a paradigmatic "Foucauldian approach to the body" (Shilling 1993: 75). However, one cannot ignore that this approach implies that the body is effectively and solely actuated by anonymous power-knowledge complexes. If these anonymous strategies constitute operations and functions of power-knowledge beyond the agency of individuals, then, to quote Judith Butler, "the subject is left behind as the relation of power to the body emerges" (2004: 184). In other words, Foucault's focus on structures of supra-subjective dispositifs and their tacit embodiment disregards the role agents play in the constitution of the body: Embodiment is conceptualized as mechanic and reactive rather than as active and productive. In the end, in the tradition of Nietzsche, Foucault claims the 'death of the subject' (cf. Allen 2000; Dreyfus/Rabinow 1982: 44ff.). Historical change is, following Foucault, primarily an effect of changing dispositifs. In the end, this perspective implies that history is never made by humans. However, Marx argued to the contrary that "history does nothing; [...] [i]t is men [...] who do all this" (qtd. in Kitching 1988: 39). With this in mind, I will now turn to Goffman's interactionism in order to focus on the relation between agency and the embodiment of tacit knowledge.

III. Embodiment as Interactional Display of Knowledge

In his book *Asylums* (1961), Goffman is concerned with the usurpation of the body by total institutions. He identifies psychiatric practices such as bodily examinations, security controls, and other restrictions to which patients on psychiatric wards are subjected as forms of "personal defacement" which pursue "mortification[s] of the self by way of the body" (ibid. 21) and violate the embodied self (cf. Raab 2008). Thus at first it seems that Goffman argues along similar lines as Foucault, as both hold that the body is a "programmed" and institutionally determined entity (Goffman 1961: 189). However, a closer reading of *Asylums* reveals that Goffman's approach is actually opposed to Foucault's supra-subjective perspective.

First, the most significant characteristic of total institutions is, following Goffman, "that the inmate lives all the aspects of his life on the premises in the close company of others who are similarly cut off from the wider world" (ibid. 203). Goffman's depiction of total institutions is in contradistinction to Foucault because for him they are not complex and ubiquitous organizational structures of dispositifs, but are separate from the everyday world (cf. Raab 2008). Second, in institutions like psychiatric hospitals there are "two broad and quite differently situated categories of participants, staff and inmates" (Goffman 1961: 203). Thus, Goffman's analytical focus is on concrete agents, with the result that "men are coming back into the picture" (Gouldner 1970: 380). For Goffman, psychiatric inmates are not completely at the mercy of the institution because they are able to utilize behaviors to resist a complete usurpation of their bodies. After a phase of 'primary adjustments' during the inmates' institutionalization, they are able to accomplish a 'secondary adjustment' by engaging in unauthorized activities, which can be read as the implementation of a knowledge of resistance (cf. Goffman 1961: 171ff.). So, diametrically opposed to Foucault, Goffman thinks that agents possess the knowledge of how to act bodily and are thus able to thwart the institution's expectations. Goffman argues that the ability of individuals to perform independently is so strong that "secondary adjustment becomes almost a kind of lodgment for the self" (ibid. 55), and agents thus are never completely immersed in their social roles. He writes: "We always find the individual employing methods to keep some distance, some elbow room [...]. [I]t is thus against something that the self can emerge" (ibid. 319f.). Goffman is interested in how individuals actively deal with role expectations in social situations and interactions which generate specific interactional orders, which, in turn, are not produced by but rather are able to produce themselves institutionalized knowledge.

In opposition to Foucault, Goffman methodically contrasts the 'normality' of everyday practices with those of total institutions as the exception to the rule (cf. Manning 1992). That is why it is worthwhile to also look at Goffman's studies of everyday life, which offer numerous microsociological insights. Goffman's basic insight is that "Wherever an individual is or goes he must bring his body along with him" (1977: 327). This point is crucial to my argument because humans appear as agents *with* bodies – hence, situations appear as material situations. From Goffman's point of view, this requires that agents know how to establish interactional orders intentionally through sophisticated techniques of the body. In Goffman's theory, the agent has the ability to intervene in everyday social life because of his intentional management of the body, that is, he is precisely *not* a passive product of dispositifs (cf. Shilling 1993). The focus is not on the body as permeated and constituted by power-knowledge, but on individuals as agents who exert control over their bodies. Social situations can consequently be understood as the materialization and non-deterministic operationalization of normative rules of behavior and action. Agents know how to regulate framed co-present social interactions through bodily practices such as oculesics, symbolic gestures (cf. Goffman 1963), and body language that serve to establish a "working consensus" "involving a degree of mutual considerateness, sympathy, and a muting of opinion differences" (ibid. 96). Moreover, through bodily enactments individuals form an image of themselves that mirrors the one attributed to them by others, which they have to modify by bodily acts in order to encourage desired responses and to overcome imposed roles (cf. Goffman 1959). In other words, Goffman pays attention to the bodily produced order instead of the social order of the body (cf. Reuter 2004).

In Goffman's conception of techniques of the body, there are similarities to Mauss's reflections on the instrumental dimension of the body. In Goffman's analysis, the body is controlled by an agent who reacts to the social environment by using techniques of the body. Nevertheless, Goffman differs from Mauss because he emphasizes specific social situations which are grounded in co-present bodies, and takes into account bodily social interaction and the importance of knowledge of how to act bodily. Whereas Mauss analyzes techniques of the body regardless of situational demands and constraints, Goffman prioritizes "on-going practices which accommodate [...] anticipated exigencies" and gives a microsociological account of the "vibrant flux of everyday social interaction" (Crossley 1995: 135; cf. Goffman 1971).

However, compared to Foucault's theory of dispositifs, Goffman's theoretical scope is narrower. While Foucault concentrates on the cultural and social construction of the body and bodily practices through tacit power-knowledge, Goffman is indifferent to those questions because he conceives social interactions and situations ahistorically as a reality *sui generis* (cf. 1983). The body appears as an ahistorical instrument for structuring sociality. Goffman's shifting of the sociological question of embodiment and its link to knowledge to the sphere of co-present interaction has the theoretical problem that it implies a "static historyless society of scenes" (Sennett 1977: 36). This lack of historicity implies that social life is altogether uncertain, so that agents are condemned to first define social reality *and then* to display bodily presentations of themselves. Therefore, the question of agency cannot be answered in terms of social processes and hence in regard to the historical genesis of the knowledge of how to act. From this point of view, Goffman is forced to posit an agent's self that has to react to situative constraints (cf. Reiger 2000); the Goffmanian agent is always confronted with situative demands that have to be dealt with. One could almost say that interaction orders are not produced by processes of socialization but by personal interpretations; bodily acts and embodiment then are in no way shaped by preceding social orders (cf. Hitzler 1992).

These reflections necessitate defining more precisely what type of knowledge Goffman actually posits as embodied. According to him, it is primarily a representational and rather conscious knowledge which is displayed in bodily actions. As suggested, Goffman's notion of embodied agency suffers from the fact that his theory implies that humans act *with* their bodies. Goffman posits an agent who knows how to behave, who is "fostering and maintaining a specific conception of self before others" (Gouldner 1970: 380), and for whom the body has a mere ancillary function. As a consequence, tacit knowledge cannot be conceived as embodied in the strict sense, as the body is merely a convenient instrument. The knowledge of how to behave can be displayed and enacted but is no longer embodied itself. Instead of tacit knowledge that is grounded in the body, Goffman conceptualizes explicit knowledge of socially acceptable behavior, and posits a subject which again and again has to perform singular and strategically planned acts on the stage of everyday life (cf. Reuter 2004). "On this," as Lofland states, "Sartre and Goffman are inseparable," because they agree that "[m]an is nothing else but that which he makes of himself" (1980: 46). This existentialist notion of self-objectification and of an ontological 'being-for-itself' tends to reproduce the Cartesian dualism of mind and body which makes a sophisticated conceptualization of the embodiment of tacit knowledge impossible. Taking Goffman seriously requires one to posit a mental substance (*res cogitans*) that holds sway over the materiality of the body (*res extensa*). In this vein, as Goffman puts it, "[t]he behavior in question is *merely* performed by bodies" (1971: 137, emphasis added). Or, as Shilling remarks with regard to Goffman's concept of the body: "Ultimately the significance of the body is determined by the mind's receptiveness [...]; the mind becomes the site in which is inscribed the body's meaning" (1993: 90). That is, the Goffmanian agent is disconnected, first, from any historical and social presuppositions of his or her mental or embodied knowledge; and second, from his or her own bodily actions and from social situations themselves. Therefore, the agent has to decide how to deal with the frame of an interaction order and to what extent he or she accepts its guidance. If an agent is compelled to question and scrutinize interaction orders continually, then the agent acknowledges and complies to it only situationally (cf. Hitzler 1992). Therefore, from Goffman's point of view, this 'knowledge to acknowledge' precedes any bodily action. As a result, bodily actions appear as ancillary to situational awareness, and (tacit) knowledge is theoretically cut off from embodiment.

IV. Practice Theories: Between Dispositifs and Interaction

As outlined above, neither a theory which conceives the body as a passive effect of tacit power-knowledge nor an ahistoric interactionistic approach which conceives the body as subordinate to an agent's mind leads to a sufficient theorization of the embodiment of tacit knowledge. As a way out of this impasse,

I suggest rereading both positions with the help of practice theory, which conceives of sociality as relational.

Foucault's aim of drawing attention to the contingent history of the embodiment of tacit knowledge is shared by practice theory: Foucault's 'social history' of the body and Bourdieu's analysis of habitus converge in their theoretical focus on historical discontinuities. The question is whether substantialist thinking can be avoided by adopting a relational and dialectical perspective (cf. Schäfer 2009). Both Bourdieu and Foucault are interested in disclosing the hidden and embodied mechanisms of power and knowledge (cf. Bourdieu 1991, 2000a, 2000b), and hold that cultural orders are contingent effects of historical balances of power (cf. Bublitz 2008). However, in contrast to Foucault's top-down approach, relational social theory incorporates the 'work' of the individual into its theoretical structure. According to Bourdieu, a "'milieu'" is not "exerting a form of mechanical causality on the agent;" instead, he refers to the "complicity between two states of the social, [...] between the history in the form of structures and mechanisms [...] and the history incarnated in bodies in the form of habitus" (2000b: 150f.). This process of incarnating history in bodies can be read as the condition of possibility for the embodiment of tacit knowledge. In Merleau-Ponty's terms, it is about practical and bodily 'being-in-the-world' (cf. 2005).[3] "The world," Bourdieu says, "is comprehensible, immediately endowed with meaning, because the body, which, thanks to its senses and its brain, has the capacity to be present what is outside itself, in the world" and "to be impressed and durably modified by it." That is, "if the agent has an immediate understanding of the familiar world, this is because the cognitive structures that he implements are the product of the structures of the world in which he acts" (2000b: 135f.). If one conceives the embodiment of tacit knowledge in this vein as a relational process of habitualization, the necessity to define the materialization of knowledge as tacit in terms of passivity becomes obsolete. The embodiment of tacit knowledge then means active acquisition of a "corporeal knowledge" which provides a "practical comprehension of the world quite different from the intentional act of conscious decoding" (ibid.).

By taking into account that subjects possess agency depending on corporeal knowledge it is possible to theorize the emergence of Foucauldian docile bodies in terms of the transmission of tacit knowledge via performative bodily practices. Foucault's notion of the 'archive' as a historic layer of discourse systems has to be thought of as linked to a repertoire of "performances, gestures, orality, movement, singing – in short, all those acts usually thought of as ephemeral,

---

3 | In opposition to Heidegger's 'In-der-Welt-sein,' which is also translated as 'being-in-the-world,' the German translation of Merleau-Ponty's term 'être au monde' as 'Zur-Welt-sein' highlights that agents are not entirely a product of sociality but are also producers of sociality.

nonreproducible knowledge" (Taylor 2003: 20). According to Diana Taylor, the concept of a "repertoire of embodied practices" allows one to understand praxis as an "important system of knowing and [especially] transmitting knowledge" (ibid. 2). Taylor's conceptualization of performances as "vital acts of transfer" of "social knowledge, memory and a sense of identity" (ibid.) can be understood as an "implicit pedagogy" (Bourdieu 1990: 69) which is actuated by mimetic praxis: children acquire in a playful way a small number of practical schematic principles (i.e., a repertoire of dispositions), which, however, generate a wide range of differentiated practices (cf. Fröhlich 2009). It is crucial that this incorporation of schemas and dispositions is transmitted through interactive praxis and requires bodily co-presence: "people participate in the production and reproduction of knowledge by 'being there,' being a part of the transmission" (Taylor 2003: 20). Tacit knowledge thus cannot be conceived as hidden, invisible knowledge, and its transmission cannot be understood solely as an act of representation. A theory of mimesis which provides an understanding of the transmission of embodied tacit knowledge thus exceeds Cooley's 'looking-glass self' (1922), which reduces corporeality to a 'body image' and disregards acquired dispositional and pragmatic 'body schemas.'[4] As "practical mastery is transmitted through practice," mimesis should neither be misunderstood as the imitation of a deliberately chosen role model nor as embodiment that is solely imposed by sociality (Bourdieu 1990: 73): It is the agent herself who is bodily engaged in the process of embodying tacit knowledge.

Moreover, positing an embodied agency enables one to reformulate Foucault's deconstruction of the embodiment of tacit knowledge in specific institutions in terms of mimetic and bodily practices. Institutions like hospitals, courts, or schools require a performance of specified and routine gestures. This is why skillful movements are the most elementary part of institutions. For example, a judge using a gavel in court performs an intelligible gesture consisting of an institutionalized sequence of bodily movements which indicates that a case has been decided, but this gesture is only intelligible against the background of shared tacit knowledge. The performance itself is a result of embodied tacit knowledge; at the same time, the embodiment of tacit knowledge occurs only through performance. With the routinized performance of a gesture the norms and values of an institution get inscribed into the bodies of agents. They gain significance through mimetic and repetitive performances (cf. Wulf 1997).

It is important to note here that the notion of routinization does not imply that bodily practices and tacit knowledge are static and unchangeable, as practices always imply both repetition and change (cf. Hörning 2004). They are

---

4 | On the relation between 'body image' und 'body schema' cf. Gallagher (2005) and Vignemont (2010).

not causations of ahistorical laws but rather products of frequently occurring performances. From an ethnomethodological perspective, they need to be performed anew every day. Bodily praxis can be understood in analogy to Ludwig Wittgenstein's description of language games and family resemblances: When "spinning a thread we twist fibre on fibre. And the strength of the thread does not reside in the fact that some one fibre runs through its whole length, but in the overlapping of many fibres" (1973: §67). The "network of [overlapping and criss-crossing] similarities" that results from mimetic and bodily practices (ibid. §66), however, does not follow explicit rules which govern all practices. In fact, as Bourdieu stresses, practical logic differs from theoretical thought and can effect surprising and unpredictable changes. Embodied practices oscillate between rigid repetition and dynamic variation (cf. Reckwitz 2003). Changes in embodied tacit knowledge can thus be described as continuous modifications of the habitus, as Bourdieu's notion of 'trajectoire' (cf. 1984) links the modification of embodied tacit knowledge to change in social position.

As social structures are not static but dynamic, embodied knowledge is not ahistorical, and its modifications depend on the involvement of bodies in social contexts. These contexts can be conceived in Bourdieu's terms as autonomous institutional fields. Every field requires specific bodily practices and hence specific tacit knowledge, which is acquired by participating actively in practices through which one is bodily socialized (cf. Bourdieu/Wacquant 1996). Through their ongoing mimetic socialization by different fields with different practical logics, individuals are bodily affected by different orders of tacitly acquired knowledge. In turn, these orders are necessary for the embodied performance of practices which are required in different social contexts (cf. Ebrecht 2004). With John Dewey, one can argue that "[c]haracter is the interpenetration of habits" that are acquired by interacting with a social environment; and "since environments overlap, since situations are continuous and those remote from one another contain like elements, a continuous modification of habits by one another is constantly going on" (1922: 38).

In regard to Goffman's theory of social interaction, the theoretical shift from supra-subjective structures to embodied praxis means that the acting subject's status in social situations needs to be reformulated. As already stated, Goffman tends to overemphasize the strategic and reflexive moments in interactions and hence risks reducing the body to a mere instrument of subjective volition. This corresponds to a mental model theory of reasoning, but it is exactly this theory that stands in contrast to the experience and performance of skillful doings in everyday life. To argue that bodily praxis primarily is the execution of mental representations posits agents who "resemble the centipede who by trying to think of the movement of each leg in relation to all the others was rendered unable to travel" (Dewey 1922: 39); Dewey also states that "[r]eason pure of all influences from prior habit is a fiction" (ibid. 31). In short, an adequate description of how tacit knowledge is embodied necessitates giving up the assumption that action follows from intention. Otherwise, the argumentation runs the risk of cutting off the body from action and hence embodiment from its relation to tacit knowledge. Instead, it needs to be stressed that volition is possible only because of the habitual incorporation of tacit knowledge: ideas, opinions, and judgments are not presuppositionless but rather are possible only through bodily involvement in the social world.

In short, conceptualizing the embodiment of tacit knowledge relies necessarily on the acceptance of Dewey's notion that "a wish gets definite form only in connection with an idea, and an idea gets shape and consistency only when it has a habit back of it." From this follows that "[t]he act must come before the thought, and a habit before an ability to evoke the thought at will" (ibid. 30). Shusterman similarly states that a "voluntary action is not a product of isolated moments of purely mental decision" because it relies on embodied "habits of feeling, thinking, acting, and desiring" (2008: 89) that can be described as tacit knowledge, which in turn is realized through and acquired by bodily actions. One can thus argue that in a way the body itself is the acting subject, or to put it the other way round: "we do not [only] *have* the body, but we *are* the body" (Ichikawa 1991: 8). If habits are necessary for the constitution of an embodied self then in "any intelligible sense of the word will, they *are* will" (Dewey 1922: 25).[5]

Nevertheless, Goffman's interactionist approach rightly points out that social situations are a crucial site of bodily practices. His notion of sociality in Merleau-Ponty's terms clearly describes bodily being-in-the-world as bodily being-in-situations.[6] The question is what this means for a relational theory of the embodiment of tacit knowledge in particular. Bourdieu's approach allows one to sketch the condition of possibility for the occurrence of interactions. Due to their habitualized tacit knowledge, individuals are habitually involved in interactional situations and as a consequence constitute them in a bodily manner. By taking into account that "the interaction itself owes its form to the objective structures which have produced the dispositions of the interacting agents" (Bourdieu 2000a: 81), an interaction can be understood formally as a constellation of competent and socialized bodies. An interpersonal situation thus cannot be understood as an "individual-to-individual" encounter (ibid.) between isolated individuals who are detached from the history of their own socialized embodiment of tacit knowledge. Instead, an interpersonal encounter

---

5 | That is why a sociology of the body that is informed by practice theory needs to be careful when using the term 'action' because of its mentalistic and representationalist connotations. For the difference between the terms 'action' and 'praxis' cf. Hirschauer (2004).

6 | The same notion in respect to Dewey can be found in Kestenbaum 1977: 19.

is always concerned with "systems of dispositions (carried by 'natural persons') such as a linguistic competence and a cultural competence [...] which are active only when embodied in a competence acquired in the course of a particular history" (ibid.). Thus, situative bodily interactions cannot be grasped merely as a framework of mental representations or as a means to achieve specific goals. I suggest instead that on the basis of Bourdieu's notion of larger social spheres as 'playing fields,' temporary and local social situations can be described as interactional fields to which socialized bodies or embodied actors bring embodied tacit knowledge which grounds and supports the coordination of interaction. While Bourdieu investigates the logics of broader social fields (cf. 1975), I am specifically concerned here with the practical logic of embodied encounters. An interactional field, to use Merleau-Ponty's example of a football player's actions, "is not given to him, but present as the immanent term of his practical intentions; the player becomes one with it and feels the direction of the 'goal,' for example, just as immediately as the vertical and the horizontal planes of his own body" (1963: 168).

As a consequence, only the theoretical assumption that individuals are bodily involved in interactions allows describing the interaction order itself as a quality *sui generis* like Goffman does. However, speaking of an interaction order *sui generis* does not imply that participants are cut off from embodied tacit knowledge or from bodily socialization. Rather, the embodiment of tacit knowledge is the condition of possibility for several special qualities of interaction. The dynamics of interactional fields, the 'vibrant flux,' is constituted by bodily doings. For instance, a 'maneuver' can be reconceptualized as an active capability to structure an interactional field: "each maneuver undertaken by the player modifies the character of the field and establishes in it new lines of force in which the action in turn unfolds and is accomplished" (ibid.). This notion of Merleau-Ponty implies that bodily praxis always involves a spontaneous and prereflexive display of embodied knowledge. Sharing a smile or exchanging glances can be understood as embodied expressions of a situational feeling; to display bodily tacit knowledge in this way does not mean expressing a preexisting state of mind or thought. Goffman's term "personal front," which refers to the "part of the individual's performance which regularly functions in a general and fixed fashion to define the situation for those who observe the performance" (1959: 22), is insufficient because it subordinates the body as displayed 'surface' to the 'inner' mind. Instead, the appearance and presence of the body in an interaction is not presuppositionless but rather an expression of embodied tacit knowledge, and vice versa: what on the fundamental level of perception is perceived as a meaningful action is rooted in socialized embodied tacit knowledge of how to perceive and assess the environment and other agents. These "schemes of perception" (Bourdieu 1990: 54) can be conceived as a Maussian 'body technique' based on embodied knowledge which is engaged in an interactional field. An interactional field accordingly always implies a 'perceptual field' (cf. Merleau-Ponty 2005) similar to the macrosociological fields Bourdieu has in mind. This means that "the meaning of any subjectively perceived object [...] is affected by the spatio-temporal background or context against which it is perceived" (Crossley 2001: 67). Hence, without this embodied modality of interaction neither the mimetic socialization mentioned above nor a general interaction order is possible. Bourdieu's notion of 'illusio' (cf. 1998), which refers to the habitual and therefore embodied emotional and implicit acknowledgment of the implicit rules of a social field, suggests that every interactional field requires such an embodied acknowledgment prior to any propositional definitions.

In consequence, the fundamental materiality of social co-present situations points to the fact that the situational quality of embodied tacit knowledge cannot be theoretically grasped by modeling interactional fields as terrains where the body is simply used as an instrument. Social stagecraft as described by Goffman cannot be thought of as presuppositionless deliberate action. Every intentional management of bodily expressions is grounded in a bodily and habitual continuity which in turn is grounded in active being-in-the-world. In a social situation, "consciousness is nothing other than the dialectic of milieu and action" (Merleau-Ponty 1963: 35). This means that Goffman's conceptualization of the presentation of the self has to be reformulated as "flexible, sensitive habit" (Dewey 2008: 51f.) or "refined, intelligent habit" (Shusterman 2008: 205), which necessitates scrutinizing Goffman's Sartrean conceptualization of social roles in interaction. Bourdieu argues in this regard that a waiter "is not playing at being a waiter, as Sartre would have it," because his "body, which contains a history, espouses his job, in other words a history, a tradition, which he has never seen except incarnated in bodies, or more precisely, in the uniforms inhabited by a certain habitus that are called waiters." Hence, "he enters into the character of the waiter not as an actor playing a part" (2000b: 153f.). A surprising event, like the accidental breaking of dishes or a complaining guest, does not push the waiter into pre-social awareness. Instead, such an event can be dealt with because of the practical creativity of the waiter's habits (cf. Hörning 2004). It is embodied tacit knowledge that enables him to deal with more or less unexpected incidents. Thus the reflection of self is not negated but rather located in bodily praxis. In this light it is pointless to analytically separate a social role from its bodily praxis. A theory of the embodiment of tacit knowledge has to avoid generalizing the exceptional case of theatrical practices in which actors have a distanced attitude to situations and use the body like an instrument. It is necessary to take more seriously Goffman's remark that "doing is being" (1961: 88): embodied praxis is an expression, actualization and transformation of tacit knowledge that has been incorporated by a history of bodily being-in-the-world and being-in-situations.

V. Conclusion

Finally we can come back to the initial question of how to overcome the apparent theoretical gap between a supra-subjective understanding of the embodiment of tacit knowledge on the one hand, and a situative understanding of embodied knowledge of how to interact in social situations on the other. While Foucault's notion of the embodiment of tacit knowledge dismisses the active contribution of agents to the process of the embodiment of tacit knowledge, Goffman's interactional framework is mindful of the bodily agent in social situations, yet at the same time neglects the tacit embodiment of knowledge. I therefore proposed a theoretical shift to a relational notion of bodily praxis which is able to avoid the aporias of both perspectives.

First, by using Foucault as a starting point, the embodiment of tacit knowledge can be conceived as the habitualization of knowledge by agents who are bodily in the world. This implies that objective supra-subjective orders like dispositifs or collective habitus are neither presuppositionless nor a mere cause; rather, they are dependent on practical doings. Hence, Foucauldian materialization is closely related to acts of mimetic transmission via bodily practices in co-presence. Agents get incorporated by their bodily practices, including perceptions and experiences. They embody tacit knowledge in the sense of dispositional body schemas. With reference to Foucault's reflections on the power of institutions, I argued that it is the gesture, the repetitive performance of embodied tacit knowledge, which serves to establish institutions' power and effectiveness. Emphasizing repetition does not rule out that embodied tacit knowledge can change. However, it is crucial to renounce the idea of a presuppositionless genius, because the transformation of embodied tacit knowledge is bound up with bodily and sensual experiences that are made when participating in various practices in different interactional fields and social contexts. In this vein, the transformation of practices and therefore of embodied tacit knowledge can be grasped without denying the agency of embodied individuals.

Second, such a notion of embodied tacit knowledge has consequences for Goffman's notions of agency in social situations. A theory of embodied tacit knowledge cannot be integrated into a narrowly representationalist theory of agency. In fact, a notion of volition is necessary for conceptualizing habitualized embodied and hence socialized tacit knowledge. Thus, to be embodied in social situations means to be habitually related to these situations. It is only embodied tacit knowledge that makes possible a field of interactional dynamics, and therefore all practical interaction. That is, the active appearance, presence, and interaction of bodies can be conceived as the expression of embodied tacit knowledge. The meaningful processing of such expressions within an interaction order in turn requires perceptual schemas as part of the embodied tacit knowledge of each participant.

Third, linking the notion of agency to embodied tacit knowledge in order to conceptualize embodied agency implies a reconceptualization of Goffman's approach to role-playing. As has been shown, it is not necessary to separate bodily acts and role-playing by positing a Cartesian separation of mind and body. The ability to play a role – i.e. to perform a bodily practice – presupposes embodied tacit knowledge, and every reflection which occurs in problematic situations depends upon it as well.

In the end, my contribution demonstrated that a relational understanding of the embodiment of tacit knowledge helps to avoid aporias and blind spots both in regard to its constitution and to its role in interactive coordination. Embodied praxis is the condition of possibility for the embodiment of tacit knowledge. At the same time, the habitualized materialization of embodied tacit knowledge is the basis of bodily practices, just as displaying and performing embodied knowledge in social situations is the prerequisite of its occurrence – but this interactive praxis is impossible without embodied tacit knowledge.

Works Cited

Allen, Amy (2000): "The Anti-Subjective Hypothesis. Michel Foucault and the Death of the Subject," in: The Philosophical Forum 31, 113-130.
Bourdieu, Pierre (1975): "The Specificity of the Scientific Field and the Social Conditions of the Progress of Reason," in: Social Science Information 14, 19-47.
—. (1984): Distinction. A Social Critique of the Judgment of Taste, Cambridge: Harvard UP.
—. (1990): The Logic of Practice, Stanford: Stanford UP.
—. (1991): Language and Symbolic Power, Cambridge: Harvard UP.
—. (1998): Practical Reason. On the Theory of Action, Stanford: Stanford UP.
—. (2000a): Outline of a Theory of Practice, Cambridge: Cambridge UP.
—. (2000b): Pascalian Meditations, Stanford: Stanford UP.
Bourdieu, Pierre/Wacquant, Loïc J.D. (1996): An Invitation to Reflexive Sociology, Cambridge: Polity.
Bublitz, Hannelore (1999): Foucaults Archäologie des kulturellen Unbewußten. Zum Wissensarchiv und Wissensbegehren moderner Gesellschaften, Frankfurt/Main: Campus.
—. (2003): Diskurs, Bielefeld: transcript.
—. (2008): "Pierre Bourdieu," in: Kammler/Reinhardt-Becker, Foucault-Handbuch, 210-213.
Butler, Judith (2004): "Bodies and Power Revisited," in: Diana Taylor/Karen Vintges (eds.), Feminism and the Final Foucault, Chicago: U of Illinois P, 183-194.

Cooley, Charles Horton (1922): Human Nature and the Social Order, Chicago: Scribner's.
Crossley, Nick (1995): "Body Techniques, Agency and Intercorporeality. On Goffman's Relations in Public," in: Sociology 29, 133-149.
—. (1996): "Body-Subject/Body-Power. Agency, Inscription and Control in Foucault and Merleau-Ponty," in: Body and Society 2, 99-116.
—. (2001): The Social Body. Habit, Identity, Desire, London: Sage.
Dewey, John (1922): Human Nature and Conduct. An Introduction to Social Psychology, New York: Henry Holt.
—. (2008): The Middle Works, Vol. 14, Carbondale: Southern Illinois UP.
Dreyfus, Hubert L./Rabinow, Paul (1982): Michel Foucault. Beyond Structuralism and Hermeneutics, Chicago: U of Chicago P.
Ebrecht, Jörg (2004): "Die Kreativität der Praxis. Überlegungen zum Wandel von Habitusformationen," in: Jörg Ebrecht/Frank Hillebrandt (eds.), Bourdieus Theorie der Praxis. Erklärungskraft – Anwendung – Perspektiven, Wiesbaden: VS, 225-241.
Foucault, Michael (1977): Discipline and Punish. The Birth of the Prison, New York: Pantheon.
—. (1978): The Will to Knowledge. The History of Sexuality 1, London: Penguin.
—. (1984): "Nietzsche, Genealogy, History," in: Paul Rabinow (ed.), The Foucault Reader, New York: Pantheon, 76-100.
—. (1996): "The Order of Things," in: Sylvere Lotringer (ed.), Foucault Live. Interviews 1961-84, New York: Semiotext(e), 13-18.
Fröhlich, Gerhard (1994): "Kapital, Habitus, Feld, Symbol. Grundbegriffe der Kulturtheorie bei Pierre Bourdieu," in: Ingo Mörth/Gerhard Fröhlich (eds.), Das symbolische Kapital der Lebensstile. Zur Kultursoziologie der Moderne nach Pierre Bourdieu, Frankfurt/Main: Campus, 55-74.
Gallagher, Shaun (2005): How the Body Shapes the Mind, New York: Oxford UP.
Gehring, Petra (2004): Foucault. Die Philosophie im Archiv, Frankfurt/Main: Campus.
—. (2008): "Der Wille zum Wissen. Sexualität und Wahrheit 1," in: Kammler/Reinhardt-Becker, Foucault-Handbuch, 85–93.
Goffman, Erving (1959): The Presentation of Self in Everyday Life, New York: Anchor.
—. (1961): Asylums. Essays on the Social Situation of Mental Patients and Other Inmates, New York: Anchor.
—. (1963): Behavior in Public Places. Notes on the Social Organization of Gatherings, New York: Free Press.
—. (1971): Relations in Public. Microstudies of the Public Order, New York: Basic.

—. (1977): "The Arrangement between the Sexes," in: Theory and Society 4, 301-331.

—. (1983): "The Interaction Order," in: American Sociological Review 48, 1-17

Gouldner, Alvin (1970): The Coming Crisis of Western Sociology, New York: Basic.

Gugutzer, Robert (2006): "Der body turn in der Soziologie. Eine programmatische Einführung," in: Robert Gugutzer (ed.), Body turn. Perspektiven der Soziologie des Körpers und des Sports, Bielefeld: transcript, 9-53.

—. (2010): Soziologie des Körpers, Bielefeld: transcript.

Hirschauer, Stefan (2004): "Praktiken und ihre Körper. Über materielle Partizipanden des Tuns," in: Hörning/Reuter, Doing Culture, 73-91.

Hitzler, Ronald (1992): "Der Goffmensch. Überlegungen zu einer dramatologischen Anthropologie," in: Soziale Welt. Zeitschrift für sozialwissenschaftliche Forschung und Praxis 4, 449-461.

Hörning, Karl H. (2004): "Soziale Praxis zwischen Beharrung und Neuschöpfung. Ein Erkenntnis- und Theorieproblem," in: Hörning/Reuter, Doing Culture, 19-39.

Hörning, Karl H./Reuter, Julia (eds.) (2004): Doing Culture. Neue Positionen zum Verhältnis von Kultur und sozialer Praxis, Bielefeld: transcript.

Hubrich, Michael (2013): Körperbegriff und Körperpraxis. Perspektiven für die soziologische Theorie, Wiesbaden: VS.

Ichikawa, Hiroshi (1991): The Body as the Spirit, Tokyo: Keiso Shobo.

Kammler, Clemens/Reinhardt-Becker, Elke (eds.) (2008): Foucault-Handbuch. Leben, Werk, Wirkung, Stuttgart: Metzler.

Kestenbaum, Victor (1977): The Phenomenological Sense of John Dewey. Habit and Meaning, New Jersey: Humanities.

Kitching, Gavin (1988): Karl Marx and the Philosophy of Praxis, Bungay: Richard Clay.

Lofland, John (1980): "Early Goffman. Style, Structure, Substance, Soul," in: Jason Ditton (ed.), The View from Goffman, London: Macmillan, 24-51.

Manning, Philip (1992): Erving Goffman and Modern Sociology, Stanford: Stanford UP.

Marx, Karl (1975): Early Writings, New York: Vintage.

Mauss, Marcel (1992 [1934]): "Techniques of the Body," in: Jonathan Crary/Sanford Kwinter (eds.), Incorporations, New York: Zone, 455-477.

Merleau-Ponty, Maurice (1963): The Structure of Behavior, Boston: Beacon.

—. (2005): Phenomenology of Perception, London: Routledge.

Meuser, Michael (2004): "Zwischen 'Leibvergessenheit' und 'Körperboom.' Die Soziologie und der Körper," in: Sport und Gesellschaft 1, 197-218.

Polanyi, Michael (2009): The Tacit Dimension, Chicago: Chicago UP.

Raab, Jürgen (2008): Erving Goffman, Konstanz: UVK.

Reckwitz, Andreas (2003): "Grundelemente einer Theorie sozialer Praktiken. Eine sozialtheoretische Perspektive," in: Zeitschrift für Soziologie 4, 282-301.
Reiger, Horst (2000): Face-to-face Interaktion. Zur Soziologie Erving Goffmans, Frankfurt/Main: Lang.
Reuter, Julia (2004): "Körperinszenierungen. Zur Materialität des Performativen bei Erving Goffman und Judith Butler," in: Das Argument. Zeitschrift für Philosophie und Sozialwissenschaften 254, 102-114.
Ruoff, Michael (2009): Foucault-Lexikon. Entwicklung, Kernbegriffe, Zusammenhänge, Paderborn: Fink.
Ryle, Gilbert (2000): The Concept of Mind, London: Penguin.
Schäfer, Hilmar (2009): "Michel Foucault," in: Gerhard Fröhlich/Boike Rehbein (eds.), Bourdieu-Handbuch, Stuttgart: Metzler, 44-46.
Sennett, Richard (1977): The Fall of Public Man, Cambridge: Cambridge UP.
Shilling, Chris (1993): The Body and Social Theory, London: Sage.
Shusterman, Richard (2008): Body Consciousness. A Philosophy of Mindfulness and Somaesthetics, Cambridge: Cambridge UP.
Siebenfeiffer, Hania (2008): "Körper," in: Kammler/Reinhardt-Becker, Foucault-Handbuch, 266-272.
Taylor, Diana (2003): The Archive and the Repertoire. Performing Cultural Memory in the Americas, Durham: Duke UP.
Vignemont, Frederique de (2010): "Body Schema and Body Image – Pros and Cons," in: Neuropsychologia 48, 669-680.
Walsh, David F. (1998): "Structure/Agency," in: Chris Jenks (ed.), Core Sociological Dichotomies, London: Thousand Oaks, 8-33.
Wittgenstein, Ludwig (1973): Philosophical Investigations, London: Pearsons.
Wulf, Christoph (1997): "Geste," in: Christoph Wulf (ed.), Vom Menschen. Handbuch Historische Anthropologie, Weinheim: Beltz, 516-524.

The Background of Moods and Atmospheres
Sociological Observations

Rainer Schützeichel

I. INTRODUCTION

In recent years, sociology has in many ways become aware of the "implicit." One might well speak of an "implicit turn" that has broken ground, for example, in the form of pre-reflective and routinized "practices" in social theory or in the form of "implicit knowledge" in epistemology. The fact that the implicit has enjoyed such a boom can be attributed to two fundamental problems: Without recourse to implicit capabilities, dispositions, skills, and rules, we can neither explain the "agency" of actors nor their actions and speech acts. Nevertheless, a number of points remain unresolved: What does "implicit" actually mean? Is knowledge the central dimension where the implicit manifests itself? How can we explain actions by means of an implicit knowledge of rules? Is there not a multitude of "implicit" dimensions that differ significantly with regard to their structure and makeup of "implicitness"? Some implicit structures arise from habitualizations and routinizations while others incorporate meaningful forms in material relations. If all such forms of the implicit have one thing in common, it is that they realize or make appear other entities without being much in evidence themselves. This paper will examine implicit references and constitutive relationships in the field of the affective, in particular affective systems such as moods and atmospheres.

With the concept of "background," this paper presents a theoretical alternative that has not been considered in previous discussions of the implicit. The background is implicit insofar as it stands in a relationship to the foreground corresponding to that of figure and ground or text and context. The background has been developed mainly in social ontology and social theory in recent years, based on the works of John Searle. Of course, this concept has a long tradition – Wittgenstein and Heidegger are just two inspirations that should be mentioned. So far, the concept has played a prominent role only in philosophical discussions. There are some related concepts in sociology, for example "frames," which have sometimes developed parallel to such major categories as "culture" or "habitus." Above all, the category of "life-world" – used among others by Husserl, Schütz, Habermas, and Luhmann – includes equivalent conceptions.

I propose that the concept of background can play a significant role in sociological research. Its nature is more complex than comparable variants of the "implicit." And this is precisely why "background" can reveal problems faced by sociology when it attempts to incorporate implicit dimensions into sociological foundations. Let us now examine a specific question applying to the concept of "background:" In recent decades, emotions and feelings have been broadly integrated into all major fields of sociology. However, sociologists have largely ignored "affective states." Affective states have been described as "moods" or life-world "familiarities," and, in recent years, as "atmospheres" or "existential feelings." It has been said that they constitute the affective foundation of "the social" as such and determine every person's individual access to the world. Only recently, sociology has developed a corresponding field of research in response to developments in other scientific disciplines. "Affective sciences" in contrast to traditional emotion research refer to basic affective qualities (cf. Gregg/Seigworth 2010; Seyfert 2011a, 2011b) "beyond personal feelings and collective emotions" (cf. Seyfert 2012).

The concept of background can serve to illustrate the affective foundations of the social. Moods and atmospheres form the affective background of our individual and collective experiences, thoughts, and actions. At the same time, the connection of affectivity and background corrects the implicit cognitivist "bias" of almost all conceptions of the implicit, including Searle's. Phenomenologically, the life-world thus has to be observed as a "perceived," "affective" frame of meaning.

Moods and atmospheres are not only of theoretical interest. In fact, sociological analysis has shown that moods and atmospheres have come more and more to the fore as implicit or latent forms of behavior and action control. They were sublime objects which posed the greatest possible contrast to everyday life.[1] This has changed considerably. Today, there are hardly any functional areas that have not been analyzed regarding the moods and atmospheres they evoke: Supermarkets, football stadiums, roads (cf. Corbineau-Hoffmann 2011), cities, pedestrian zones, theater productions, museum exhibitions, hospitals (cf. Lorenz/Penzel 2007), liturgies and spiritual practices (cf. Huppertz 2007; Patzelt 2007), service rooms, and workshops. The many forms of cultural communitization, such as unions ("Bünde") (cf. Schmalenbach 1922), youth cultures (cf. Kimminich 2007), and various 'scenes' (cf. Hitzler/Honer/Pfadenhauer 2008),

---

1 | Even where 'moods' were being created in a special way, namely in the interior of the bourgeois home of the 19th century, decoration work was still regarded as workmanship, sometimes even as artistic activity (cf. Haag 2012).

can be understood as generators of moods and atmospheres. Because moods and atmospheres cannot be created ad hoc and arbitrarily, the question arises how moods can be influenced and controlled.

In the following, I will examine the implicit background of moods. Since sociology has not yet found an access to moods and atmospheres, I will first review the current state of interdisciplinary research with the aim to provide an analytical frame for approaching the "background of moods" from a sociological perspective.

II. The 'Background' of Intentionality

In Searle's philosophy and social theory, the concept of background plays an important role not least because he aims to avoid certain aporias in the construction of a naturalistic and yet intentionalist theory of society, language, and mind (cf. Radman 2012; Schmitz/Kobow/Schmid 2013). According to Searle, the construction of social reality, the structure of social institutions, and the practices of human activity are based on constitutive rules, i.e. rules that determine the function of given entities in social contexts. However, actors are rarely if ever guided by such rules. Constitutive rules function without the actors following them intentionally. So how can we explain the existence of such constitutive rules? Searle tries to find a new solution to the old problem of rule compliance. The point of this problem is that rules are never exhaustive. Searle argues for a third approach between behaviorist theories (that reduce social phenomena to physical mechanisms and thereby reduce the control character of social phenomena to regularities) and cognitivist theories (that – like most action and rationality theories – ascribe social phenomena and actions to rational deliberations and decisions).

II.1 Background and Understanding

Searle initially introduces the concept of background with respect to problems of semantics. His criticism aims at the principle of compositionality (or "Frege principle") that derives the meaning of a complex statement from the meanings of its components:

> The reason that the same semantic content, "cut," derives not from any ambiguity of a semantic kind, but rather from the fact that as members of our culture we bring to bear on the literal utterance and understanding of a sentence a whole background of information about how nature works and how our culture works. (Searle 1980: 226f)

The meaning of an expression cannot be determined without reference to a background of institutions, practices, cultural rules, or facts of nature. Intentions are not atomic, as their conditions of possibility exist only relative to a variety of other intentional states. References, truth conditions, and meanings presuppose some 'pre-intentional assumptions' or 'presuppositions.' Different background beliefs lead to different meanings. The sentence 'The cat is on the mat,' for example, presupposes the background belief of a gravitational field (cf. Searle 1978) as well as an advanced and culturally contingent understanding of 'cat.' Thus, Searle claims that "the literal meaning of a sentence only determines a set of truth conditions given a set of background practices and assumptions. Relative to one set of practices and assumptions, a sentence may determine one set of truth conditions, relative to another set of practices and assumptions" (Searle 1980: 227). Not only meanings of sentences or of general linguistic entities are context-dependent but beliefs and opinions of speakers are as well. This equally applies to truth conditions of convictions and desires. The intention to run for a seat in the German Bundestag presupposes the understanding that the Federal Republic of Germany is a parliamentary democracy, that elections are secret, that there is an active and passive right to vote – and so on. Each intention is embedded in a network of further intentions, attitudes, and practices. This is also true for someone else whom the candidate tells about his intentions: He can only understand his running for parliament if he shares a sufficiently overlapping network with the candidate. Searle (1991: 180) characterizes such networks as holistic. A holistic network does not only consist of other intentional states or, as Searle – using 'intentionalist' expressions – prefers to say, of skills and practices. Rather, it also comprises affective states: "secondary intentions, hopes, fears, anxieties and expectations, feelings of disappointment and satisfaction, and so on" (Searle 1980: 226).

This 'background' fulfills a variety of functions. It serves to understand metaphors, to remember events, and to train physical skills. It provides our experience with a narrative structure and is responsible for our pre-intentional realism. It is also responsible for the function of 'taken-for-granted' and everyday realism – described in particular by social phenomenology or ethnomethodology. The background manifests life-world familiarities. It provides us with a complete, matter-of-course metaphysics (cf. Searle 2001: 132). The background shapes our attitude ('stance') toward things, giving us (according to Searle 1995) a "sense" of the world, a sense that – to use Heidegger's terminology – can be seen as a specific 'condition' or, sociologically more prominent, as a 'practical sense' (in Bourdieu's sense). Searle describes background as the total of 'knowing how:'

This set of skills, abilities, propensities, habits, dispositions, as a matter of course prerequisites and general "knowing how" is what I have referred to as "background" […].

Only against this background of "knowing how" that allows us to cope with the world, all our intentional states, all our individual beliefs, hopes, fears, etc., play the role they are playing – i.e. only against such a background, they determine their truth conditions. (Searle 2001: 130f.)

II.II Background, Intentionality, and Rules

Searle's later works, however, increasingly conceive of the background as constituted by non-conceptual intentional contents or frames of reference (cf. Rust 2009; Schmitz 2013; Stueber 2005; Stroud 1991). The background is "sensitive to rule structure" (Searle 1995: 145). It is even causally sensitive to rule structures without disposing of representations for these rules. According to Searle, it is the background of manifest dispositions that allows actors to follow rules, since its dispositions are trained in dealing with the institutional rules of societies in a learning or imitation process. The background allows for intentional states as well as practices of rule-following.

Searle attempts to differentiate these background grids. As "deep background" (Searle 1991: 183) he denotes the skills given to all humans as biological beings – the physiological processes, physical skills such as gripping or eating, perception, and others. From this 'deep background' he distinguishes 'local backgrounds' rooted in specific cultures and cultural practices, such as the behavioral norms of groups, communities, and societies (cf. Searle 2010: 157). In particular, all social institutions require such cultural backgrounds, which in turn can be highly generalized – for example, the knowledge that a piece of paper is money – or highly specific – for example, the communication order of a family at the dinner table. According to Searle, the background is formed by anthropological or biological potentials, by cultural practices and rules. It emerges from "the entire conglomerate of relationships, in which each biological-social creature lives within its environment" (Searle 1991: 195).

Searle devotes comparatively little attention to the question whether and how the background can be socially shared. The fact that the background is socially split is derived largely functionally from the theorem of collective intentionality which Searle understands as primary and anthropologically anchored in contrast to individual intentionality. Recently, Searle has also derived the concept of 'background power' in this way:

The basic concept of background power is that there is a set of background presuppositions, attitudes, dispositions, capacities, and practices of any community that set normative constraints on the members of that community in such a way that violations of those constraints are subject to the negative imposition of sanctions by any member of the community. (Searle 2010: 160)

Searle (1995) also introduces 'background' as a theoretical entity to explain actions. The background of actions is formed by the (constitutive) rules that guide actors and their actions. But how can we understand this rule aspect of actions? Searle offers two possible explications:

(RR) Representational or Intentional Rule-Following: In a representational-intentionalist reading, actors can intentionally follow certain rules. Rules are represented as rules in the intentional network of actors; rules function as rules insofar as actors intend to follow certain rules.

This interpretation, however, raises serious doubts regarding its scope and applicability. When and under what circumstances are actors 'aware' of the rules on which their actions are based? Searle questions the validity of this argument of intentional rule-following for basic logical reasons. Like Wittgenstein, Searle assumes that rules cannot define their own application and therefore are caught in a regress of reasoning. Searle also dismisses a solution favored by many representationalist theories, which from Chomsky and Fodor to sociological approaches are all aware of the paradox that the existence of constitutive rules cannot be explained intentionally. They all rely on latency in terms of an "unconscious" – the rules are so deeply rooted that speakers and actors practice them unconsciously. The unconscious, however, is a very 'dark category' for Searle.

It is also unacceptable for Searle to resort to "habitualization," as it reduces a rule-following action to a rule-compliant behavior. The difference between the two lies in the fact that only a rule-following behavior is an action that is causally triggered by reference to rules. Only such actions account for both the normativity of rules and for the causality triggered by rules. Moreover, in contrast to rule-compliant behavior only rule-following behavior ensures that we can distinguish between the correct and incorrect compliance with rules.

But how do we find a way out of this dilemma? Is there a third way between representational intentionality on the one hand, and non-intentional behaviorism on the other? The common alternative in sociology – to invoke unconscious intentions – is not acceptable to Searle (cf. Searle 1992). Searle instead introduces the concept of pre-intentional cognitive phenomena that in their entirety constitute the background of intentional acts: Dispositions, skills, and 'capacities,' which are neither intentional nor unintentional, but rather pre-intentional or non-conceptual. They manifest themselves in neurophysiological structures.

(NRR) Non-Conceptual or Pre-Intentional Rule-Following: A background of mental, physiologically anchored dispositions and skills allows intentional beings to follow pre-intentional institutional rules in such a way that the institutional rules are part of the causal history of the background.

In our context, however, the most important function is that the background allows intentional beings to follow pre-intentional rules. How can we explain this relation between background and institutional rules? Why is it a question of a pre- or even non-intentional compliance with rules?

Searle sees the reference to rules in the fact that this 'background' develops evolutionary in dealing with institutional rules (cf. Searle 1995, 2002; for critiques of Searle's position cf. Dreyfus 2012; Margolis 2012). For two reasons, the reference to the theory of evolution here is not a coincidence.

First, Searle considers the Darwinian theory of evolution as the central caesura in which teleological explanations are replaced by causal ones. Second, Searle puts physiological or psychological mechanisms into a diachronic perspective. The perpetuation of background mechanisms in the diachronic perspective means that they can assume their causal role. Consequently, the balancing between non-representational mechanisms and social rules does not occur in a process of rule transfer, habitualization, internalization, or unconscious transfer, but by a practical exercise through which mechanisms adapt to rules causally and functionally. Searle illustrates this with the example of a skier. A skier does not learn the rules of skiing through the internalization of rules, but by practical exercise that makes rules become ever less relevant. Through exercise, the body is equipped with skills "to assume command of itself, and the rules can then retire to the background" (Searle 1991: 191). Searle rejects intentionalist, representationalist, and cognitivist models, e.g. the model of unconscious rule learning. He replaces them with a model of a physical, pre-representational background of 'skills.' According to Searle, the RR model fails because it is unable to explain how something is done:

Suppose my ability to walk really would be due to internalization of rules for walking. What rules could that be? Well, let's try to give such a walking-rule: "First, move the left foot forward, then the right, then the left, and then go on like that!" However, we have already seen that each of the semantic contents just put forward can be interpreted in many ways. (Searle 1991: 194)

How can we proceed under these conditions from the interpretation of semantic contents to action without being caught in an infinite regress of interpretations of interpretations? The representations or propositional contents do not apply themselves. Searle's solution is one originally proposed by Wittgenstein: "As Wittgenstein suggested: We simply act" (ibid.; cf. also Searle 2011).

Just how can we integrate affective states into this background? Searle certainly would not disregard them completely and he also assumes the inevitability of moods. People are always in some mood – consciousness is always 'toned' in some way (cf. Searle 2005: 150). He distinguishes between moods and emotions – emotions are intentional acts, whereas moods usually have no intentional content. Moods, however, predispose individuals to have certain emotions (ibid. 151). If you are irritated, certain causes will make you angry.

However, Searle leaves open the connection between background and affective qualities as well as the causal role of moods for actions and social phenomena. Thus, an important component of the background is not accounted for, namely the affective component of moods and atmospheres as selection parameters for our experiences and actions as well as as a resource for understanding experiences and the actions of others.

III. The Background of Moods and the Presence of Emotions

In the following, I will show how the concept of background can be fruitfully used in sociological affect research. The term 'affect' is used here as a generic term for all phenomena that go along with or are based on phenomenal qualities, on certain forms of feeling and sensing. Affects thus include moods as well as emotions or feelings.

III.I Moods and Emotions

The German term 'Stimmung' can hardly be translated with just one word into other languages (cf. Gumbrecht 2012; Mullhall 1996; Welsh 2012; Wimmer 2011). It combines the meaning of two English words, namely 'mood' as an inner feeling and 'climate' (cf. de Rivera 1992) as an objective affective quality that pertains to both individuals and groups. Moods are 'passions.' They occur with a persistent presence and have their own objectivity that cannot simply be generated, constructed, or stimulated because they form a relational phenomenon. It is evident that there are differences between those qualities, not only because of everyday experiences but also because they have been the subject of a long theoretical debate. Usually, moods or atmospheres are distinguished from feelings or emotions. In academic discourse, you will find the following distinctions:

- Diffusivity and globality of moods versus specificity of emotions (cf. Bollnow 2009 [1941]). This position is shared in particular by the so-called cognitive theories of emotion. Although moods, too, have a minimal intentional content, in contrast to emotions it remains diffuse and global.
- Durability of moods versus the episodicity of emotions (cf. e.g. Beedie/Terry/Lane 2005; Beedie/Terry/Devonport 2011) – a view that is widely held in sociology.
- Lower experience intensitivity of moods versus higher intensitivity of emotions (cf. Frijda 1993).
- Moods as pure states of feeling or 'affects' without propositional content

versus emotions as affects arising from cognition (cf. Oatley/Johnson-Laird 1989, 1990) – this position has particularly been held by the so-called 'feeling theories.'
- Moods as affective states to which no conscious cause can be attributed versus emotions as caused episodes.
- Poor expressiveness of moods versus expressiveness of emotions (cf. Ekman 1994).

One difference between the two affective phenomena can be seen in the fact that moods are global, diffuse, and without intentional object, whereas emotions are intentional acts or are accompanied by intentional acts. According to Ratcliffe (2010: 350), "'moods' are part of the background structure of intentionality." For example, if you are in an angry mood, usually you will find neither an occasion nor an object that has caused this mood; you simply meet the objects in the world in an angry mood. Phenomena that we all know from our everyday experience like 'shame,' 'fear,' 'happiness,' 'anger,' or 'worry' are prototypical emotions or feelings (cf. Slaby 2012). We also know non-intentional affective phenomena from our daily experience. Examples of such moods are 'serenity,' 'sadness,' or 'calm.' As these terms indicate, they refer to states rather than to events.

Another distinction between moods and emotions is that the former denote non-episodic, non-intentional qualities while the latter refer to episodic and intentional qualities. For Robert Solomon (1993: 15) moods form "generalized emotions," i.e. emotions that have lost their specific object in the course of habituation. Emotions are a primary, moods a secondary quality. Emotions are intentional states in relation to specific objects; moods, however, are intentional states in relation to non-specific, generalized objects (cf. Solomon 1993; Goldie 2000; Roberts 2003).

The concept of background allows for a further differentiation between phenomenal qualities such as moods on the one hand and emotions and feelings on the other hand. Moods form the background of our experiences and actions, while emotions and feelings act in the foreground. As explained above, moods form part of the background structure of our intentional life, in which the formation of emotions and feelings occurs. Emotions and feelings impose themselves on us; they are immediately present to us while moods remain rather diffuse in the background. Emotions "are only intelligible in the context of mood" (Ratcliffe 2010: 354). According to Ratcliffe (ibid. 353), moods form a "pre-intentional background to intentional states." He describes them not as non-intentional – as is common in the phenomenological tradition – but as pre-intentional because they determine the scope of possibilities for emotional experiences and episodes. In an affective manner, moods reflect how things appear in the world, i.e. their meaning and relevance. Or to rephrase it in a more sociological way: If we find ourselves in a situation in which our satisfied or unsatisfied desires in relation to objects and events provide us with certain emotions, then this situation in itself is an affective space. Therefore, moods and emotions can be described as two dimensions of the affective. According to Ratcliffe (2010), they do not differ so much in their affective qualities but in their phenomenological features.

Moods and emotions can thus be functionally distinguished; they play different phenomenal roles. The relationship can in general be defined as a background-relationship. However, it remains controversial just how far this background-relationship is going. On the one hand, especially in phenomenological studies, we find the thesis that the background of moods implies that emotions and other intentional types of actions have their foundation in moods. On the other hand, only few sociological studies assume that moods differ from emotions mainly in their permanence and that the difference between the two is thus a temporary and therefore only a gradual one. They reduce the difference of moods and emotions primarily to self-attributions and to social resources to make affective states a subject of discussion and thus make it available for reflection.

III.II Moods

Moods arise from the fact that subject and object or subject and subject are each in a mood and are thus also keyed in a mood to each other.[2] This situation has been pointed out especially in the phenomenological tradition – moods transcend the difference between subject and object. Even if the possibility of the spontaneous generation of moods – in contrast to the spontaneous generation of emotions – may be assessed differently, Geiger (1911: 53) has pointed out an important, almost paradoxical fact: Moods have a communal character that results from the mutual interrelationship of the moods of subject and object or of subject and subject. Moods are not inside or outside of people but comprise the interior and the exterior, embrace it, and form totalities and thus also social constellations in which a person experiences him- or herself. Moods thus have different aspects. First, they take an intermediary position between subject and object, or between subject and subject. And second, they form experiential, af-

---

2 | Becker (2012) points out the close conceptual-historic association of 'mood' and 'harmony.' As Leo Spitzer (1963) outlines in his classic study, in the history of ideas, the word 'mood' denotes totalities of the kind that include different, heterogeneous, and differing components (cf. also von Arburg/Rickenbacher 2012b; Gisbertz 2009, 2011; Meyer-Sickendiek 2011). They do not only integrate an inside and an outside but also transverse such distinctions as 'activity' or 'passivity;' they so to speak correspond to the diathesis of 'middle voice.'

fective totalities or systems. Dilthey, finally, draws attention to another feature of moods: He mentions "fundamental moods" (cf. Dilthey 1931 [1911]: 33; my transl.) to point out the integrative and structuring power of moods for the various psychic powers. Moods are fundamental and comprehensive. They form the lower layer of spiritual life, especially of knowledge and worldviews (cf. Große 2008). Beyond that, they are a basis for all objectivations of the human mind in religion, myth, art, and literature. As such, moods are also exempt from the classical triad of thought, feeling, and action, and, even more, superordinate to them. From Dilthey's 'basic moods' it is now only a short step to Heidegger's foundations for an ontology of the condition of existence or to the 'existential feelings' of current research (cf. Ratcliffe 2008).[3]

In the tradition of Kierkegaard (1991 [1844]), who probably introduced the term into modern philosophy, Heidegger defined moods and in particular fear as a fundamental mode of the existentiality of existence (cf. Ferreira 2002; Elpidorou 2013; Merker 2008; Taylor 1993). Existence finds itself in fact always "thrown" into a world from where it must project its possibilities. Existence is always 'in a mood,' it lives in its moods in a way that precedes all differences of the inner world and the outer world, of self and world. Moods are subdivided into 'elevated moods' such as serenity, contentment, or happiness, which he only briefly touches upon, and 'depressed,' in which the burden of existence manifests itself. Moods are a prerequisite for things in our world to become meaningful to us. Moods characterize the relevance of our relationship to the world. And finally, this foundation also applies to the relationship between moods and emotions (or affects, as Heidegger called them). Since moods determine how things and events mean something to us, they also restrict our emotions relative to these things.

Bollnow has integrated this relationship of moods and emotions into a layer model of the soul. According to Bollnow, moods form the lowest level of this model. They are the original form in which life becomes aware of its qualities and values. All higher mental powers, both cognitive and affective, such as emotions, are rooted in this primary layer. Moods even precede any subject-object difference according to Bollnow. In a pre-conceptual way, they create a reality in such a way that the perception of objects and these objects themselves are mutually dependent on each other. Perception is not something that is directed from the outside to a reality but is realized in a world that already is 'in a

---

3 | The important phenomenology of feelings by Max Scheler (1916 [1913]) does not distinguish between moods and emotions, but its distinction of four different emotional levels (sensational feelings, body and life feelings, emotional feelings, and mental feelings) nevertheless has a high functional affinity. This is true in particular for the layer of body and life feelings (such as freshness, rest, tenseness, anxiety, or fatigue), which, as the name suggests, have their basis in the body.

mood.' Bollnow also makes an attempt to classify moods. In a polar taxonomy he distinguishes between elevated moods (ecstasy, serenity, joy, exuberance, love, happiness, etc.) on the one side and depressed moods (fear, despair, irritability, solicitude, gloom, melancholy, etc.) on the other side. Between them are moods that can have both elevated and depressed parts (e.g. security, serenity).

According to Stephan Strasser (cf. 1956: 110), moods are a form of feeling that precedes any division into separate feelings. Strasser refers to such an affective background of all feelings as 'thymic.' 'Thymic experience' transmits all feelings. Moods are the primary sphere of phenomenal experience. According to Strasser, moods are the basic foundation of human experience; they support all intentional 'directedness,' from simple perceptions to acts of thought. Similar to Bollnow's distinction of moods and 'feelings in the proper sense,' Strasser distinguishes between the 'thymic experience' and intentional feelings. Yet, Strasser goes even one step further. Moods are at the same time a feeling of the self and a feeling of the world (cf. ibid. 115). They are a total experience in which the boundaries between self and world, between I and object become blurred. They are trans-subjective and at the same time trans-objective phenomena. Strasser formulates concisely that in moods the pre-predicative and pre-intentional unity of subject and object can be experienced (cf. ibid. 117). It is a consciousness different from object-consciousness. Moods, however, are not directed at anything. Melancholy, cheerfulness, emptiness, depression, abjectness, euphoria, and other moods may in turn be the result of something, but their 'causes' are not conscious, they do not become phenomena of consciousness. And, in contrast to feelings, moods are always present. There is no such thing as a mood-less state. Even seemingly emotion-neutral states are, according to Strasser, not without a 'feel-in' [zumute sein]. Strasser, like Heidegger, Bollnow, Tugendhat[4] (1979), Lormand (1985), and Ratcliffe, holds that moods are not objects of intentional experience but possibility spheres of intentional experiences. The fact that we are 'in a mood' only makes itself felt in problematic situations, when our moods meet with resistance or other moods. Otherwise we are with the things and events that trigger certain emotions in us and demand our attention, and moods and atmospheres remain in the background.

In contemporary psychological research, moods and emotions are not examined regarding their foundational conditions – in contrast to the phenomenological discussion (cf. Reisenzein/Döring 2009; Siemer 1999, 2009).

---

4 | According to Ernst Tugendhat (1979), affects (in the tradition of Heidegger) refer to a specific situation or a particular object. Moods, however, refer evaluatively to an entire life situation. Tugendhat highlights the self-referential character of moods: they disclose what the general shape of a person is. Emotions tell us something about the world, moods something about the way the subject perceives this world (cf. also Parkinson et al. 2000).

Although two affective qualities are distinguished, the main challenge is to develop a comprehensive theory of the genesis of affective states that integrates moods and emotions. Accordingly, 'feeling theories' and 'dispositional theories' are distinguished. Feeling theories regard moods as 'qualia,' as objectless phenomenal experiences that occur when the sensing person does not pay attention to eliciting moments. However, they form the affective core of all higher emotions. Moods and emotions are closely related in so far as moods form the affective or 'phenomenal' core of emotions. It is commonly accepted that certain fundamental or basic emotions can occur both as moods and emotions. Moods are basic emotions without any cognitive content, reduced to their affective quality only:

Moods are affective reactions distinct from emotions. Emotions are usually considered responses to a distinct event. They are intentional states: They are about some objects or events. Mood, by contrast, is the appropriate designation for affective states that refer to nothing specific or to everything, to the world in general. (Frijda 2009: 2)

Emotions are accordingly linked to cognitions to which they owe their intentional directedness. Moods, however, are purely affective states. In the more cognitivist-oriented dispositional theories however, moods are assessment dispositions. "Moods are temporary dispositions – more precisely, temporarily heightened dispositions – to have or to generate particular kinds of cognitions, specifically to make particular kinds of emotion-relevant appraisals" (Siemer 2009: 257). If such assumptions pertain to a concrete object, they are transformed into emotions. If they remain general, they are reduced to their phenomenal, affective qualities. Thus, moods are generalized dispositions of assessments which may affect the respective emotions concerning concrete objects. Richard Lazarus (1994: 84) argues: "Moods are products of appraisals of the existential background of our lives. This background has to do with who we are, now and in the long run, and how we are doing in life overall." Psychological theories do not address a relationship between moods and emotions but consider moods to be the background for the genesis of cognitions and emotions. Also in neurophysiological research, we find the metaphor of background and foreground. Damasio (1999: 190) replaced the term 'mood' with 'background emotions.' They are the feelings and moods of everyday life that are more in the background and rarely available for reflection.

Moods are often understood as background in sociology in a temporal sense. Moods are more durable than the episodic emotions (cf. Doan 2012; Smith-Lovin 1995; Stets 2003; Thoits 1985). This durability is sometimes attributed to the fact that they are hardly available reflexively, that their events are rarely in the focus of attention, and that they have comparatively low intensity. Affect control theory (cf. Heise 2006), according to which emotions are triggered by the non-confirmation of identities in action situations, also attributes the durability of moods to the fact that they are strongly linked to the identities of actors and arise from the permanent self-verification processes of actors in interactive situations. Self-labeling theory (cf. Thoits 1985), according to which the difference of moods and emotions is due to identifications and attributions, attributes the classification of affective states as moods to the fact that they are less controllable than emotions. Moods are affective states that an emotional subject attributes to him- or herself as 'passions,' as uncontrolled and therefore potentially deviant states.

III.III Atmospheres, Moods, and Bodily Feelings

In contrast to moods, atmospheres have only recently been introduced into an almost exclusively affective theoretical framework. Especially the phenomenology of Hermann Schmitz (1969, 1978) has contributed significantly to this. Furthermore, the philosophy of atmospheres of Gernot Böhme (2004, 2006, 2007; cf. Hauskeller 1995) has a particularly strong affinity to sociology. Böhme uses the term to capture a sensual aesthetic perception. In contrast to Schmitz, who considers atmospheres to be powers that become manifest independent of actual objects and persons, Böhme ties the presence of things and persons to atmospheres. For Böhme, atmospheres form a joint reality of the perceived and the perceiver. Atmospheres are spaces of the sensual. For example, we speak of the atmosphere of a house, a celebration, a political event, a summer evening, a friendly encounter, a shopping mall, or a landscape. Atmospheres are not cognitive but affective or emotional, body-centered structures with a 'holistic character.' In this sense, atmospheres are the central objects of aesthetics. And this includes not just images, but especially sounds and music, which form basic atmospheric conditions. According to Böhme, describing and perceiving atmospheres requires an object ontology different from the usual everyday or scientific ontology. He speaks of "ecstasies of things" (Böhme 2013: 225; my transl.) to denote that things have their properties not as abstract, self-sufficient, narrowing designations, but as relations that extend into their environment, determine their presence, and therefore give rise to atmospheres. Atmospheres are ordered spatially. The space of atmospheres is not a mathematical or functional space (cf. Böhme 2004) nor a cognitive space, but a space that is organized and centered on bodily presence. Atmospheres have a "quasi-objectivity" (Böhme 2007: 281). Although they only become atmospheres for a subject that perceives or feels them, they cannot be reduced to the subject's mere perception and feeling. They remain available even if one evades them. This quasi-objectivity also exists – and here we have to contradict Böhme (ibid.) – in atmospheres in social relations.

Many properties are attributed to moods and atmospheres, such as their non-conceptual content or their 'media character.' However, one property appears to be undisputed, namely their embodiment or incorporation. They manifest themselves primarily as a bodily sensation. Metaphors such as feeling 'depressed,' 'laid low' or 'upright' clearly indicate this. Bodily sensation does not mean that what we feel in our moods is only our body; it means that through the way our body feels, we find access to the objects and events in the world. It is actually the body that feels. So it is not only a feeling of internal states, but a bodily feeling and feeling of external states.

This again points to another important property of the implicit. Like many dimensions of the 'implicit,' the body forms the background of a person's world relationship within the affective. Recent research has therefore introduced the term of 'enactive' processes: The perception of some entity is based on proprioceptive, physical activities embedded in their environment (cf. Gallagher 2005; Noë 2004; Fingerhut/Hufendiek/Wild 2013). Enactivism, split into conservative and radical positions (cf. Hutto 2005), has criticized older ideas of cognitive science that understood cognition as representations and not as embodied interactions with the environment. The mental and affective life, according to enactivism, is not instrumentally dependent on a body but constitutive of it. And although we are rarely aware of our body, we are only aware of things in the world with and in our bodies. The same applies to the affective phenomena associated with mental processes (cf. Maiese 2011). Their bodily embeddedness is responsible for the fact that moods as well as emotions can hardly be modulated or selected.

There is one more aspect moods and atmospheres have in common: They are binary-coded. Almost all studies refer to 'positive' and 'negative' dimensions, i.e. to an elementary affective coding of states and events in the world as 'comfortable' or 'uncomfortable,' filled with pleasure or pain. Thereby, they address dimensions that form the core of the new 'affect studies' or 'cultural studies of affect.' They, too, assume that there is no (cognitive or evaluative) relationship to the world out there which is emotionally neutral. They stand in the tradition of Spinoza, Bergson, or Deleuze and describe the basic affectivity as 'élan vital,' as 'forces' that bind people to or dissociate them from things or situations (cf. Gregg/Seigworth 2010; Grossberg 2009; Adamowsky et al. 2011). Especially for Seyfert (2011a, 2011b), this has led to the conclusion that all social relations, cultural symbols, and social institutions have an affective foundation and that this affective foundation is a necessary precondition for the existence of institutions. Affects are affective or dissociative.

IV. Sociological Links

I have so far called attention to 'backgrounds' as a central form of the implicit and to moods and atmospheres as affective forms of such backgrounds. Using the theoretical concept of 'background,' it is possible to integrate moods and atmospheres into sociological theory. And using the concept of 'mood' or 'atmosphere,' it is possible to determine backgrounds as affective and free them from their cognitivist bias. From a sociological perspective, the central role of such affective backgrounds can be seen in the fact that affective backgrounds constitute spaces of possibility for the experience and action of individuals and social configurations (cf. Silver 2011). They characterize certain attitudes and approaches to persons, things, and events and therefore pre-determine possibilities of how you can experience and act with respect to persons, things, and events (cf. Schützeichel 2010b). They open possibilities and close them as well, represent opportunities and constraints of experience and action, and have a symbolic as well as a diabolical function. The affective dimension of moods can finally be seen in the fact that – in a more diffuse way – they binary-code general situations of experience and action. Their encoding occurs in different dimensions of factual, social, and temporal nature – as pleasant or unpleasant, in a dimension of concern or hope, trust or caution, pleasure or pain, calmness or excitement, tension or relaxation. As such, they represent a fundamental dimension of all social configurations.

But what is meant by 'background' in the context of moods and atmospheres? Why are moods and atmospheres background phenomena? A look at the phenomena will make this clear. In the previous chapter we discussed the various conceptual distinctions. From a sociological perspective, you can differentiate these affective phenomena in the following way:

- Sensations such as pain, hunger, or dizziness are physical conditions that can be triggered by specific internal states and processes.
- Feelings or emotions such as hatred, anger, resentment, shame, pride, or disgust are affective evaluations of certain events, objects, persons, or situations.
- Moods such as tenseness, depression, euphoria, or sadness are permanent or momentary attitudes towards action or life. They can occur individually or collectively.
- Atmospheres, which can be described like moods, are affective phenomena that arise from the material as well as from the social context of our experience and action.

Moods or atmospheres are background phenomena because they form the affective context of intentional reference to things. As such, they are rarely available for reflection because they are only given in addition [mit-gegeben]. They form the 'pre-intentional' background of our intentional experience and action (cf. Ratcliffe 2008, 2010). As is true of all background phenomena, we are most likely to become aware of moods, atmospheres, and existential feelings when they dissatisfy our expectations (cf. Adloff 2013). It is no coincidence that background affects are met with a high degree of pathologization. They are sometimes described as depression, neurosis, or deviance. However, for sociology, a general methodological motto can be derived from this: moods, atmospheres, and existential feelings can best be investigated when they are faced with resistance.

Communication does not only consist of the mere exchange of information, but has also a relational aspect in which the atmosphere between the communication partners plays a special role. Each communicative act has an effect on the atmosphere and affects the space of subsequent opportunities. It opens up and widens or narrows it. Atmospheres or moods can be understood according to communication theory as symbolically generalized media. They have the function to transform improbable into more probable communicative acts by suggesting or initiating certain connections (cf. Baecker 2005, 2011; Hiebler 2012). Moods and atmospheres, however, are not to be understood only as symbolic media but also as diabolical media. They do not only link but also separate communication partners. They close opportunities. Moods are therefore means functionally equivalent to money, power, truth, or love. Moods accomplish this by allowing for a 'consonance' of communicating souls by generating a joint 'background' of communicative processes.[5] To quote communication pragmatics: moods characterize a particular 'how' of communicating and thus open spaces of possibilities for what can or cannot be communicated. In such interaction situations the 'materiality' of a voice is of special importance for the genesis of moods (cf. Schützeichel 2010a, 2014). Moods and atmospheres thus act sym- as well as diabolically; they associate and they dissociate. Therefore, they are suited to form environments as places for consensual reality production (cf. Patzelt 2007).

How do moods form in interactions? Doan (2012) considers this question within the framework of symbolic interactionism. He differentiates between long-lasting moods and episodic emotions and argues that crucial mechanisms for the formation of moods are first intensity and second attention regarding the cause or the occasion of emotions. Doan sees moods as dispositions that an individual ascribes to him- or herself if he or she cannot meet required standards and in particular standards of emotions. Moods are thus quasi deviant affective states. Whether affective states are more likely to manifest as emotions

---

5 | This is particularly emphasized in Theodor Lipps's and John Volkelt's 'empathy aesthetics' as well as recently in the 'presence aesthetics' of Hans Ulrich Gumbrecht.

or as moods can be understood using Kemper's structural theory of emotion (1978): It depends on the status of a person in social relationships and the resulting opportunities to verbalize affective states. According to Doan (2012), people with low social status are far less capable of verbalizing their affective states than people with high social status. Therefore, they are much more likely to be controlled by moods.

V. Conclusion: Moods, Atmospheres, and 'Materialities'

The analysis of moods and atmospheres in cities and landscapes forms part of the traditional inventory of sociology, although they only recently have become a subject of research. Georg Simmel was a pioneer in this field. Simmel used the term 'mood' in a variety of academic studies, for example about religious attitudes or about the experience of works of art. Simmel associated moods with the experience of landscapes and generally with the experience of natural phenomena. Moods are links between the experiencing subject and the experienced nature. However, Simmel notes that it is difficult to locate moods. Feeling and idea of a landscape cannot be separated like cause and effect, they are mutually dependent. Simmel also refers to the individuality of such moods – every mood is uniquely toned (cf. 2001 [1913]). Like Simmel, art historian Alois Riegl (1929 [1899]) took the experiences related to landscapes as the 'paradigm' for the experience of moods. According to Martina Löw, each city displays specific areas of experience or atmospheres that form an integral part of its private logic [Eigenlogik]. The intrinsic logic of cities refers to implicit forms of meaning that prompt specific thoughts, feelings and actions (cf. Löw 2012: 59) and also physically inscribe them (cf. Göbel 2012). For example, based on the experience of its citizens, Darmstadt can be described as a city striving for harmony, deceleration, order, and routine because they allow familiarities (cf. Löw/Noller 2010). Each city has a specific feeling structure.

Certain social configurations, however, are of particular interest because they not only have moods or atmospheres but also depend on the necessity to produce certain moods or atmospheres. The relevance of such affective institutions and configurations in postmodernism has been growing steadily, as I emphasized in the introduction. This applies for example to rituals – rituals can delimit their experience and action sphere against the commonplace only by creating certain atmospheres and moods. This affective dimension is often overlooked in older as well as in more recent ritual and symbol research. Thus, a different social function of moods and atmospheres becomes apparent: they delimit social situations and structures in spatial and temporal terms. This becomes noticeable in our physical reactions: We breathe better when we leave a situation, and we tense up when we enter a new situation.

This function of delimitation also applies to all institutions that 'show' or 'stage' something. Such 'deictic institutions' – from liturgies to art institutions – rely on the generation and direction of attentions. And this requires that correspondingly favorable atmospheres and moods are being created. This also applies to configurations for which communicative order and the moods and atmospheres generated therein are essential for the achievement of specific objectives, for example in professional working relationships. The following conclusion is drawn: atmospheres and moods constitute the background of our social interactions and our communication. Contrary to Searle's considerations, a background is not a purely cognitive but also an affective phenomenon. Affective phenomena show how situations are experienced and how speech acts can or should be recognized.

Works Cited

Adamowsky, Natascha, et al. (eds.) (2011): Affektive Dinge. Objektberührungen in Wissenschaft und Kunst, Göttingen: Wallstein.
Adloff, Frank (2013): "Gefühle zwischen Präsenz und implizitem Wissen," in: Christoph Ernst/Heike Paul (eds.), Präsenz und implizites Wissen, Bielefeld: transcript, 97-124.
Baecker, Dirk (2005): Form und Formen der Kommunikation, Frankfurt/Main: Suhrkamp.
—. (2011): "Kulturen der Furcht," in: Thomas Kisser/Daniela Rippl/Marion Tiedtke (eds.), Angst. Dimensionen eines Gefühls, München: Fink, 47-58.
Becker, Alexander (2012): "Die verlorene Harmonie der Harmonie," in: von Arburg/Rickenbacher, Concordia Discors, 261-279.
Beedie, Christopher J./Terry, Peter C./Lane, Andrew M. (2005): "Distinctions between Emotion and Mood," in: Cognition and Emotion 19, 847-878.
Beedie, Christopher J./Terry, Peter C./Devonport, Tracey J. (2011): "Differential Assessment of Emotions and Moods," in: Personality and Individual Differences 50, 228-233.
Böhme, Gernot (2004): "Der Raum leiblicher Anwesenheit und der Raum als Medium von Darstellung," in: Sybille Krämer (ed.), Performativität und Medialität, München: Fink, 129-140.
—. (2006): Architektur und Atmosphäre, München: Fink.
—. (2007): "Atmosphären in zwischenmenschlicher Kommunikation," in: Debus/Posner, Atmosphären im Alltag, 281-293.
—. (2013): Atmosphäre. Essays zur neuen Ästhetik, 7th extended and rev. ed., Frankfurt/Main: Suhrkamp.

Bollnow, Otto Friedrich (2009 [1941]): Das Wesen der Stimmungen, Würzburg: Königshausen und Neumann.
Corbineau-Hoffmann, Angelika (2011): "Passanten, Passagen, Kunstkonzepte. Die Straßen großer Städte als affektive Räume," in: Lehnert, Raum und Gefühl, 118-134.
Damasio, Antonio (1999): The Feeling of What Happens. Body, Emotion and the Making of Consciousness, London: Heinemann.
Debus, Stephan/Posner, Roland (eds.) (2007): Atmosphären im Alltag, Bonn: Psychiatrie-Verlag.
De Rivera, Joseph (1992): "Emotional Climate. Social Structure and Emotional Dynamics," in: K.T. Strongman (ed.), International Review of Studies on Emotion, Chichester: Wiley, 197-218.
Dilthey, Wilhelm (1931 [1911]): "Weltanschauungslehre. Abhandlungen zur Philosophie der Philosophie," in: Wilhelm Dilthey, Gesammelte Schriften, Vol. VIII, Leipzig: Teubner.
Doan, Long (2012): "A Social Model of Persistent Mood States," in: Social Psychology Quarterly 75.3, 198-218.
Dreyfus, Hubert L. (2012): "The Mystery of Background qua Background," in: Radman, Knowing without Thinking, 1-11.
Ekman, Paul (1994): "Moods, Emotions, and Traits," in: Ekman/Davidson, Nature, 56-58.
Ekman, Paul/Davidson, Richard J. (eds.) (1994): The Nature of Emotion, New York: Oxford UP.
Elpidorou, Andreas (2013): "Moods and Appraisals. How the Phenomenology and Science of Emotions Can Come Together," in: Human Studies 36.4, 1-27.
Ferreira, Boris (2002): Stimmung bei Heidegger. Das Phänomen der Stimmung im Kontext von Heideggers Existenzialanalyse des Daseins, Dordrecht: Kluwer.
Fingerhut, Jörg/Hufendiek, Rebekka/Wild, Markus (eds.) (2013): Philosophie der Verkörperung, Frankfurt/Main: Suhrkamp.
Frijda, Nico H. (1993): "Moods, Emotion Episodes, and Emotions," in: Michael Lewis/J.M. Haviland (eds.), Handbook of Emotions, New York: Guilford, 381-403.
—. (2009): "Mood," in: David Sander/Klaus R. Scherer (eds.), The Oxford Companion to Emotion and the Affective Sciences, Oxford: Oxford UP, 258-259.
Gallagher, Shaun (2005): How the Body Shapes the Mind, Oxford: Oxford UP.
Geiger, Moritz (1911): "Zum Problem der Stimmungseinfühlung," in: Zeitschrift für Ästhetik und allgemeine Kunstwissenschaft 6, 1-42.
Gisbertz, Anna Katharina (2009): Stimmung – Leib – Sprache. Eine Konfiguration in der Wiener Moderne, München: Fink.

—. (ed.) (2011): Stimmung. Zur Wiederkehr einer ästhetischen Kategorie, München: Fink.
Göbel, Katharina (2012): "Urbanes Design von Atmosphären. Ästhetische und sinnengeleitete Praktiken mit Gebäuden," in: Stephan Moebius/Sophia Prinz (eds.), Das Design der Gesellschaft. Zur Kultursoziologie des Designs, Bielefeld: transcript, 337-358.
Goldie, Peter (2000): The Emotions, Oxford: Clarendon P.
Gregg, Melissa/Seigworth, Gregory J. (eds.) (2010): The Affect Theory Reader, Durham: Duke UP.
Grossberg, Lawrence (2009): "Postmodernity and Affect. All Dressed Up with No Place to Go," in: Jennifer Harding/E. Deidre Pribam (eds.), Emotions. A Cultural Studies Reader, London: Routledge, 69-83.
Große, Jürgen (2008): Philosophie der Langeweile, Stuttgart: Metzler.
Gumbrecht, Hans Ulrich (2012): Atmosphere, Mood, Stimmung, Stanford: Stanford UP.
Haag, Saskia (2012): "'Stimmung' machen. Die Produktion des Interieurs im 19. Jahrhundert," in: von Arburg/Rickenbacher, Concordia Discors, 115-126.
Hauskeller, Michael (1995): Atmosphären erleben, Berlin: Akademie.
Heise, David (2006): Expressive Order. Confirming Sentiments in Social Actions, New York: Springer.
Hiebler, Heinz (2012): "'Tuning In.' Stimmung als medienästhetisches und epistemologisches Konzept," in: von Arburg/Rickenbacher, Concordia Discors, 163-182.
Hitzler, Ronald/Honer, Anne/Pfadenhauer, Michaela (eds.) (2008): Posttraditionale Gemeinschaften, Wiesbaden: VS.
Huppertz, Michael (2007): "Spirituelle Atmosphären," in: Debus/Posner, Atmosphären im Alltag, 157-185.
Hutto, Daniel D. (2005): "Knowing What? Radical versus Conservative Enactivism," in: Phenomenology and the Cognitive Sciences 4, 389-405.
Kemper, Theodore D. (1978): A Social Interaction Theory of Emotions, New York: Wiley.
Kierkegaard, Sören (1991 [1844]): Der Begriff Angst, Gesammelte Werke, Vol. 11/12, Gütersloh: Gütersloher Verlagshaus.
Kimminich, Eva (2007): "Kairos, Actionality and Flow – Wie, wozu und warum in Jugendkulturen Atmosphäre hergestellt wird," in: Debus/Posner, Atmosphären im Alltag, 141-156.
Lazarus, Richard S. (1994): "The Stable and the Unstable in Emotion," in: Ekman/Davidson, Nature, 79-85.
Lehnert, Gertrud (ed.) (2011): Raum und Gefühl, Bielefeld: transcript.
Löw, Martina (2012): "'Jede Stadt ist ein Seelenzustand.' Über städtische Vergesellschaftung und Identitätsforderung," in: Rainer Goetz/Stefan Graupner (eds.), Atmosphären II, München: Kopaed, 55-67.

Löw, Martina/Noller, Peter (2010): "Eine Insel der Glückseligen? Gefühltes Darmstadt. Zufriedenheit, Phlegma und Entschleunigung," in: Martina Löw/Peter Noller/Sabine Süß (eds.), Typisch Darmstadt? Eine Stadt beschreibt sich selbst, Frankfurt/Main: Campus, 256-273.

Lorenz, Claudia/Penzel, Joachim (2007): "Gestimmte Räume. Ein atmosphärischer Rundgang durch ein Kinderkrankenhaus," in: Debus/Posner, Atmosphären im Alltag, 53-65.

Lormand, Eric (1985): "Toward a Theory of Moods," in: Philosophical Studies 47, 385-407.

Maiese, Michelle (2011): Embodiment, Emotion, and Cognition, Houndmills: Palgrave Macmillan.

Margolis, John (2012): "Contesting John Searle's Social Ontology. Institutions and Background," in: Radman, Knowing without Thinking, 98-114.

Merker, Barbara (2008): "Heidegger und Bollnow. Theorie der Befindlichkeit und ihre Kritik," in: Hilge Landweer/Ursula Renz (eds.), Klassische Emotionstheorien, Berlin: de Gruyter, 635-660.

Meyer-Sickendiek, Burkhard (2011): "Gefühlstiefen. Aktuelle Perspektiven einer vergessenen Dimension der Emotionsforschung," in: Lehnert, Raum und Gefühl, 26-48.

Mullhall, Stephen (1996): "Can There Be an Epistemology of Moods?," in: Anthony O'Hear (ed.), Verstehen and Human Understanding, Cambridge: Cambridge UP, 191-210.

Noë, Alva (2004): Action in Perception, Cambridge: MIT P.

Oatley, Keith/Johnson-Laird, P.N. (1989): "Emotion, Moods, and Conscious Awareness," in: Cognition and Emotion 3, 125-137.

—. (1990): "Semantic Primitives for Emotions," in: Cognition and Emotion 4, 129-143.

Parkinson, Brian, et al. (2000): Stimmungen. Struktur, Dynamik und Beeinflussungsmöglichkeiten eines psychologischen Phänomens, Stuttgart: Klett-Cotta.

Patzelt, Werner J. (2007): "Stimmung, Atmosphäre, Milieu. Eine ethnomethodologische Analyse ihrer Konstruktion und Reproduktion," in: Debus/Posner, Atmosphären im Alltag, 196-232.

Radman, Zdravko (ed.) (2012): Knowing without Thinking, Baskingstoke: Palgrave Macmillan.

Ratcliffe, Matthew (2008): Feelings of Being. Phenomenology, Psychiatry and the Sense of Reality, Oxford: Oxford UP.

—. (2010): "The Phenomenology of Mood and the Meaning of Life," in: Peter Goldie (ed.), The Oxford Handbook of Philosophy of Emotion, Oxford: Oxford UP, 349-371.

Reisenzein, Rainer/Döring, Sabine (2009): "Ten Perspectives on Emotional Experience," in: Emotion Review 1, 195-205.

Riegl, Alois (1929 [1899]): "Die Stimmung als Inhalt der modernen Kunst," in: Alois Riegl, Gesammelte Aufsätze, Augsburg: Filser, 28-39.
Roberts, Robert C. (2003): Emotions. An Essay in Aid in Moral Psychology, Cambridge: Cambridge UP.
Rust, Joshua (2009): John Searle, London: Continuum.
Scheler, Max (1916 [1913]): Der Formalismus in der Ethik und die materiale Wertethik, Bern: Francke.
Schmalenbach, Herman (1922): "Die soziologische Kategorie des Bundes," in: Die Dioskuren. Jahrbuch für Geisteswissenschaften 1922, 35-105.
Schmitz, Hermann (1969): Der Gefühlsraum. System der Philosophie III.4, Bonn: Bouvier.
—. (1978): Die Wahrnehmung. System der Philosophie III.5, Bonn: Bouvier.
Schmitz, Michael (2013): "Social Rules and the Social Background," in: Schmitz/Kobow/Schmid, Background, 107-126.
Schmitz, Michael/Kobow, Beatrice/Schmid, Hans Bernhard (eds.) (2013): The Background and Social Reality, Dordrecht: Springer.
Schützeichel, Rainer (2010a): "Soziologie der Stimme. Über den Körper in der Kommunikation," in: Reiner Keller/Michael Meuser (eds.), Körperwissen, Wiesbaden: VS, 85-104.
—. (2010b): "Die Logik des Sozialen. Entwurf einer intentional-relationalen Soziologie," in: Gert Albert/Rainer Greshoff/Rainer Schützeichel (eds.), Dimensionen der Sozialität, Wiesbaden: VS, 339-376.
—. (2014): "Materialitäten und Atmosphären," in: Herbert Kalthoff, et al. (eds.), Materialitäten, München: Fink. forthcoming.
Searle, John R. (1978): "Literal Meaning," in: Erkenntnis 13, 207-224.
—. (1980): "The Background of Meaning," in: John R. Searle/Ferenc Kiefer/Manfred Bierwisch (eds.), Speech Act Theory and Pragmatics, Dordrecht: Reidel, 221-232.
—. (1991): Intentionalität, Frankfurt/Main: Suhrkamp.
—. (1992): The Rediscovery of the Mind, Cambridge: MIT P.
—. (1995): The Construction of Social Reality, New York: Free Press.
—. (2001): Geist, Sprache und Gesellschaft, Frankfurt/Main: Suhrkamp.
—. (2002): "Skepticism about Rules and Intentionality," in: John R. Searle, Consciousness and Language, Cambridge: Cambridge UP, 251-264.
—. (2005): Geist, Frankfurt/Main: Suhrkamp.
—. (2010): Making the Social World, Oxford: Oxford UP.
—. (2011): "Wittgenstein and the Background," in: American Philosophical Quarterly 48.2, 119-128.
Seyfert, Robert (2011a): Das Leben der Institutionen, Weilerswist: Velbrück.
—. (2011b): "Atmosphären – Transmissionen – Interaktionen. Zu einer Theorie sozialer Affekte," in: Soziale Systeme 17.1, 73-96.

—. (2012): "Beyond Personal Feelings and Collective Emotions. A Theory of Social Affect," in: Theory, Culture and Society 29.6, 27-46.
Siemer, Matthias (1999): Stimmungen, Emotionen und soziale Urteile, Frankfurt/Main: Lang.
—. (2009): "Mood Experience. Implications of a Dispositional Theory of Moods," in: Emotion Review 1, 256-263.
Silver, Daniel (2011): "The Moodiness of Action," in: Sociological Theory 29, 199-222.
Simmel, Georg (2001 [1913]): "Philosophie der Landschaft," in: Georg Simmel, Aufsätze und Abhandlungen 1909-1918, Vol 1, Frankfurt/Main: Suhrkamp, 471-482.
Slaby, Jan (2012): "Matthew Ratcliffes phänomenologische Theorie existentieller Gefühle," in: Annette Schnabel/Rainer Schützeichel (eds.), Emotionen, Sozialstruktur und Moderne, Wiesbaden: VS, 75-91.
Solomon, Robert C. (1993): The Passions. Emotions and the Meaning of Life, rev. ed., Cambridge: Hackett.
Smith-Lovin, Lynn (1995): "The Sociology of Affect and Emotion," in: Karen S. Cook, et al. (eds.), Sociological Perspectives on Social Psychology, Boston: Allyn and Bacon, 118-148.
Spitzer, Leo (1963): Classical and Christian Ideas of World Harmony. Prolegomena to an Interpretation of the Word "Stimmung," Baltimore: Johns Hopkins.
Stets, Jan E. (2003): "Emotions and Sentiments," in: J. Delamatger (ed.), Emotions and Sentiments, New York: Springer, 309-335.
Strasser, Stephan (1956): Das Gemüt, Freiburg: Herder.
Stroud, Barry (1991): "The Background of Thought," in: Ernest Lepore/Robert van Gulick (eds.), John Searle and His Critics, Oxford: Blackwell, 245-258.
Stueber, Karsten R. (2005): "How to Think about Rules and Rule-Following," in: Philosophy of the Social Sciences 35, 307-323.
Taylor, Charles (1993): "Engaged Agency and Background in Heidegger," in: Charles B. Guignon (ed.), The Cambridge Companion to Heidegger, Cambridge: Cambridge UP, 317-336.
Thoits, Peggy A. (1985): "Self-Labeling Processes in Mental Illness. The Role of Emotional Deviance," in: American Journal of Sociology 91, 221-249.
Tugendhat, Ernst (1979): Selbstbewußtsein und Selbstbestimmung, Frankfurt/Main: Suhrkamp.
von Arburg, Hans-Georg/Rickenbacher, Sergej (eds.) (2012a): Concordia Discors. Ästhetiken der Stimmung zwischen Literaturen, Künsten und Wissenschaften, Würzburg: Königshausen und Neumann.
—. (2012b): "Einleitung," in: von Arburg/Rickenbacher, Concordia Discors, 7-20.

Welsh, Caroline (2012): "'Stimmung.' The Emergence of a Concept and Its Modification in Psychology and Physiology," in: Brigit Neumann/Ansgar Nünning (eds.), Travelling Concepts for the Study of Culture, Berlin: de Gruyter, 267-289.

Wimmer, Manfred (2011): "Stimmungen im Spannungsfeld zwischen Phänomenologie, Ontologie und naturwissenschaftlicher Emotionsforschung," in: Kerstin Andermann/Undine Eberlein (eds.), Gefühle als Atmosphären. Neue Phänomenologie und philosophische Emotionstheorie, Berlin: Akademie, 97-123.

Tacit Knowledge in a Differentiated Society

David Kaldewey

I. Introduction

In the discourse of sociological theory, the issue of tacit knowledge has become increasingly relevant, especially in the context of interactionist, phenomenological, pragmatist, and praxeological approaches.[1] There is an emerging consensus that *social theories* have to pay heed to the manifold weak and strong forms of tacit knowledge, such as relational or not-yet-explicated knowledge, practical skill-based knowledge, embodied tacit knowledge, affective and emotional understanding, and collective, that is socially shared forms of tacit knowledge.[2] In *theories of society* however, that is, in macrosociological theories based on an understanding of society as a reality *sui generis*, the issue of tacit knowledge figures less prominently. A basic assumption of these theories shared by most classical sociologists is that modern society is functionally differentiated and as such is no longer determined by stratification or inequality, but rather by a plurality of autonomous value spheres, systems, or fields that operate according to their own logic. If we accept this diagnosis and are at the same time interested in evaluating the relevance of tacit knowledge for sociological theory, then we have to reflect about the role tacit knowledge plays in a differentiated society. Hence, the following considerations build on two assumptions: First, if society is as fragmented as differentiation theory suggests, then we must assume that the tacit knowledge of actors, especially their knowledge about the society they live in, is equally fragmented; and second, if tacit knowledge is constitutive for everyday social practice and interaction on a micro level, then we must assume that the macro structure of society is not independent of this 'hidden' stock of knowledge.

---

[1] | See for example the contributions of Antony, Hubrich, Loenhoff, and Renn in the present volume.

[2] | Typologies of tacit knowledge have been proposed, among others, by Collins (2010) and Shotwell (2011).

In the following, I will first discuss different notions of societal differentiation and elaborate on the distinction between two prominent approaches, namely cultural differentiation and functional differentiation. Taking up a suggestion by Joachim Renn (2006), the two forms of differentiation can be distinguished from each other not least in regard to whether they focus on tacit or on explicit forms of knowledge. These two approaches have different ideas about what constitutes the basic unit of differentiation in modern societies and about the role tacit knowledge plays in integrating these units. In theories of cultural differentiation, the units of analysis are *cultural forms of life* (CFLs), while theories of functional differentiation are built on a notion of *macrosocial supercategories* (MSCs). I will then examine how these concepts are used in the theories of Max Weber, Talcott Parsons, Jürgen Habermas, Niklas Luhmann, and Pierre Bourdieu, and I will specifically ask whether and how these theories are able to conceptualize the relevance of tacit knowledge for differentiation processes. Finally, after comparing these different theoretical frameworks, I will ask how the nexus between tacit knowledge and societal differentiation could be further theorized.

II. Cultural Differentiation and Functional Differentiation

In sociology, the concept of differentiation has several meanings. In a very general sense, social differentiation often refers to dimensions of inequality, such as class, race, and gender. What is at issue here is *vertical stratification*, which implies that some people have more material resources and power at their disposal than others. However, differentiation theories in a stricter sense usually deal with *horizontal differentiation*, for example in regard to different social worlds, cultures, or different kinds of subsystems that coexist without establishing a hierarchical order. Both the vertical and the horizontal perspectives are constitutive for sociological thinking (cf. Schwinn 2004), the first being more prominent in many fields of empirical research, the second in theoretical discussions about the evolution and structure of modern societies.

I will now concentrate on differentiation theories in the strict sense and consider what kind of social units are of relevance to them. Here, two approaches can be distinguished again. The first approach focuses on the plurality and heterogeneity of cultural units or forms of life. There is no common definition of what exactly these units represent – sometimes they are understood as collectives or communities, sometimes as "social worlds" (Strauss 1978) or, from a phenomenological perspective, as "provinces of meaning" (Berger/Luckmann 1966: 25). Joachim Renn recently proposed the concept of "milieus," which he defines as cultural forms of life that, building on a common tacit background knowledge, differ from each other in regard to their habitual and practical dimension (2006: 410ff.). When several of these internally integrated milieus fall apart, Renn speaks of *cultural differentiation* (ibid. 106f., 399). Due to the fact that concepts such as 'social worlds,' 'provinces of meaning,' and 'milieus' denote different and heterogeneous phenomena, I will use the label *cultural form of life* (CFL) as an umbrella term in the following. On the one hand, CFLs can refer to more or less isolated subcultures *within* an encompassing societal context, and on the other to radically different and spatially separated cultures *beyond* the horizon and societal context of the observer. Traditionally, sociologists have been interested in the first aspect, whereas anthropologists have concentrated on the second. However, the two meanings are not necessarily contradictory, as modern multicultural societies reveal. Here, groups of immigrants may be regarded as subcultures that are at least partially integrated into the culture of the host country, and as members of a migrant or diasporic culture at the same time. As a result, they deal with multiple identities and participate in heterogeneous cultural forms of life. Against this background, it is evident why theories of cultural differentiation often revolve around the problem of *intercultural communication*. Following Jens Loenhoff, this problem is systematically connected to tacit knowledge. Like Renn, Loenhoff conceives of CFLs in terms of tacit knowledge. Arguing from a pragmatist perspective, he states

that it is the intuitive knowledge of practical consequences and presuppositions of speaking and acting, as well as the connected implicit knowledge of the adequacy of this acting and experiencing, that guarantees agents acting within their own cultural form of life a chance to participate in this world, provides them with the feeling of normality in this world, and ensures familiarity with everyday affairs in this world. (2011: 61)

In short, CFLs are integrated by means of everyday practical actions, which themselves are primarily grounded in tacit knowledge. *Cultural differentiation* can thus be understood as the differentiation of social groups that share a specific and sometimes esoteric tacit knowledge.

In contrast to the first approach, the second approach focuses on abstract and large-scale societal units such as the economy, politics, science, or religion. These social systems are based on specific rationalities, codes, and values, and have monopolized specific functions that are crucial for modern society. Again, there is no common definition of these macrosocial units; they have been described as 'cultural systems' (Wilhelm Dilthey), 'value spheres' (Max Weber), 'subsystems' (Talcott Parsons), 'function systems' (Niklas Luhmann) or 'social fields' (Pierre Bourdieu). Although these concepts are not synonymous, the approaches from which they derive have enough in common to be subsumed under the general label of *functional differentiation*.³ In order to maintain impartiality in regard to the competing theories of functional differentiation, I will in the following refer to the differentiated entities in question as *macrosocial supercategories* (MSCs), a label proposed by Roy Harris (2006, 2007) to explain how language in practice functions to integrate social complexes such as art (Harris 2003) or science (Harris 2005). Since Harris's approach is not linked to sociological theories, his term may serve as a neutral placeholder for the heterogeneous sociological concepts. It is worth noting here that even though there is no agreement on how exactly to conceptualize and to label the various MSCs, there is little disagreement in regard to which of these units are the most relevant members in the club.⁴ Most authors agree that politics, the economy, the law, science, religion, and art are indispensable constituents of modern society, while the mass media, the education system, the health system, and sports are not universally accepted as relevant MSCs, but are at least plausible candidates; the sphere of love, eroticism, and intimate relationships has also been conceptualized as an MSC (cf. Weber 1988; Luhmann 1986b).

Given these two approaches towards differentiation, the questions arise whether and how cultural differentiation and functional differentiation are interconnected, and whether and how it is possible to systematically distinguish between CFLs and MSCs as distinct types of social entities. Actually, many sociological theories do not make this distinction. This is not surprising, because conventional concepts such as 'groups,' 'communities,' 'cultures,' or 'institutions,' can be easily applied to small-scale as well as large-scale social entities. A good example is the afore-mentioned social-worlds perspective, which understands 'huge' entities such as politics, science, or medicine as well as 'small' networks of interaction and interests, such as opera, baseball, or stamp collecting as social worlds (cf. Strauss 1978: 121). However, if we turn from theories of the *social* to theories of *society*, the distinction between cultural and functional differentiation can no longer be ignored. Its most systematic analysis can be found in the work of Joachim Renn. Even though it is beyond the scope of this paper to explain Renn's theoretical framework (2006) in its entirety, I will briefly sketch some of his distinctions that are of interest here. The crucial point is

---

3 | Another label that has sometimes been used is "structural differentiation" (cf. Rueschemeyer 1974, 1977; Colomy/Rhoades 1994). However, this concept is mainly associated with the Parsonian tradition and ignores certain crucial developments in the German tradition, which in the end radically departed from the premises of Parsons' structural functionalism.

4 | Roth (2012) for example presents a list with ten systems, while Schimank speaks about "a collection of about a dozen partial systems" (2011: 261, my transl.), and Stichweh claims "that more than ten global function systems definitely exist in world society" (2013: 58).

that Renn conceives of functional differentiation as a specific form of cultural differentiation. As a consequence, he states that "function systems" (in our terms: MSCs) grow out of socio-cultural "milieus" (in our terms: CFLs), that is, out of life-world contexts, in a process of semanticization that results in abstraction, generalization, and specialization. In this process, knowledge becomes explicit, reflexive, and discursive (cf. Renn 2004: 247; 2006: 403f.). Thus, MSCs can be understood as systems of explicated knowledge. This knowledge is the outcome of a translation process in which different forms of implicit cultural background knowledge have been transformed into the fragmented semantics of modernity. Following Renn, these "function systems" differ from each other only semantically, that is, in regard to their explicit knowledge (cf. Renn 2006: 403, 407). In other words, Renn uses the distinction between tacit and explicit knowledge to clarify the distinction between cultural and functional differentiation, as well as the distinction between CFLs and MSCs. In short, MSCs are purified from tacit knowledge.

Evaluating critically the plausibility of Renn's framework, the question arises whether the definition of an MSC as a system of explicated knowledge adequately explains the emergence and stabilization of diverse and complex entities such as the economy, politics, science, and religion. Do these MSCs really operate in the medium of semantics and discourse only, that is, without building on tacit knowledge and the cultural practices that rely on it? Furthermore, does the emergence of a MSC out of a CFL necessarily imply the decoupling of these two units of integration? To answer these questions, I will take a closer look at how classical theories of functional differentiation conceive of MSCs; I will examine how Weber, Parsons, Habermas, Luhmann, and Bourdieu connect the idea of functional differentiation to the issue of cultural differentiation, and whether and how their theories pay heed to tacit knowledge. As mentioned above, I will use the terms 'MSC' and 'CFL' in my account of these theoretical frameworks in order to provide an impartial perspective from which the different vocabularies of these authors can be interpreted as contributions to the same theoretical discourse.

III. MAX WEBER'S VALUE SPHERES AND LIFE ORDERS

Although Max Weber himself did not use the term 'differentiation' systematically in his diagnosis of modernity, many authors agree that he actually developed a strong differentiation theory (cf. Habermas 1984; Schluchter 1988; Tyrell 1998; Schwinn 2001; Schimank 2002; Schmidt 2005; Darmon 2011). Weber's differentiation theory in a way is a byproduct of his sociology of religion and his theory of rationalization. The most important reference here is the "intermediate reflection" (*Zwischenbetrachtung*) in his collected essays on the sociology of religion (cf. Weber 1988). In this short text, Weber describes the tensions and conflicts between the world-rejecting forms of religious ethics on the one hand, and the worldly orders that shape human action on the other. Weber specifically mentions a set of "value spheres" (*Wertsphären*) that emerged historically and developed a certain autonomy and inner logic (*Eigengesetzlichkeit*): Beside religion, which appears as the prototypical value sphere, there is the economic sphere, the political sphere, the aesthetic sphere, the erotic sphere, and the intellectual sphere.[5] Weber's notion of value spheres is at least partly influenced by Wilhelm Dilthey (cf. Tyrell 1998: 138ff.; Schneider 2010: 206f.), who can generally be read as a precursor to modern sociological differentiation theories. Dilthey repeatedly pointed to the differentiation and isolation of "cultural systems" (*Kultursysteme*) such as education, the economy, the law, politics, religion, sociability, art, philosophy, and science (cf. 1970: 203f.). A cultural system in this sense emerges when the interrelated actions of individuals materialize in certain shared values. The common denominator of Dilthey and Weber is their strong notion of culture and their reference to individual subjects: 'cultural systems' or 'value spheres' are conceived of as horizons of meaning that structure the actions of individuals and are at the same time reproduced by these actions. However, Weber departs from Dilthey insofar as the notion of value spheres refers more radically to *culture*, and not to *society*. In contrast to later theories of functional differentiation, the idea is not that society splits into a set of subsystems; Weber instead proposes a "differentiation without society" (cf. Schwinn 2001). Thus, the label *cultural differentiation* may be more appropriate here than the label *functional differentiation*. At first sight it seems that there is no systematic distinction between CFLs and MSCs in Weber's framework, because Weber's definition of culture as "a finite segment of the meaningless infinity of the world process, a segment on which human beings confer meaning and significance" (1949: 81) is very broad. Following this definition, what counts as a cultural value is not restricted to ethically valuable or socially important aspects of reality: According to Weber, "[p]rostitution is a cultural phenomenon just as much as religion or money" (ibid.). What Weber has in mind when he speaks about 'value spheres' thus is a closed set of cultural ideas that have been rationalized and universalized in a historically unique way. As a consequence, and in regard to Renn's approach discussed above, a 'value sphere' can be interpreted as a MSC that has emerged historically out of a CFL.

The concept of value spheres marks the starting point for Weber's differentiation theory. However, Weber also talks about "life orders" (*Lebensordnungen*),

---

5 | It is interesting to note that whereas most differentiation theories also conceptualize the law as a MSC, Weber conceives of it as a coordination mechanism into which the other value spheres are embedded (cf. Habermas 1984: 242; Schwinn 2001: 198).

a complementary concept that is sometimes used synonymously with 'value spheres' (cf. Darmon 2011: 109f.). Nevertheless it is possible to distinguish precisely between these two concepts: Whereas value spheres are condensations of cultural ideas and values, life orders are the result of the structural materialization and stabilization of these value spheres (cf. Schluchter 1988: 107, 146; Schwinn 2001: 47, 153ff.; Schmidt 2005: 420). The basic idea is that if large numbers of people orient their actions towards specific values, then these values become institutionalized in the form of modern organizations, associations, and roles on the one hand, and in the inner ethos and lifestyle of individuals on the other. In this process, cultural differentiation turns into "institutional differentiation" (Schluchter 1988: 146, 148ff.). This theoretical framework is very close to what later theoreticians describe as functional differentiation. To sum up, Weber understands MSCs as a result of the interplay between an ideal or cultural level ('value sphere') and a material or structural level ('life order').

What is the role of tacit knowledge in Weber's differentiation theory? Although Weber did not use the term, we can now see that tacit knowledge is relevant to his approach. First, the whole notion of cultural ideas and value spheres cannot be reduced to explicit forms of knowledge. Of course, value spheres depend at least partially on explicit semantics, such as religious texts, formal laws, or scientific methods and theories, but they necessarily build on shared tacit knowledge as well. Especially in regard to religion – which for Weber is the prototypical value sphere – one can further suppose that it is rooted in both a "collective consciousness" (Émile Durkheim) and a "collective unconscious" (C.G. Jung).[6] Second, if value spheres materialize in life orders, the respective values will be embedded in everyday practices and will be embodied by individuals. This point is particularly obvious in the case of "innerworldly asceticism," which plays a central role in Weber's analysis of both religion and the economy (cf. Weber 1988: 539). The relevance of implicit and embodied knowledge is also evident in Weber's conception of the value sphere of eroticism, which according to him is the "biggest irrational power of life" (1988: 556, my transl.). For Weber, this value sphere is rooted in what today we would call sexual *practices* rather than in explicit *knowledge* about love.[7]

---

6 | See Greenwood (1990) for a discussion of the interrelationship of these two concepts.

7 | Weber in this regard markedly differs from Luhmann, who conceptualizes love as a function system that primarily builds on the semantics of romantic love (cf. Luhmann 1986b).

IV. Talcott Parsons' Decomposition Paradigm

While Weber and other classical sociologists appear today as differentiation theorists *avant la lettre*, Talcott Parsons is usually depicted as the actual inventor of the theory of functional differentiation. In Parsons' system-functional framework, every system can be analytically decomposed into four subsystems which each fulfill a specific function. The four functions are codified in the so-called AGIL scheme: adaption (A), goal attainment (G), integration (I), and latent pattern maintenance (L).[8] Societies are conceived of as specific social systems, and as such they are differentiated into four subsystems (cf. Parsons/ Smelser 1956; Parsons 1966, 1971), namely the 'economy' (A), the 'polity' (G), the 'societal community' (I), and the 'fiduciary system' (L). All of these systems may be decomposed into further subsystems. It is neither possible here to discuss in detail how these subsystems are nested into each other, nor is it necessary to repeat the well-known critique of this approach. What matters for the moment is only the basic idea of "functional prerequisites" that have to be fulfilled at the level of society as well as at the level of the subsystems (cf. Parsons 1951: 26ff.). Following this premise, functional differentiation is basically defined as the "decomposition of a functionally diffuse unit [...] into several, functionally more specific units" (Schimank 2002: 3664). This idea has its roots in organicist theories of society on the one hand (e.g. Herbert Spencer) and in theories that see the division of labor as a central constituent of modernization processes on the other (e.g. Émile Durkheim). Today, Parsons' approach is therefore often characterized as a "decomposition paradigm" and contrasted with other theories of functional differentiation (such as Weber's or Luhmann's) that conceive of social systems as contingently emerging and increasingly autonomous systems (cf. Mayntz 1988: 14; Schimank 2002: 3664; Stichweh 2013: 56). The conceptualization of functional differentiation as a decomposition process is apparent both in the term "partial social system," which Parsons introduced in his general theory of action systems (cf. Parsons 1951: 19), and in the term "subsystem," which he preferred later on.[9]

In contemporary sociology, Parsons' attempt to analytically break down every social phenomenon into a four-part functional system is viewed with skep-

---

8 | It is important to note that Parsons actually uses this scheme for every system, that is, not only for social systems. On the most abstract level, the late Parsons conceives of the 'human condition' as a system in which the 'general action system' functions as the integrative subsystem (cf. Parsons 1978). This general action system is subdivided into the 'behavioral organism' (A), the 'personality system' (G), the 'social system' (I), and the 'cultural system' (L).

9 | Interestingly, several German authors still talk about partial social systems (*Teilsysteme*) although they do not agree with the decomposition paradigm.

ticism and indeed often almost with hostility. At the same time, however, several of his categorizations have remained tremendously influential until today. Ironically, even if his differentiation theory is completely banned from today's theoretical discourse, it persists tenaciously in many concepts and categories of authors that do not even mention his name.

The tacit impact of Parsons' differentiation theory is demonstrated, first, by the lasting influence of his distinction between the "social system" and the "cultural system" as two subsystems of the general action system. It is instructive to look at how Parsons assorts the different MSCs: The economy and politics are, as already noted, subsystems of the social system, and the same goes for the law, while religion, art, and science are subsystems of the cultural system. In other words, Parsons does not differentiate between MSCs and CFLs, but between *social* MSCs and *cultural* MSCs. At this point Parsons departs from Weber, who conceptualizes all MSCs as *conglomerates* of social and cultural structures. According to Weber, it makes no sense at all to distinguish between *cultural* value spheres on the one hand and *social* life orders on the other, because in his view, all relevant spheres are culturally grounded and at the same time institutionalized in social structures. Of course, Parsons himself was quite aware of the fact that the cultural and the social intermingle in myriad ways (cf. Kroeber/Parsons 1958), and in reference to the AGIL scheme it is no problem to reintroduce the one into the other – for example, the 'fiduciary system' can be interpreted as a kind of re-entry of the formerly excluded cultural system into the social system. Parsons nevertheless relies on a strong distinction between society and culture, and it is this distinction that still influences the disciplinary landscape of sociology today: Cultural sociologists usually do not concern themselves with questions of social structure, while many sociologists focusing on social structure do not pay heed to culture as a constituent aspect of the very structures they examine. In other words, the notorious dualism of 'social structure' and 'culture' (cf. Sewell 1992; Hays 1994; Kaldewey 2011) is at least in part a legacy of Parsonian differentiation theory.

The lasting influence of Parsonian categories is visible, second, in the fourfold differentiation of societies. The primary subsystems of a society are labeled by Parsons, as we have seen, as the 'economy' (A), the 'polity' (G), the 'societal community' (I), and the 'fiduciary system' (L), the first two of which are clearly identifiable as the most prominent MSCs. The 'societal community' represents the "core of a society" and is defined as "the patterned normative order through which the life of a population is collectively organized" (Parsons 1966: 10) – here, the system seems closer to a CFL than to a MSC. The strangely labeled 'fiduciary system' finally is, as we have seen, a kind of placeholder for the cultural system, and is responsible for the maintenance of cultural patterns (cf. Parsons 1971: 14f.). What is interesting about this specific application of the AGIL scheme is that it has been gradually popularized and transformed into a nutshell differentiation theory. Today, many authors refer to four similar social spheres without even thinking about the Parsonian legacy: Helga Nowotny, Peter Scott, and Michael Gibbons (2001) for example formulate a diagnosis of modernity in which processes of differentiation have been replaced by processes of dedifferentiation. They argue explicitly and aggressively against authors such as Parsons and Luhmann, but they refer constantly to the four "fundamental categories of the modern world," namely the state, the economy, society, and culture (ibid. 47), and thus contradict performatively their own hypothesis that these categories are no longer relevant. In other words: Even critics of functional differentiation theories build systematically on a simplified Parsonian framework. Thus the question arises whether it would not be more honest and productive to make this latent Parsonian framework explicit and to consider replacing it with less rigid differentiation theories.

Finally, the question remains whether there is a role for tacit knowledge in the system-functional framework. Parsons did not use the term, but it may be possible to integrate the tacit into the AGIL scheme: For instance, we could say that in regard to the 'behavioral organism' (A) there is a place for embodied knowledge that helps serving the adaptive function. However, probably more important in regard to tacit knowledge is the 'cultural system' (L), which is the place where latent patterns are maintained. Although it would be problematic to simply equate the 'latent' with the 'tacit,' it is evident that this is the point where Parsons comes closest to the concept of collective tacit knowledge. The problem still remains that at the level of the general action system Parsons excludes the cultural from the social. At the level of the social system of society, the 'fiduciary system' (L) is responsible for latent pattern maintenance, but its relationship to the cultural system as part of the environment of society is far from clear. Nevertheless it is theoretically possible at this level to interpret the distinction between latently maintained 'values' and system-integrating 'norms' in analogy to the distinction between tacit and explicit knowledge. To summarize, the problem with Parsons' system-functionalism is the tendency to define the 'cultural' not as part of social subsystems but as their environment. However, the AGIL scheme makes it possible to switch to another level at which the latency function reappears as an internal dimension of every subsystem.

V. Jürgen Habermas' Differentiation of Lifeworld and System

Even if Jürgen Habermas is rarely systematically treated as a differentiation theorist, his *Theory of Communicative Action* (1984, 1987) is of great interest in regard to the distinction between cultural and functional differentiation.

Habermas builds on both Weber and Parsons, but finally develops his own perspective on societal differentiation. As we have seen, Weber's theory is framed primarily in terms of *cultural* differentiation, whereas Parsons' theory is framed primarily in terms of *functional* differentiation. Against this background, Habermas develops a symmetric perspective in which the two forms of differentiation are separated and necessarily complementary at the same time, resulting in a conception of society that is internally differentiated into the two spheres of 'lifeworld' and 'system' (cf. Habermas 1987: 113ff.). For Habermas, society consists of action patterns and contexts that are 'symbolically' and 'socially' integrated on the one hand (the lifeworld), and of action patterns and contexts that are 'systemically' stabilized and relatively independent of the lifeworld on the other (cf. Renn 2006: 47).[10] Using our terminology, we could say that the Habermasian 'lifeworld' consists of CFLs, and that his 'systems' are equivalent to MSCs.

Both parts of society – lifeworld and system – are internally structured in a complex way. Following Habermas, the lifeworld consists of three "structural components," namely (1) *culture*, that is "the stock of knowledge from which participants in communication supply themselves with interpretations as they come to an understanding about something in the world;" (2) *society*,[11] here understood in the specific sense of "the legitimate orders through which participants regulate their memberships in social groups and thereby secure solidarity;" and (3) *personality*, defined as "the competences that make a subject capable of speaking and acting" (Habermas 1987: 138; cf. Baxter 1987: 47f.). In modern societies, all of these components are further differentiated (cf. Habermas 1984: 159ff.). First, culture splits into (1a) the *cognitive* sphere, in which modern science emerges, (1b) the *evaluative* sphere, in which universal notions of law and morality are developed, and (1c) the *expressive* sphere of autonomous art, which may also include the Weberian sphere of eroticism. These three cultural spheres are complemented, second, by a plurality of formal institutions that secure the coordination of action, namely (2a) the institutions of the science system, such as universities and research institutes, (2b) the formal law and its organizations, religious communities, and the bourgeois family, and (2c) the art business and art market. Furthermore, the sphere of society contains the two most dominant institutions of modernity, namely the 'economy'

---

10 | With this conception Habermas at least partly builds on Lockwood's (1964) distinction between 'social integration' and 'system integration.' For a critique of Habermas' reformulation of these terms, see Mouzelis (1992).

11 | This terminology, which is borrowed from Parsons, is confusing, since 'society' refers to the whole of lifeworld and system on the one hand, and stands for a specific aspect of the lifeworld on the other. For a detailed discussion of the relationship between Habermas' and Parsons' terminologies, see Baxter (1987).

and the 'political/administrative order.' Both of these systems tend to decouple from the lifeworld, that is, following Habermas, they no longer are integrated institutions of the lifeworld, but rather autonomous and rationalized 'systems' operating beyond communicative rationality. Third, there are the differentiated spheres of socialization at the level of personality,[12] for example (3a) preschool, primary, and secondary educational institutions, (3b) again the family and religious organizations, and last but not least (3c) counter-cultural lifestyles through which people express their individuality.

To summarize, Habermas sketches a complex differentiation pattern of the lifeworld. Some of the resulting units are conceived of as cultural or value spheres in the Weberian sense, and others as networks of formal institutions resembling the Weberian notion of life orders. All in all, the differentiated units of the lifeworld may best be conceptualized as CFLs.[13] Unlike Weber, Habermas does not systematically construct societal macro units that integrate cultural and institutional aspects. Only the economy and the political/administrative order are described as 'systems,' which furthermore appear as MSCs devoid of culture, as they are radically decoupled from the cultural background of the lifeworld. Here, the differentiation between the economy and the state is conceived of as functional differentiation in the sense of Parsons' distinction between adaption and goal attainment. However, it is important to remember that the basic differentiation between lifeworld and system is conceived of as functional differentiation as well: CFLs are responsible for the "symbolic reproduction" of society, while MSCs secure the "material reproduction" of society (Habermas 1987: 138, 151, 204, 232; cf. Braaten 1991: 78f.). In other words, Habermas explicitly distinguishes between cultural and functional differentiation, and does not reserve the concept of functional differentiation for the differentiation of 'systems' or MSCs.

Finally, we have to ask about the role of tacit knowledge in Habermas' theory of society. As his conception of society as both lifeworld and system is dualistic, the question should be answered in regard to each sphere separately. At first sight, it seems that the lifeworld is the place where tacit understandings of the world, the social, and the self are of crucial relevance. However, this is

---

12 | Baxter speaks about a "socialization system" (cf. 1987: 74f.); in my view however, Habermas would not use the notion of system here.

13 | Baxter (1987: 73) points to an ambiguity in Habermas' usage of the term lifeworld: On the one hand, the concept means "the resources of culture, society, and personality that serve as background to social action," while on the other the term also denotes "informally organized spheres of action, such as the family, voluntary associations, neighborhoods, friendships, and the like." However, for the present context this ambiguity is not problemetical, since both aspects fit quite well with the notion of CFLs sketched above.

not the case. If one compares the lifeworld's differentiation into the structural components of 'culture,' 'society,' and 'personality' to the AGIL scheme, then it becomes apparent that the fourth element of Parsons' general action system, the 'behavioral organism,' is missing in Habermas' triad. This omission hints at Habermas' more restricted sociological perspective, which no longer claims to be compatible with the abstract and interdisciplinary framework of a general systems theory (cf. Habermas 1987: 237, 250). One consequence of this narrower framework is that it becomes more difficult to integrate the notion of embodied tacit knowledge. Thus, the question arises whether the concept of communicative action is biased towards explicit acts of communication. This suspicion is corroborated by Renn's discussion of this issue, who argues that Habermas' notion of the lifeworld builds on a "cognitivist picture" of tacit background knowledge (2006: 254). Tacit knowledge is conceived of as "not yet or no longer 'thematic' knowledge," and therefore as in principle explicable in the medium of rational discourse (ibid. 250). With Collins we could say that Habermas deals with 'relational tacit knowledge,' rather than with 'collective tacit knowledge' in a strong sense (cf. Collins 2010). Similarly, Renn holds that, according to Habermas there is actually no strong distinction between tacit and explicit knowledge (2006: 255). This bias towards explicit forms of knowledge is at least partly due to Habermas' interest in the possibility of a non-instrumental rationalization of the lifeworld. The whole idea of "communicative rationality," understood as the "liberation of the rational potential inherent in communicative action" (Baxter 1987: 50), forces Habermas to believe that in principle every aspect of the social world can be made explicit and thus be introduced into public discourse. In this neo-enlightenment framework, tacit knowledge must appear as an obstacle to overcome.

In regard to the 'system' aspect of society, one might expect that there is even less room for tacit knowledge. The narrow definition of the formalized spheres of the economy and politics comes very close to Renn's description of function systems as systems operating in terms of explicit semantics only. Thus, if we follow Renn, Habermas indeed is of no use at all for anybody who is interested in issues of tacit knowledge. However, the process which Habermas describes as the "colonization" of the lifeworld by system imperatives (1987: 301ff.) points to aspects of the lifeworld that are not controlled by rational discourse and that insofar operate somehow implicitly. In other words, following the colonization thesis, it may be instructive to continue thinking about whether and how the *explicit semantics* of rationalized systems (or MSCs) become influential as *implicit structures* of lifeworld contexts (or CFLs).

VI. Niklas Luhmann's Strong Notion of Function Systems

Many authors agree that today Luhmann represents the most comprehensive theory of functional differentiation. At the same time, his system-theoretical approach has been criticized for several reasons. First, Luhmann's differentiation theory is often perceived as "the 'German wing' of contemporary post-Parsonianism" especially in Anglo-Saxon contexts (Colomy/Rhoades 1994: 552). This interpretation is basically a misunderstanding. Luhmann's conceptualization of functional differentiation actually builds on a radically different paradigm which is much closer to Weber than to Parsons. Systems theory in the Luhmannian tradition does not conceive of society as a jigsaw puzzle of subsystems (cf. Mölders 2012: 480f.), but rather as the historically contingent emergence of autonomous function systems (cf. Mayntz 1988: 14; Schimank 2002: 3664; Stichweh 2013: 56). It is therefore important to note that Luhmann usually labels the MSCs as 'function systems' and not, like Parsons, as 'partial systems' or 'subsystems.' Luhmann's notion of functionality also differs from Parsons', as Luhmann does not believe in 'functional prerequisites,' but conceives of functionality as a relative category which only indicates that a certain system can be observed in regard to the function it fulfills in the context of society. For this reason there can never be a finite list of functions and corresponding MSCs (cf. Renn 2006: 404f.; Ziemann 2007: 223; Stichweh 2013: 58). Second, authors in the Weberian tradition have also been critical of systems theory, because they generally dismiss the idea that the primary reference points of differentiation theory are abstract systems instead of concrete individual or collective subjects (cf. Schwinn 2001; Schmidt 2005). This dissent is an effect of the diverging paradigms of action theory and systems theory. However, this conflict should not detract our attention from the fact that there are intriguing parallels between Luhmann and Weber that may further guide the development of differentiation theory. Third, Luhmann's claim that the basic element of social systems is *communication* rather than *action* has been criticized as a "semanticization of the social," that is, as neglecting the material structures of society (Peters 1993: 16f., 31f.; Berger 1996: 235ff., 2003: 218ff.). Evidently, this criticism parallels Renn's critical assessment of theories of functional differentiation and their notion of MSCs as systems of *explicit knowledge* that are purified from *tacit knowledge* in a process of abstraction, generalization, and specialization.

The most important difference between Luhmann and the differentiation theorists discussed so far is that he does not distinguish between culture and society. Luhmann has always had doubts about the conceptual strength of the concept of culture (cf. Luhmann 1995: 31ff.) and strictly avoided conceiving of culture as a separate subsystem in the sense of Parsons (cf. Burkart 2004: 17). Luhmann also was skeptical about the lifeworld concept, especially as conceived by Habermas (cf. Luhmann 1997: 874f.).[14] Consequently, Luhmann's system-theoretical approach has no concept coming close to that of a CFL. Instead, he distinguishes between three kinds of social systems that are constituted by different modes of communication (ibid. 595ff.): 'Interaction systems' are the result of communication between people that are co-present to one another, 'organizations' are systems that reproduce themselves on the basis of decisions, and 'function systems' communicate through specific codes and symbolically generalized media. While we can easily label function systems as MSCs, it would be a mistake to think of interactions or organizations as CFLs. Compared to the above-mentioned notions of 'social worlds' (Strauss), 'provinces of meaning' (Berger/Luckmann), and 'milieus' (Renn), Luhmann's conceptualization of social systems does not pay much heed to the manifold implicit and explicit cultural background knowledge that integrates such units. Thus at first sight it seems that there is no place for culture, tacit knowledge, and cultural differentiation in Luhmann's systems theory.

Whereas Luhmann has no concept of CFLs, his concept of MSCs is much more complex than his critics assume. Actually it would be a misunderstanding to think of function systems merely as systems of *explicit knowledge*. Contrary to the Habermasian notion of 'systems' that are decoupled from the lifeworld and devoid of culture, Luhmann's function systems not only consist of rationalized operations guided by non-linguistic media such as power or money, but also of complex semantic structures (cf. Kaldewey 2013: 122ff.). Strictly speaking, Luhmann's term 'semantics' takes up what mainstream sociology calls 'culture.' Since every system develops its own semantics, we could translate this into non-Luhmannian terms by saying that "every function system has its own culture" (Burkart 2004: 28, my transl.). Also, the system-theoretical concept of semantics is very broad: Beyond discursive semantics and textual self-descriptions one can also refer to, for example, the *material semantics* (cf. Guggenheim 2011) or the *visual semantics* (cf. Stäheli 2007) of function systems.

In regard to the charge that Luhmann reduces the social to its semantic or symbolic dimension, it is important to note that he basically conceives of social systems as operating on two levels at the same time: The *operative level*, which is "generated by currently occurring communications," and the *semantic level*, which consists of "meanings worthy of retention" that enable a kind of "self-monitoring" of the system (Luhmann 1996: 60). This distinction is of crucial relevance for the present discussion: The concept of operationality explains communications as real-world events that are coupled with other levels of reality, for example the biological and physical substratum of communication. In other words, the notion of operationality makes clear that Luhmann

---

14 | Luhmann nevertheless tried to redefine the lifeworld concept in system-theoretical terms (cf. 1986a, 1990: 160ff.).

has never intended to conceive of communication only in terms of explicit semantics, which allows us to think about whether and how embodied and tacit forms of knowledge may be relevant at the operative and/or semantic level.

In order to be able to understand function systems as MSCs, some further remarks are necessary. First, for Luhmann all function systems are *structurally comparable*. As we have seen, Parsons and Habermas distinguish more or less precisely between cultural spheres and rationalized systems, with the result that for example science or art appear as 'soft' MSCs, while the economy and politics appear as 'strong' MSCs. Luhmann argues closer to Weber at this point: All MSCs are equivalent in regard to their autonomy and can therefore be compared to each other in regard to certain common characteristics, which implies that "an abstract catalogue of (necessary) constituents of any function system" (Stichweh 2013: 58) can be applied to *all* function systems, that is, to religion as well as to the economy, to love as well as to politics, etc. Second, function systems *monopolize* the communicative competence for a certain aspect of the social. This is what makes them unique, and this is what distinguishes the form of functional differentiation from traditional forms of differentiation, such as segmentary or stratificatory differentiation. Furthermore, this monopolization of functions happens at the level of world society, that is, function systems are global systems not confined to national boundaries (cf. Luhmann 2012: 83ff.; Stichweh 2000). Both Parsons and Habermas were less radical at this point, as they conceived of functional differentiation mainly as something that happens within nation states. Finally, MSCs do not only monopolize certain forms of communication, but also constitute universal perspectives or "global modes of access to the world" (Greve/Kroneberg 2011: 10, my transl.). Luhmann proposed the term *polycontexturality* to make this point clear. Polycontexturality means that function systems are not so much parts of a whole but rather radically different contextures or "contexts of understanding" (Mölders 2012: 480, my transl.) which construct exhaustive worlds of their own (cf. Luhmann 2012: 13, 46). Thus, for the economy, the world is a network of payments and markets, for science, it is made up of explicable events, for politics, it consists of relationships of power and collectively binding decisions. In other words: The point is not to distinguish between economic, scientific, political etc. events, but to reconstruct the *same* event within the diverging perspectives of the function systems. For example, an opera performance can be observed as art, but also as an economic event (people buying tickets, artists earning money), as a political statement (a municipality demonstrating its political relevance by affording an opera house), as an object of academic inquiry (intellectual discourse on the respective play), etc.

To summarize, Luhmann develops a strong and multifaceted concept of historically emerging 'function systems' that have become constituent structures of modern world society. Although he did not reflect about the role that tacit knowledge plays in the emergence and reproduction of such MSCs, his theoretical framework allows in principle to consider their tacit dimension. However, Luhmann's theory of *functional differentiation* is not complemented by a theory of *cultural differentiation*. Consequently, there is no notion of CFLs as basic units of social reality. Rather, the cultural dimension of society is radically reconceptualized as the semantic dimension of the function systems. However, since both the semantic and the operative levels of function systems further differentiate into diverse discourses and subsystems (cf. Kaldewey 2013: 140ff.), CFLs may be conceived of as subsystems of MSCs.[15]

VII. Pierre Bourdieu's Conception of Field and Habitus

Like Weber and Habermas, Pierre Bourdieu did not think of himself as a differentiation theorist. Nevertheless, his theory of fields can be read as an important contribution to the theorization of differentiation (cf. Bongaerts 2008, 2011), and several authors have pointed out similarities between Luhmann's theory of functional differentiation and Bourdieu's theory of fields (cf. Kneer 2004; Hillebrandt 2006; Kieserling 2008; Hartard 2010). Furthermore, it is important to note that the theory of fields at least partly builds on an interpretation of Weber's sociology of religion (cf. Bourdieu 1987, 1991). The notion of 'fields' in general has been gaining ground in contemporary sociological theorizing against older notions such as 'value spheres' or 'systems' – some authors for example recently proposed to develop a general theory of fields and a corresponding methodological approach that integrates Bourdieu's theory into several other social sciences paradigms (cf. Bernhard/Schmidt-Wellenburg 2012; Fligstein/McAdam 2012). As it goes beyond the scope of this essay to discuss the potential of the theory of fields in general, I will concentrate on how Bourdieu himself uses the notion of 'field' and the complementary concept of 'habitus.'

The basic assumption of Bourdieu's theory of fields is that the social cosmos is differentiated into a number of "relatively autonomous social microcosms" (Bourdieu/Wacquant 1992: 97) which are governed by a specific logic and a fundamental law (*nomos*) that makes them independent of the economic and political powers governing the social universe as a whole (cf. Bourdieu 1995: 61; 2000: 96). Analytically, a field can be defined "as a network, or a configuration, of objective relations between positions" (Bourdieu/Wacquant

---

15 | For example, Karin Knorr-Cetina's "epistemic cultures" (1999) can be understood as CFLs that are embedded in the function system of science and serve to integrate the latter as a MSC.

1992: 97). These positions are occupied by actors that have different amounts and kinds of 'capital' at their disposal. Since these actors usually try to improve their relative position in the field and to increase their field-specific capital, every field necessarily is a "field of struggles" (ibid. 101). At the same time, the competing actors share a common interest (*illusio*) and certain values, norms, and presuppositions (*doxa*) that are constitutive for the field. The terms *illusio* and *doxa* rely on a strong notion of tacit knowledge that comes close to Collins' notion of 'collective tacit knowledge' (cf. Collins 2010): Bourdieu for instance describes the *illusio* as a "tacit belief" in the value of the game (1995: 167) and as "tacit adherence to the *nomos*" (2000: 101),[16] and the *doxa* as constituting "the tacit condition of argument" in the scientific field (1975: 34). In short, the actors in a field are guided by common tacit background knowledge, and it is this knowledge that integrates and reproduces the field. Thus it is evident that Bourdieu's 'fields' come very close to the conception of CFLs as discussed above.

Following Bourdieu, we cannot talk about 'fields' without considering the complementary notion of 'habitus' at the same time. The habitus is the embodiment of the social or, in the context of social fields, of the specific logic of the field. Analytically, a habitus can be defined as "the durable and transposable systems of schemata of perception, appreciation, and action that result from the institution of the social in the body" (Bourdieu/Wacquant 1992: 126f.). This understanding demonstrates the habitus' relation to the concept of embodied or somatic tacit knowledge. However, it would be a mistake to conceive of the habitus as the *product* of a field, because it is *structured* and *structuring* at the same time. The relation between habitus and field thus is one of co-construction: While "the field structures the habitus," the habitus "contributes to constituting the field as a meaningful world, a world endowed with sense and value, in which it is worth investing one's energy" (ibid. 127). In other words, historical action, or more generally, historical social reality, manifests itself at two levels, "in things and in minds, in fields and in habitus, outside and inside of agents" (ibid.). By the way, transferring this theoretical figure from an action-theoretical to a system-theoretical framework, we come close to Luhmann's distinction between an operative and a semantic level of systems.

Tacit knowledge figures much more prominently in Bourdieu's framework than in the theories discussed so far. However, Bourdieu's fields are conceptualized as CFLs, not as MSCs, which begs the question whether Bourdieu delivers a theory of *functional differentiation* that goes beyond a theory of *cultural differentiation*. If we follow Renn, then Bourdieu does not manage to conceive of complex social orders or systems that are integrated no longer by their habitual basis but by explicit rules and communication media (cf. Renn 2006: 357f.).

---

16 | The notion of 'game' and the notion of 'nomos' are to some extent related, as both are used by Bourdieu to denote the basic structure of a social field.

Renn argues that unlike Habermas, Bourdieu does not meet the challenge of systems theory (ibid. 362), but if we take a closer look at the fields that are at the center of Bourdieu's interest, we see that they are more or less the same systems as those described as MSCs by (other) differentiation theorists: the economy, politics, the law, religion, art, philosophy, science, education, etc. Renn is certainly right when he states that it is problematic to describe these fields as basically integrated by a specific habitus. Bourdieu furthermore is unable to conceive of MSCs beyond the national level, because his notion of fields implies that these MSCs are networks of actors interacting and competing with each other on a local level – whereas for Luhmann, function systems are by definition global systems, Bourdieu's notion of society thus is bound to the nation state (cf. Bongaerts 2008: 261).

Nevertheless, the theory of fields goes far beyond the classical theories of cultural differentiation and their concepts of CFLs, and although Bourdieu strictly avoids a functionalist perspective and therefore never speaks of functional differentiation, his theory of modernity comes very close to those of other differentiation theorists. Gregor Bongaerts (2008) has reconstructed this more or less implicit aspect of Bourdieu's work; in his reading, Bourdieu theorizes modern societies as "differentiated into autonomous sub-fields" which are the result of a specific differentiation mechanism: "the great repression" (ibid. 338, my transl.). Bourdieu's metaphor of the "great repression" describes the historical process in which the fields of cultural and symbolic production differentiated and emancipated themselves from the economic universe (2000: 17ff.). In other words: The cultural fields of religion, philosophy, science, and art became autonomous, that is, (relatively) independent from the economic field, and later also (relatively) independent from the political field. In this basic conception of the historical differentiation process, there are intriguing parallels to the theories of Parsons and Habermas – all of them conceive of the economy and of politics as one kind of MSC, and of the cultural spheres as another kind of MSC that comes conceptually close to the notion of CFLs. Bourdieu's 'field of power' is what Habermas calls the 'system.' The difference is that Habermas assumes that the rationalized systems of the economy and politics emerge out of the 'lifeworld,' whereas Bourdieu holds that the 'field of power' is the basic structure of society out of which the autonomous cultural fields emerge in a process of permanent struggle. However, it is evident that both describe processes of functional differentiation.

VIII. Conclusion

The discussion of the differentiation theories of Weber, Parsons, Habermas, Luhmann, and Bourdieu demonstrated that distinguishing between cultural and functional differentiation and between *cultural forms of life* (CFLs) and *macrosocial supercategories* (MSC) is helpful for assessing these heterogeneous theoretical paradigms. However, it also became obvious that the distinction between the two forms of differentiation is complex and at times precarious. Against this background, Renn's proposal to define CFLs as integration units that build on *tacit forms of knowledge,* and MSCs as integration units that are constituted by *explicit forms of knowledge* is both promising and problematic; it is promising because it distinguishes precisely between two types of social entities and their respective forms of differentiation, and it is problematic because the resulting conceptualization of CFLs and MSCs is too abstract to fit the realities of modern differentiation processes. While Renn conceptualizes MSCs in terms of explicit semantics only, that is, as purified from culture and from tacit knowledge, most theories of functional differentiation have developed less purified notions of MSCs and include different aspects of tacit knowledge. As we have seen, neither Weber, nor Parsons, nor Luhmann conceive of functional differentiation in terms of explicit knowledge only, and Bourdieu builds his theory of fields strictly on the tacit dimension of social practice. The only exception is Habermas, whose conception of 'system' fits quite well with Renn's framework. However, Habermas uses this notion of systems as radically decoupled from the lifeworld only to describe the economy and the political/administrative order, but not in regard to other MSCs such as religion, art, and science.

I want to conclude with some remarks on the consequences of my inquiry for further theory-building. Instead of arguing for the advantages of one theoretical framework over another, I want to point to a question that all theories of differentiation have to address, namely whether and how tacit knowledge is relevant to the process of differentiation and integration of social units. While most authors agree on the relevance of tacit knowledge in regard to *cultural differentiation* and CFLs, its relevance in regard to *functional differentiation* and MSCs remains unclear. In my view, there are basically three options for dealing with this question. First, we can give up the distinction completely: Parsons' general notion of 'system' and Bourdieu's general notion of 'field' could then be used both to describe CFLs and MSCs. Many sociological theories that deal exclusively with cultural differentiation avoid making the distinction between CFLs and MSCs anyway, as revealed for example in notions such as 'social worlds' or 'provinces of meaning.' Second, we can combine a *strong* notion of CFLs with a *weak* notion of MSCs. This is the solution chosen by Renn and Habermas, who consider the milieus of the lifeworld to be the place where sociality takes place, and MSCs to be abstract spheres of rationalized semantics. Third, we can combine a *strong* notion of MSCs with a *weak* notion of CFLs. In this case, the cultural as well as the tacit dimension of the social are seen as integral parts of every MSC. Different kinds of CFLs may then figure as subsystems of MSCs or operate in the environment of MSCs, but do not constitute the primary structure of modern society. This is the approach taken by Weber and Luhmann.

Currently, the first two options seem to be the most popular, as can be seen for example in the enduring prominence of cultural studies, the turns to practice and performativity, and the recent development of a theory of fields that concentrates on 'mesolevel' social orders (cf. Fligstein/McAdam 2012). The third option in contrast appears as a kind of German *Sonderweg* that has been viewed with skepticism not least in regard to the ideological blind spots of theories of functional differentiation: Some critics argue that functional differentiation goes hand in hand with the problems of modernization theory (cf. Tilly 1984; Tiryakian 1992), while others think that the idea of functional differentiation reduces the social to abstract forms of explicit semantics (cf. Peters 1993; Berger 2003; Renn 2006). Against this background it seems unpromising to continue elaborating a theory of functional differentiation vis-à-vis the theory of cultural differentiation. However, the problem is not the idea of functional differentiation per se, but rather *the reduction of functional differentiation to a differentiation of explicit semantics*. Now, what makes the third option interesting after all is that it replaces a *weak* notion of MSCs with a *strong* notion of MSCs and thereby integrates cultural and tacit forms of knowledge. I want to conclude my discussion by pointing to some consequences of this conceptual strategy.

Authors advocating the second option, such as Habermas and Renn, focus on the process of translating tacit knowledge into the rationalized and explicit structures of MSCs. For them, the lifeworld is where sociality is grounded. However, taking the third option by working out some insights of Weber and Luhmann would allow for the idea that in modern societies the lifeworld itself is in a very basic way structured by differentiated forms of tacit knowledge. Thus, if we admit that MSCs in a functionally differentiated society build at least partly on system-specific or field-specific forms of tacit knowledge, then the tacit knowledge of a society would itself be differentiated in a polycontextural way. In other words, tacit knowledge may not only be rooted in the lifeworld or in CFLs, but also in macrosocial structures or MSCs. Furthermore, if we assume that there are not only culturally but also functionally differentiated forms of tacit knowledge, then there might also be (implicit or explicit) forms of knowledge about basic structures of functional differentiation: People for instance know about the difference between the economy and the state or between religion and art without having studied sociology. We can interpret this kind of knowledge as an *implicit proto-differentiation theory*, which is part of the lifeworld of modern individuals. Of course, this proto-differentiation theory is also given in the cognitive structure of sociologists, in whose case this 'implied' theory in a way mixes with explicit theories of functional differentiation. As a consequence, the theory of functional differentiation is not only a *theoretical tool* for sociology, but also a basic form of everyday knowledge, and therefore an *object* of empirical analysis. This object, that is to say, the real-world tacit presuppositions people have about functional differentiation, is neglected in most theories of cultural differentiation.

Works Cited

Baxter, Hugh (1987): "System and Life-World in Habermas's 'Theory of Communicative Action,'" in: Theory and Society 16.1, 39-86.

Berger, Johannes (1996): "Entfernung von der Truppe. Realanalytische Grenzen des Konstruktivismus in der Soziologie," in: Max Miller/Hans-Georg Soeffner (eds.), Modernität und Barbarei. Soziologische Zeitdiagnose am Ende des 20. Jahrhunderts, Frankfurt/Main: Suhrkamp, 231-245.

—. (2003): "Neuerliche Anfragen an die Theorie der funktionalen Differenzierung," in: Hans-Joachim Giegel/Uwe Schimank (eds.), Beobachter der Moderne. Beiträge zu Niklas Luhmanns 'Die Gesellschaft der Gesellschaft,' Frankfurt/Main: Suhrkamp, 207-230.

Berger, Peter L./Luckmann, Thomas (1966): The Social Construction of Reality. A Treatise in the Sociology of Knowledge, Garden City: Doubleday.

Bernhard, Stefan/Schmidt-Wellenburg, Christian (eds.) (2012): Feldanalyse als Forschungsprogramm, Band 1: Der programmatische Kern, Wiesbaden: Springer VS.

Bongaerts, Gregor (2008): Verdrängungen des Ökonomischen. Bourdieus Theorie der Moderne, Bielefeld: transcript.

—. (2011): "Grenzsicherung in sozialen Feldern. Ein Beitrag zu Bourdieus Theorie gesellschaftlicher Differenzierung," in: Schwinn/Kroneberg/Greve, Soziale Differenzierung, 113-133.

Bourdieu, Pierre (1975): "The Specificity of the Scientific Field and the Social Conditions of the Progress of Reason," in: Social Science Information 14.6, 19-47.

—. (1987): "Legitimation and Structured Interests in Weber's Sociology of Religion," in: Scott Lash/Sam Whimster (eds.), Max Weber. Rationality and Modernity, London: Allen and Unwin, 119-136.

—. (1991): "Genesis and Structure of the Religious Field," in: Comparative Social Research 13, 1-44.

—. (1995): The Rules of Art. Genesis and Structure of the Literary Field, transl. Susan Emanuel, Stanford: Stanford UP.

—. (2000): Pascalian Meditations, Stanford: Stanford UP.

Bourdieu, Pierre/Wacquant, Loïc J.D. (1992): An Invitation to Reflexive Sociology, Chicago: U of Chicago P.

Braaten, Jane (1991): Habermas's Critical Theory of Society, Albany: State U of New York P.
Burkart, Günter (2004): "Niklas Luhmann: ein Theoretiker der Kultur?" in: Günter Burkart/Gunter Runkel (eds.), Luhmann und die Kulturtheorie, Frankfurt/Main: Suhrkamp, 11-39.
Collins, Harry M. (2010): Tacit and Explicit Knowledge, Chicago: U of Chicago P.
Colomy, Paul/Rhoades, Gary (1994): "Toward a Micro Corrective of Structural Differentiation Theory," in: Sociological Perspectives 37.4, 547-583.
Darmon, Isabelle (2011): Max Weber's Science of Reality. Types of Human Being and the Possibility of Life Conduct in Contemporary Culture, Manchester: unpubl. diss.
Dilthey, Wilhelm (1970): Der Aufbau der geschichtlichen Welt in den Geisteswissenschaften, introd. Manfred Riedel, Frankfurt/Main: Suhrkamp.
Fligstein, Neil/ McAdam, Doug (2012): A Theory of Fields, Oxford: Oxford UP.
Greenwood, Susan F. (1990): "Émile Durkheim and C.G. Jung. Structuring a Transpersonal Sociology of Religion," in: Journal for the Scientific Study of Religion 29.4, 482-495.
Greve, Jens/Kroneberg, Clemens (2011): "Herausforderungen einer handlungstheoretisch fundierten Differenzierungstheorie – zur Einleitung," in: Schwinn/Kroneberg/Greve, Soziale Differenzierung, 7-23.
Guggenheim, Michael (2011): "(Un-)Building Social Systems. The Concrete Foundations of Functional Differentiation," in: Ignacio Farías/José Ossandón (eds.), Comunicaciones, semánticas y redes. Usos y desviaciones de la sociología de Niklas Luhmann, México: Universidad Iberoamericana, 245-277.
Habermas, Jürgen (1984): The Theory of Communicative Action, Vol. 1: Reason and the Rationalization of Society, transl. Thomas McCarthy, Boston: Beacon.
—. (1987): The Theory of Communicative Action, Vol. 2: Lifeworld and System. A Critique of Functionalist Reason, transl.Thomas McCarthy, Boston: Beacon.
Harris, Roy (2003): The Necessity of Artspeak. The Language of the Arts in the Western Tradition, London: Continuum.
—. (2005): The Semantics of Science, London: Continuum.
—. (2006): "Integrational Linguistics and Semiology," in: Keith Brown (ed.), Encyclopedia of Language and Linguistics, 2nd ed., Oxford: Elsevier, 714-718.
—. (2007): "Integrational Linguistics," in: Jan-Ola Östman/Jef Verschueren (eds.), Handbook of Pragmatics Online, Amsterdam: John Benjamins.
Hartard, Christian (2010): Kunstautonomien. Luhmann und Bourdieu, München: Silke Schreiber.

Hays, Sharon (1994): "Structure and Agency and the Sticky Problem of Culture," in: Sociological Theory 12.1, 57-72.

Hillebrandt, Frank (2006): "Funktionssysteme ohne Praxis oder Praxisfelder ohne System? System- und Praxistheorie im Vergleich," in: Berliner Journal für Soziologie 16.3, 337-354.

Kaldewey, David (2011): "Das Realitätsproblem der Sozialwissenschaften. Anmerkungen zur Beobachtung des Außersozialen," in: Soziale Systeme 17.2, 277-307.

—. (2013): Wahrheit und Nützlichkeit. Selbstbeschreibungen der Wissenschaft zwischen Autonomie und gesellschaftlicher Relevanz, Bielefeld: transcript.

Kieserling, André (2008): "Felder und Klassen. Pierre Bourdieus Theorie der modernen Gesellschaft," in: Zeitschrift für Soziologie 37.1, 3-24.

Kneer, Georg (2004): "Differenzierung bei Luhmann und Bourdieu. Ein Theorienvergleich," in: Armin Nassehi/Gerd Nollmann (eds.), Bourdieu und Luhmann. Ein Theorienvergleich, Frankfurt/Main: Suhrkamp, 25-56.

Knorr-Cetina, Karin (1999): Epistemic Cultures. How the Sciences Make Knowledge, Cambridge: Harvard UP.

Kroeber, A.L./Parsons, Talcott (1958): "The Concepts of Culture and of Social System," in: American Sociological Review 23, 582-583.

Lockwood, David (1964): "Social Integration and System Integration," in: George K. Zollschan/Walter Hirsch (eds.), Explorations in Social Change, London: Routledge and Kegan Paul, 244-257.

Loenhoff, Jens (2011): "Tacit Knowledge in Intercultural Communication," in: Intercultural Communication Studies 20.1, 57-64.

Luhmann, Niklas (1986a): "Die Lebenswelt – nach Rücksprache mit Phänomenologen," in: Archiv für Rechts- und Sozialphilosophie 72.2, 176-194.

—. (1986b): Love as Passion. The Codification of Intimacy, transl. Jeremy Gaines/Doris L. Jones, Stanford: Stanford UP.

—. (1990): Die Wissenschaft der Gesellschaft, Frankfurt/Main: Suhrkamp.

—. (1995): Gesellschaftsstruktur und Semantik. Studien zur Wissenssoziologie der modernen Gesellschaft, Band 4, Frankfurt/Main: Suhrkamp.

—. (1996): "Complexity, Structural Contingencies and Value Conflicts," in: Paul Heelas/Scott Lash/Paul Morris (eds.), Detraditionalization. Critical Reflections on Authority and Identity, Cambridge: Blackwell, 59-71.

—. (1997): Die Gesellschaft der Gesellschaft, Frankfurt/Main: Suhrkamp.

—. (2012): Theory of Society, Vol. 1, transl. Rhodes Barrett, Stanford: Stanford UP.

Mayntz, Renate (1988): "Funktionelle Teilsysteme in der Theorie sozialer Differenzierung," in: Renate Mayntz, et al. (eds.), Differenzierung und Verselbständigung. Zur Entwicklung gesellschaftlicher Teilsysteme, Frankfurt: Campus, 11-44.

Mölders, Marc (2012): "Differenzierung und Integration. Zur Aktualisierung einer kommunikationsbasierten Differenzierungstheorie," in: Zeitschrift für Soziologie 41.6, 478-494.
Mouzelis, Nicos (1992): "Social and System Integration. Habermas' View," in: British Journal of Sociology 43.2, 267-288.
Nowotny, Helga/Scott, Peter /Gibbons, Michael (2001): Re-Thinking Science. Knowledge and the Public in an Age of Uncertainty, London: Polity.
Parsons, Talcott (1951): The Social System, Glencoe: Free Press.
—. (1966): Societies. Evolutionary and Comparative Perspectives, Englewood Cliffs: Prentice-Hall.
—. (1971): The System of Modern Societies, Englewood Cliffs: Prentice-Hall.
—. (1978): Action Theory and the Human Condition, New York: Free Press.
Parsons, Talcott/Smelser, Neil J. (1956): Economy and Society. A Study in the Integration of Economic and Social Theory, London: Routledge and Kegan Paul.
Peters, Bernhard (1993): Die Integration moderner Gesellschaften, Frankfurt/Main: Suhrkamp.
Renn, Joachim (2004): "Wissen und Explikation. Zum kognitiven Geltungsanspruch der 'Kulturen,'" in: Friedrich Jaeger/Liebsch Burkhard (eds.), Handbuch der Kulturwissenschaften. Grundlagen und Schlüsselbegriffe, Vol. 1, Stuttgart: Metzler, 232-250.
—. (2006): Übersetzungsverhältnisse. Perspektiven einer pragmatistischen Gesellschaftstheorie, Weilerswist: Velbrück.
Roth, Steffen (2012): Die zehn Systeme. Ein Beitrag zur Kanonisierung der Funktionssysteme, unpubl. manuscript.
Rueschemeyer, Dietrich (1974): "Reflections on Structural Differentiation," in: Zeitschrift für Soziologie 3.3, 279-294.
—. (1977): "Structural Differentiation, Efficiency, and Power," in: American Journal of Sociology 83.1, 1-25.
Schimank, Uwe (2002): "Differentiation, Social," in: Neil J. Smelser/Paul Baltes (eds.), International Encyclopedia of the Social and Behavioral Sciences, Vol. 6, Oxford: Pergamon, 3663-3668.
—. (2011): "Gesellschaftliche Differenzierungsdynamiken – ein Fünf-Fronten-Kampf," in: Schwinn/Kroneberg/Greve, Soziale Differenzierung, 261-284.
Schluchter, Wolfgang (1988): Religion und Lebensführung, Band 1: Studien zu Max Webers Kultur- und Werttheorie, Frankfurt/Main: Suhrkamp.
Schmidt, Volker H. (2005): "Die Systeme der Systemtheorie. Stärken, Schwächen und ein Lösungsvorschlag," in: Zeitschrift für Soziologie 34.6, 406-424.
Schneider, Wolfgang Ludwig (2010): "Systemtheorie, hermeneutische Tradition und die Theorie funktionaler Differenzierung," in: René John/Anna

Henkel/Jana Rückert-John (eds.), Die Methodologien des Systems. Wie kommt man zum Fall und wie dahinter, Wiesbaden: VS, 203-224.

Schwinn, Thomas (2001): Differenzierung ohne Gesellschaft. Umstellung eines soziologischen Konzepts, Weilerswist: Velbrück.

—. (ed.) (2004): Differenzierung und soziale Ungleichheit. Die zwei Soziologien und ihre Verknüpfung, Frankfurt/Main: Humanities Online.

Schwinn, Thomas/Kroneberg, Clemens/Greve, Jens (eds.) (2011): Soziale Differenzierung. Handlungstheoretische Zugänge in der Diskussion, Wiesbaden: VS.

Sewell, William H. (1992): "A Theory of Structure: Duality, Agency, and Transformation," in: American Journal of Sociology 98.1, 1-29.

Shotwell, Alexis (2011): Knowing Otherwise. Race, Gender, and Implicit Understanding, University Park: Pennsylvania State UP.

Stäheli, Urs (2007): "Die Sichtbarkeit sozialer Systeme. Zur Visualität von Selbst- und Fremdbeschreibungen," in: Soziale Systeme 13.1/2, 70-85.

Stichweh, Rudolf (2000): Die Weltgesellschaft. Soziologische Analysen, Frankfurt/Main: Suhrkamp.

—. (2013): "The History and Systematics of Functional Differentiation in Sociology," in: Mathias Albert/Barry Buzan/Michael Zürn (eds.), Bringing Sociology to International Relations. World Politics as Differentiation Theory, Cambridge: Cambridge UP, 50-70.

Strauss, Anselm (1978): "A Social World Perspective," in: Studies in Symbolic Interaction 1, 119-128.

Tilly, Charles (1984): Big Structures, Large Processes, Huge Comparisons, New York: Russell Sage Foundation.

Tiryakian, Edward A. (1992): "Dialectics of Modernity. Reenchantment and Dedifferentiation as Counterprocesses," in: Hans Haferkamp/Neil J. Smelser (eds.), Social Change and Modernity, Berkeley: U of California P, 78-94.

Tyrell, Hartmann (1998): "Zur Diversität der Differenzierungstheorie. Soziologiehistorische Anmerkungen," in: Soziale Systeme 4.1, 119-149.

Weber, Max (1949): The Methodology of the Social Sciences, transl. and ed. Edward A. Shils/Henry A. Finch, Glencoe: Free Press.

—. (1988): "Zwischenbetrachtung," in: Gesammelte Aufsätze zur Religionssoziologie I, Tübingen: Mohr Siebeck, 536-573.

Ziemann, Benjamin (2007): "The Theory of Functional Differentiation and the History of Modern Society. Reflections on the Reception of Systems Theory in Recent Historiography," in: Soziale Systeme 13.1/2, 220-229.

Questions to Theodore R. Schatzki

In regard to your manifold contributions to social theory as well as to the philosophy of social sciences, my first, very general question is: What kind of theories do we need to understand tacit knowledge? Do we need a genuinely interdisciplinary approach that integrates, for instance, insights from philosophy, sociology, and cultural studies? Or can we tackle the issue with more traditional disciplinary approaches?

Students of tacit knowledge should accept help from any quarter on issues such as differences between knowledge and understanding, the distinction between tacit and implicit, the relationships of tacit knowledge to the body and to human activity, noncognitive and social dimensions of the phenomenon, and the possibilities of explicitization. Philosophers were central to the first wave of attempts to theorize the tacit dimension, but there is no reason that theorists with other disciplinary or multidisciplinary training cannot contribute today. I hesitate to circumscribe potential contributions by prioritizing or favoring disciplinary or interdisciplinary approaches.

Basic issues concerning tacit knowledge are transdisciplinary. They form a single problem nexus with implications for work in many disciplines. Individuals with different disciplinary (or multidisciplinary) backgrounds can study this nexus, and their analyses, focused on a common good, point beyond individual fields. What's more, because contributions from different disciplines build on, refer to, and often are compatible with one another, they can, over time, compose integrative "interdisciplinary approaches." In this sense, I advocate the likelihood that accounts of tacit knowledge will constitute genuinely interdisciplinary approaches. But this outcome is not inevitable or guaranteed. Disciplines might delimit what scholars and students read, and incompatibilities between accounts emanating from different disciplines might outweigh compatibilities. To the extent, however, that those studying tacit knowledge are multidisciplinarily schooled and inclined, networks of studies of this phenomenon will likely be multidisciplinary.

Of course, contributions emanating from different disciplines might reveal characteristic differences. Philosophers, for instance, gravitate toward basic distinctions and large generalities. Sociologists and cultural theorists tend to study things as social or cultural phenomena. They might be better than philosophers at identifying the different forms of tacit knowledge, at mapping its presence in different walks of social or cultural life (and in social or cultural life generally), and at studying the differences it makes to proceedings in particular social or cultural arenas, for example, science, artistic production, human interaction, financial markets, and ritual. But care is in order here. The interests and reading habits of some scholars lead them to address topics and to study literatures nominally assigned to others in the established academic division of labor. The humanities writ large are much more cross-disciplinary in character today than was the norm decades ago. So approaches to tacit knowledge are likely to form a multidisciplinary nexus if for no other reason than that multidisciplinarity is the way of much academia today – and the transdisciplinary nature of the basic phenomenon facilitates this.

If we turn to sociology in particular, what kind of sociological theories do we need to understand tacit knowledge? Do we need a sociology of the body? Do we need a sociology of emotions or a sociology of the affective? Furthermore: Is tacit knowledge relevant only for microsociological theories (for example, phenomenology, symbolic interactionism, pragmatism, practice theories), or is it relevant as well for macro-sociological theories, especially theories of cultural and/or functional differentiation?

I am wary of the phrase "sociology of X" in this context. Sociologists who study X might propagate a circumscribed body of literature with which to do so. But it is an open question whether this body of literature – and not some other that is either associated with a different discipline or the multi- or transdisciplinary possession of many disciplines – offers the best illumination of X, for example, emotions or bodies. So whether sociologists should reach for a "sociology of X" if they want to study X or something related to X is questionable. Moreover, in cases where sociological work on X has become common property of multiple disciplines – such as Marx on class, Durkheim on religion, or Weber on power – "sociology of X" should be replaced by "theory of X."

I think that it is illuminating, and also more in line with my response to the first question, to repose the question as "What kind of (social) theories do we need to understand tacit knowledge? Do we need a (social) theory of the body? Do we need a (social) theory of emotions or a (social) theory of the affective?" I place "social" in parentheses to warn against prejudging the sort of theory that might be required in a given context.

My answer to these questions is that theories about many things will contribute to fuller understandings of tacit knowledge. Theories of the body are needed since tacit knowledge as a feature of individuals, however it is conceptualized as a mental entity, must be embodied somehow if one is not a Cartesian dualist. Bodies are a crucial object of study also because tacit knowledge subtends human activity, and activities of all sorts – mental as well as interventions in the world – either are carried out by bodies or expressed in their features and movements. Emotions, too, are an important topic since they can be tacit and thus components of the broader realm of the nonexplicit. In their bearing on human activity, emotions also get tangled up with tacit knowledges and understandings construed as cognitive phenomena. For reasons just suggested, theories of human activity are likewise important for understanding the tacit dimension. And theories of interaction, practices, or of whatever social phenomena a theorist believes immediately engage with mind and activity will also prove useful. Some might hold that this is also true of the broader social contexts that encompass these social phenomena.

I am not sure whether the theories needed will be social, cultural, neuropsychological, evolutionary, phenomenological, humanistic, or scientific. I suspect that those advancing useful ideas will have different disciplinary backgrounds. Consider the body. Disciplines as disparate as performance studies, phenomenology, and neuroscience are likely to illuminate the tacit dimension as a bodily phenomenon; the trick will be to find ways of connecting their ideas. So, too, regarding each phenomenon mentioned in the previous paragraph: one should draw on whatever theories help advance one's work. If that means drawing on work emanating from the discipline in which one is trained because doing this is familiar and easiest (sociology of X), fine. The more scholars move in multidisciplinary circles, however, the more they will find their work informed by ideas from different disciplines or multidisciplinary contexts.

I also think that the tacit dimension is relevant to both the "micro" and "macro" levels, or rather, to both small and large phenomena. Because tacit knowledge supports activity and itself is transformed by activity, it bears on all social phenomena that characterize or are constituted by small nets of human actions and interactions. Examples are workplaces, families, community meetings, and sporting events. Because such phenomena are routinely studied by phenomenology, symbolic interactionism, pragmatism, and practice approaches, accounts or conceptions of tacit knowledge have a place in such theories. Whether, moreover, they are construed as a property of individuals or as a background dimension of sociality, tacit knowledges, understandings, feelings, emotions, and ways of doing things pervade larger phenomena such as financial networks, international supply chains, sports confederations, the global entertainment industry, world religions, and educational systems, probably varying along such parameters as location, nation, culture, economic system, and denomination. They affect how these larger phenomena work and bear upon possibilities and forms of social change. Stock market cascades and reforms illustrate the centrality that the tacit dimension and its explicitization can play in social events and changes.

What does the discourse about tacit knowledge tell us about the state of the art of sociological theory? Following the recent debates, one might get the impression that sociologists are unsatisfied with their basic terms and theories. There seems to be a need, maybe even a desire for more fundamental concepts. Is "tacit knowledge" such a fundamental category, comparable to categories such as "agency," "structure," "practice," or "communication"?

To answer this question, one must first realize that agency, structure, practice, and communication are fundamental because theorists take them to be a – or the – basic component or dimension of social existence. From the beginning of modern social thought in Hegel and Mill, individualists have treated action as the sole or most central component of social life. For equally long, other theorists have complemented the concept of action with that of structure to suggest that action is caught up in broader contexts that limit and determine it. Of late, the concept of practices has been advanced both as underlying agency and structure and as the basic constituent of social phenomena. Meanwhile, a longer tradition dating to G.H. Mead and encompassing such apparent opposites as symbolic interactionism and systems theory has treated communication as the basic social phenomena out of which larger social organizations are composed.

I do not think that tacit knowledge is this sort of category. Tacit knowledge is not the central component of social life or the most basic social phenomenon out of which social phenomena are composed. But this absence does not imply that tacit knowledge is not fundamental to social life. On the contrary, actions, interactions, practices, and, thus, what transpires in social affairs are beholden to tacit knowledge. Tacit knowledge, consequently, is a crucial component of the social, a dimension of social life that theoretical and empirical analyses should acknowledge. Its importance lies partly in challenging accounts of actions and practices that invoke entities such as norms, beliefs and desires, or utility calculating apparatuses as the sole determinants of what people do. Its importance also lies in the idea that human activity rests on something inexplicit or unformulated, with all the attendant challenges to self-knowledge and to identifying what is tacit in particular cases. The idea that social contexts have a tacit dimension also offers diagnostic paths into cultural and intercultural phenomena. For all these reasons, social analysts do well to acknowledge and to be on the outlook for the bearing of tacit knowledge on their subject matters. As long as we recognize that tacit knowledge will not play the ontological role assigned to other "fundamental" concepts, it can be labeled a "fundamental" category.

In the last decades, the diagnosis of a theory deficit has led various scholars to introduce new terms and aspects of reality and to proclaim theoretical "turns:" For example, the body, space, time, performativity, practices, or materiality have entered the arena of theoretical and methodological discourse. Thus the question is whether theories of tacit knowledge simply continue this "one more turn"-tradition or whether they may help on the contrary to understand what these turns are about.

The metaphor of the turn aims to capture something fundamental. A turn to X connotes a major reorientation of research based on the centrality of X to the subject matter of some discipline. As such, turns should be relatively infrequent and draped in controversy. A second, different kind of turn embraces changes in attention, switches from one topic or phenomenon to another as a leading object of discussion in some discipline or set thereof. Commentators sometimes dismiss certain changes of this sort as fads, thereby suggesting that there was something more solid about scholarly pursuits before these turns. They might be concerned that nothing more than a search for novelty and effect lies behind these turns and convinced that earlier topics held greater and longer-lasting significance for their disciplines. It is clear that academia prizes novelty and innovation and that rapid assimilations of new literatures as well as sudden annexations of new concepts and topics can be based on insufficient immersion in existing approaches to subject matters. But although shallow turns do occur, many turns are solid and are the work of scholarly curiosity unearthing topics that had been hitherto ignored or underexamined.

Not many turns of the first, more consequential sort exist. A heralded "linguistic turn" occurred in the middle of the twentieth century in social thought. Its partisans either took features of linguistic phenomena as analogues of fundamental features of social life, treated language (e.g., communication) as the central social phenomenon, or held that language was the key to understanding all manner of human phenomena, for example, thinking or worldviews. Few turns, and none since, have been as consequential or as broad as this one was. Although, for example, the contemporary "practice turn" has sought to be as consequential as the linguistic one was, practice theoretical concepts and approaches have not disseminated as widely through the social disciplines as did linguistic analogues, phenomena, and concepts in an earlier era.

Meanwhile, many turns of the second sort occur. Turns to the body and to materiality are two prominent examples: each has become a prominent object of attention for social investigators. These turns are not fads since they spotlight dimensions of social life that were not being adequately attended to. What, then, about a turn to tacit knowledge? Because considerable attention was paid to tacit knowledge in earlier decades, any contemporary focus on the topic might be better described as a return to it. For reasons aired in the answer to the third question, moreover, I doubt that a return to tacit knowledge will qualify as a major reorientation around a fundamental phenomenon. It will instead amount to refocusing attention on something important that has been insufficiently studied.

Moreover, the question might be right to suggest that the concept of tacit knowledge helps clarify what is going on with turns of the second sort. Each turn, it might be said, focuses attention on a phenomenon that is present in social life but that social investigation had been overlooking even as the phenomenon contributed to the shape and course of social affairs. One might even go a step further and speculate that investigations of phenomena other than any such phenomenon were facilitated by its remaining in the background. If so, then, as this volume suggests, the phenomenon functioned as a background grounded in a "from-to" structure parallel to the one that Michael Polanyi – and gestalt theorists before him – attributed to perception and that contemporary theorists attribute to tacit knowledge. The question then arises about the fate of previously highlighted topics when attention moves on to new ones: do they recede into the background, and does this help facilitate attending to new topics? Or do they stay in focus, not as the center of attention, but as an acknowledged dimension of the subject matter that must find a place in accounts about it? I suspect that the second case lies closer to the truth, though topics also fade sometimes never to return. Just how such shifts, fadings, and reappearances contribute to an overall account of tacit knowledge is a question for contemporary students of the phenomenon.

Questions by David Kaldewey

Part II
Translations

First- and Second-Order Tacit Knowledge
Sociological Consequences of Consequent Pragmatism

Joachim Renn

I. A STRONG VERSION OF TACIT KNOWLEDGE

What do we know about tacit knowledge? And what does it mean to know something about tacit knowledge? At least there seems to be a relevant difference between *knowing that* tacit knowledge has certain properties and functions and *knowing how* it is to have tacit knowledge (cf. Ryle 2002). The more radical we conceptualize the constitutive distinction between tacit knowledge and propositional belief, the more the second-order features of knowledge about knowing lead to serious methodological problems with regard to the possibility of access and explication. If there is reason to believe that tacit knowledge either in part or entirely escapes representation through explicit propositional reconstruction, the menacing paradox of explicating the inexplicable calls for a closer look at the *performative* foundations of propositional reconstruction.

In order to reveal this frequently disregarded methodological challenge of explicating tacit knowledge, the distinction between those two basic modes of *knowledge about knowledge* – between knowing *that* tacit knowledge has certain properties and knowing *how* it is to know how to do something – needs to be carefully conceptualized. In the first case, with regard to knowing that – i.e., on a conceptual level – we may distinguish with reference to Michael Polanyi between certain elements of constitutive relations such as the "proximal" and the "distal" (cf. 1983). Whatever the structure of tacit knowledge in principle may be, we know tacit knowledge in general to be generated by processes of incorporation and to be preserved as a bodily habitus (cf. Bourdieu 1979). Due to this genetic and structural mode, tacit knowledge is conceived as being *inexplicable* (cf. Polanyi 1983; James 1950).[1]

---

[1] That means that explicating tacit knowledge seems to be a transforming substitution rather than a representation. A solid criterion for the difference between representation and substitution is the fact that tacitly grounded competence cannot be

On the one hand, this inexplicability is a necessary condition; on the other hand, it is an enabling condition, for it seems to provide actors with certain potential advantages in terms of situational adaptability. Avoiding the detour of drawing on explicit and conceptual calculations may guarantee an adequate reaction time in unprecedented and rapidly occurring situations. From this functional perspective, a similarity between tacit knowledge and physiological reflexes seems to be likely, but John Dewey already argued convincingly in his well-known analysis of the "reflex-arc" that even non-reflective "behavior" transcends a simply causal relation between "stimulus" and "response" (cf. 1896). The central argument here is that the "non-explicability" of habitual dispositions does not imply that those dispositions constitute a merely "natural" relation between organisms and physical environments. On the contrary, inexplicable tacit knowledge has a meaning dimension which includes the normative distinction between adequate and inadequate "rule-following" (cf. Brandom 1994). Knowing how to do something includes the possibility of failure and therefore points to a certain rational dimension of types of action which are based on tacit knowledge (cf. Renn 2012, 2013). Otherwise, habitual dispositions would hardly deserve to be called a mode of 'knowledge' at all. Although this ascription of a rational structure to the connection between knowing how to do something and the problem of rule-following in Wittgenstein's sense seems to be necessary, two types of access to this kind of knowledge are puzzling at first: first, the social process of achieving this kind of knowledge by someone who participates in a certain practice; second, the reconstructive access to someone's tacit knowledge by the so-called "observer" (cf. Nagel 1974). If we assume with Bourdieu that tacit knowledge is a sort of unconscious disposition, then in both cases – socialization and reconstruction – the 'invisibility' of this knowledge seems to impede its transmission to others, including by socializing practices (cf. Turner 1994; Schmidt 2012). But this argument obviously presupposes a narrow and restrictive concept of social 'influence' that confines any access to tacit knowledge to the intentional communication of *explicit* knowledge by presupposing a conventional view of causality. In contrast to these conventional restrictions, the clue is to be found in the self-referential relation of 'knowing how.'

In comparison with explicit knowledge about tacit knowledge, the second, self-referential case seems to be quite different: knowing 'how' it is to know how to do something presumably excludes the possibility of an adequate conceptual 'representation' of this knowledge, for 'knowing how' by definition precludes being able to give an explicit account of this knowledge. Of course many scholars still hesitate to agree to this theoretical hypothesis. Some argue

---

substituted by explicit planning and making inferences from propositional beliefs. We do not improve skills like playing the piano by learning the general physiological rules of turning a score into finger movement.

that the difficulty of 'representing' tacit knowledge may be an epistemological rather than an ontological problem and hence only a temporary restriction. They hold that at some point in the future it might be possible to reconstruct e.g. every single element of a bodily constituted process of behavior (cf. Turner 1994) by using general rules and well-defined categories.[2] Even if this argument may seem to be plausible at first, it nevertheless underestimates the very nature of a primordially *performative* mode of access 'to the world.' In terms of a Heideggerian account of "being in the world," one has to acknowledge that the transformation of "ready-at-hand-ness" into "ready-before-hand-ness" – as modes of the "objective" correlate of knowledge – includes a "translation" of pre-conceptually available "stuff" (in Heidegger's terms: "Zeug") into an "object" which is identified by a – maybe definite – conjunction of general properties in a conceptual mode (cf. Heidegger 1984; Dreyfus 1991). Thus, to assume that tacitly well-known aspects of a practical situation and tacit knowledge as such can in principle be represented conceptually without loss simply distorts the peculiar characteristics of tacit knowledge.

Furthermore, this peculiarity of tacit knowledge does not only apply to examples of bodily competences such as riding a bike or telling the tone of a clarinet from that of an oboe. It is rather part of much more complicated contexts of action which also include 'social action,' i.e. the problematic relation between at least two mutually intransparent intentional horizons. A good example is the frequently reported experience of cultural anthropologists with the limits of translation between cultural backgrounds: at first, there is a serious gap between their conceptual framework and the so-called 'emic' perspective, which after a long period of practical participation may be bridged on a practical level. The anthropologists by and large become part of the form of life (Wittgenstein) they want to explore, but as a consequence cannot adequately express their insights gained through participant observation with the scientific vocabulary they need to use in order to publish the results of their research. This problem of a 'one-way' accomplishment of understanding basically results from a lack of adequate conceptual terms, for example with regard to the classification of emotional modes, feelings and affections (cf. Röttger-Rössler 1997).

In this case the problem of representation hardly originates simply from the anthropologists' lack of imagination. Even if there may be a way out in the

---

2 | Future scientific progress may provide the tools to decipher bodily competences like riding a bike, recognizing individual faces and so on as fine-grained logical inferences from a complex set of explicitly known states of affairs. Thus the technical reproduction of seemingly human-specific practical competences may be just around the corner as soon as cognitive psychology develops the theory of prototypes as schemata of cognition, and connectionist neuroscience manages to help developing robots which even know how to climb stairs.

direction of imagination and good scientific poetry, the basic and general difficulties posed by the indeterminacy of translation and hence of meaning, which Quine exemplified by analyzing the tremendous difficulties of understanding the expression 'gavagai,' are irreducible (cf. 1960). One needs to admit that there is a real problem of transforming 'knowing how it is to know how to be a native' into 'knowing that.' The distinction between tacit knowledge and explicit knowledge of tacit knowledge thus necessarily is of great methodological importance, because these two sorts of knowledge are by no means logically equivalent versions of the same relation between knowledge and its 'object.' And this difference leads to different conditions with regard to the conceptualization of the two modes of knowing about tacit knowledge. The given examples are just *pars pro toto* of a broad discussion (cf. e.g. Loenhoff 2012), hence we might take for granted that tacit knowledge *cannot* be adequately articulated in terms of justified propositional belief – at least if we define 'adequacy' here quite ambitiously as the strict identity between the properties of the 'object' itself and the properties which are ascribed to the object by the descriptive expression referring to the object.[3]

II. Second-Order Entanglements – Explication as Transformation

If we start from this insight, that is, if there indeed is something within tacit knowledge which escapes in principle its explicit articulation, the aforementioned difference between knowing that and knowing how with regard to tacit knowledge indicates a severe problem for theories of tacit knowledge: developing a satisfying conceptual (theoretical) account of tacit knowledge becomes a paradoxical enterprise as soon as it entails efforts to explicate the inexplicable.[4] Although much has been said about the peculiar properties of tacit knowledge, there is still a lack of sufficient reflection on this paradox within the extensive scientific discourse about tacit knowledge, because the rules of the game within the scientific community still maintain a propositional bias: the criteria of validity

---

3 | Which is pretty much in accord with the classical correspondence theory of truth, and this implies – just by the way – that the truth-value relation of tacit knowledge is not in principle jeopardized by neglecting its propositional structure just because the truth-value-guaranteeing properties of a 'truth-carrying' element of knowledge do not necessarily fit into the categories of the correspondence theory of truth and by no means exclusively presuppose a propositional structure.

4 | It is disputable whether R. Brandom (1994) successfully manages to avoid this problem by presupposing a propositional or conceptual structure of the 'outward' objects even of performative reference.

for propositions about tacit knowledge remain criteria of rational justification in the sense that the logical coherence between explicit utterances and valid inferences is derived either from explicit rules (deductive relation) or from explicit descriptions (hypothetical inductions) which have to represent objective states of affairs; hence, the criterion of coherence between theoretical utterances projects the propositional structure onto these outward 'objects' by connecting the internal relation between elements of the scientific discourse with the referential dimension of 'correspondence' with outward states of affairs.[5] But talking about *tacit* knowledge inevitably refers to a unique form of experience, and thus to an empirical basis, which is quite different from 'observation:' in the midst of the empirical evidence on which scientific or theoretical accounts of 'knowing how' rest we inevitably come upon a *second order of tacit knowledge* about tacit knowledge. This again is a necessary conclusion following from the argument that an explication of tacit knowledge 'distorts' the peculiar mode of knowing how, because this argument presupposes the possibility of experiencing knowing how at least relatively independently from conceptually structured apperception. We need to know how it is to know how (i.e., to have a pre-conceptual, non-predicative but reflexive stance) in order to be able to experience the shortcomings of conceptual description and explanation. Hence, there is no conceptual 'invention' of fictitious objects which have no reference outside of the recursive relation between elements of the inventing process (e.g. discourse) – as constructivism tries to make us believe – but an experiential foundation of 'making it explicit' according to which explicit knowledge seems to be a special sort of 'translation' rather than a representation.

Every conceptual account of tacit knowledge includes a set of 'transforming' inferential and referential moves. These moves lead to an employment of propositional expressions of properties, which means that an important threshold is crossed: Referring with a conceptual vocabulary to experiences with tacit knowledge translates a performative stance into categorical observation. In terms of modes of rational acceptability, practical certainty (cf. Wittgenstein 1969) has to be transformed into potentially justified rational belief. In his revision of his own epistemology, Habermas relies explicitly on exactly this translation as a "translation" in order to complete his consensus theory of truth-validity by including the dimension of "external" influence on rational acceptability (by means of reference to real "objects" or objective states of affairs) (cf. 1999).[6] The

---

5 | Cf. footnote 2) above, as well as Husserl (1982) on the alienating selectivity of science in relation to the "lifeworld" ("Lebenswelt").

6 | It remains quite unclear in Habermas's account (1999), which explicitly refers to Heidegger's "being-in-the-world," whether the "real" correlate of terms within propositional expressions consists of "things" or of "states of affairs" (cf. Renn 2000). This is a tricky question, because the simple argument that every statement which refers to

idea of a revisionary force of practical experience with regard to propositional belief, Habermas holds, might be sufficient to anchor propositional content within the world. But Habermas does not make clear what kind of translation this may be, what precisely connects the two modes of knowledge, and what exactly defines a *valid* translation between practical experience immersed in situational immediacy and propositional belief justified within rational discourse.

The problem is that there is no third language available with which we could compare the *adequacy* either of practical certainty or of propositional validity (with regard to each other) by simply 'representing' the objects of 'co-reference' of two related incidents of 'knowing that' and 'knowing how' which are conceived of as translations of each other in the paradigmatic case of comparison. In the case of the anthropologist – who is paying for achieving the intended 'knowing how' by losing the ability to express this knowledge – there is no neutral report of substantial affections by which we could evaluate either the adequacy of knowing 'how it feels' or the validity of knowing 'that this feeling has such and such (general) properties.' Hence, we can neither simply compare those two relations to the 'affections as such,' nor can we evaluate the translational relation between these incidents of related knowing how and knowing that by neutrally referring to the 'objective' thing as such, at least if we admit that 'objective' accounts of basic emotions and needs (e.g. Maslow's hierarchy of pristine affections) are inadequate – for such accounts (being explicit knowledge about emotions) undoubtedly already belong to one of the two parts which are to be compared.

These deliberations may appear to be of little relevance for sociological theorizing, as sociologists might be hardly concerned about the correspondence theory of truth while doing empirical work. However, persistent methodological concerns evoke similar questions: with regard to tacit knowledge, theoretical as well as empirical sociology must take into account that there is a problem of access to and of 'representing' this peculiar mode of knowledge. Exclusively adopting the paradigm of knowing, that tacit knowledge has certain properties 'by observation' is insufficient, because the experiential justifications of such knowledge about tacit knowledge necessarily include at least some features of knowing how themselves (cf. Nagel 1974), as has been argued above. Thus we are confronted with a sort of second-order tacit knowledge with regard to the empirical basis of sociology as soon as we resist the seduction to restrict this empirical basis to simple models of 'observation.' This calls for further investigation, because now it has become unclear how to justify valid passages of reflection and articulation between knowing how and knowing that.

"things" necessarily presupposes the primacy of the state-of-affairs structure by employing at least the predication of existence does not really match with Heidegger's ontological investigations to which Habermas alludes (and Habermas himself uses Heidegger to advocate an anti-empiricist stance towards reference).

With reference to the preceding remarks, tacit knowledge escapes adequate representation in terms of explicit (propositional) knowledge. But making the assumption that we cannot adequately and without loss transform tacit knowledge into propositional or explicit knowledge does not exclusively rely on the peculiar mode of 'being-in-the-world' articulated exclusively with reference to individual cases of 'Dasein' and its internal mode of understanding. It has been said already that explicating knowing how often means shifting from the description of the particular *content* of knowledge (which is hard enough, because it is pre-predicative 'content') to the analysis of the *functional role* of tacit knowledge. Even if we cannot represent the content of a particular case of knowing how, we are able to circumscribe the mode of having and using such knowledge by reconstructing the role this knowledge plays in a broader social context.

Actually sociology has a special capability for this enterprise of circumscription, because it places the functional role of tacit knowledge in a broader picture of related contexts of action instead of confining its analysis to parochial situations of individual behavior: *Thus in sociological terms, the crucial functional aspect of tacit knowledge is related to the phenomenon of the social differentiation between contexts of action as a differentiation between contexts of different sorts of knowledge.* While explicitly knowing that this or that is at stake within a situation (social context) does not suffice in *every* case, there are special contexts of social action and communication which are factually based on and mediated by explicit knowledge. The theoretical discourse is a good example, but the more relevant cases are contexts of abstraction (generalization and explication) of meaning (of types of action) such as jurisdictional, administrative or economic 'systems' of social coordination. The rules of law and the principles of markets by definition determine just general types of action-events or commodities, which obviously presupposes the abstraction of types from situational particularities. With regard to those contexts, tacit knowledge provides the (second-order) possibility of *mediation* between situation-transcending regularities, typifications and categories (of action), and unprecedented occurrences in specific/individual situations (cf. Renn 2006: 443ff.). At this point the analysis benefits from relating tacit knowledge not only to bodily competences but also to structures of social interactions.

Of course 'there is' explicit knowledge, and it is constitutive both for the rationalization of social structures of action (or action-coordination) and for the reconstructive enterprise of defining "rational" types of acting (M. Weber). But explicit 'knowing that' and propositional cognition cannot *replace* tacit knowledge by rationalizing human conduct in regard to its functional role. The transformation of opaque habits, routines, and pre-predicative capabilities into technical applications of well-justified general rules, norms, and concepts only tells half of the story of modernization, because the established regimes of rational knowledge still need a reliable anchoring in situated practice.[7] Hence, explicit knowledge constantly has to be *translated* into tacit knowledge (cf. Renn 2006: 443ff.), i.e. into knowing how to apply explicit knowledge under particular circumstances.

This special type of re-specification – the application of generalized knowledge to concrete circumstances – re-embeds the fetish of sociological theories of modernity, i.e., the vanishing point of rationality and rationalization (M. Weber) by emphasizing the hermeneutical dimension of the re-translation of explicit rules and meanings and its function in light of situational adequacy.[8] Such a re-embedding by no means advocates the abolishment of justified knowledge and the (normative) claim of rational justification (cf. Habermas 1981). On the contrary, it simply implies that the strong version of tacit knowledge is neither a hasty prejudice nor only a result of the confusion between epistemological and ontological constraints, but the necessary correction of confusing the two main modes of knowing, i.e. the possibility of explication and the possibility of application. As Quine puts it: we have to distinguish between the direction of fit and the direction of guide: explicit principles, rules, laws, and concepts may fit with the observable conduct of acting individuals, but that does not mean at all that these individuals are guided exactly and exclusively just by those explications. The confusion between explication and application consists in the false presupposition that those two directions are equivalent and thus invertible. According to this false assumption, we can turn the move from practical knowledge to plausible explications backwards, and deduce from explicit knowledge determined acts that are based on tacit knowledge. But this is an invalid conclusion, because theoretical knowledge and practical certainty call for different criteria of justification: assertive utterances prove to be valid in relation to other assertive utterances, whereas practical knowledge proves to be valid by performative success. Therefore, the distinction of directions is relevant, because elaborat-

---

7 | This is so because this transformation institutionalizes with great effect an incomplete rationality of action: the instrumental rationality which 'in case of an accident' compensates the lack of adequacy of the 'object' of action by delegating the need for compensation to the object, forces it to surrender and to tolerate being treated as a mere example of some general type. Of course this sounds like Adorno. But the point can be made less emphatically: explicit knowledge tends to foster instrumental rationality, and thus to establish technical adaptations and standardizations instead of putting into question the accomplishments of general tools of problem solving.

8 | In contrast to classical critiques of social 'alienation,' which subsumed action, labor, and identity under the general categories of e.g. "abstract labour" (Marx) or the enforcement of instrumental rationality and the barter of equivalents (Adorno), the need of re-translation points to the limits of the transformation of "traditional" action into symbolically generalized media of communication (Parsons).

ing theoretical knowledge does not simply bring acting to perfection. On the contrary: acting *exclusively* on the basis of explicit knowledge leaves the actor completely helpless, because explicating the adequate *application* of explicit knowledge here and now calls for further applications of those explications of applications, and so on: of course this is Wittgenstein's argument with regard to the problem of rule following. This argument has to be systematically embedded in a theory of meaning. What does an action event 'mean' in terms of possible and probable successions of chains of action? Following Wittgenstein with special regard to the problem of rule following points to another basic vantage point of the theory of meaning: to the 'meaning-as-use' perspective. Hence, the meaning of an action event is not a substantial entity which ought to be irreversibly connected with a general action type, but always appears to be dependent on a whole "life-form" based horizon of practices.

Social differentiation and the distinction between modes of knowledge create the background for the polysemy of action events as signs. This point deserves attention. But first one has to make sure that the distinction between the two modes of knowing is not a classification of distinct realms of action, but rather a distinction between phases of a complex bow of reflected and rational conduct. Hence, reflection and calculation may emerge from performatively experienced crises of acting (cf. Dewey 1922; Mead 1938) and may interrupt the sequence of events we interpret as actions of an actor, but even the creative reconstruction of the respective situation of action needs to be complemented by an additional move which *retranslates* explicit knowledge about what is at stake here and now into the tacitly effective capacity to transform justified beliefs into practical certainty about how it is to *performatively* draw conclusions. 'Knowing that' does not amount to some sort of evil reification, but however sophisticated our explicit cognition may be, we always have to turn back to tacitly knowing how this knowledge is to be made effective in action. Therefore 'knowing that' does not precede intelligent acting, but is a period within a circle of numerous steps of translation between explicit and tacit knowledge.

III. Contesting Monological Accounts of Tacit Knowledge

Drawing attention to the functional role of tacit knowledge (cf. Renn 2013) and to the polysemy of action-tokens in relation to social differentiation might be an adequate reaction to the paradox of explicating the 'inexplicable.' But still the question remains from where we derive the knowledge that tacit knowledge is not represented by explicit reconstructions of its content. What kind of knowledge comes into play as soon as we know that knowing that and knowing how are substantially different? The answer may be put forth initially in a metaphorical manner; in order to know that tacit knowledge escapes and transcends knowing that, we need to have *two different kinds* of knowledge about knowing how at once: we need to know that knowing how has certain properties and we need to know how it is to have or to employ tacit knowledge in order to detect the difference between tacit knowledge and its explication. The explicit reconstruction of tacit knowledge presupposes the practical experience not only with objects of some kind (not only the participant's attitude towards Heideggerian *pragmata*: cf. Heidegger 1984; Dreyfus 1991), but also the somewhat miraculous reflective experience of tacit knowledge *in the mode of tacit knowledge*, i.e., *second-order* tacit knowledge.

This becomes much more plausible as soon as one keeps one's distance from a well-established convention of many theories of tacit knowledge. This convention may be called a *monological* focus on practical knowledge. It is not by accident that paradigmatic examples of tacit knowledge typically do not cover 'social action,' as has been stated before in this essay. Bodily capacities transcend the paradigm of the classical rational agent, because in this case action is not the conclusion of dis-embedded calculation but is a sort of seemingly automatically performed conduct. Examples like riding a bike implicitly cut off the social dimension of acting, which traditionally includes the intentional orientation of one actor to the intentionality of another. While there is knowledge without rationally justified explicit belief, there is no rational knowledge without tacitly presupposed, normative expectations concerning one's conduct, for if there were no *expectation* which one may possibly disappoint, there would be no action, but only behavior. Riding a bike is a poor example of tacit knowledge, but knowing how to apologize in an appropriate manner is a good one, because it includes tacit expectations of tacit expectations of someone else who may show by his or her further performance that one's apology suffers from infelicities in the sense of J. L. Austin (cf. 1962).

Taking this for granted and in accordance with a pragmatist theory of action we may state that the performative stance of an organism embedded in cooperative practice precedes the reflective attitude of explicitly knowing that something is the case, but we have to add that this primordial attitude – in contrast e.g. to George H. Mead's concept of role-taking (cf. 1934) – from scratch includes tacitly knowing about the tacit knowledge of someone else. Hence, there is good reason to modify the classical account of intersubjectivity in sociological pragmatism. The 'inter' between two subjective intentional horizons simply cannot consist of mutually shared 'meaning-intentions,' for knowing how to act is not based on the explicit meaning of articulated linguistic expression (otherwise we could not explain language acquisition in 'prelingual' infants at all).

Wherever the modification of the theoretical account of intersubjectivity may lead, *scientific* knowledge about tacit knowledge has to be related to and justified by an adequate reconstruction of this *basic feature* of second-order tacit knowledge. The passage from the *practical* experience with tacit knowledge to an explicit knowledge about properties of tacit knowledge simply were impossible if there was no primordial reflexivity concerning tacit knowledge in the participant's performative attitude itself. What's more, we have to grant that there simply is no first-order tacit knowledge at all without the second-order iteration, because the social character of tacit knowledge calls for the primordial status of at least two instances of tacit knowledge that are related to each other.[9] The main aspect of this argument is the very possibility of entering the reflective stance with reference to the self instead of to the object of action (which is a matter of the condition of possibility which remains quite unclear in G. H. Mead's account of the genetic aspect of the 'self'). The monological capacity of knowing how to tell apart edible and inedible things does not include any property by which the passage to the reflective stance leads to the self-referential reflection of knowing *as knowing* – it simply leads to a better classification of vegetables and prey. Here George Herbert Mead's concept of taking in the attitude of the other (cf. 1934) lacks grounding with respect to second-order *tacit* knowledge. Unfortunately, Mead explains the condition of possibility of role taking by interpreting the identity of meaning of significant gestures as an *objective* correspondence between responses. This begs the question how a self in non-naturalistic terms emerges, and it is furthermore misleading, because it assimilates the tacit knowledge of how to act to explicitly knowing what kind of objective event a gesture refers to. Mead thus explains intersubjectivity by presupposing intersubjectively identical *explicit* meaning. This vicious circle does not even touch on the question of how the reflective stance of the self may emerge from a pre-theoretical performative stance.

In contrast to this circle, one can argue that 'taking in the *explicit* attitude of others' presupposes on a primordial level *tacit knowledge of being addressed by tacit knowledge*.[10] Before reflection is able to make sure that my implicit expectation really was *my* expectation, I must already have known (tacitly) that others tacitly presuppose that I am the author of my action. To put it differently: tacit knowledge which does not include tacit knowledge *about* tacit knowledge offers no passage to any *reflective* articulation of knowledge as tacit knowledge.

In order to be able to give a somewhat plausible account of second-order tacit knowledge therefore necessitates a revision of the pragmatist tradition within sociology. But explaining the consequences of pragmatism for the sociological

---

9 | Otherwise we would have good reason to agree with the skeptics who deny that tacit knowledge is knowledge at all, for action without reference to the contingent action of an 'alter ego' remains behavior.

10 | Some examples of this kind of pre-predicative sociality can be found in phenomenological descriptions of the tricky structure of the "gaze," e.g. in Sartre's account of the keyhole-observer (cf. 1984).

theory of action and knowledge with special regard to tacit knowledge leads to a more technical sort of analysis by drawing attention to the theory of linguistic meaning.

IV. Meaning as Use and Knowing about Tacit Knowledge

Presupposing the necessity of second-order tacit knowledge on the level of pre-predicative sociality has one basic and simple implication: tacit knowledge is more than a mental correlate to automatized behavior, because it has a *meaning* dimension (including an implicit normativity). Hence, its main aspect of relevance is meaning attribution with reference to action events. Traditionally, what an action 'is' or what it means has either been considered to be determined subjectively ("constituted" as a subjective *noema* according to A. Schütz's reading of M. Weber; cf. Schütz 1974) or it has been taken to be generalized semantic content, i.e. a property of a general action type which functions as a 'class' of action events and transforms situational discontinuity (the *kairos* of concrete action) into (teleologically explainable) examples of *general* means for general ends.

Mainstream *pragmatist* sociology by and large has replaced the empiricist model of acting (and speaking) by turning the tables with regard to the direction of constitution: whereas empiricists explain social order by presupposing a subject of preferences and choices (and by explaining the subjective utility of contracts), pragmatists stress the primacy of *intersubjective* relations and thus justify the claim of normative social integration (in contrast to game theory models of order) by focusing on the primordial cooperation of practically immersed, dependent organisms (cf. Mead 1934; Habermas 1981; Honneth 1992). Additionally, *pragmatism* of course radicalizes the concept of action-event-*meaning* by turning an idealistic (platonic) or truth-semantic account of meaning into a pragmatic account. Hence action-*categories* – like all generalized concepts – are *derived* from action as performance and are related to performative implications of the use of the respective concept. Explaining, determining, and understanding 'action' by employing action-categories as generalized concepts with determined, explicit meanings therefore presupposes a preceding *practical* understanding of action, and tacit knowledge about the implicit criterion of an adequate use of explicit categories. In order to avoid a vicious circle of explanation, the 'understanding' of action (including the comprehension of regular performative implications) must primordially mean something different than subsuming a single event of action under clearly specified general terms.

I do not know 'what' you are doing right now by applying a general term, e.g. 'apologizing,' to a single event attributed to you, but I understand what 'apologizing' means by tacitly knowing which (kind of) practical implications your act as a member of a 'family' of equivalent acts should have or have not; to me, your *specific* act is not primarily a *noema*, i.e., an example (or mere token) of a general type (cf. Schütz 1974), but a *pragma* (cf. Heidegger 1984) which I know how to 'handle' before I know how to reconstruct it explicitly by applying well-defined categories of general action types – otherwise, I would not have the slightest idea of how to apply the general rule of apologizing to a concrete situation that is determined by unprecedented situational conditions.

A pragmatist stance consequently stresses the primacy of the *performative* character of signs, social acts, and reflections. Thoughts and propositional content have significant meaning in relation to action (cf. Peirce 1878), because we know the meaning of a term (we may add: the meaning of one single action-event as a token of an action type) as soon as we know what consequences are (probably) related to the use of the term (and to the realization of the action type's token). Referential and differential aspects of meaning – i.e., meaning as a 'name' for a 'distinct object' of thought or a class of material 'things' on the one hand, and meaning as a result of a set of constitutive structural differentiations on the other – are based on implicit (not logical!) *inferential* relations, which implies that denotative relations and the descriptive function (furthermore: meaning as a function of truth as correspondence) are grounded in life-form-relative knowledge of use (Wittgenstein), because conceptual meaning is grounded and embedded in practical knowledge, and knowing what exactly a given propositional content may 'designate' means to *know how* concepts are to be applied (correctly or intelligibly) in situated contexts (including specialized contexts of justification, where propositional content is warranted by propositional content). Even the inferential mode of "abduction" (cf. Peirce 1878) presupposes tacit knowledge, because the transgression from single events to a generalized principle (or even law) that explains the occurrence of these events and other events of the same 'type' implicitly presupposes the tacit knowledge of 'family resemblance' between those events.[11]

With reference to linguistic meaning, such an account of 'knowing how' hence reveals that understanding signs and symbols, sentences and speech acts on a basic level includes pre-predicative knowledge of *using* those items within specific situations (if criteria of adequate use or application weren't a matter of practical judgement based on tacit knowledge, they would lead into an infinite regress of justifying just applications); hence, to 'understand' the meaning of a sign, a sentence, or a speech act does not mean to subsume tokens of (speech-)action under types, but to relate "ready-at-hand-ness" of significant

---

11 | Otherwise the articulation of the respective principle or generalizing hypothesis – i.e., the product of abduction – would be nothing but a representation of an ontologically pre-existing regularity and of a pre-existing 'objective' class of events.

"stuff" (Heidegger) with dispositional practical knowledge conceived as part of a collective cultural form of life (Wittgenstein).

With regard to the first level of second-order tacit knowledge, that is, with regard to knowing how others know and expect how to act, we can see that the performative turn in linguistic philosophy perfectly fits into this account, because the concept of 'meaning as use' quite adequately expresses the fact that even linguistic competence (not only practical abilities that allow one to cope with a material environment) includes the mode of tacit knowledge of how to use linguistic expressions. The road from the participants' attitude to a *sociological* reconstruction of the mode of tacit knowledge now is open, because the *theoretical* use of explicit concepts also *includes* features of second-order tacit knowledge: first, the knowledge of how it is to performatively employ tacit linguistic knowledge, and second, the knowledge of how to use and to justify explicit categories of and assertions about action and knowledge.

Thus the object-related revision of what one may call constitutive social ontology has important implications for the reflective conceptualization of sociological knowledge, because this knowledge itself – following the course of pragmatist action analysis –becomes epistemologically intelligible as a special type of tacitly motivated reflective refraining from the level of performative participation or taken-for-granted conduct. In addition to this, in reversed direction, the use of *sociological* concepts comes back to tacit knowledge, for using sociological knowledge in order to interpret *specific* social 'facts,' 'structures,' and 'changes' again becomes an application of general terms which is at least in part based on tacit knowledge.

V. Second-Order Tacit Knowledge and Theoretical Reconstruction

The notion of second-order tacit knowledge primarily refers to the level of pre-predicative, primordial sociality. But in addition to this, it also refers through a 'reflexive turn' to the *sociological* stance *towards* tacit knowledge as an 'object' of investigation. As I already mentioned, tacit knowledge escapes direct representation in terms of the propositional vocabulary of conventional theorizing (cf. Polanyi 1983). Explicating, that is, giving a propositional description of defining properties – e.g. "how a clarinet sounds"– may use metaphorical descriptions of secondary properties (more "wooden" than "metallic") or metaphorical localizations (the clarinet may be "located" somewhere "between the English horn and the oboe") (cf. Wittgenstein 1969), but these obviously do not 'represent' the tacitly well-known qualitative experience. Due to the paradox of explicating the non-explicable, pragmatism necessarily has to presuppose an experiential foundation of its own conceptual framework of reflection which is inaccessible to propositional vocabulary even on the basic level of idealized meaning (cf. Dewey 1922), although it really does provide for the experiential 'input' of the theoretical reconstruction, which we now dare to call an operation of "worlddisclosure" (cf. Heidegger 1980), for it is keeping equal distance to conceptual representation (discovery) and to conceptual construction (invention). Hence, *explicating the inexplicability* of tacit knowledge leads to the scientific prerequisite of methodologically reflected *second-order tacit knowledge*. The pragmatist sociologist reverts to her own experiential access to tacit knowledge – which as habitualized knowledge about how it is to be a member of a 'lifeform' is a form of tacit knowledge itself – in order to experience the difference between her own explicit or conceptual account of the object (the tacit knowledge of social actors) and its 'properties' which escape propositional and conceptual representation (thus the idea that 'reconstruction' is not a representation but a *transformation* of the reconstructed, and is performatively motivated and tacitly warranted).

This seemingly helter-skelter epistemology in fact is a coherent part of sociological self-reference and of its reflection of its own conceptualizing work as an emergent subcontext of the social symbolical order of a complex society. In fact, conceptualizing the empirical access of sociological efforts to tacit knowledge as second-order tacit knowledge which is not representable in a closed framework of hierarchical justifications may simply be what Thomas Kuhn (cf. 1996) refers to as a paradigm: its main part is the set of taken-for-granted patterns of plausibility which is constitutive for rational discourse and its internal criteria of acceptable justifications, and therefore is not justified by this discourse itself (for justifying criteria through themselves obviously would constitute a vicious circle). The hierarchy of justifications – including the justification of criteria of justification – leads to life-form specific, hence socially shared *tacit knowledge*.

Thus tacit knowledge about tacit knowledge finally becomes an appropriate indication for the non-representational characteristics of scientific world-disclosure, i.e., a translation of tacitly accessible experience into the emergent vocabulary of sociology which is neither a form of representation (according to the false model of true description as the one adequate account with no alternative; cf. Putnam 1991), nor a merely self-referential invention in the sense of radical constructivism, which confuses being "theory-laden" (cf. Quine 1990) with the denial of any referential relation between emergent vocabularies and the *pragmata* they 'reconstruct.' The translational character of the relation between conceptual language and tacit knowledge in a methodological sense can be shown to be an implication of pragmatism as soon as we focus our attention again on the pragmatist account of the performative character of language.

Tacit knowledge and explicit, propositional knowledge neither represent nor 'invent' each other, but are connected by different types of translation. Such a position is central for the understanding of the dynamics of distancing (reflection and conceptual typification), for there is no reflection without distance from the performative stance, and no referential relation to the social by sociology without at least *some* sort of performative anchoring of sociological knowledge in the 'world' of practical conduct which this knowledge pretends to be knowledge about.

From this perspective, sociology is related to the concept of tacit knowledge in a twofold way: first, the disclosure of the role of tacit knowledge for social conduct helps to clarify the somewhat old-fashioned question about the relation between 'structure' and 'actor;' and second, reconstructing the emergent but influential role of reflective intentionality within and for social conduct and the situational context-transcending social order sheds some light on the problem of *sociological validity conditions*. The pragmatist account of the performative prerequisites of knowledge provides the ground for overcoming the tradition of the scientifically restricted correspondence theory of truth (the still widespread orthodoxy of the propositional or 'apophantic' structure of truth-value), which is either positively (empiricist position) or negatively (constructivist position) still taken for granted as the only alternative for the scientific type of social reflection. Second-order tacit knowledge may advance to a key concept of sociological epistemology as soon as we conceptualize the relation between first- and second-order tacit knowledge as a matter of mutual translation. Hence, the 'truth' of a pragmatist sociological account of society neither lies in a simple correspondence between theories and 'facts' nor in a normatively justified concept of legitimate forms of the 'good life,' but becomes a matter of *'appropriate' translation*. This calls for a different set of criteria of validity with regard to the pragmatic role of theoretical vocabularies in a poly-contextualized society – but this is another story.

Works Cited

Austin, John Langshaw (1962): How to do Things with Words. The William James Lectures Delivered at Harvard University in 1955, ed. J.O. Urmson/ Marina Sbisà, Oxford: Clarendon P.
Bourdieu, Pierre (1979): Entwurf einer Theorie der Praxis, Frankfurt/Main: Suhrkamp.
Brandom, Robert (1994): Making It Explicit, Cambridge: Harvard UP.
Dewey, John (1896): "The Reflex Arc Concept in Psychology," in: Psychological Review 3, 357-370.
—. (1922): Human Nature and Conduct, New York: Holt.
Dreyfus, Hubert (1991): Being-In-The-World. A Commentary on Heidegger's Being and Time, Division I, Cambridge: MIT P.

Habermas, Jürgen (1981): Theorie des kommunikativen Handelns, 2 vols., Frankfurt/Main: Suhrkamp.
—. (1999): Wahrheit und Rechtfertigung, Frankfurt/Main: Suhrkamp.
Heidegger, Martin (1980): "Zeit des Weltbildes," in: Holzwege, Frankfurt/Main: Klostermann, 73-117.
—. (1984 [1927]): Sein und Zeit, Tübingen: Niemeyer.
Honneth, Axel (1992): Kampf um Anerkennung. Zur moralischen Grammatik sozialer Konflikte, Frankfurt/Main: Suhrkamp.
Husserl, Edmund (1982): Die Krisis der europäischen Wissenschaften und die transzendentale Phänomenologie, Hamburg: Meiner.
James, William (1950 [1890]): The Principles of Psychology, 2 vols., New York: Dover.
Kuhn, Thomas (1996): The Structure of Scientific Revolutions, Chicago: U of Chicago P.
Loenhoff, Jens (ed.) (2012): Implizites Wissen, Velbrück: Weilerswist.
Mead, George Herbert (1934): Mind, Self, and Society, Chicago: Chicago UP.
—. (1938): The Philosophy of the Act, Chicago: Chicago UP.
Nagel, Thomas (1974): "What Is It Like to Be a Bat?" in: The Philosophical Review 83.4, 435-450.
Peirce, Charles S. (1878): *How to Make* Our Ideas *Clear*, in: Popular Science Monthly 12, 286-302.
Polanyi, Michael (1983 [1966]): The Tacit Dimension, Gloucester: Peter Smith.
Putnam, Hillary (1991): Repräsentation und Realität, Frankfurt/Main: Suhrkamp.
Quine, Willard Van Orman (1960): Word and Object, Cambridge: Wiley.
—. (1990): Pursuit of Truth, Cambridge: Harvard UP.
Renn, Joachim (2000): "One World is Enough," in: European Journal of Social Theory 3.4, 485-499.
—. (2006): Übersetzungsverhältnisse. Perspektiven einer pragmatistischen Gesellschaftstheorie, Weilerswist: Velbrück.
—. (2012): "Was ist rational am impliziten Wissen. Zum theoretischen Status der praktischen Gewissheit zwischen Handlungs- und Gesellschaftstheorie," in: Loenhoff, Implizites Wissen, 150-177.
—. (2013): "Praktische Gewissheit und die Rationalität zweiter Ordnung. Zur gesellschaftstheoretischen Analyse des impliziten Wissens," in: ZTS – Zeitschrift für Theoretische Soziologie 1.2, 56-81.
Röttger-Rössler, Birgit (1997): "Die Wortlosigkeit des Ethnologen. Zum Problem der Übersetzung zwischen den Kulturen am Beispiel indonesischer Gefühlstermini," in: Doris Bachmann Medick (ed.), Übersetzung als Repräsentation fremder Kulturen, Berlin: Schmidt, 199-215.
Ryle, Gilbert (2002): The Concept of Mind, Chicago: U of Chicago P.

Sartre, Jean Paul (1984): Being and Nothingness, New York: Washington Square.
Schmidt, Robert (2012): Soziologie der Praktiken, Frankfurt/Main: Suhrkamp.
Schütz, Alfred (1974): Der sinnhafte Aufbau der sozialen Welt, Frankfurt/Main: Suhrkamp.
Turner, Stephen (1994): The Social Theory of Practices. Tradition, Tacit Knowledge and Presuppositions, Chicago: Chicago UP.
Wittgenstein, Ludwig (1969): On Certainty/Über Gewissheit, ed. G.E.M. Anscombe/Georg H. von Wright, New York: Harper and Row.

Tacit Knowledge and Analytic Autoethnography
Methodological Reflections on the Sociological Translation of Self-Experience[1]

Alexander Antony

I. INTRODUCTION

In 1978 David Sudnow published *Ways of the Hand: The Organization of Improvised Conduct*, an ethnographic account of his journey of becoming a jazz pianist which he refers to in the introduction to the book as a "close description of the handicraft of improvisation, of the knowing ways of the jazz body [...], a phenomenologically motivated inquiry into the nature of handwork *from the standpoint of the performer*" (xiii, emphasis added). Sudnow for instance describes how his experience of melody while playing the piano was practically and sequentially interconnected with his acquisition of fine motor skills:

[A] manner of bodily engagement describes how "listening" and "sounds" are to be described within the context of the activity at hand. [...] I began to find that I knew what the next notes would sound like. But I did not know what a next note sounded like or where a sounding note lay on the keyboard, apart from how I was engaged with this terrain. As I found the next sounds coming up, as I set out into a course of notes, it was not as if I had learned about the keyboard so that looking down I could tell what a regarded note would sound like. I do not have that skill, nor do many other musicians have. I could tell what a note would sound like because it was a next sound, because my hand was so engaged with the keyboard that it was given a setting of sounding places in its own configurations and potentialities. (Ibid. 45)

---

1 | I wish to thank Frank Adloff, Martin Fuchs, Katharina Gerund, Peter Isenböck, David Kaldewey, Robert Schmidt, Gerd Sebald, and Yasemin Yilmaz for their helpful comments on and critiques of earlier versions of this paper.

This example of Sudnow's subtle, precise, and theoretically informed descriptions bring to the foreground aspects of musical action coordination that could hardly be described by jazz musicians themselves and/or observed by audience members.[2] Sudnow's method of active participation and self-observation allowed him to articulate some of the 'tacit' and 'invisible' dimensions of the practice of improvisation. He was thus able to multi-modally experience the object of investigation, i.e. the empirical reference of his descriptions, firsthand. Such a research strategy of "deep immersion in the profession or activity under consideration" (Pollner/Emerson 2010: 119) establishes an 'unmediated' relationship between ethnographers' scholarly knowledge and their embodied experiences 'in the field,' which allows for an empirical reconstruction and sociological translation of concretely situated 'tacit' social practices. Even though Sudnow himself did not call his approach analytic autoethnography, I argue that it can be characterized as such because autoethnographers too not only *use* their tacit knowledge and acquired bodily skills in and for their research, but also make it the object of their sociological studies.

Analytic autoethnography in particular is concerned with the multiple relationships and tensions between theoretical concepts and empirical phenomena in regard to at least three important dimensions, which however do not exclusively apply to analytic autoethnography, but to analytically oriented qualitative research in general: First, analytic autoethnography breaks with *tabula rasa* conceptualizations of social research as put forward for instance in early Grounded Theory (cf. Glaser/Strauss 2006);[3] just as sociological research in general, autoethnography is necessarily a theory-laden enterprise which has its starting point in sociological discourse (or at least in everyday folk theories of social phenomena). Second, analytic autoethnographers try to "tap and translate what they have comprehended viscerally into the *conceptual language* of their scholarly discipline" (Wacquant 2005: 467, emphasis added). Thus as members of scientific thought collectives (cf. Fleck 1979: 38ff.) they make use of the practice of theoretical abstraction, which allows them to link their findings to scholarly discourse and enables them "to use empirical data to gain insight into some broader set of social phenomena than those provided by the data themselves" (Anderson

---

2 | In a small research project on improvisational action coordination I conducted unstructured interviews with jazz musicians to learn about their improvisational practice, during which it soon became obvious how difficult it is to make discursively accessible what in improvisational practice mainly remains tacit or implicit.

3 | There is a tension between naive empiricism and 'theoretical sensitivity' in Glaser and Strauss (2006) which has led to the demand that qualitative researchers dismiss *all* prior knowledge, especially theoretical concepts and hypotheses derived from sociological discourse; this is neither tenable from an epistemological standpoint nor from the standpoint of scientific practice (cf. Kelle 2007; Meinefeld 2004: 153f.).

2006a: 387). Third, analytic autoethnographers aim at "theoretical development" (Snow/Morrill/Anderson 2003: 185); they do not only use theoretical concepts as 'translational resources' to describe the phenomena they study, but attempt to gain new theoretical insights, refine existing theories, and try to extend the use of theoretical concepts from one context or case to other contexts and phenomena (cf. ibid. 186ff.). What is of special interest here is the aspect of theoretical refinement, because it implies the question if and how general sociological concepts may be challenged by empirical research. In the following, I will argue that analytic autoethnography could be used to overcome the often asserted indifference of empirical practice toward theory, and vice versa (cf. Amann/Hirschauer 1997: 7), and could thus help stimulate an empirically controlled 'communication' between these two dimensions of sociological work. In this sense this paper follows Herbert Blumer, who was quite sensitive to "the difficulty of bringing social theory into close and self-correcting relation with its empirical world so that its proposals about that world can be tested, refined and enriched by the data of that world" (1986: 151; cf. Hammersley 1989; Maines 1989).

I suggest that analytic autoethnography is especially promising in regard to researching social practices based on tacit knowledge, because it allows to overcome some of the limitations of other methods like interviewing or 'conventional' participant observation as *the* method of ethnography. The actual performance of specific practices "in real time and space" (Wacquant 2005: 465) "enables access to vital aspects of human experience that cannot be accessed using other available methods" (Vryan 2006: 407; cf. Duncan 2004: 34, Pollner/Emerson 2010: 123f., 126f.). The problem inherent in empirically reconstructing tacit knowledge provides a good opportunity to discuss the methodological implications of analytic autoethnography. The goal of this paper is therefore to sharpen the conceptual tools that allow for a self-reflective research practice and to reveal some of the methodological complexity that often remains implicit in qualitative social research by bringing together different theoretical strands that have so far been discussed separately. Even though the reflections presented here are meant to be suggestive rather than conclusive, they may help to throw light on methodological problems which are not only of interest to autoethnographers in particular but to ethnographers and qualitative researchers in general.

In the following, I will first conceptualize tacit knowledge within a pragmatist action theoretical framework by showing how the tacit dimension of action coordination can be specified by means of John Dewey's concept of primary experience and his sub-concepts of habit and immediate quality (II). Second, I draw a distinction between different types of theoretical concepts in order to methodologically reflect on the problem of the relationship between empirical observation/analysis and theoretical concepts (III), as even authors who pursue an analytical agenda (cf. Snow/Morrill/Anderson 2003; Anderson 2006a) seldom spell out the methodological implications of differentiating between distinct types of theories. I will show that the concept of primary experience (including the above-mentioned sub-concepts) cannot simply be falsified due to its high level of abstraction; however, since such general sociological concepts necessarily serve as "seeing instruments" (Lindemann 2008: 114, my transl.) in social research and are therefore co-constitutive of the subject-matter of sociology, it is nonetheless possible to ask how theoretical concepts and empirical phenomena 'fit' together. This question concerns the empirical reference of theoretical concepts, and in section IV I argue that some methods, like interviewing or "detached observation" (Pollner/Emerson 2010: 126), are less suitable than analytic autoethnography for establishing the empirical reference of concepts like primary experience or tacit knowledge. In section V, I contrast analytic autoethnography with evocative research strategies and argue for the necessity of sociological translation by means of acts of theoretical abstraction; the point here is that sensory engagement with 'the field' and theoretical analysis are not antagonistic but mutually informative. Again drawing on pragmatism, I argue that the concept of translation – which can be said to transcend the realist/constructivist dichotomy – is suitable for conceptually grasping the complex relationships between theoretical concepts and empirical phenomena (VI). In section VII, I bring together my lines of argument and present analytic autoethnography as an answer to the questions posed in the sections before. In the next-to-last section, I discuss the problem of tacit sociological translation as a specific analytic 'moment' where theory and empirical phenomena come together in the fieldwork of autoethnographers in real-time (VIII). The paper closes with the presentation of some topics that may be worth discussing in the future (IX).

II. Tacit Knowledge and Primary Experience

Pragmatist action theory is an anti-cognitivist and anti-intellectualist undertaking which puts the conception of *experience* at the heart of theorizing action and social practices.[4] By cognitivism I mean a reductionist decomposition of the mind-body dualism which often manifests itself in an overemphasis of cognitive or mental activity with respect to the conceptualization of action coordination; by subordinating the bodily basis of being-in-the-world, cognitivist approaches not only fall short of capturing phenomena such as bodily skills, practical knowledge, feelings, etc., but also miss the opportunity to examine the complex *relations* between – analytically separable – bodily and mental phenomena. By

---

4 | Dewey and also George Herbert Mead, as I would argue, share this anti-cognitivism and anti-intellectualism with newer theories of social practices (cf. e.g. Reckwitz 2002; Schatzki/Knorr Cetina/von Savigny 2001).

intellectualism I mean the claim that all human action coordination basically rests upon reflective-intentional anticipations of future action consequences, and hence on what Dewey calls thought or "knowledge experience" (1917: 48);[5] knowledge experiences, as they operate on the basis of symbol-using processes, enable actors to consciously and reflectively plan action coordination and to partially transcend situational circumstances (cf. e.g. Dewey 1984a). Dewey does not deny the importance of knowledge experiences or thought processes, yet he holds that conceptualizations of human action coordination which take acts of knowing as their theoretical starting point put the cart before the horse (cf. also Joas 1996: 157ff.). He argues for a broader conceptualization of action coordination which emphasizes the habitual, dispositional, bodily, and affective dimensions of experience. Thought or knowledge experiences based on the usage of "significant symbols" (cf. Mead 1922) can thus be regarded as one special mode of experience which arises only under specific conditions, namely when habitual action coordination becomes problematic (cf. Dewey 1983: 128ff.). Knowing in this pragmatist sense should therefore not be over-generalized as an explication of all forms of action coordination. Dewey thus rejects "the notion that *every* experience must be a cognitive noting" (1917: 49, emphasis added), and therefore a knowledge experience; rather, "things [in the most general sense; A.A.] are objects to be treated, used, acted upon and with, enjoyed and endured, even more than things to be known. They are things *had* before they are things cognized" (Dewey 1981: 28, emphasis in the original). Consequently, Dewey argues for a primary form of experience and action coordination and an immediate, pre-reflective mode of meaning constitution which underlies secondary and therefore reflective knowledge experiences.[6] 'Higher' cognitive processes (thinking, knowing, reflective imagination, etc.), so Dewey's claim, genetically and functionally presuppose pre-reflective or primary forms of experience (affect, emotion, habits, bodily knowledge, etc.).[7] I argue that Dewey's conception of primary experience is highly relevant to those phenomena Michael Polanyi refers to as acts of tacit knowing, first, because Dewey's claim that pre-reflective

---

5 | Dewey writes: "By 'intellectualism' as an *indictment* is meant the theory that all experiencing is a mode of *knowing*, and that all subject-matter, all nature, is, in principle, to be reduced and transformed till it is defined in terms identical with the characteristics presented by refined objects of science as such" (1981: 28, emphasis added). Dewey's critique of this "great intellectualist fallacy" (1984a: 175) parallels Pierre Bourdieu's and Karl Mannheim's critiques of intellectualism (cf. Bourdieu 1990: 29, 34ff.; Mannheim 1982: 185ff).

6 | Dewey uses the terms "primary" and "secondary" experience to denote two different but *interrelated* forms of experience (cf. 1981: 15ff.).

7 | For current cognitive science research supporting this claim, cf. Johnson 2010; cf. also Jens Loenhoff's contribution in the present volume.

forms of primary experience cannot be (fully) verbally explicated (cf. Dewey 1981: 74f.) corresponds with Polanyi's conception of tacit knowledge;[8] and second, because primary experiences constitute a fundamental characteristic of being-in-the-world, and are for that reason – as a theoretical concept – relevant to (sociological) action theory in general.

How does Dewey theoretically specify what he calls primary experience? To answer this question, one has to begin with his understanding of experience in general. Dewey understands every experience as a "trans-action," and therefore as a *co*-constitutive relationship between human organism and environment (cf. Dewey/Bentley 1989, ch. 4).[9] The theoretical core of this conception of experience has two dimensions. On one side, all primary experiences are based on an *active-dispositional* dimension. Dewey here speaks of habit, which he describes, quite similar to Bourdieu's concept of habitus (cf. 2000: 72-87), as

a predisposition to *ways* or modes of response, not to particular acts except as, under special conditions, these express a way of behaving. Habit means special sensitiveness or accessibility to certain classes of stimuli, standing predilections and aversions, rather than bare recurrence of specific acts. (Dewey 1983: 32)

Habits for Dewey cannot be simply considered as "physiological functions, like breathing, [or] digesting" (ibid. 15), even though they work in a similar 'instinctive' way, because they are "acquired" (ibid.) in specific social environments and thus are products of "shared" conduct (ibid. 16). It necessarily follows from

---

8 | In this sense, Dewey conceptualizes what Loenhoff and Renn (see their contributions in the present volume) call a "strong" version of tacit knowledge. However, in line with Dewey, I would propose not to speak of tacit *knowledge* but of primary *experience* or primary action coordination, because knowing can be regarded as an analytically separable and temporally specifiable mode or phase of experience/action coordination. Anticipating Ryle (cf. 2009), Dewey at some point speaks of "*know[ing] how* by means of our habits" (1983: 124, emphasis in the original) in contrast to "knowledge that involves reflection" (ibid. 125).

9 | Dewey and Bentley distinguish between "trans-action" and "inter-action:" in inter-action, "thing is balanced against thing in causal interconnection" (1989: 101), whereas in trans-action, "systems of description and naming are employed to deal with aspects and phases of action, without final attribution to 'elements' or other presumptively detachable or independent 'entities,' 'essences,' or 'realities,' and without isolation of presumptively detachable 'relations,' from such detachable 'elements'" (ibid. 110f.). For a discussion of the idea of co-constitution in Dewey's philosophy, cf. also Kestenbaum (1977).

this that they are a collective property and have a normative structure.[10] Furthermore, Dewey does not understand habits as mechanical routines in a behavioristic sense. Routines of this sort are regarded by him only as one specific type of habit (cf. Dewey 1983: 50f., 121), first, because habits more generally can be considered as *"cooperation[s]* of organism and environment" (ibid. 15, emphasis added) where both dimensions are in a co-constitutive relationship which should not be misunderstood as causality; and second, because habits can be regarded as flexible and impulsive (cf. ibid. 69ff.) and potentially enable actors to pre-reflectively adapt to new situations and to altered circumstances (in this sense, 'creativity' is not only an intrinsic quality of secondary knowledge experiences but a potentiality of habitual action coordination too).

On the other side, Dewey's conception of primary experience implies what he calls *"immediate* quality" (1984a: 180, emphasis in the original; cf. also 1984b), which for Dewey is related to the *passive-receptive* dimension of primary experience and action coordination in general, and encompasses what he elsewhere calls "feeling" (1984b: 248; 1981: 198) or simply "hav[ing]" (1981: 28). Important here is that the conception of immediate quality not only applies to the pre-reflective (and in this sense: immediate) perception of the environmental dimension of experiences, but also to the conscious or unconscious self-perception of the actor in regard to for example phenomenal or bodily aspects of emotional experiences, different forms of proprioception, the perception of preparedness or tendencies to act, and even intuition or a sense of moral or aesthetic adequacy.

Together, the active-dispositional dimension in the form of habits and the passive-receptive dimension in the form of immediate qualities co-constitute in their trans-action (e.g. in sensorimotor coordination as a basic type of action coordination) the core of primary experiences and "immediate meanings" (Dewey 1981: 198), i.e. meanings that are intimately related to our pre-reflective mode of being-in-the-world that are more a matter of doing and feeling than of knowing. However, it can be quite difficult, for instance in the case of kinesthesia, to analytically distinguish between habits and qualities. Dewey himself speaks of the "feeling of habits" (1983: 26) and brings closely together the habitual and qualitative aspects of action coordination: "Immediate, seemingly instinctive, feeling of the direction and end of various lines of behavior is in reality the feeling of habits working below direct consciousness" (ibid.). Moreover, from another analytical perspective, which may be particularly productive for sociological research, habits and qualities can be regarded as *processually* and *transsituationally* related to each other, which requires asking how the reciprocal co-constitution of habits and qualities may temporally and spatially transcend situational boundaries: how can, for instance, habits acquired in one

---

10 | Cf. Jens Loenhoff's contribution in the present volume for an elaboration of this aspect.

specific social setting become the preconditions for immediate qualities in another setting under different circumstances?

Dewey's concepts of habit and immediate quality indeed provide us with a theoretical heuristic for empirically investigating and describing primary experiences as a basic mode of action coordination,[11] but these sometimes vague but nonetheless "sensitizing concepts" (Blumer 1986: 140-152) undoubtedly call for their empirical specification and application in research practice (cf. Kelle/Kluge 2010: 28ff.). This leads to the methodological question as to what type of concepts we are dealing with here, and how these concepts function in research.

III. General Sociological Concepts and the Theory-Ladenness of Scientific Practice

To think about tacit knowledge or, more generally, primary experience in Dewey's sense means to reflect on a specific *type* of theory, namely "general sociological concepts" (Meinefeld 2004: 157) or "social theory" (Joas/Knöbl 2009: 1-19; cf. Lindemann 2008: 108f.). Such concepts contain basic assumptions concerning the 'nature' of the social, social practices, social structure, action, and interaction, to name a few examples. General sociological concepts have to be distinguished from theoretical concepts in the hypothetico-deductive (H-D) model of research as well as from "object-related concepts" (Meinefeld 2004: 157), which are specifically relevant in qualitative research. This ideal-typical differentiation is of importance because the three mentioned types of theory differ from each other with regard to 1) their level of abstraction, 2) their function in the research process, and 3) their relation to empirical phenomena.

In the H-D model, theory takes the form of "sound scientific hypotheses" (Kelle 2007: 147): "In this context one regards only clear-cut and precisely formulated hypotheses whereas concepts and hypotheses which lack empirical content and thus cannot be falsified are considered as highly problematic" (ibid.). Object-related concepts have, in contrast to general sociological concepts, a high level of empirical content, and therefore a lower level of abstraction;[12] they logical-

---

11 | For discussions of pragmatism that touch upon aspects I discuss above, cf. Gronow 2011; Jung 2010; Kestenbaum 1977; Ostrow 1990, as well as Loenhoff's and Renn's articles in the present volume.

12 | This is of course a quite broad claim, because their level of abstraction can vary greatly; cf. e.g. Strauss' differentiation between "substantive" and "formal" theories (1987: 241f.). Moreover, the transition from object-related to general sociological concepts has to be thought of as fluent. For an overview on the topic of prior knowledge and different types of theory in qualitative research, cf. Kelle/Kluge 2010, ch. 2.

ly and functionally presuppose general sociological concepts. Asking for the relation of theory to empirical phenomena, it can thus be argued that object-related concepts can at least be falsified bit by bit even though their use in research does not follow a falsificationist logic in the strict sense (cf. Lindemann 2008: 108).[13] As general sociological concepts have a higher level of theoretical abstraction and thus lower empirical content than object-related concepts, they are neither falsifiable in a strict sense nor bit by bit (cf. Kelle 2007: 147; Lindemann 2008: 113f.). To give an example: Giddens' definition of structure as "always both constraining and enabling" conditions of social action (2008: 25, 169) cannot, at least on this level of abstraction and without taking into account his more specific sub-concepts of rules and resources, be proven wrong – at best, it can be contrasted or complemented with other, possibly more comprehensive conceptualizations. As already indicated in the introduction, general sociological concepts thus should rather be judged by whether their use as translational resources is pertinent, i.e. whether they aptly describe (or explain) social phenomena. To use an admittedly theoretically erroneous metaphor: If general sociological concepts serve as "lenses" (Kelle 2007: 147, my transl.) or as "seeing instruments" (Lindemann 2008: 114, my transl.), one may well wonder how accurate the image is that they produce (cf. ibid.); this points to another important characteristic of general sociological concepts: they are (co-)constitutive of the phenomena under investigation, a fact that is often referred to as the inevitable theory-ladenness of empirical observation and analysis. In this sense, general sociological concepts function as *"heuristic concepts* [...] through which researcher[s] perceive facts and phenomena in their research field" (Kelle 2007: 147, emphasis in the original; cf. Scheffer 2002: 370ff.; Abbott 2004); researchers thus are always equipped with a specific "scientific habitus," i.e. a theoretically 'incorporated' "program of perception and action [...] which is disclosed only in empirical work that actualizes it" (Bourdieu/Wacquant 1992: 161). Therefore, scientific practice in the social sciences in general as well as (auto)ethnographic practice in particular is always a *constructive* enterprise, which, however, is not to say that scientific practice is arbitrary: Theoretical perspectivism does not necessarily lead to relativism.

IV. THE PROBLEM OF ESTABLISHING EMPIRICAL REFERENCE

Even though there seems to be a broad consensus in qualitative research that empirical practice is theory-laden, according to Lindemann, little effort is taken

---

13 | As in Grounded Theory, for instance, "the research phases induction/abduction, deduction and verification/falsification" merely "are no longer strictly isolated from each other," its methodology does not provide an "alternative to falsificationism" (Lindemann 2008: 108, my transl.).

to empirically question general sociological concepts which guide qualitative research practice: "They are used, but they are not considered as assumptions that can be questioned by means of empirical research" (2008: 113, my transl.). This topic has quite a long history in qualitative research (cf. Blumer 1986), and has remained relevant to this day; in Germany, for example, there have been attempts to initiate a dialog between theory and empirical practice under the label of "Theoretische Empirie" (cf. Kalthoff/Hirschauer/Lindemann 2008; Kalthoff 2006: 147, 149; Scheffer 2002: 353, 366ff., 370ff.); in the U.S., representatives of "analytic ethnography" (cf. Lofland 1995; Snow/Morrill/Anderson 2003, Vaughan 2009) and autoethnography (cf. Anderson 2006a) have taken the view that

> ethnographers need to be oriented toward larger theoretical concerns from the outset of their projects by, at the very least, being sensitive to the range of theoretical relevancies of their orienting research questions and of the alternative paths through which those questions might be linked to theoretical development" (Snow/Morrill/Anderson 2003: 185).

However, any attempt to 'connect' general sociological concepts and empirical phenomena is problematical, especially when researchers are faced with what Stefan Hirschauer calls "the silence of the social" (cf. 2006): In researching phenomena of *tacit* knowing, primary experiences based on habits and immediate quality, etc., the problem of the "verbalization" (ibid. 422) or "translation" (ibid. 430) of these tacit dimensions of action coordination has to be solved.[14] For Hirschauer, "the core problem of all forms of empirical research is how social reality finds *access* to sociological discourse" (ibid.; cf. Samudra 2008: 668ff.). "Access" in this regard especially refers to the problem of *using* theory – and particularly, general sociological concepts – in empirical research. Using general sociological concepts is related to two dimensions of qualitative research: First, data-producing methods (e.g. participant observation and writing field notes, conducting, recording, and transcribing interviews, etc.), and second, the 'nature' of phenomena under investigation. Both aspects are, or rather, should be inextricably related to each other, which means that specific social phenomena need specific data-producing methods to study them with. *The co-constitutive establishment of this relation between method and subject-matter through the practice of research is the condition of possibility for a methodically controlled use of theory.* From this follows that the *use* of theory, not to speak of its specification, modifi-

---

14 | For Hirschauer, what I refer to as primary experience is only one aspect of the 'silent' dimensions of action coordination, which he calls the "pre-lingual" (2006: 431); others include the voiceless, speechlessness, the indescribable, things taken for granted, and muteness.

cation, and so on, is quite a critical matter – particularly with regard to general sociological concepts like tacit knowledge or primary experience.

To give an example: What happens when we conduct interviews with jazz musicians in order to learn about their improvisational practice? The major problem here is that everything the interviewees say about their musical practice is already, to use Jörg Bergmann's phrase, a "preservation by *reconstruction*" (in contrast to "preservations by *registration*") (qtd. in Hirschauer 2006: 417; emphasis in original).[15] With preservations by registration, Bergmann means the "fixation of a social event in vision and sound" (1985: 305, my transl.), while preservation by reconstruction refers to the "verbal realization of past events" (ibid., my transl.). Preservations by reconstruction can therefore be understood as interviewees' *ex post* interpretations of specific phenomena or practices, e.g. musical improvisation. Thus, when improvisational practice *per se* rather than the practice of *speaking about* improvisation is the object of investigation, researchers conducting interviews necessarily rely on the interviewees' interpretive verbalizations to get access to the phenomenon. Two problems result from this situation: First, because musical practice in general and musical improvisation in particular is primarily based on forms of bodily and practical knowledge, verbalizing them is quite difficult for the players (cf. Gibson 2006; Sudnow 1978; Wilf 2010). From this follows, second, that researchers who want to learn about improvisational practice through interviews not only have to interpret what is said, but also have to reconstruct the *relation* between the interviewees' verbalizations of the experience, and the experience of the phenomenon itself. In other words: Researchers need to understand how primary experiences (improvisational practice) are translated into linguistic concepts by the interviewees.

Similar problems may arise when ethnographers for instance attend jazz jam sessions to learn about improvisational practice. Primary experiences not only are hard to translate into linguistic concepts or written accounts but are also quite difficult to observe, as they involve 'invisible' dimensions which cannot simply be reconstructed empirically by just looking at how practices are performed. Researchers who focus primarily or exclusively on the visual (and auditory) dimensions of social practices may thus be able to study players' performances (cf. Goffman 1959: 22ff.), but they will not be able to empirically reconstruct the "practical mastery" (Bourdieu 2000: 118) or the *experience* of improvisational action coordination from the standpoint of the performer.

Both examples show that it is often hardly possible to establish an empirical reference of (presumably) relevant theoretical concepts like tacit knowledge or primary experience, because it is quite difficult (though certainly not impossible) to empirically reconstruct practitioners' *ex post* interpretations of their

---

15 | For a discussion of the concept of preservation by registration in relation to ethnographic writing and recording techniques, cf. Hirschauer 2006: 417-422.

primary action coordination, and to gain access to the tacit and often 'invisible' aspects of primary experiences. The empirical reconstruction of primary action coordination therefore requires other, more suitable methods, which brings autoethnography into play.[16]

V. A Plea for *Analytic* Autoethnography

Whereas there is not just one type of autoethnography (cf. Charmaz 2006),[17] in the last years – at least in sociology – the term has become particularly associated with a specific type of ethnographic research practice which was developed and promoted by Carolyn Ellis (cf. 1991) and her colleagues: "evocative" (cf. Ellis 1997) or "he*art*ful" autoethnography (cf. Ellis 1999, emphasis in the original). Ellis and Bochner's demand that the term autoethnography "should be reserved for work that ties sociology to literature, expresses fieldwork evocatively, and has an ethical agenda" (2006: 445; for a critique cf. Anderson 2006a: 374; Delamont 2009: 57ff.; Duncan 2004: 36) led some scholars to completely reject the term as a label for their own work (cf. e.g. Wacquant 2005: 469)[18] and to use labels such as "carnal sociology" (ibid. 466) or "thick participation" (Samudra 2008: 667) instead, or formulate alternative methodological approaches to autoethnography such as Anderson's "analytic autoethnography" (cf. 2006a; 2006b: 455ff.).[19] Personally, I prefer the term analytic autoethnography (even though I differ from Anderson in some respects), because it aptly describes a specific type of ethnographic practice in which the ethnographers' own experiences become (part of) the phenomenon under investigation.

The main difference between evocative and analytic autoethnography lies in their research aims. While evocative autoethnographers aim primarily at evoking emotional responses by means of producing "personal narratives" (Ellis

---

16 | The statements above do not indicate that researchers know from the outset which methods are suitable; figuring out which ones are will of course always rely on experimentation.

17 | For short historical overviews of autoethnography, cf. Reed-Danahay (1997); Anderson (2006a: 375ff.).

18 | Wacquant even goes so far as to characterize his book *Body and Soul* (2004) as "*anti-autoethnographic* in design and spirit" (2005: 470, emphasis in the original) in order to distance himself from that "ill-defined genre" (ibid. 469) that e.g. Reed-Danahay, Ellis, and Bochner promote as autoethnography.

19 | Also cf. Honer's approach of ethnographic life-world analysis and in particular her notion of "existential commitment" (2004: 115f.) and the emphasis of "active participation and the acquisition of indigenous skills and knowledge as means of capturing the lived order" (Emerson/Pollner 2010: 123) in ethnomethodology.

1999: 678; cf. Sparkes 2000: 34), analytic autoethnography is concerned with the trans-actional relationship between theoretical concepts and empirical phenomena. Ellis and Bochner, who advocate evocative autoethnography, are highly critical of "distanced theorizing" (2006: 433) and focus instead "on aesthetics and our link to arts and humanities rather than Truth claims and our link to science" (ibid. 434, capitalization in the original). They aim at opening up "conversations about how people live, rather than close down with a definitive description and analytic statements about the world as it 'truly' exists outside the contingencies of language and culture" (ibid. 435). Thus, evocative autoethnography's aims are 'critical,' 'political,' and even therapeutic (cf. Ellis 1999: 677).

In contrast, analytic autoethnography is concerned with pushing forward theoretical development (cf. Snow/Morrill/Anderson 2003: 185ff.) and takes into account the productive function of abstraction or theoretical distancication. For analytic autoethnography, theoretical distancication (also from membership perspectives) through the use of sociological concepts often allows insights that would not have been possible without these conceptual tools, as "estrangement" (Hirschauer 1994: 340) by means of theoretical verbalization enables sociologists to "explicate local knowledge that for members neither in action situations, nor through vague asking is verbally available" (Amann/Hirschauer 1997: 24, my transl.; cf. Hirschauer 1994; Schmidt/Volbers 2011: 431f.). However, this also means that in analytic autoethnography, theoretical *abstraction* through sociological translation is intimately connected to bodily and sensuous *engagement*; abstraction in this sense functionally presupposes engagement, for only engagement or "apprenticeship" (Wacquant 2005: 465) – i.e., *active* participation (cf. Pink 2009: 63ff.; Pollner/Emerson 2010: 126f.) – ensures access to primary experiences. In this way, the empirical reference of general sociological concepts (e.g. habit or immediate quality) can be established.

VI. Realism, Constructivism, and Sociological Translation

The fact that analytic autoethnographers aim at theoretical descriptions/translations does not mean that they take a naïve realist or representational position,[20] as evocative autoethnographers allege,[21] but neither does their accepting of the theory-ladenness of all empirical observation and analysis necessarily lead to radical forms of constructivism. From a pragmatist point of view, real-

---

20 | Cf. Renn's contribution in the present volume.
21 | However, it is not clear whether Ellis and Bochner (cf. 2006: 433ff.) think about epistemological realism, or ethnographic realism as a specific literary genre, or both (on this topic in general cf. Fuchs/Berg 1993: 38ff.).

ism and constructivism can be regarded as different and analytically separable *dimensions* or *modes* of experience. The observer and the observed for pragmatists are always in trans-action; the same is true for theoretically sensitive researchers and their data. Therefore, asking how trans-actions actually (that is, on empirical grounds) look like is an empirical question rather than one of epistemological dogma. Such a theoretical starting point allows for an outline of sociological translation which neither loses its realist "experiential foundation"[22] nor has to deny its constructive dimension.[23]

In the most abstract sense, sociological translation can be understood with Hirschauer as "transferring" what is observed "into the public sphere of *scientific* communication" (2006: 423, emphasis added; cf. Kalthoff 2006: 163, 170f.); and I would add: *vice versa*. It should have become clear that a constructive dimension is inevitably implied in all acts of translation in general and acts of sociological translation in particular (e.g. because of the scientific habitus in participant observation and the use of theoretical concepts as translational resources in ethnographic writing). Acts of sociological translation are thus constructive in the sense that they co-constitute sociologically relevant phenomena and data. Moreover, when acts of translation appear as verbalizations, as is commonly the case in ethnographic practice, they abstract from the immediate quality of individual experiences and therefore necessarily transcend (some of) the characteristics of situations (what is felt, sensed, etc.); Renn in this context speaks of "selective explication" (2004: 236, my transl.; cf. Fuchs 2002: 125f.; Stanley 1990: 622). Primary experiences are thus only vicariously present in language (cf. Dewey 1983: 132). Translations furthermore are necessarily contingent in the sense that there cannot be the one and only 'right' translation (cf. Renn 2004: 233).

Although acts of sociological translation thus have a constructive dimension, they are not arbitrary, because trans-actions between general sociological concepts and empirical phenomena in research rest upon a 'realist' or 'objective' dimension of action coordination. George Herbert Mead argues that the world "in its unanalyzed state must serve to test the observations and hypothe-

---

22 | Cf. Renn's contribution in the present volume.

23 | From this also follows that one can ask how these 'real' and 'constructive' *dimensions* and *modes* of experience relate to one another. For a critique of crude forms of epistemological realism in ethnography, cf. e.g. Hammersley 1992: 50ff.; for a broad discussion of the relation between epistemology, the philosophy of science, and the sociology of scientific knowledge, cf. Meinefeld 1995. While there seems to be a consensus that naïve and crude forms of realism can be overcome by acknowledging the theory-ladenness of empirical observation and analysis, there are quite contradictory positions when it comes to the question of relativism and the establishment of (scientific) criteria (cf. e.g. Smith/Deemer 2000; Sparkes 2000; Hammersley 1992: 57ff.).

ses which formulate and undertake to solve the problems of science" (1972: 43). This presupposition is necessary to access a world which *may* become problematic, and then becomes a world of scientific discovery. For Mead,

> the data of observation and experiment never lose the *actuality of the unquestioned world* because they can happen for the time being only in the lives of particular individuals, or because they are fitted to serve in the mental processes of discovery. They are *solid realities* that can bridge the gaps between discredited theories and the discoveries of science. [...] What gives to the observation or experiment its validity is its position in the *world that is there, that is not questioned*. It is indeed carefully isolated from what has fallen into question. (Ibid. 47f., emphasis added)

Long before the dichotomization between subject and object, which is an intellectual product of secondary knowledge experience and constitutes the starting point of many epistemological discussions, the world is given, Mead argues, in a mode of pre-reflective, unarticulated, and therefore immediate existence. That the world at the same time is also perspectivated on the level of primary experience due to the trans-action of habits and immediate quality is not a contradictory statement. On the contrary: The active-dispositional dimension of action coordination in the form of habits and the passive-receptive dimension in the form of immediate quality allow one to take the world for granted as a "world of immediate experience" in the first place (Mead 1972: 31; cf. Dewey 1983: 25f., 127f.; Kestenbaum 1977: 19f.). In pragmatist thought, realism and constructivism are not mutually exclusive standpoints but denote different dimensions and modes of experience and action coordination;[24] what is 'real' therefore depends on the *attitudes* of actors towards their environment rather than on universal and over-generalized definitions of the real. But why, one may ask, are all these considerations relevant for a methodology of analytic autoethnography?

VII. SPECIFYING AUTOETHNOGRAPHIC PRACTICE

I would now like to bring together the "theoretical construction" (Boudieu/ Wacquant 1992: 160) of phenomena of primary experience and Mead's methodologically relevant argument about the irreducibility of the unquestioned world of immediate experience. Studies show, and this proves true for 'natives' as well as for autoethnographers, that "thick" (Samudra 2008: 667) or "active"

---

24 | Also cf. Kalthoff 2006: 147, who argues similarly without mentioning pragmatism.

(Emerson/Pollner 2010: 123) participation in specific "social worlds"[25] leads to a specific conditioning of action coordination *even on the level of primary experience* – or to speak with Bourdieu again: not only with regard to "symbolic" but also with regard to *"practical* mastery" (2000: 118, emphasis added);[26] these acquired forms of primary action coordination through active participation in social worlds provide the above-mentioned access point (concerning the relationship between method and research object; cf. section IV) as well as the 'realist' foundation (concerning the relationship between theoretical concepts and research object; cf. section VI) of autoethnographic inquiry. In other words, through *experiencing* specific practices on the level of primary action coordination, autoethnographers can produce an empirical world that is resistant to acts of theoretical abstraction, which means that these practices have the potential to *constrain* the necessarily contingent acts of sociological translation. Therefore autoethnographers are able to ask – *in actu* or *ex post*, tacitly or reflectively – whether certain general sociological concepts can adequately capture the specific practices experienced by them; performing diverse practices thus allows autoethnographers to establish the *empirical reference* (cf. section III) of general sociological concepts (e.g. primary experience or tacit knowledge). While this makes analytic autoethnography a suitable method for researching primary action coordination, one should keep in mind that different translations of experienced phenomena into general sociological discourse are possible.[27]

To summarize, the condition of possibility for establishing a 'resistant' empirical world is that autoethnographers simultaneously perform specific practices (like boxing or glassblowing) as participating members in social worlds *and* carry out the empirical work of sociological translation, which begins

---

25 | For the interactionist concept of social worlds, cf. Strauss 1991, 2008: 209ff.; Becker 2008. Autoethnographers (regardless of whether they identify as such) have for example studied the social world of jazz music (Gibson 2006; Sudnow 1978; Wilf 2010), glassblowing (O'Connor 2007a, 2007b), meditation (Pagis 2009, 2010), martial arts (Samudra 2008), and boxing (Wacquant 2004).

26 | One can say with Mannheim that through the participation in specific "experiential space[s]" (1982: 193), one acquires specific conjunctive knowledge. Mannheim's notion of conjunctive knowledge as a "pre-theoretical and pre-reflective ascription of meaning" (ibid. 230) comes quite close to Dewey's conceptualization of primary experience and immediate quality, and he similarly argues for the *"essential perspectivity* of conjunctive knowledge" (ibid. 252, emphasis added).

27 | This opens up the question of how one should deal with the relationship between 'native' *first-order* translations and sociological *first-order* translations (cf. e.g. Fuchs 2002: 115ff.; Hirschauer 1994: 339f.; Renn 2005: 219), which also touches upon the problem of using multiple theoretical frameworks (e.g. pragmatism and phenomenology).

with their primary experiences in the field. One can say that autoethnographers, as well as ethnographers in general, need to belong to two or more "contexts" (Fuchs 2009: 26), or require, metaphorically speaking, a "split identity" (Hirschauer 1994: 345; cf. Stanley 1990: 623). As the autoethnographer in a way has 'direct' (i.e. pre-lingual) access to the primary experiences under investigation and actively co-constitutes her research object, she is able to methodically control her acts of translation and ensure that the theoretical concepts she uses aptly describe the investigated phenomenon. Autoethnographers thus do not rely on first-order translations to produce second-order translations, because they are able to produce sociological *first*-order translations based on their first-hand experience. This implies that relevant data are neither 'given' exclusively as text, as is the case in transcription-based interpretive analysis (cf. Soeffner 2004: 68f., 82, 92ff.), nor solely through visual and auditory sensory modalities, as is often the case in participant observation (cf. Scheffer 2002: 353; Pink 2009: 64; Pollner/Emerson 2010: 126): instead, as the 'case' is immediately and multi-sensory co-constituted *in* autoethnographic practice, data are extended to a *non-textual dimension* and *transcend the limitations of visual and auditory modes of data production* (cf. Ó Riain 2009).[28]

Even while acknowledging that, first, conventional forms of participant observation are based on multi-modal action coordination and are therefore necessarily rooted in bodily and pre-reflective experiences (cf. Kalthoff 2006: 152f.; Scheffer 2002: 353, 362), and second, that ethnography in general may involve self-observational elements (cf. Atkinson 2006: 400, 402f.; Hirschauer 2006: 426), the point is that *autoethnography* as I define it *makes ethnographers' world-specific embodiments, their acquired tacit knowledge, bodily skills, habits, and felt qualities thematic in the written text* (cf. Anderson 2006a: 384). This means that even though ethnographers may *use* their primary experiences – tacit, unverbalized, and maybe unverbalizable "membership knowledge" (ten Have 2005) which they acquired while working in the field – to co-constitute their research objects (e.g. in the act of observation), this does not necessarily mean that these experiences become the investigated phenomenon (or part of it) *itself*. In contrast, autoethnographers' ways of 'being-in-social-worlds' consequently become part of their research objects. Their primary experiences are therefore not only instruments of observation and data-production but also the 'material' of sociological translations. In other words: When, as pragmatism teaches us, experience can always be considered as a trans-action between organism and environment, then conventional participant observation in ethnography tends to be mainly concerned with analyzing the *environment dimension*, whereas

---

28 | The point here is not that autoethnographic field notes cannot be regarded as relevant data, but that sociological analysis or translation does not *begin* with the process of writing (cf. Hirschauer 2006: 430; Pink 2009: 121).

autoethnography particularly, though not exclusively, focuses on the *organism dimension* of ethnographic experience.[29] Thus whereas all strands of ethnography necessarily and tacitly *use* the organism aspect of experience in and for ethnographic research, autoethnography not only uses it, but turns it into its research object. The differentiation between conventional participant observation and autoethnography is of course only a gradual and ideal-typical one (cf. Anderson 2006a: 383). Autoethnography should be regarded as a specific form or dimension of ethnographic practice in general; in actual research practice, there may be a lot of overlap between the two.

VIII. Trans-Actions between Theoretical and Empirical Practice in Autoethnographic Experience

The 'real-time encounter' of general sociological concepts and empirical phenomena in autoethnographers' experience of social world-specific practices can be seen as *one* moment of the trans-action between theoretical and empirical practice in autoethnographic research; other trans-actional moments include e.g. the *ex post* writing down, interpretation, and coding of different types of theoretically predetermined field notes. In all of these practices, theory and empirical phenomena come together in a functional and co-constitutive relationship (cf. Blumer 1986: 155ff., 165f.; Maines 1989: 169ff.). Furthermore, theoretical reflection as a form of secondary knowledge experience, be it in the form of writing, interpreting, or memoing, will always have effects on autoethnographic real-time practice, since it continually shapes and recursively *re*shapes autoethnographers' theoretical sensitivity and pre-reflective perception, which in turn co-constitutes the phenomena of primary experiences under investigation (cf. Blumer 1986: 155; Hirschauer 2006: 430). Thus the diversity and recursiveness of translation processes in different phases of research practice – e.g. from primary experience to verbalization as well as from (secondary) theoretical reflection to primary experiences – has to be taken into account when reflecting on the methodological foundations of analytic autoethnographic practice.

I will concentrate here on those trans-actional 'moments' that occur while autoethnographers actually execute the practices which they investigate. The fact that autoethnographic research into primary experiences itself relies on pre-reflective forms of primary experiences/tacit knowledge to stay functional-

---

29 | Of course, determining what belongs to the 'environment' or to the 'organism,' respectively, may in some cases prove difficult. One could probably use Polanyi's differentiation between the proximal and distal term of tacit knowing to get a sharper analytic differentiation (cf. 1983: 10ff.); another possibility would be the differentiation between *Leib* and *Körper* (cf. e.g. Gugutzer 2012: 17f.).

ly operational parallels Mead's argument that scientific practice operates in an unquestioned world of immediate experience. However, it is necessary to further expand and specify this argument with regard to the problem of the relation between general sociological concepts and empirical observation/analysis; I argue that there are two different modes in which the primary experiences under investigation can trans-act with general sociological concepts, namely tacit and reflective sociological translation.

Tacit sociological translation is a mode of trans-action between general theoretical concepts and empirical phenomena that functions on the basis of primary experiences, which means that the (un)suitability of theoretical concepts for empirical phenomena is not subject of intentional-reflective acts of interpretation (propositional acts of knowing), but is itself based *in actu* on processes of primary experiences which cannot even *ex post* be (fully) verbally articulated and therefore remain (partially) tacit. One can draw here again on Polanyi's distinction between the proximal and distal term of tacit knowing (1983: 10ff.): Assessing the adequateness of sociological translation can be conceived as the proximal term of tacit knowing; this operation remains tacit and can only be experienced through its consequences, i.e. the distal term of tacit knowing (e.g. to have the feeling that specific concepts fit without being able to fully articulate why). Polanyi writes: "we know the first [proximal; A.A.] term only by relying on our awareness of it for attending to the second [the distal term; A.A.]" (ibid. 10, emphasis removed). Following Dewey, one can add that the assessment of the adequateness of sociological translations with regard to investigating primary experiences and acts of tacit knowing is more a matter of feeling than knowing. This leads to the somewhat paradoxical situation that autoethnographic investigations of primary experiences themselves, even with regard to the assessment of the analytically important process of sociological translation, depend on primary experiences or acts of tacit knowing. With Renn, one could call this a "second order feature of tacit knowledge about tacit knowledge."[30] These considerations point to a number of relevant methodological aspects which I will broadly outline in the last section.

Reflective sociological translation can be regarded as a temporary 'switch' from the mode of tacit sociological translation on the level of primary experience to a mode of secondary reflective knowledge experience based on propositional knowledge or at least on significant symbols (cf. Mead 1910, 1922; Dewey 1983: 127ff.). The mode of reflective sociological translation is a phase in autoethnographic practice in which the trans-action of general sociological concepts and empirical phenomena becomes the object of interpretive processes; thus, reflective sociological translation partially abstracts from tacit sociological translation as well as from the primary experiences under investigation.

---

30 | Cf. Renn's contribution in the present volume.

Especially in the second case – abstracting from primary experiences – there can be problems with "multiple foci" (Anderson 2006a: 380); this means that reflective sociological translation may inhibit the primary experiences which constitute the research object, for example when practices under investigation themselves operate in a fully pre-reflective mode of action coordination (e.g. sensorimotor coordination in boxing, cf. Wacquant 2004: 95ff.). In this case, secondary knowledge processes may interfere with the very practice that is analyzed.

Even though this second mode of sociological translation can be analytically distinguished from the tacit mode, one should keep in mind that secondary knowledge experiences and therefore acts of reflective sociological translation (cf. section II) are always dependent on primary forms of action coordination that remain partially tacit. The two modes of translation should therefore not be opposed to each other; instead, one should ask how both 'interact' and rely on each other.

As *analytic* autoethnography is concerned with trans-actions between sociological theory and empirical phenomena and therefore not only *uses* theory but furthermore has the potential to challenge even general sociological concepts, it is necessary to understand how these trans-actions operate. The concept of sociological translation can be quite useful here, first, because it helps avoid crude forms of realism and constructivism; and second, because it captures different forms of trans-action between theoretical concepts and empirical observation/analysis, e.g. acts of verbalization or the shaping of pre-reflective sensitivity through the acquisition of theoretical knowledge.

IX. Further Considerations and Perspectives – a Non-Conclusion

In this paper, I used the concept of translation as a theoretical heuristic for thinking about some methodological implications of analytic autoethnography. This concept without doubt needs further refining; even though it is used quite often in ethnographic texts and texts on the methodology of ethnography (cf. e.g Kalthoff 2006: 163; Samudra 2008: 668; Stanley 1990: 619; Wacquant 2005: 467) as well as for instance in Actor-Network Theory (cf. Latour 1999: ch. 2) and interactionism (cf. Star/Griesemer 1989; Fujimura 1992), its definitions and applications are quite heterogeneous. The concept of sociological translation as suggested here shares some characteristics with Hammersley's concept of sociological *description* (cf. 1992: ch. 1; Stanley 1990) and Hirschauer's conceptualization of ethnographic writing as *verbalization* (cf. 2006). Acts of sociological translation (and translation in general), sociological description, and verbalization all are constructive, and thus selective and contingent, but the concept of translation in comparison to description and verbalization seems to be more extensive insofar as it not only captures translations from primary experiences into language but also vice versa; it therefore allows taking into account diverse 'directions' of translation and thus opens up the possibility to reflect on how general sociological concepts actually shape pre-reflective forms of perception (theoretical sensitivity) that in autoethnographic real-time practice co-constitute research objects. Furthermore, the concept of translation takes into account translations between different 'media' (primary experiences, sociological discourse, images, etc.) (cf. Fuchs 2009: 25).

Tacit sociological translations do not only imply the *use* of theoretical concepts as translational resources but also entail judging the adequateness of these translations. Since the operation in question has a pre- or extra-lingual character, the question is how it is possible to have tacit knowledge about the adequateness of sociological translations of tacit knowledge/primary experiences if the relevant theoretical concepts which allow for sociological translations are not given – at least not *in actu* – in propositional or symbolized form. The following ideal-typical chain of translations in autoethnographic practice allows contextualizing this question:

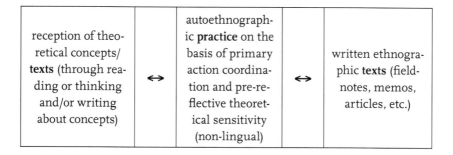

reception of theoretical concepts/ **texts** (through reading or thinking and/or writing about concepts)	↔	autoethnographic **practice** on the basis of primary action coordination and pre-reflective theoretical sensitivity (non-lingual)	↔	written ethnographic **texts** (fieldnotes, memos, articles, etc.)

I will focus in particular on the middle link of the chain, even though the question of how theory becomes 'incorporated' (i.e. translated into theoretical sensitivity) is more or less implicit in the following considerations. One has to understand the operation of pre-reflective theoretical sensitivity in order to be able to understand how the adequateness of tacit sociological translation (or lack thereof) is assessed. In my view, there are two possible conceptualizations of this operation; one explanation draws on a theoretical figure from the psychology of emotions, which conceptualizes the constitution of emotional experience as a co-constitutive interplay between core affect, which includes e.g. dispositions and feelings (in short: primary experiences), and emotion categories, i.e. pre- or extra-lingual conceptual knowledge based on "context-sensitive representations" (Barrett 2006: 41). As emotion categorization can operate on a pre-reflective and even unconscious level, emotional *experiences* can be considered as a kind of pre-reflective alignment between emotion concepts and core affect, with both *constraining* each other: "The idea is that conceptual and affective processing proceed in parallel, with the processing in each limiting, shaping and constraining the way in which the brain achieves a single coherent 'solution'" (ibid. 35), which implies that the alignment of emotion categories and core affect is not arbitrary. This "constraint satisfaction logic" (ibid.) in my view is applicable not only in emotion research, but can also be used to describe the relationship between general sociological concepts and empirical phenomena of primary experiences. From this point of view, pre-reflective theoretical sensitivity (i.e., conceptual theoretical knowledge) and autoethnographers' social world-specific primary experiences can be understood as mutually constraining dimensions of analytic autoethnographic practice.

The second explanation points out that the translation of general sociological concepts into pre-reflective theoretical sensitivity directly shapes the primary action coordination of autoethnographers, which leads to a kind of *conjunctive knowing of general sociological concepts* (cf. Mannheim 1982: 190). Thus sociological concepts would, at least in the case of practiced autoethnography, rather be immediately felt than conceptually known. Assessing the adequacy of sociological translations then could be conceptualized not as an alignment of pre- or extra-lingual *conceptual* knowledge with the primary experiences under investigation, but as an immediate comparison of *felt* primary experiences. The question – which, however, cannot be posed *in actu* by the practicing autoethnographers – is whether the practices (or specific aspects of these practices) performed and investigated by them 'feel' the way relevant general sociological concepts 'feel.' Depending on how 'conceptual knowledge' is grasped analytically in the first model (e.g. on the basis of embodied cognition models; cf. Ignatow 2007), the two explanations may be more similar than it seems at first glance, as both allow one to conceptualize the experienced adequateness of sociological translations as acts of tacit knowing. These tacit assessments are experienced through their consequences, which in turn can be partially verbalized (at least with regard to *what* concepts are deemed adequate). However, the 'why' remains (partially) inexpressible.

Such considerations are important, because in my opinion it is not sufficient to leave the operational functionality of tacit sociological translations unquestioned. Since analytic forms of autoethnography claim to be able to challenge general sociological concepts and thereby to give impulses for their modification, specification, refinement, and/or extension (cf. Snow/Morrill/Anderson 2003), one must not be satisfied with merely gesturing toward their functionality without questioning how they actually operate. Since the autoethnographer as 'constructive' and embodied observer and his "lived sense" (Ostrow 1990: 9) of what may or may not be an adequate sociological translation is the methodical and methodological epicenter of analytic autoethnography (cf. Spry 2001:

720), the validity of its scientific operations cannot be simply retraced through logical or rational reasoning, because autoethnographic practice does not lead to argumentative validity but to "conjunctive validity" through participating in specific "experiential space[s]" (Mannheim 1982: 193). Functionally, the resulting conjunctive knowledge about specific practices is non-theoretical and can therefore not be *represented* by but only *translated* into sociological discourse (cf. Renn 2004: 236). The same holds true for the tacit assessments of the adequateness of sociological translations. The conjunctive knowledge or lived sense of whether theoretical concepts adequately relate to empirical phenomena is not (or at best partially) verbalizable and thus only attainable through analytic autoethnographic *experience*; as it is conjunctively valid, "one cannot avoid letting the ultimate support of evidentness rest on elements in the experienced object which are *qualitative* in content" (Mannheim 1982: 251, emphasis added). This results in the fact that to retrace acts of tacit sociological translation "is in any case not so much a question of demonstration or proof (*Beweis*) as it is of exhibition or showing (*Aufweis*)" (ibid. 252), from which follows that "understanding" (ibid. 204) the primary experiences under investigation as well as experiencing the adequateness of sociological translations presupposes actively *"participating* in the fabric of life of an experiential community" (ibid., emphasis added). The fact that even *ex post*, only some of the underlying conditions of autoethnographic practice can be verbally articulated may trigger further controversial methodological discussions in the future.

Finally, analytic autoethnography has to meet the challenge of situationalist fallacies. Of course, autoethnographic studies have to account for the interactive attunements, negotiations, instructions, and subtle aspects of communication which take place in the field and which may be relevant for acquiring primary action coordination (cf. e.g. O'Connor 2007b: 63; Sudnow 1978: 29ff.; Wacquant 2004: 77ff.); the autoethnographer will seldom act in complete isolation. But autoethnographers should avoid only taking into account what is immediately 'given' in present situations; instead, they should also follow the *trans*situational "associations" of situated practices (Latour 2005: 287ff., 343ff.; cf. Schmidt/Volbers 2011). Thus if analytic autoethnography claims sociological relevance, it has to deal with questions of *social organization* and *collective action coordination* (cf. Becker 2008; Latour 2005: 299ff.; Strauss 1978: 78ff., 2008: 209ff.), and has to ask how specific practices are embedded in wider, spatially and temporally interconnected social contexts.[31] Of course, there is not just one way to a sociological analytic autoethnography.

---

31 | Cf. Kaldewey's contribution in the present volume.

Works Cited

Abbott, Andrew (2004): Methods of Discovery. Heuristics for the Social Sciences, Chicago: U of Chicago P.

Amann, Klaus/Hirschauer, Stefan (1997): "Die Befremdung der eigenen Kultur. Ein Programm," in: Stefan Hirschauer/Klaus Amann (eds.), Die Befremdung der eigenen Kultur. Zur ethnographischen Herausforderung soziologischer Empirie, Frankfurt/Main: Suhrkamp, 7-52.

Anderson, Leon (2006a): "Analytic Autoethnography," in: Journal of Contemporary Ethnography 35.4, 373-395.

—. (2006b): "On Apples, Oranges, and Autopsies. A Response to Commentators," in: Journal of Contemporary Ethnography 35.4, 450-465.

Atkinson, Paul (2006): "Rescuing Autoethnography," in: Journal of Contemporary Ethnography 35.4, 400-404.

Barrett, Lisa Feldman (2006): "Solving the Emotion Paradox. Categorization and the Experience of Emotion," in: Personality and Social Psychology Review 10.1, 20-46.

Becker, Howard S. (2008 [1982]): Art Worlds, Berkeley: U of California P.

Bergmann, Jörg R. (1985): "Flüchtigkeit und methodische Fixierung sozialer Wirklichkeit. Aufzeichnungen als Daten der interpretativen Soziologie," in: Wolfgang Bonß/Heinz Hartmann (eds.), Entzauberte Wissenschaft. Zur Relativität und Geltung soziologischer Forschung, Special Issue of the Journal Soziale Welt, Göttingen: Schwarz, 299-320.

Blumer, Herbert (1986 [1969]): Symbolic Interactionism. Perspective and Method, Berkeley: U of California P.

Bourdieu, Pierre (1990 [1980]): The Logic of Practice, Stanford: Stanford UP.

—. (2000 [1972]): Outline of a Theory of Practice, Cambridge: Cambridge UP.

Bourdieu, Pierre/Wacquant, Loïc J.D. (1992): An Invitation to Reflexive Sociology, Cambridge: Polity.

Charmaz, Kathy (2006): "The Power of Names," in: Journal of Contemporary Ethnography 35.4, 396-399.

Cochran, Molly (ed.) (2010): The Cambridge Companion to Dewey, Cambridge: Cambridge UP.

Delamont, Sara (2009): "The Only Honest Thing. Autoethnography, Reflexivity and Small Crises in Fieldwork," in: Ethnography and Education 4.1, 51-63.

Dewey, John (1917): "The Need for a Recovery of Philosophy," in: John Dewey et al., Creative Intelligence. Essays in the Pragmatic Attitude, New York: Henry Holt, 3-69.

—. (1981 [1925]): Experience and Nature, The Later Works, 1925-1953, Vol. 1: 1925, Carbondale: Southern Illinois UP.

—. (1983 [1922]): Human Nature and Conduct. An Introduction to Social Psychology, The Middle Works, 1899-1924, Vol. 14: 1922, Carbondale: Southern Illinois UP.
—. (1984a [1929]): The Quest for Certainty. A Study of the Relation of Knowledge and Action, The Later Works, 1925-1953, Vol. 4: 1929, Carbondale: Southern Illinois UP.
—. (1984b [1930]): "Qualitative Thought," in: John Dewey, The Later Works, 1925-1953, Vol. 5: 1929-1930, Carbondale: Southern Illinois UP, 241-262.
Dewey, John/Bentley, Arthur F. (1989): Kowing and the Known, The Later Works, 1925-1953, Vol. 16: 1949-1952, Carbondale: Southern Illinois UP.
Duncan, Margot (2004): "Autoethnography. Critical Appreciation of an Emerging Art," in: International Journal of Qualitative Methods 3.4, 28-39.
Ellis, Carolyn (1991): "Sociological Introspection and Emotional Experience," in: Symbolic Interaction 14.1, 23-50.
—. (1997): "Evocative Autoethnography. Writing Emotionally about Our Lives," in: William G. Tierney/Yvonna S. Lincoln (eds.), Representation and the Text. Reframing the Narrative Voice, Albany: State U of New York P, 116-139.
—. (1999): "Heartful Autoethnography," in: Qualitative Health Research 9.5, 669-683.
Ellis, Carolyn S./Bochner, Arthur P. (2006): "Analyzing Analytic Autoethnography. An Autopsy," in: Journal of Contemporary Ethnography 35.4, 429-449.
Fleck, Ludwik (1979 [1935]): Genesis and Development of a Scientific Fact, Chicago: U of Chicago P.
Flick, Uwe/von Kardorff, Ernst/Steinke, Ines (eds.) (2004): A Companion to Qualitative Research, London: Sage.
Fuchs, Martin (2002): "The Praxis of Cognition and the Representation of Difference," in: Heidrun Friese (ed.), Identities. Time, Difference and Boundaries, New York: Berghahn, 109-132.
—. (2009): "Reaching Out; or, Nobody Exists in One Context Only. Society as Translation," in: Translation Studies 2.1, 21-40.
Fuchs, Martin/Berg, Eberhard (1993): "Phänomenologie der Differenz. Reflexionsstufen ethnographischer Repräsentation," in: Martin Fuchs/Eberhard Berg (eds.), Kultur, soziale Praxis, Text. Die Krise der ethnographischen Repräsentation, Frankfurt/Main: Suhrkamp, 11-108.
Fujimura, Joan H. (1992): "Crafting Science. Standardized Packages, Boundary Objects, and 'Translation,'" in: Andrew Pickering (ed.), Science as Practice and Culture, Chicago: U of Chicago P, 168-211.
Gibson, Will (2006): "Material Culture and Embodied Action. Sociological Notes on the Examination of Musical Instruments in Jazz Improvisation," in: The Sociological Review 54.1, 171-187.

Giddens, Anthony (2008 [1984]): The Constitution of Society. Outline of the Theory of Structuration, Cambridge: Polity.

Glaser, Barney G./Strauss, Anselm L. (2006 [1967]): The Discovery of Grounded Theory. Strategies for Qualitative Research, New Brunswick: Transaction.

Goffman, Erving (1959): The Presentation of Self in Everyday Life, New York: Anchor/Doubleday.

Gronow, Antti (2011): From Habits to Social Structures. Pragmatism and Contemporary Social Theory, Frankfurt/Main: Lang.

Gugutzer, Robert (2012): Verkörperungen des Sozialen. Neophänomenologische Grundlagen und soziologische Analysen, Bielefeld: transcript.

Hammersley, Martyn (1989): "The Problem of the Concept. Herbert Blumer on the Relationship between Concepts and Data," in: Journal of Contemporary Ethnography 18.2, 133-159.

—. (1992): What's Wrong with Ethnography? Methodological Explorations, London: Routledge.

Hirschauer, Stefan (1994): "Towards a Methodology of Investigations into the Strangeness of One's Own Culture. A Response to Collins," in: Social Studies of Science 24.2, 335-346.

—. (2006): "Putting Things into Words. Ethnographic Description and the Silence of the Social," in: Human Studies 29.4, 413-441.

Honer, Anne (2004): "Life-World Analysis in Ethnography," in: Flick/von Kardorff/Steinke, Companion, 113-117.

Ignatow, Gabriel (2007): "Theories of Embodied Knowledge. New Directions for Cultural and Cognitive Sociology?," in: Journal for the Theory of Social Behaviour 37.2, 115-135.

Joas, Hans (1996 [1992]): The Creativity of Action, Cambridge: Polity.

Joas, Hans/Knöbl, Wolfgang (2009): Social Theory. Twenty Introductory Lectures, Cambridge: Cambridge UP.

Johnson, Mark (2010): "Cognitive Science and Dewey's Theory of Mind, Thought, and Language," in: Cochran, Cambridge Companion, 123-144.

Jung, Matthias (2010): "John Dewey and Action," in: Cochran, Cambridge Companion, 145-165.

Kalthoff, Herbert (2006): "Beobachtung und Ethnographie," in: Ruth Ayas/Jörg Bergmann (eds.), Qualitative Methoden der Medienforschung, Reinbek: Rowohlt, 146-182.

Kalthoff, Herbert/Hirschauer, Stefan/Lindemann, Gesa (eds.) (2008): Theoretische Empirie. Zur Relevanz qualitativer Forschung, Frankfurt/Main: Suhrkamp.

Kelle, Udo (2007): "'Emergence' vs. 'Forcing' Empirical Data? A Crucial Problem of 'Grounded Theory' Reconsidered," in: Historical Social Research, supplement 19, 133-156.

Kelle, Udo/Kluge, Susann (2010): Vom Einzelfall zum Typus. Fallvergleich und Fallkontrastierung in der qualitativen Sozialforschung, Wiesbaden: VS.

Kestenbaum, Victor (1977): The Phenomenological Sense of John Dewey. Habit and Meaning, Atlantic Highlands: Humanities.

Latour, Bruno (1999): Pandora's Hope. Essays on the Reality of Science Studies, Cambridge: Harvard UP.

—. (2005): Reassembling the Social. An Introduction to Actor-Network-Theory, Oxford: Oxford UP.

Lindemann, Gesa (2008): "Theoriekonstruktion und empirische Forschung," in: Kalthoff/Hirschauer/Lindemann, Theoretische Empirie, 107-128.

Lofland, John (1995): "Analytic Ethnography. Features, Failings, and Futures," in: Journal of Contemporary Ethnography 24.1, 30-67.

Maines, David R. (1989): "Herbert Blumer on the Possibility of Science in the Practice of Sociology. Further Thoughts," in: Journal of Contemporary Ethnography 18.2, 160-177.

Mannheim, Karl (1982): Structures of Thinking, London: Routledge and Kegan Paul.

Mead, George Herbert (1910): "Social Consciousness and the Consciousness of Meaning," in: Psychological Bulletin 7.12, 397-405.

—. (1922): "A Behavioristic Account of the Significant Symbol," in: The Journal of Philosophy 19.6, 157-163.

—. (1972 [1938]): The Philosophy of the Act, Chicago: U of Chicago P.

Meinefeld, Werner (1995): Realität und Konstruktion. Erkenntnistheoretische Grundlagen einer Methodologie der empirischen Sozialforschung, Opladen: Leske und Budrich.

—. (2004): "Hypotheses and Prior Knowledge in Qualitative Research," in: Flick/von Kardorff/Steinke, Companion, 153-158.

O'Connor, Erin (2007a): "Embodied Knowledge in Glassblowing. The Experience of Meaning and the Struggle towards Proficiency," in: Chris Shilling (ed.), Embodying Sociology. Retrospect, Progress and Prospects, Malden: Blackwell, 126-141.

—. (2007b): "Hot Glass. The Calorific Imagination of Practice in Glassblowing," in: Craig Calhoun/Richard Sennett (eds.), Practicing Culture, London: Routledge, 57-81.

Ó Riain, Seán (2009): "Extending Ethnographic Case Study," in: David Byrne/Charles C. Ragin (eds.), The Sage Handbook of Case Based Methods, London: Sage, 289-306.

Ostrow, James M. (1990): Social Sensitivity. A Study of Habit and Experience, Albany: State U of New York P.

Pagis, Michal (2009): "Embodied Self-Reflexivity," in: Social Psychology Quarterly 72.3, 265-283.

—. (2010): "From Abstract Concepts to Experiential Knowledge. Embodying Enlightenment in a Meditation Center," in: Qualitative Sociology 33.4, 469-489.

Pollner, Melvin/Emerson, Robert M. (2010): "Ethnomethodology and Ethnography," in: Paul Atkinson, et al. (eds.), Handbook of Ethnography, London: Sage, 119-135.

Pink, Sarah (2009): Doing Sensory Ethnography, Los Angeles: Sage.

Polanyi, Michael (1983 [1966]): The Tacit Dimension, Gloucester: Peter Smith.

Reckwitz, Andreas (2002): "Toward a Theory of Social Practices. A Development in Culturalist Theorizing," in: European Journal of Social Theory 5.2, 243-263.

Reed-Danahay, Deborah (1997): "Introduction," in: Deborah Reed-Danahay (ed.), Auto/Ethnography. Rewriting the Self and the Social, Oxford: Berg, 1-17.

Renn, Joachim (2004): "Wissen und Explikation. Zum kognitiven Geltungsanspruch der 'Kulturen,'" in: Friedrich Jaeger/Burkardt Liebsch (eds.), Handbuch der Kulturwissenschaften, Band 1: Grundlegung und Schlüsselbegriffe, Stuttgart: Metzler, 232-250.

—. (2005): "Die gemeinsame menschliche Handlungsweise. Das doppelte Übersetzungsproblem des sozialwissenschaftlichen Kulturvergleichs," in: Ilja Srubar/Joachim Renn/Ulrich Wenzel (eds.), Kulturen vergleichen. Sozial- und kulturwissenschaftliche Grundlagen und Kontroversen, Wiesbaden: VS, 195-227.

Ryle, Gilbert (2009 [1946]): "Knowing How and Knowing That," in: Gilbert Ryle, Collected Papers, Vol. 2: Collected Essays 1929-1968, London: Routledge, 222-235.

Samudra, Jaida Kim (2008): "Memory in Our Body. Thick Participation and the Translation of Kinesthetic Experience," in: American Ethnologist 35.4, 665-681.

Schatzki, Theodore R./Knorr Cetina, Karin/von Savigny, Eike (eds.) (2001): The Practice Turn in Contemporary Theory, London: Routledge.

Scheffer, Thomas (2002): "Das Beobachten als sozialwissenschaftliche Methode. Von den Grenzen der Beobachtbarkeit und ihrer methodischen Bearbeitung," in: Doris Schaeffer/Gabriele Müller-Mundt (eds.), Qualitative Gesundheits- und Pflegeforschung, Bern: Huber, 351-374.

Schmidt, Robert/Volbers, Jörg (2011): "Siting Praxeology. The Methodological Significance of 'Public' in Theories of Social Practices," in: Journal for the Theory of Social Behaviour 41.4, 419-440.

Smith, John K./Deemer, Deborah K. (2000): "The Problem of Criteria in the Age of Relativism," in: Norman K. Denzin/Yvonna S. Lincoln (eds.), The Sage Handbook of Qualitative Research, 2nd ed., Thousand Oaks: Sage, 877-896.

Snow, David A./Morrill, Calvin/Anderson, Leon (2003): "Elaborating Analytic Ethnography. Linking Fieldwork and Theory," in: Ethnography 4.2, 181-200.
Soeffner, Hans-Georg (2004): Auslegung des Alltags – Der Alltag der Auslegung. Zur wissenssoziologischen Konzeption einer sozialwissenschaftlichen Hermeneutik, Konstanz: UVK.
Sparkes, Andrew C. (2000): "Autoethnography and Narratives of Self. Reflections on Criteria in Action," in: Sociology of Sport Journal 17.1, 21-43.
Spry, Tami (2001): "Performing Autoethnography. An Embodied Methodological Praxis," in: Qualitative Inquiry 7.6, 706-732.
Stanley, Liz (1990): "Doing Ethnography, Writing Ethnography. A Comment on Hammersley," in: Sociology 24.4, 617-627.
Star, Susan Leigh/Griesemer, James R. (1989): "Institutional Ecology, 'Translations' and Boundary Objects. Amateurs and Professionals in Berkeley's Museum of Vertebrate Zoology, 1907-1939," in: Social Studies of Science 19.3, 387-420.
Strauss, Anselm L. (1987): Qualitative Analysis for Social Scientists, Cambridge: Cambridge UP.
—. (1991 [1978]): "A Social World Perspective," in: Anselm L. Strauss, Creating Sociological Awareness. Collective Images and Symbolic Representations, New Brunswick: Transaction, 233-244.
—. (2008 [1993]): Continual Permutations of Action, New Brunswick: Transaction.
Sudnow, David (1978): Ways of the Hand. The Organization of Improvised Conduct, Cambridge: Harvard UP.
ten Have, Paul (2005): "The Notion of Member Is the Heart of the Matter. On the Role of Membership Knowledge in Ethnomethodological Inquiry," in: Historical Social Research 30.1, 28-53.
Vaughan, Diane (2009): "Analytic Ethnography," in: Peter Hedström/Peter Bearman (eds.): Oxford Handbook of Analytical Sociology, Oxford: Oxford UP, 688-711.
Vryan, Kevin (2006): "Expanding Analytic Autoethnography and Enhancing Its Potential," in: Journal of Contemporary Ethnography 35.4, 405-409.
Wacquant, Loïc (2004): Body and Soul. Notebooks of an Apprentice Boxer, Oxford: Oxford UP.
—. (2005): "Carnal Connections. On Embodiment, Apprenticeship, and Membership," in: Qualitative Sociology 28.4, 445-474.
Wilf, Eitan (2010): "Swinging within the Iron Cage. Modernity, Creativity, and Embodied Practice in American Postsecondary Jazz Education," in: American Ethnologist 37.3, 563-582.

Racial Formation, Implicit Understanding, and Problems with Implicit Association Tests

Alexis Shotwell

I.   INTRODUCTION

In this paper, I argue that the concept of 'implicit understanding' includes affective, bodily, presuppositional, and socially-situated forms of understanding. I claim that implicit understanding is politically and epistemically salient to race, racism, and racial formation, and that it can supplement, sharpen, and enrich accounts of, among other things, implicit bias. Theorizing the political transformation of racialized implicit bias benefits from such an account of understanding and knowing. First, I offer some definitions of race and racism and focus my attention on personally-held understandings of race in relation to systemic injustice; second, I lay out an account of implicit understanding; third, I argue that Implicit Association Tests (IATs), along with cognate experimental instruments, rely on a relatively imprecise definition of the implicit – an imprecision mirrored even in philosophical discussions of the issues IATs raise. I conclude by offering some suggestions for both philosophical and empirical work on 'racism without words.'

II.   RACIAL FORMATION AND RACISM

In thinking about race and racial cognition, it is useful to have a working definition of race and racism. I follow a tendency in sociology that understands the production of racial categories and subjectivities to be ongoing and foundationally relational. Sociologists Michael Omi and Howard Winant canonically call this racial formation, "the process by which social, economic and political forces determine the content and importance of racial categories, and by which they are in turn shaped by racial meanings" (1994: 61). On this account, race acquires meaning through social processes, rather than accruing to something 'underneath' them. So, racial formation names a process through which physical and material things in the world, alongside social and cultural relations, become differentiated and categorized as racial; the social category we call race just *is* this process of formation. To adopt a racial formation view of race is not to deny that race exists, carries meaning, and has effects, yet it is to deny that those meanings are the natural result of phenotype, that culture arises from particular bodies, or that biology is destiny. Instead, such a view is compatible with evidence that our biological being takes form through social practices (cf. Fausto-Sterling 2005, 2008).

'Race' can thus be seen as an unstable and mutable category. Likewise, 'racism' can be understood in a range of ways. It is common to think about racism as explicit, verbal expressions of prejudice, intolerance, or hatred (cf. Garcia 2004). More recent critical race theory has begun to articulate the sense that racism could be understood as a form of active ignorance (cf. Mills 1998, 2007; Outlaw 2007: 197; Sullivan/Tuana 2007; Alcoff 2007: 39), although even these conceptions of "epistemologies of ignorance" (cf. Sullivan/Tuana 2007; Alcoff 2007) focus on propositional content (as e.g. when someone makes an 'ignorant judgment' or an unintentionally racist remark; of course, people and policies can be explicitly racist even when they claim the opposite).

As I will discuss below, there are other, non-verbal sorts of racism; for example, a person might shrink away from physical contact with people of color on the bus, or reach out to feel a black stranger's hair. This sort of racism articulates with other, perhaps equally unstated, forms. Tacit racism, which could be made propositional, might be 'unpacked' in these cases; perhaps on some level the person shrinking away or reaching out to touch has the unspoken belief that people of color are dirty, or that their hair is socially available to touch. The affect underlying these beliefs may take the form of disgust, discomfort, curiosity, entitlement, and more (cf. Blum 2002; Valls 2009). Sally Haslanger (2004) would, I think, understand these forms of racism as 'agent oppression.'

At the same time, as Haslanger (ibid.) argues, we should worry about structural oppression as well as individual wrongdoing; consider for example US mandatory sentencing laws: given the disproportionate arrests levied in communities of color, often because of implicit racism, people of color will be more likely to enter the criminal justice system. Once in, mandatory sentencing predicts and perpetuates – alongside less bureaucratic means – the vast overrepresentation of people of color in prisons, jails, and on permanent probation (cf. e.g. Davis 2003). Along these lines, geographer Ruth Gilmore defines racism as "the state-sanctioned and/or extra-legal production and exploitation of group-differentiated vulnerabilities to premature death, in distinct yet densely interconnected political geographies" (2007: 28). Notice that Gilmore's definition does not rule out a role for traditional understandings of racism as expressed prejudice; people enact systems, after all, and can perpetuate or resist their effects. Notice also that there is a perhaps surprising lack of reference to race in Gilmore's definition of racism. The emphasis is on group-differentiation and death, and we could read the claim here as an ostensive definition: how do we tell if racialization is at work, and thus if race is at issue? Look at who is dying prematurely.[1] This is a way to talk about the sense in which racism involves *group*-differentiated harm; pointing to a single counter-example (e.g., someone who has not been harmed in the ways at issue) will not defeat the claim. 'Death' here means physical death – as a result of violence, illness, inadequate health care, and so on – but also, I think, the more ineffable sense of a 'death of spirit' arising from the daily denial of the possibility to live with dignity. It also means the civil death of being classified as a nonperson (as were blacks in the antebellum US South), a civic child (as are many Aboriginal peoples in contemporary Canada), or a noncitizen unable to participate in fundamental self-determining civic activities (as are undocumented migrants, forced refugees, or people on parole and permanently denied the exercise of the vote, again in the US). Orlando Patterson (1982) has compellingly articulated an account of "social death" as a key piece of US chattel slavery.

There is real work to do on the question of how we ought to understand the relationship between oppression enacted by individual agents on the one hand, and by systemic or structural means on the other. I believe that structural change has had, and will have, significant antiracist effects – perhaps more significant ones than changes in individual people's racism. I affirm Sally Haslanger's claim that

[l]iving together in peace and justice does not require that we love each other, or that we even fully respect each other, but rather that we conform our actions to principles of justice... for many of those who suffer injustice, "private" attitudes are not the worst problem; systemic institutional subordination is. (2004: 121-122)

However, because racialization arises from complex social relations among people, it will be important to transform people's understanding of racial formation and its connection with structural oppression. The recursive movement between agent-level understanding and structure-level conditions for dignity or oppression means that it is justified to attend to how people personally experience and transform their own and other's racism. Indeed, oppression is fundamentally enacted by individual agents, and individual affects and networks

---

1 | Ladelle McWhorter offers a similarly heterodox reading of racism in her defense of Foucault's claim that ableism and heterosexism can be coherently understood as forms of racism; each, along with other social practices, is grounded in a eugenic understanding of 'good genes' and thus aims at an imagined ideal of whiteness (cf. McWhorter 2004, 2009).

of understanding are always to some extent social.² To get at that level, it is worth attending to our implicit understanding of racialization.

III. Implicit Understanding: Skill-based, Somatic, Tacit, and Affective

Elsewhere I have attempted to articulate a more precise nomenclature and lineage for thinking about the cluster of concepts I have only gestured toward so far in this paper (cf. Shotwell 2011). I will reprise the kernel of that analysis here, but without tracing the philosophical genealogies that provide the backstory for my taxonomy. Note, though, that philosophers have been talking about this topic for a very long time and in a wide range of subdisciplines from phenomenology and hermeneutics to political theory and, more recently, psychology.

I suggest the umbrella term 'implicit understanding.' 'Implicit' here carries the meaning of something not (or not currently) expressed in words, whereas 'understanding' is meant to name an epistemic state that in general may not achieve the status of knowledge traditionally defined. Implicit understanding, then, may not meet the epistemic requirements we apply to propositions about the world and the belief states we expect from good knowers. However, such understanding is epistemically salient, particularly to our capacities to address the 'ingredients' contributing to things like implicit bias. It is plausible to think that there is a relationship between our explicit beliefs, our actions, and salient implicit ingredients in our political and moral orientation toward the world. We can distinguish between four sorts of implicit understanding: practical or skill-based forms of understanding, socially-situated habitus, tacit but propositionalizable beliefs, and affective or emotional understanding. While they might run alongside or underneath propositional knowing and be conceptually separable from it, these forms of understanding are inextricable – they can be teased apart conceptually, but from the point of view of a subject enacting understanding or knowledge, they will all be present to one degree or another.

The notion of practical, skill-based, or 'knowing-how' understanding has received a resurgence of attention in the last ten years.³ Against prevailing trends in that literature, I understand skilled knowledge to centrally involve ability. We can know *about* how to do something – i.e., possess and correctly apply propositional knowledge about how one might do something – without hav-

---

2 | I thank Jeanine Weekes Schroer for helping me clarify this point. For an extended engagement with this idea from a Deleuzean perspective see Protevi (2009).

3 | On the question of whether knowing-how is a form of knowing-that, or propositional knowledge, see Fantl (2008); Koethe (2002); Stanley (2010, 2011); Stanley/Williamson (2001); Tsai (2011); Williams (2008); and Young (2008).

ing the relevant ability. As I am using the idea of skilled know-how, it is a kind of ability, a capacity to do things. Generally, skills are embodied and prototypically include capacities like swimming or playing a musical instrument, but they also include non-physical abilities like holding a chess game in mind and making moves without a board present. Skilled abilities intersect with political categories like class – the ability to fix cars shows up more in working-class communities than does the ability to play the piano. In other respects, though, this form of nonpropositional knowledge is less central to the kinds of political categories I discuss here (for example race).

Skilled knowledge is often somatic, but there is another layer of somatic implicit understanding: that of socially-situated embodiment. Pierre Bourdieu calls this incorporated expression of social norms and mores 'habitus' – the bodily understanding of, for example, how far apart it is appropriate to stand in casual conversation with a co-worker, how loudly it is acceptable to speak in a library, etc. Note that this form of currently-implicit embodied understanding includes content that may be explicit in the sense of being obvious, particularly when social norms of embodiment are violated or unfamiliar. Consider for example the social expectations governing hand-holding between men in the US and Afghanistan: In the US, hand-holding between men usually signifies either a family relationship (in which case it is mostly limited to fathers and young sons), or, more often, a gay relationship. Straight men as a rule do not hold hands with each other. In Afghanistan, in contrast, for unrelated men to hold hands with one another does not signify that they are gay. This is not a matter of skilled bodily knowledge, but rather of the habitus, or socially-situated embodiment, which names the bodily expression and experience of social practices.

Tacit or presuppositional knowledge names contingently unspeakable or not-currently-explicit but propositionalizable understanding. We might think of this as commonsensical understanding, presupposition, or prejudice. Beliefs that are not consciously asserted, go without saying, or have been internalized but nevertheless *could* be verbally expressed fall into this category of implicit understanding. We rely on such currently tacit former propositions to the extent that we do not treat them as claims: they are foundational, beyond or beneath question. For example, take Wittgenstein's discussion of things about which we are certain, such that it would be unusual in ordinary conversation to make observations like "every human has parents," or (looking at one's own hand) "this is my hand!" (1986: §412). At some point, we did not take for granted the idea that everybody has parents, or other equally commonsensical beliefs. There are also commonsensical beliefs that are incorrect, which become perceptible as such at moments of epistemic crisis or during a paradigm shift (think for example of the shift from a Ptolemaic [geocentric] to a Copernican [heliocentric] cosmology).

Finally, affective or emotional understanding forms a significant part of epistemically salient but nonpropositional knowing. This sort of understanding names both accepted emotions (like love, anger, jealousy, and so on) as well as more inchoate or idiosyncratic feelings that are less easy to name.[4] Feeling can be both an epistemic resource – a guide for reason and knowledge – and a more direct site for meaningful understanding. It is distinct from skills, habitus, and tacit knowledge in that it does not necessarily follow or involve any of those categories, which can manifest without carrying any feeling in particular.

Indeed, these four types of unspeakable or unspoken understanding have significant dissimilarities, and are distinguishable from propositional knowledge: Whereas skills involve abilities to perform specific tasks like swimming, or landing an airplane, merely being able to make correct propositional claims about those tasks will not equate with actually swimming, or landing a plane. Likewise, having a feeling is significantly unlike socially-situated understanding; we may dread or adore formal dinner parties in ways that do not depend on knowing which fork to use, or how to gracefully pick up chana masala with our fingers. Commonsense understandings are frequently not subjected to tests of truth and justification that we expect propositional knowledge to withstand, and they may contrast with other forms of implicit understanding, as when someone loves their working-class family but holds as commonsense that they are not as smart as middle-class people.[5]

However, it would be a mistake to characterize the four sorts of implicit understanding I have been delineating as different species of knowledge, or as ontologically separate. They may be distinguishable but I do not believe that they can be finally disentangled, because understanding is at root a social relation – understandings are held by individual agents, but are not restricted to the scale of the individual. Since individuals enter into consciousness and maintain their subjectivity as persons always in relational contexts, we are ontologically interdependent; and our knowledge claims must track this. We are embodied, feeling, thinking, socially responsive beings, and our experience of social and political realities like race engages us on all of those levels. So, even if the four sorts of implicit understanding are not separable I still offer a taxonomy, because while delineating them helps clarify the terms we use to theorize phenomena like implicit bias and racism without words, the main point is not a

---

4 | Sue Campbell (1998) discusses examples like the "Sunday morning" feeling as a particular affect experienced especially in North America, or the "white master's well-fed dog" feeling of nonwhites working for white people in apartheid-era South Africa; see also Massumi (2002).

5 | On class and the category of 'stupidity' see Kadi (1999) and Heldke (2006). On the mechanisms by which people internalize harmful views of groups to which they belong, see Inzlicht/Schmader (2012) and Steele (2010).

critique of definitional unclarity: As I will discuss further below, the main use of distinguishing among different sorts of implicit understanding is to first better conceive of and then transform politically important categories defined by complex systems of oppression, such as racialization.

IV. WHAT DOES A CONCEPTION OF IMPLICIT UNDERSTANDING OFFER IATs AND ASSOCIATED STUDIES?

Implicit Association Tests (IATs) have captured people's attention in a wide range of fields. They are arguably the most popular and frequently-cited instrument for measuring implicit attitudes, beliefs, orientations, or feelings. Most IATs aim to measure the degree to which research subjects associate two concepts (usually social categories, like 'Democrats' and 'Republicans') with two attributes (usually value judgments like 'good' and 'bad') (cf. Nosek et al. 2007: 36; Project Implicit; Greenwald/McGhee/Schwartz 1998; Greenwald/Banaji 1995). In the case of IATs assessing implicit racism – which researchers tend to characterize as racist views that the subject would or does deny holding – the measure of racism is the degree of difficulty which subjects exhibit in grouping 'positive' words with images of racialized (non-white) faces. This degree of difficulty is gauged by the length of time it takes subjects to pair, for example, Black faces with a positive word like 'wonderful.' Images and words flash on a computer screen, and subjects press one of two keys on the keyboard to associate the image with a noun or descriptor.

In the discipline of philosophy, most of the papers citing work in psychology about IATs have relied on data from them to either assess the ethical significance of implicit bias (cf. Kelly/Roedder 2008: 522) or to argue for the need to redress the effects of implicit bias on social groups inside or outside the profession (cf. Saul n.d.). As yet, this literature lacks a clearly delineated and widely-shared vocabulary for the various kinds of racism without words that right now are gesturally named by the concepts of 'unconscious racism,' 'implicit attitudes,' or 'implicit bias,' among other terms. As Kelley and Roedder, two philosophers writing about the ethical implications of implicit bias, ask:

[W]hat exactly is the nature of these implicit attitudes? Implicit racial attitudes raise a number of novel moral issues; getting a grip on them will require a better understanding of the character of the implicit attitudes themselves. As we pointed out earlier, they might be construed as Freudian unconscious states or as very minimal mental associations, and these options are far from exhaustive. Resolving this question will take both experimental and conceptual work. (2008: 530)

They do not, however, attempt to answer the question of what the nature of "implicit attitudes" might be, instead moving on to assess the ethical implications of these unspecified attitudes. Similarly, consider Tamar Gendler's article "On the Epistemic Costs of Implicit Bias," which characterizes the enactment of implicit bias as showing a gap between the "automatic or habitual or default responses on the one hand, and our reflective commitments on the other" (2011: 38). In this paper Gendler builds on her important work on 'aliefs,' which on her account name these non-reflective commitments, or what she frames as a 'representational-affective-behavioral' triad. Gendler characterizes the salient epistemic content of aliefs as consisting in "implicit associations and habitual patterns of response" (ibid. 42). Gendler's account of the effects of this gap between belief and alief is a good example of a more general tendency in the current literature on implicit bias.[6] It would be useful to advance this work to arrive at an account of the differences among *automatic, habitual,* and *default* responses.

As I will discuss in more detail below, the psychological literature also offers very gestural ideas of what kind of implicitness it treats. In a recent article summarizing data from 2.5 million completed Implicit Association Tests, Nosek et al. say that this work "provides a glimpse" of what they frame as "implicit social cognition – thoughts and feelings of which the respondent may be unaware or unable to control" (2007: 36). Greenwald, McGhee, and Schwartz define the 'implicit' in their version of the IAT thus: "Implicit attitudes are manifest as actions or judgments that are under the control of automatically activated evaluation, without the performer's awareness of that causation" (1998: 1464). Again, the nature of this "automatically activated evaluation" controlling actions or judgments is unspecified. "Awareness" is the salient epistemic notion in much of this discussion.

The proliferation of accounts that draw upon a distinction, however wooly, between what is and what is not reflective, explicit, and propositional in our experience indicates that theorists need an account of the implicit, because there is no widely-held consensus on what exactly the implicit is yet. We should worry about the unspecified character of this non-reflective, inexplicit epistemic content. Or, to put it in positive terms: We can offer thicker and more adequate accounts of this content; more specific delineations will help our theoretical work in perhaps unexpected ways. That we are talking about something inarticulate does not mean that we cannot articulate more precisely what we are talking about.[7] This is a good example of a situation in which philosophy can

---

6 | For more on the gesture without sufficient explication toward non-semantic conditions for truth claims and action, including political action, see Shotwell 2011: 4-7.

7 | It is useful to have an expanded terminology of implicit understanding rather than the more specific concept of implicit bias, because the epistemically and politically

help move other disciplines – sociology and psychology in particular – towards conceptual clarity and precision. If it is important for our scientific measures of attitudes and their effects to express strong objectivity, it is as important for our theoretical accounts to have similar precision. The proliferation of names for this epistemic category, particularly as it shows up in thinking about politicized inequality and injustice, indicates the usefulness – perhaps the need – for a more rigorous terminology, as all of these formulations are somewhat unwieldy and quite imprecise. What does it mean for something to 'go without words'? What is a bias? Does 'implicit' refer to something that can never be made explicit, or to something that is implied? How ought we to think about 'implicit associations'? Are 'habitual patterns of response' socially created? What does it mean for something to be 'unconscious'? And so on.

As in the philosophical literature, there has not been a thorough assessment of what exactly psychologists include in the category of 'implicit bias.' Indeed, there is frequently a slippage between the terms 'implicit' and 'unconscious' – a fact that has given traction to critics of IATs as meaningful psychological instruments. Recall the definition from one of the first academic publications on the IAT: "Implicit attitudes are manifest as actions or judgments that are under the control of automatically activated evaluation, without the performer's awareness of that causation" (Greenwald/McGhee/Schwartz 1998: 1464). Here the authors claim that implicit *attitudes* are manifest as judgment or action, and the locus of the implicit is an "automatically activated evaluation." They express, then, intertwined notions of something being automatic and something manifesting without our self-reflective awareness of what caused our action or evaluation. In an earlier, widely-cited article, Greenwald and Banaji write that they are interested in the "indirect, unconscious, or implicit mode of operation for attitudes and stereotypes" (1995: 4). These definitions are not so much definitions as clusters of labels for related but different phenomena – attitudes, 'automatic' responses, indirect *or* unconscious *or* implicit modes of operation that manifest as attitudes *or* stereotypes *or* prejudices.

There are two main effects of this kind of conceptual unclarity. First, lacking precise conceptual delineation leaves researchers working on implicit bias within psychology open to critiques arising from misapprehension rather than genuine scientific worry (though such worries are sometimes also present). Second, overly general definitions of the sort exemplified above may limit the experimental results offered by IATs and similar tests.

On the first point, consider an example that attempts to give very explicit definitions of the terms in question. Blanton and Jaccard's (2008) critical review of studies of what they frame as 'unconscious racism' posits that the

---

salient contents of our consciousness do not all take the form of bias (in the sense of politically harmful orientations to the social world).

primary characteristic of this sort of racism is that it is outside of consciousness – that subjects who manifest unconscious racism do not know (or are not aware) that they have racist orientations toward the world. They offer a close analysis of three ways in which we might understand something to be 'unconscious:' we may not accurately predict the potentially racist effects of our actions, we may not understand the causes of our racialized preferences, or, finally, we may exhibit what they characterize as 'inaccessible attitudes.' They judge that it is this final sort of racism that IATs aim to reveal. Blanton and Jaccard are to be congratulated for attempting to give explicit definitions of the key terms in the field they critique, but their reading of the terms is itself faulty: They offer no justification for their characterization of the object in question as 'unconscious racism.' Their slide from the term 'implicit beliefs,' used in the review essay they cite as a lead-in to their discussion, to the terminology of 'unconscious racism' has significant theoretical effects. Repeatedly, the authors they cite as examples of proponents of the view that there is racism not in words use terms like 'beliefs,' 'feelings,' 'emotions,' and 'attitudes.' Blanton and Jaccard subsume all these terms under the 'unconscious' without discussion or justification, and then proceed to critique the notion of the unconscious. If researchers on implicit bias and its effects offered clearer definitions, this sort of generalization would be more difficult for critics to make.

The more important result of an insufficiently fine-grained definition of the components IATs and similar instruments aim to measure is experimental. Tests aiming to measure implicit associations do, I believe, measure something meaningful: they show that there is something we can call implicit bias. But what they measure could be more nuanced and more meaningful. That is, there is a proliferation of data points tracking social objects other than race – gender and professionalization, disability, gender and science, fatness, sexuality, and more. But because what comprises implicit bias *and* what comprises each of the social categories tested is unspecified, the data gathered cannot answer important questions: Do people's emotional responses line up with their common-sense understandings? When currently tacit racist beliefs based on incorrect information are directly brought into explicit conversation and challenged with correct information, do they change? What role do socially-situated and embodied experiences play in shaping people's first-pass responses to social categories like racialization? What is the relationship between association, stereotype, prejudice, and action?

V. Test Driving the Taxonomy

The answer to questions like these matter for people who want to change the harmful effects of racism and other social relations based on oppression. Having established that there are implicit biases and that they operate in a number of different scenarios, experimenters could fruitfully build on this insight. They could assess, first, whether a taxonomy of the sort I lay out here in fact shows up in experimental contexts; whether people's emotions, presuppositions, and bodily responses are measurable and relevant, and how we might measure patterned bodily responses of the sort that Bourdieu calls the habitus to determine whether and how they might be involved in potentially propositional responses to racial situations. Second, they could begin to present their results in terms that would offer more traction for action. For example, imagine that most people who exhibit racist implicit biases (i.e., almost everybody) demonstrate emotional aversion to non-white people and also tacit prejudice based on inaccurate information. In order to counteract these wrong propositions, the emotional aversion involved would also need to be addressed. Similarly, if people have socially-shaped somatic responses that manifest racism in ways that articulate with wrong beliefs, it would be useful to examine how such social cognition is shaped.

I am not a psychological researcher, and so I offer only speculations on how studies might be designed to address the questions with which I closed section IV. Consider, though, one of the paradigmatic Implicit Association Tests about race. Reading this study using a conception of implicit understanding demonstrates how such a conception might nuance and clarify the empirical work. In the 'Race-Weapons IAT,' participants are tested to determine the degree to which they associate Black American and White American faces with either weapons or harmless objects. The weapons include axes and maces as well as more common ones like guns. The harmless objects include things like wallets and water bottles. The majority of people who take this test reveal a predominant implicit association between Black Americans and weapons, and between White Americans and harmless objects.[8] This test is significant, because it suggests that quick, non-reflective judgments are more shaped by implicit associations than are reflective, considered assessments. Since police officers, among others, are called upon to make very fast responses to stimuli and to respond differently to people holding weapons or harmless objects, we can see how these kinds of implicit associations can – and do – have life-or-death effects.[9] How might thinking about the implicit understanding mobilized in the case of assessing whether someone is holding a dangerous weapon help advance work on implicit bias? Examples from the US context abound. One example would be the case of Oscar Grant, who was killed on January 1, 2009,

---

8 | See Project Implicit at harvard.edu: https://implicit.harvard.edu/implicit/Launch?study=/user/education/weapons/weapons.expt.xml.

9 | For research on the possibly racialized basis of police-involved shootings, see Correll et al. (2002), Correll et al. (2007), and Doerner/Ho (1994).

by BART police officer Johannes Mehserle. Grant was face-down on the ground and unarmed when Mehserle shot him in the back. Mehserle was convicted of involuntary manslaughter and served less than two years for the killing. Consider also George Zimmerman's February 26, 2012 killing of Trayvon Martin, a young African-American man walking home from the store; Zimmerman was not a law enforcement officer but led a neighborhood watch organization for a gated community and had a permit to carry a gun. Zimmerman was acquitted on July 13, 2013.[10]

Perhaps the main way my conception of implicit understanding helps advance an analysis of the effects of implicit bias is that it requires us to consider non-experimental contexts in which implicit bias has effects. At least two of the four kinds of understanding I delineate are not directly at play in most laboratory contexts: skills and habitus. A base-line condition for the effects of race-weapons associations is skill – the ability to accurately aim and fire a weapon, e.g. in the case of police-involved shootings. The habitus that activates that skill involves the non-reflexive, socially-shaped, bodily response to people who officers read as having hostile intent and the means to cause harm. The capacity to recognize and respond to threat is a vital component of policing, and so it matters very much that this capacity is so strongly torqued by racism – particularly to the people who are killed and hurt by its effects. That is, when the police enact the well-documented tendency to associate people of color with threat at the level of their first-pass bodily schemas, they are mobilizing their socially-situated embodied response, or habitus. These two forms of implicit understanding, which are not explicitly measured in the IAT about race and weapons, articulate with the other two forms, which are measured. So, there are likely commonsense, tacit racist beliefs at play in the association of black faces with weapons – that Black Americans are dangerous, hate cops, have weapons more often than White Americans, and so on.

Alongside those commonsense understandings is a network of feeling – threat, fear, anger, and so on. At this writing, the tests referenced to substantiate worries about implicit bias have no way to measure or talk about the emotions involved in responding to racial (and other) difference. It seems reasonable to assume that most people will have different responses in experimental situations, such as sitting in front of a computer and classifying images on a screen, than they do in everyday situations, such as walking down the street. Perhaps they will have still different affective orientations if they are, for example, a police officer on duty carrying a loaded weapon. Investigating how these differences might be in play would give us valuable traction for addressing what might shift the effects of people's implicit understanding, including their tacit but propositionalizable knowledge, their emotions, their skills, and their social-

---

10 | For useful thinking on the Martin case, see Yancy/Jones (2013).

ly-situated orientation toward the world. When people use the term 'implicit bias,' they may gesture toward an amalgam of these four aspects of our implicit understanding, but I believe we would enrich our conception of implicit understandings were we to consider, and research, them separately.

Racist implicit understanding has effects. It may shape our conscious and articulate decisions, as in the case of potential employers who judge resumes that code as racialized more harshly than resumes that code as white (cf. Bertrand/Mullainathan 2003). It may manifest explicitly but without words or propositional explanation, as in the case of police who kill unarmed Black people out of a somatic response shaped by their perception that non-weapons are weapons. It may shape the systematic and procedural undertakings of courts of law (cf. Levinson n.d.; Kang/Lane 2010; Jolls/Sunstein 2006) or health practitioners (cf. Hill 2010). Clearer theoretical perspectives can help shape how we gather data about the effects of oppression's connection with implicit understanding. Better delineations and clearer definitions of terms may help researchers craft modes of inquiry that shape new, less-harmful implicit understandings and explicit ways of knowing; this kind of approach might help us understand the relationship between theoretical accounts of implicit understanding and the real-life effects of bias and the social relations we call race.

Works Cited

Alcoff, Linda Martin (2007): "Epistemologies of Ignorance. Three Types," in: Sullivan/Tuana, Race, 39-58.
Bertrand, Marianne/Mullainathan, Sendhil (2003): "Are Emily and Greg More Employable Than Lakisha and Jamal? A Field Experiment on Labor Market Discrimination," in: National Bureau of Economic Research Working Paper Series No. 9873, http://www.nber.org/papers/w9873, accessed 27 Aug. 2011.
Blanton, H./Jaccard, J. (2008): "Unconscious Racism. A Concept in Pursuit of a Measure," in: Annu. Rev. Sociol. 34, 277-297.
Blum, Lawrence A. (2002): I'm Not a Racist, But–. The Moral Quandary of Race, Ithaca: Cornell UP.
Campbell, Sue (1998): Interpreting the Personal. Expression and the Formation of Feelings, Ithaca: Cornell UP.
Correll, J., et al. (2002): "The Police Officer's Dilemma. Using Ethnicity to Disambiguate Potentially Threatening Individuals," in: Journal of Personality and Social Psychology 83.6, 1314.
Correll, J., et al. (2007): "Across the Thin Blue Line. Police Officers and Racial Bias in the Decision to Shoot," in: Journal of Personality and Social Psychology 92.6, 1006.

Davis, Angela Y. (2003): Are Prisons Obsolete? New York: Open Media.
Doerner, W.G./Ho, T. (1994): "Shoot-Don't Shoot. Police Use of Deadly Force under Simulated Field Conditions," in: Journal of Crime and Justice 17, 49–68.
Fantl, Jeremy (2008): "Knowing How and Knowing That," in: Philosophy Compass 3, 451-470.
Fausto-Sterling, Anne (2005): "The Bare Bones of Sex," in: Signs 30, 1491-528.
—. (2008): "The Bare Bones of Race," in: Social Studies of Science 38, 657-694.
Garcia, J.L.A. (2004): "Three Sites for Racism. Social Structures, Valuings and Vice," in: Levine/Pataki, Racism, 35-55.
Gendler, Tamar Szabó (2011): "On the Epistemic Costs of Implicit Bias," in: Philosophical Studies 156.1, 33-63.
Gilmore, Ruth Wilson (2007): Golden Gulag. Prisons, Surplus, Crisis, and Opposition in Globalizing California. Berkeley: U of California P.
Greenwald, Anthony G./Banaji, Mahzarin R. (1995): "Implicit Social Cognition. Attitudes, Self-Esteem, and Stereotypes," in: Psychological Review 102.1, 4-27.
Greenwald, Anthony G./McGhee, Debbie E./Schwartz, Jordan L.K. (1998): "Measuring Individual Differences in Implicit Cognition. The Implicit Association Test," in: Journal of Personality and Social Psychology 74.6, 1464-1480.
Haslanger, Sally (2004): "Oppressions. Racial and Other," in: Levine/Pataki, Racism, 97-123.
Heldke, Lisa (2006): "Farming Made Her Stupid," in: Hypatia 21, 151-165.
Hill, Terry E. (2010): "How Clinicians Make (or Avoid) Moral Judgments of Patients. Implications of the Evidence for Relationships and Research," in: Philosophy, Ethics, and Humanities in Medicine 5, 11.
Inzlicht, Michael/Schmader, Toni (2012): Stereotype Threat Theory, Process, and Application, Oxford: Oxford UP.
Jolls, C./Sunstein, C.R. (2006): "The Law of Implicit Bias," in: California Law Review 94, 969.
Kadi, Joanna (1999): Thinking Class. Sketches from a Cultural Worker, Cambridge: South End.
Kang, J./Lane, K. (2010): "Seeing Through Colorblindness. Implicit Bias and the Law," in: UCLA Law Review 58, 465.
Kelly, D./Roedder, E. (2008): "Racial Cognition and the Ethics of Implicit Bias," in: Philosophy Compass 3, 522.
Koethe, John (2002): "Comments and Criticism. Stanley and Williamson on Knowing How," in: Journal of Philosophy 99, 325-328.
Levine, Michael P./Pataki, Tamas (eds.) (2004): Racism in Mind, Ithaca: Cornell UP.

Levinson, Justin (n.d.): "Forgotten Racial Equality. Implicit Bias, Decision-Making and Misremembering," in: bepress Legal Serie, Working Paper 1630, http://law.bepress.com/expresso/eps/1630, accessed 19 Oct. 2013.
Massumi, Brian (2002): Parables for the Virtual. Movement, Affect, Sensation, Durham: Duke UP.
McWhorter, Ladelle (2004): "Sex, Race, and Biopower. A Foucauldian Genealogy," in: Hypatia 19, 38-62.
—. (2009): Racism and Sexual Oppression in Anglo-America. A Genealogy, Bloomington: Indiana UP.
Mills, Charles W. (1998): Blackness Visible. Essays on Philosophy and Race, Ithaca: Cornell UP.
—. (2007): "White Ignorance," in: Sullivan/Tuana, Race, 11-38.
Nosek, B., et al. (2007): "Pervasiveness and Correlates of Implicit Attitudes and Stereotypes," in: European Review of Social Psychology 18, 36.
Omi, Michael/Winant, Howard (1994): Racial Formation in the United States. From the 1960s to the 1990s, New York: Routledge.
Outlaw, Lucius T. (2007): "Social Ordering and the Systematic Production of Ignorance," in: Sullivan/Tuana, Race, 197-212.
Patterson, Orlando (1982): Slavery and Social Death. A Comparative Study, Cambridge: Harvard UP.
Project Implicit: http://www.projectimplicit.net, accessed 19 Oct. 2013.
Project Implicit at harvard.edu: https://implicit.harvard.edu/implicit/Launch?-study=/user/education/weapons/weapons.expt.xml, accessed 19 Oct. 2013.
Protevi, John (2009): Political Affect. Connecting the Social and the Somatic, Minneapolis: U of Minnesota P.
Saul, Jennifer (n.d.): "Implicit Bias, Stereotype Threat and Women in Philosophy," http://www.sheffield.ac.uk/content/1/c6/03/49/18/BiasAndPhilosophy11.doc, accessed 19 Oct. 2013.
Shotwell, Alexis (2011): Knowing Otherwise. Race, Gender, and Implicit Understanding, University Park: Pennsylvania State UP.
Stanley, Jason (2010): "Knowing (How)," in: Noûs 45, 207-238.
—. (2011): Know How, New York: Oxford UP.
Stanley, Jason/Williamson, Timothy (2001): "Knowing How," in: Journal of Philosophy 98, 411-444.
Steele, Claude (2010): Whistling Vivaldi, and Other Clues to How Stereotypes Affect Us, New York: Norton.
Sullivan, Shannon/Tuana, Nancy (eds.) (2007): Race and Epistemologies of Ignorance, Albany: State U of New York P.
Tsai, Cheng-hung (2011): "The Metaepistemology of Knowing-How," in: Phenomenology and the Cognitive Sciences 10, 541-556.
Valls, Andrew (2009): "Racism. In Defense of Garcia," in: Philosophy of the Social Sciences 39.3, 475-480.

Williams, John (2008): "Propositional Knowledge and Know-How," in: Synthese 165, 107-125.
Wittgenstein, Ludwig (1972): On Certainty/Über Gewissheit, ed. G.E.M. Anscombe/G.H. von Wright, transl. Denis Paul/G.E.M. Anscombe, New York: Harpercollins.
Yancy, George/Jones, Janine (eds.) (2013): Pursuing Trayvon Martin. Historical Contexts and Contemporary Manifestations of Racial Dynamics, Lanham: Lexington.
Young, Garry (2008): "Case Study Evidence for an Irreducible Form of Knowing How to. An Argument against a Reductive Epistemology," in: Philosophia 37, 341-360.

For a Sociology of Flesh and Blood
Questions to Loïc Wacquant

How important is it in your view to focus on the implicit dimensions (tacit knowledge, knowing-how, sens pratique, *etc.) of social interaction?*

It is crucial if we are to overcome three perennial flaws that cramp social science and prevent us from developing vibrant, full-color accounts of society and history: a dualistic and disincarnated vision of the *agent*, constituted of an active mind mounted on an absent, inert, and dumb body; a flattened and negative notion of *structure* construed as a set of external constraints; and a mentalist understanding of *knowledge* as made up of chunks of information and stocks of representations. These three conceptions are mutually reinforcing and conjoin to literally take the life out of social life, leaving us with an incomplete and inadequate grasp of the social as a fluid albeit patterned conative domain.

Consider each of these elements briefly. Conceptions of the agent across the social sciences are polarized by an opposition between *homo economicus*, the rational computing machine that maximizes individual utility, descended from Bentham and developed by neo-classical economics, and *homo culturalis*, the symbol-manipulating individual motivated by moral norms, inherited from Kant and lionized by cultural anthropology, with sociology clumsily stretched across the two poles. These two reigning models, "rational man" and "plastic man," as Martin Hollis (1977) once characterized them, are equally mutilated and mutilating. What is it that they share over and beyond their frontal clash? Both are disembodied and erase from analysis the flesh, desire, and passion as a modality of social existence. These are the ingredients of action that William James wrangled with and that Sigmund Freud's depth psychology sought to capture, but only at an ontogenetic level. The embodied strands of contemporary cognitive science, cutting across artificial intelligence, psychology, neurobiology, linguistics, and philosophy, are fast rediscovering them at the phylogenetic level (Clark 1999, Chemero 2013, Shapiro 2014). But they continue to be censored, ignored, or sidelined in standard social scientific accounts.

However "polythetic and polymorphic" the notion may be according to Merton (1976), the predominant conception of social structure locates it squarely outside of the agent, in the guise of a fence or funnel, and this is similarly truncated and limiting. For structures do not exist simply as Durkheimian facts that persons encounter in their extant environment, in the form of invisible relations, objective distributions of resources, or systems of constraints and opportunities that press or limit them from without. They are also dynamic webs of forces inscribed upon and infolded deep within the body as perceptual grids, sensorimotor capacities, emotional proclivities, and indeed as desire itself. Structures are internal springs or propellers as much as they are external containers, beams, or lattices. They are limber and alive, not inert and immobile.

Finally, the social sciences work with an excessively cerebral and passive notion of knowledge. We grant the dignity of knowledge to propositional information carried by language and located in the mind. We overlook procedural or practical knowledge acquired and manifested in concrete deeds (*pragmaticos* in ancient Greek means active, adroit in affairs or public business). We must eschew this top-down conception to overcome what Elizabeth Anscombe (1957) rightly diagnosed as the "incorrigibly contemplative conception of knowledge" inherited from the rationalist revolution, and thence break with the mentalist (or discursivist) concept of culture associated with it. We need to recognize the reality and potency of *carnal know-how*, the bottom-up, visceral grasp of the social world – in the double sense of intellectual understanding and dexterous handling – that we acquire by acting in and upon it.

What properties of the human actor need to be spotlighted to catch this embodied practical knowledge?

Ernst Cassirer (1944) was right to characterize "man" as a "symbolic animal" and to see in language, myth, art, religion, and science the main symbolic systems that human beings have invented to grapple with and shape their environment. But this property alone does not make a viable philosophical anthropology. I would supplement it with an additional five properties, all conveniently starting with S, so what we might call this expanded vision the "Six S" conception of the agent.

In addition to being a wielder of symbols, the human animal is sentient, suffering, skilled, sedimented, and situated. *Sentient*: the agent is not only endowed with senses, exteroceptive, proprioceptive, and interoceptive; she also makes sense of what her sensorium captures. She is both capable of feeling and conscious of those feelings; and the body is the synthesizing medium of this feeling awareness, as neurobiologist Antonio Damasio shows in *The Feeling of What Happens* (1999). *Suffering*: the agent is exposed to the threats and blows of the natural and social worlds; she has needs, yearnings, and desires that do not get fulfilled; she is constantly subjected to the judgment of others and faces the inescapable coming of death. As such, she lives in anguish, distress, and pain, and yet she endures. *Skilled*: the social agent can "make a difference" (the original meaning of the Old Norse *skil* is to discern and adjust) because, through experience and training, she acquires capacities to act and the dexterity to do things competently. *Sedimented*: all of these elements, our senses, suffering, and skills are not given at birth, generic, or constituted in a solipsistic relation to self. Rather, they are implanted, cultivated, and deployed over time through our engagement in the world, and they are gradually deposited in our body as the layered product of our varied individual and collective histories (Merleau-Ponty [1945], relying on Husserl, calls the "habitual knowledge of the world" lodged in the body proper an "implicit or sedimented science"). *Situated*: this sedimentation is shaped by our unique location and peregrinations in physical and social space, precisely because we are both protected by and locked in the fragile physical envelope of our mortal organism, which cannot be at two places at a given time but integrates the traces of the many places we have occupied over time.

Lastly, all six of these elements are jointly *structured* and flowing as well as growing through *time*. Our conception of the agent, structure, and knowledge all need to be radically temporalized, as Bourdieu (1980/1990: 98-111) urged long ago in "The Work of Time." Once we acknowledge that cognition is a situated activity growing out of a tangled dance of body, mind, activity, and world, we can begin to retrieve the tacit knowledge enfolded in cultural and social practices, and thereby enrich our descriptions and deepen our explanations of them. Put these three revamped ingredients together – an incarnate being engaging practical know-how as she navigates active and mobile configurations of affect, action, and powers – and you have the building blocks for a *flesh-and-blood sociology*, capable of producing multidimensional, polychrome accounts of social life that seize life as it actually unfolds, instead of the torpid reports in black and white that we now read in academic journals.

Which research methods do you recommend to detect the invisible dimensions of action, structure, and knowledge?

On principle, the four main methods of social science, ethnographic, hermeneutic (encompassing interviewing and textual analysis), historical, and statistical, can all tackle any object. But it is clear that they are unequally equipped to ferret out those components of practice that do not get articulated, symbolized, and objectified as such: doxic categories, phronetic abilities, and ordinary ways of being, feeling, and acting. One method is the royal road to the tacit texture of social action and cognition: close-up observation by means of pragmatic involvement in the activity studied.

Ethnography – that particular technique of data production and analysis that relies on the skilled and sensate organism of the observer as chief investigative tool – is uniquely suited to helping us *re-incarnate society* by restoring the praxeological dimensions of social existence. But for this we must, first, come to a clearer understanding of the distinctiveness and special virtues (as well as the correlative limitations) of ethnography as *embedded and embodied social inquiry* based on physical co-presence with(in) the phenomenon in real time and space and, second, we must reform our practice of it in two complementary if seemingly contradictory ways. On the one hand, we must *bind ethnography more firmly to theory*, against the epistemological illusions of Geertzian "thick description," the philosophic naïveté of Chicago-style empiricism, and the glamorous seductions of postmodern story-telling. On the other hand, we need to foster long-term, *intensive, even initiatory, forms* of ethnographic involvement liable to allow the investigator to master in the first person, *intus et in cute*, the prediscursive schemata that make up the competent, diligent, and appetent member of the universe under examination.

To make the most of ethnography, the field sociologist must methodically mine and thematize the fact that, like every social agent, he comes to know his object *by body*; and he can leverage carnal comprehension by deepening his social and symbolic insertion into the universe he studies. This means that we can and should work to become "vulnerable observers" in our practice of fieldwork – and not on paper, in "writing vulnerably" by injecting large doses of "subjectivity into ethnography," as proposed by Ruth Behar (1996: 16 and 6). The methodological stipulation here is to dive into the stream of action to the deepest possible degree, rather than watch it from the bank; but to dive with method and purpose, and not with reckless abandon that would cause us to drown in the bottomless whirlpool of subjectivism.

In your book Body and Soul (Wacquant 2004 [2000], new expanded edition 2014) and related essays, you have sought to develop what you call "carnal sociology:" what differentiates it from a sensual ethnography inspired by phenomenology?

Put tersely, carnal sociology is a sociology not *of* the body as sociocultural object but *from* the body as fount of social intelligence and sociological acumen. It starts from the brute fact that, as argued above, the human agent is a sentient and suffering being of flesh and blood (flesh refers here to the visible surface of the lived body while blood points to the inner circuitry of life pulsating in the depths of the visceral body, as in Leder's [1990] revision of Merleau-Ponty). It situates itself *not above or on the side of action but at its point of production*. Carnal sociology strives to eschew the spectatorial viewpoint and to grasp action-in-the-making, not action-already-accomplished. It aims to detect and document the deployment of the practical schemata that fashion practice: the cognitive, conative, and affective building blocks of habitus, whose layering and operations are fully open to empirical investigation (Wacquant 2014a and 2014b). It diverges from sensual ethnography as the field study *of* the senses, which has a distinguished lineage running from Simmel, Mauss, and Lucien Febvre, to Elias and the *Lebensphilosophie* of Arnold Gehlen and Helmut Plessner, to contemporary strands of medical and phenomenological anthropology, in that it takes "sensory formations" not as its object of study (as does Howes 2003) but as its means of study.

Carnal sociology applies to any object and can use a variety of methods so long as these treat the social agent as embodied and embedded. For instance, practitioners of *Alltagsgeschichte*, microhistory, and the recent historiography of sensibilities frequently come into its ambit, although they might not know it or intend to. When Carlo Ginsburg (1976) reconstructs the lived cosmos of the sixteenth-century miller Menocchio before he was burned at the stake for being a suspected heretic in *Il formaggio e i vermi*; when Alf Lüdtke (1993) tracks the social roots and effects of *Eigensinn*, the obstinate "self-will" feeding strategies of recalcitrance midway between accommodation and resistance to power among German laborers in the first half of the twentieth century; when Alain Corbin (1988) maps the changing sensorial and epistemic cultures that turned the seaside from an object of revulsive fear to an attractive site of contemplation and spawned a new posture toward "nature," they are doing carnal historical sociology.

For contemporary objects, the best method is what I call *enactive ethnography*, that is, immersive fieldwork through which the investigator *acts out (elements of) the phenomenon* in order to peel away the layers of its invisible properties and to test its operative mechanisms. I adapt the term *enactive* from my Berkeley colleague, the philosopher Alva Noë in his book *Action in Perception* (2004: 2), in which he proposes that perception is "a skillful activity on the part of the animal as a whole," which I find to be a very apt characterization of the ethnographer at work (Noë himself borrows the adjective from the influential "embodied mind" theory of Francesco Varela, Evan Thompson and Eleanor Rosch, 1991). The first commandment of incarnate inquiry, then, is to *enter the theater of action* and, if possible, apprentice in the ways of the people studied – be they pugilists, professors, or politicians – so as to gain a visceral apprehension of their universe as materials and springboard for its analytic reconstruction.

Carnal sociology is premised on a syllogism and a dare. The syllogism is the following: if it is true that the body is not just a socially construct-*ed* product but also a socially construc-*ting* vector of knowledge, practice, and power, then this applies to the body of the sociologist as inquirer. The dare is to overcome two millenia of "scorn for the body," to quote Nietzsche, that have led us to construe the sensate organism as an obstacle to knowledge and to turn it into a bountiful resource for social scientific inquiry.

Is "enactive ethnography" a new way of practicing the craft?

I am tempted to say, on the contrary, that it is an old and venerable brand of ethnography, harking back to its origins and golden age, which stressed "learning by doing" through lasting and intimate contact with "the natives" – in his *Poetics*, Aristotle reminds us that men acquire their first knowledge through mimesis. Enactive ethnography does no more than make explicit and then intensify the two distinctive features of any ethnography worthy of the name: that the investigator is embodied and has embedded herself into the social and symbolic structure examined. Another way to characterize it is to say that it uses habitus as both object and method of analysis (Wacquant 2011). In that regard, it goes against those currents of contemporary anthropology that have become so obsessed with tropes, positionality, ethics, the openness and multiplicity of sites (or "para-sites" lodged in "the complexities of our time," no joke), and the foibles of professionalization that they have reached a state of ethnographic paralysis by meta-analysis (Faubion and Marcus 2009).

I previously proposed that, whenever the practical configuration permits, we can and should "go native, but go native *armed*, and return" (Wacquant 2009: 119). I wish now to amend this formulation because "going native" is an ambiguous slogan that gets us off on the wrong epistemic footing. For what is "the native's point of view" that Malinowski (1922) canonized in *The Argonauts of the Western Pacific* and that Geertz (1974) invited us to honor as the standpoint of ethnography? Whose point of view is it and taken at what moment in time? Even in a small-scale, kinship-based society approximating Durkheim's "mechanical solidarity" such as the Trobriand Islands, there is social differentiation and hierarchy. Indeed, Malinowski stresses distinctions of rank and power between districts, tribes, and totemic clans. Obviously, the point of view of the village chief is not that of a commoner; the perspective and dispositions of an elderly male widower from a high-ranking lineage are not those of an unmarried teenage girl from a lower totemic clan. In any system of action there is a division of labor such that there are native *points of views, plural*, as views taken from evolving points in the objective structure of the local social space. Moreover, there is a struggle, at any moment, to determine what properties and position qualify as native. As I show in *The Prizefighter's Three Bodies*, any singular point of view, such as the pugilistic one, is always a *selective synthetic construction by the analyst* that captures a moment in this dynamic contest of situated perspectives, not a raw empirical induction from ethnographic observation (Wacquant, forthcoming, chapter 1).

In his book Pascalian Meditations, *Bourdieu (1997/2000) deepens his theory of implicit knowledge through a shadow dialogue with Pascal. What are we to make of this self-affiliation of Bourdieu with the author of Les Pensées (Pascal 1976 [1670])?*

This connection has surprised many because Pascal is an obscure and enigmatic thinker who, aside from his contributions to geometry and probability theory, is best known as an apologist of Christianity, a thinker of existential abyss, and a master prose stylist. Few social scientists have encountered him in their intellectual tribulations and Bourdieu rarely mentioned him openly in his writings. But the connection operates at several nested levels. It is first a prophylactic reference intended to ward off false genealogies (late McCarthyite accusations about Bourdieu being a crypto-Marxist) and bad readings (Bourdieu as the advocate of a strategic vision of action in the mold of rational choice theory, of which he was a tireless opponent). Next, it is an ironic wink to the philosophy of the subject as sovereign consciousness, running from Descartes to Sartre via Husserl (and his *Cartesian Meditations*, whose title Bourdieu riffs on), with which the French sociologist crossed swords for the better part of forty years. With Leibniz and especially Spinoza, another major inspiration of Bourdieu and forceful advocate of a monist conception of human activity, Pascal represents the non-Cartesian wing of the rationalist revolution, which the author of *Distinction* sought to reinforce and extend.

But there is above all a deep affinity at the level of philosophical anthropology and social ontology: the human creature is a suffering being, caught in and by the world, who tears herself from the utter absurdity of her condition, caught "between infinity and nothingness," through knowledge and action, even as this knowledge can never be grounded. This being and this world are kneaded by antinomies, hierarchical couples liable to be turned upside down on a dime: the human is both "angel and beast," submitted to the determinisms of the universe and yet capable of escaping them by the very fact that she can know them and thus know herself; institutions present themselves as founded in nature when they are nothing but "custom" ("this second nature which destroys the first one"); the social order seems necessary even as it is fundamentally contingent.

The arbitrariness of hierarchies and the incommensurability of powers ("the order of bodies, the order of minds, the order of charity"), the centrality of the symbolic, the role of deception and belief (in the sense of *fides*, faith that things are the way they appear to be: "to deny, to believe, and to doubt well, these are to men what galloping is to horses") as springs of action and glue of collective life: Pascal offers Bourdieu not a system – the author of *Les Provinciales* never produced one – but pillars and levers to "confront in its truth the enigma of fiction and fetishism" (Bourdieu 1997/2000: 6) that are at the basis of society and thus to operate a triple historicization, of social being, of the social world which makes him and which he makes, and of the knowledge that one may produce of it.

Can one draw on Pascal to deepen our understanding of the manifold ways in which tacit knowledge operates in everyday life by both veiling and unveiling itself? Can he help us develop a sociology of the implicit?

"The sensibility of man to small things and his insensibility to great things, sign of a strange reversal," writes Pascal (1976 [1670]), and yet "it is the condition of men." Bourdieu enrolls the Jansenist philosopher mostly to advance his thinking on symbolic power, its modalities and effects, and for rethinking recognition as a commutator of social existence. This leads him to cast the conceptual triad of *cognition, recognition, and misrecognition* in everyday life as well as in institutional functioning at the epicenter of his social ontology. One can go a step further and deploy the quarrelling couple of the "reasons of the heart and of reason" to take seriously profane beliefs and develop a political microsociology fusing rationality and sentiments. Likewise, with the concept of *"divertissement"* and the corollary idea that "it is the chase, and not the catch" that people seek in any activity, Pascal opens wide the doors of a sociology of passion as a modality of our relation to the world, implying love, desire, and suffering, which can assume an infinite variety of forms (philosophical, political, pugilistic, amorous, etc.).

Finally, at the outset of his *Pensées*, Pascal broaches a subtle but luminous distinction between *"esprit de géométrie"* and *"esprit de finesse,"* two modalities of reasoning that social scientists would be well advised to reflect upon (see Force 2003 for pointers). Our geometric mind proceeds from a small number of principles to cut up the world, deduce with logic, and conclude with clarity; by contrast, intellectual acuteness feeds on a multitude of implicit principles embedded in experience and riding on local intuition and felt analogy. The former is abstract and artificial, born of the specialized training of the mind; the latter is concrete and natural, springing synthetically from the flow of life. Pascal likens the geometric spirit to the gaze and the spirit of acuteness to the palpation of the hand. This opposition can help us discern the particular quandary of social science that the study of the implicit exacerbates: normal science runs on the spirit of geometry while social life runs on the spirit of acuteness. The task of an incarnate social science, then, must be to reconcile these two forms of reason. "We are automatons as much as minds," Pascal points out, and for this reason we must strive to avoid "two excesses: to exclude reason, to admit only reason." Not a bad starting axiom for a sociology of flesh and blood.

Questions by Frank Adloff

WORKS CITED

Anscombe, G.E.M. (2000 [1957]): Intention, Cambridge: Harvard UP.
Behar, Ruth (1996): The Vulnerable Observer. Anthropology That Breaks Your Heart, Boston: Beacon.
Bourdieu, Pierre (1990 [1980]): The Logic of Practice, Cambridge: Polity.
—. (2000 [1997]): Pascalian Meditations, Cambridge: Polity.
Cassirer, Ernst (1944): An Essay on Man, New Haven: Yale UP.
Chemero, Anthony (2013): "Radical Embodied Cognitive Science," in: Review of General Psychology 17.2, 145-150.
Clark, Andy (1999): "An Embodied Cognitive Science?," in: Trends in Cognitive Sciences 3.9, 345–351.
Corbin, Alain (1988): Le territoire du vide. L'Occident et le désir du rivage, 1750-1840, Paris: Aubier.
Damasio, Antonio R. (1999): The Feeling of What Happens. Body and Emotion in the Making of Consciousness, New York: Harcourt Brace.
Faubion, James D./Marcus, George E. (eds.) (2009): Fieldwork Is Not What It Used to Be. Learning Anthropology's Method in a Time of Transition, Ithaca: Cornell UP.
Force, Pierre (2003): "Géométrie, finesse, et premiers principes chez Pascal," in: Romance Quarterly 50.2, 121-130.
Geertz, Clifford (1974): "'From the Native's Point of View.' On the Nature of Anthropological Understanding," in: Bulletin of the American Academy of Arts & Sciences 28.1, 26-45. Reprinted in: Local Knowledge. Further Essays in the Interpretation of Cultures, New York: Basic, 55-71.
Ginzburg, Carlo (1976): Il formaggio e i vermi, Torino: Einaudi.
Howes, David (2003): Sensual Relations. Engaging the Senses in Culture and Social Theory, Ann Arbor: U of Michigan P.
Hollis, Martin (1977): Models of Man. Philosophical Thoughts on Social Action, New York: Cambridge UP.
Leder, Drew (1990): "Flesh and Blood. A Proposed Supplement to Merleau-Ponty," in: Human Studies 13.3, 209-19.
Lüdtke, Alf (1993): Eigen-Sinn. Fabrikalltag, Arbeitererfahrungen und Politik vom Kaiserreich bis in den Faschismus, Hamburg: Ergebnisse.
Malinowski, Bronislaw (2014 [1922]): Argonauts of the Western Pacific. An Account of Native Enterprise and Adventure in the Archipelagoes of Melanesian New Guinea, London: Routledge.
Merleau-Ponty, Maurice (1962 [1945]): Phenomenology of Perception, New York: Humanities.
Merton, Robert (1976): "Structural Analysis in Sociology," in: Peter Blau (ed.), Approaches to the Study of Social Structure, London: Open Books, 21-52.
Noë, Alva (2004): Action in Perception, Cambridge: MIT P.

Pascal, Blaise (1976 [1670]): Pensées, Paris: Garnier-Flammarion.
Shapiro, Lawrence (ed.) (2014): The Routledge Handbook of Embodied Cognition, London: Routledge.
Varela, Francesco/Thompson, Evan/Rosch, Eleanor (1993 [1991]): The Embodied Mind. Cognitive Science and Human Experience, Cambridge: MIT P.
Wacquant, Loïc (2004 [2000]): Body and Soul. Notebooks of an Apprentice Boxer, New York: Oxford UP. New expanded ed. 2014.
—. (2009): "The Body, the Ghetto and the Penal State," in: Qualitative Sociology 32.1, 101-129.
—. (2011): "Habitus as Topic and Tool. Reflections on Becoming a Prizefighter," in: Qualitative Research in Psychology 8.1, 81-92.
—. (2014a): "*Homines in extremis*. What Fighting Scholars Teach Us about Habitus." in: Body & Society 20.2, 3-17.
—. (2014b): "Putting Habitus in Its Place. Response to the Symposium," Body & Society: 20.2, 118-139.
—. Forthcoming. The Prizefighter's Three Bodies. Steps to a Carnal Sociology, New York: Oxford UP.

Part III
Presentifications

Tacit Knowledge, Public Feeling, and the Pursuits of (Un-)Happiness

Heike Paul

> We hold these truths to be self-evident, that all men are created equal, that they are endowed by their Creator with certain unalienable Rights, that among these are Life, Liberty and the pursuit of Happiness.
> Thomas Jefferson, The Declaration of Independence

> Depressed? It Might Be Political.
> Feel Tank Protest Slogan

I. Introduction

The two epigraphs to this essay refer to happiness and unhappiness, respectively, as emotions that transcend the realm of the private. In the first quote, the pursuit of happiness is declared to be a fundamental right; in the second, unhappiness – to feel depressed – is suggestively connected to politics. Both examples are cases of 'public feeling,' a concept that has been used in recent cultural studies scholarship to describe and analyze the intersections of supposedly private spheres of intimate affect and emotion on the one hand, and public spheres of communication and political practice that are conventionally seen as primarily rational on the other. By linking the latter spheres to the former, the term 'public feeling' thus problematizes the distinction and the connection between the private and the public. Public feeling takes place out in the open, so to speak, yet draws on – and in fact presentifies – an 'affective economy' (cf. Ahmed 2004) that appears to be based on a collectively shared tacit knowledge. In this essay, I will argue that tacit knowledge is a key concept for grasping and analyzing public feelings as explications of quasi-subliminal rules; it is "knowledge people have at the intersection of their bodily and conceptual systems" (Shotwell 2011: xii) and that organizes individuals into groups. In turn, tacit knowledge also accounts for processes of sedimentation and incorporation that result in the continued impact of those unspoken rules on private lives and public conduct. The repertoire of public feeling appears as a paradigmatic instance of the presentification of tacit knowledge and as a culturally specific, socially intelligible way of expressing emotions that creates an intersubjective realm in which these feelings appear to be naturally shared and exchanged. In the context of this process we may think of presence as a medium of exchange, negotiation, and re-formulation. In what follows, I will first briefly outline the contours of different perspectives on the concept of tacit knowledge, secondly, introduce the field of public-feeling scholarship that has developed in the wake of the so-called 'turn to affect,' and thirdly, address (un-)happiness as a public feeling in American culture before I conclude with some notes on further possible research agendas.

Tacit knowledge has been described in various, at times almost diametrically opposed ways in different disciplinary contexts and from different disciplinary perspectives: on the one hand, it has been seen as a kind of knowledge that enables us to perform certain tasks (like riding a bike or using a tool) and that empowers us in necessary, intuitive, and useful ways, and on the other hand, as knowledge we make use of subliminally in ways that may be considered as stifling, regulating, and controlling (rather than as creating and enhancing) agency. The first conceptualization is at the center of Michael Polanyi's work, the eminent scholar of "tacit knowing" who suggested that "we know more than we can say" (1969: 159), and that much of what we know we cannot say. In making a strong case for the centrality of the tacit dimension in any form of knowledge production, Polanyi critically engaged with positivistic notions of knowledge acquisition that he saw as dominant particularly in the natural sciences. In turn, he elevated tacit knowledge and the "tacit powers of the mind" (1959: 19) to the status of "the dominant principle of all knowledge" (ibid. 13), even if in his view, tacit knowing ultimately remains tied to utilitarian and largely practical purposes. The second definition of tacit knowledge stands in considerable tension to the first. Here, the interiorization of knowledge as a kind of tacit knowledge is not necessarily enabling, as it primarily serves the purpose of a lastingly effective incorporation of external rules and norms. Pierre Bourdieu's concept of habitus is a prominent example of grasping tacit knowing in this way (although the term itself is never used by Bourdieu); it attempts to explicate the role of tacit knowledge in stabilizing and affirming, for instance, possibly oppressive social, political, and cultural hierarchies (cf. Bourdieu 1984). Thus, with a view to both Polanyi's and Bourdieu's work, tacit knowing "can create the conditions for political transformation, but it can also block such transformation" (Shotwell 2011: xviii);[1] as phenomena of tacit know-

---

1 | Of course, there have also been other conceptualizations of tacit knowledge, which tend to fall somewhere in between the two discussed above; for various typologies of tacit knowledge cf. Collins 2010; Shotwell 2011; Ernst/Paul 2013a: 14.

ing tend to have (or oscillate between) both an enabling as well as a restraining dimension, it is safe to argue that both of these conceptualizations should be taken into account when analyzing forms of the tacit in social, political, and cultural realms.

In addition to accounting for the contradictions in these conceptualizations of tacit knowledge, first we also have to slightly recast Polanyi's and Bourdieu's approaches by adding a sense of cultural difference to their rather universalistic conceptualizations of tacit knowing in order to be able to use the concept of tacit knowledge for an understanding and/or a critique of culturally specific phenomena; second, we have to address more closely the intersubjective dimension of tacit knowing within a given culture, community, or nation with regard to questions of collective identity formation; and third, we need to account for the ways in which tacit knowledge manifests itself and becomes present, i.e. explicated and part of a wider circulation/dissemination. In order to analyze tacit knowledge in its particular presentifications as both empowering articulations *and* experiences that are ideologically contained within pre-existing cultural scripts, I will address the particular arena anticipated already in the epigraphs to this article: the discourse about (un-)happiness that is constituted at the intersection of the private and the public, the individual and the collective and that is explored and negotiated under the arc of 'public feeling' and 'public feeling projects.' In order to do so, I will use 'public feeling' as a concept that is posited on the verge, i.e. on the "charged border" (Stewart 2000: 407) between interiorization and exteriorization, between articulation and dis-articulation, between notions of subjectivity on the one hand and the always already ideologically interpellated quality of that subjectivity on the other.

The oxymoronic term 'public feeling' itself is characterized by a split duality "that simultaneously captures how it feels and provides an analysis of why and how its feelings are produced by social forces" (Cvetkovich 2012: 14). Focusing on one of the two dimensions – feeling or the production of feeling – it always seems "like there is something else happening" as well (ibid. 6). Perhaps not surprisingly, scholars of public feeling often focus on negative feelings such as shame and depression (and the stigmatization, privatization, and medicalization of 'feeling bad') in a society devoted to the 'pursuit' and 'promise of happiness' (cf. Ahmed 2012) in a spirit of what Lauren Berlant has called 'cruel optimism' (cf. 2010). Yet, the latter – happiness, optimism, utopia – have also been addressed critically in their submerged ambivalences, and I will tap into this work in my own treatment of happiness.

The concepts of tacit knowledge and public feeling both share a similar tension that has often been considered productive: tacit knowledge describes the implicit dimension of something we usually consider explicit, formal, and propositional: knowledge; public feeling – or public sentiment, as Glenn Hendler calls it (cf. 2001) – similarly focuses on an explicit dimension and the exteriorization of something we consider private, informal, and often unspoken. Thus, there appears to be an analogy between both concepts. But I will move beyond this analogy and claim that – as 'feeling' belongs to the realm of the tacit, and 'public' to the realm of presence and presentification – an interdependency exists between public feeling and tacit knowledge in the medium of presence. Situated between and partaking in both tacit knowledge and presence, public feelings may be addressed as incorporating a tacit as well as a presentist dimension which are subject to communications and negotiations within a particular nation/community/culture. Public feelings must be addressed in their cultural specificity and their intersubjective scope and appeal through which they interpellate individuals as subjects *feeling something*. That *something* is specified as positive or negative, as adequate or inadequate, as happiness, depression, grief, fear, love, etc. From a constructivist perspective, the latter are never naturally given emotions/feelings/sentiments – they are culturally pre-fabricated, and sustained individually and collectively by a (shared) tacit knowledge that, in turn, is affirmed, re-constituted, or re-calibrated (cf. Berlant 2010) through the public display of feeling(s) that as such constitutes a form of explicating practice. In my understanding, the term 'feeling' covers both and joins affect and emotion. Whereas affects are "nonconscious and unnamed, but nevertheless registered, experiences of bodily energy and intensity that arise in response to stimuli impinging on the body" (Gould 2010: 26), emotion is "the expression of affect in gesture and language, its conventional or coded expression" (Massumi qtd. in Gould 26-27), yet, as Gould points out, no expression is ever "complete," ever an "exact representation of our affective experience" but only an "approximation" (2010: 27). Thus 'feeling' has both a tacit as well as an explicit dimension.[2]

Following a brief overview of the work on public feeling in American cultural and literary studies, postcolonial studies, and feminist/gender/queer studies by Lauren Berlant, Sara Ahmed, and Ann Cvetkovich, I will show how the debates in the field draw attention to "the sensoriums of public culture" and to how "public spectres have grown intimate" (Stewart 2000: 405, 406); the above-mentioned scholars are also interested in the blurring of the lines between the protocol and the performance of public feeling. The concept of public feeling allows us to focus both on the ways in which tacit knowledge is explicat-

---

2 | Philosopher Hermann Schmitz has pointed out the 'double meaning' of feeling (cf. 1993: 48); he qualifies feelings as (shared) atmospheres and situations (cf. ibid. 41) rather than as an individual's experience of emotion (cf. ibid. 47). Even as Schmitz's work in what he calls neo-phenomenology is somewhat controversial and has been strongly and convincingly criticized, among others, by Bernhard Waldenfels (cf. 2006), I find Schmitz's notion of feeling as atmosphere and co-presence useful for a delineation of public feeling.

ed and on the way in which public feelings become part of intimate spheres that appear to be inexplicable. Public feeling offers paradigmatic instances of the co-construction of intimacy and other emotional worlds by/through individual and collective investments. Clearly, these processes are all about the presentification of tacit knowledge and the incorporation of certain 'presences' into forms of implicit understanding; they describe the percolation and sedimentation of cultural practices and expressions into a kind of embodied knowledge that exists and is perpetuated and reiterated below the level of awareness. It is in the sharing of the lived experiences of public feeling that the tacit dimension 'appears' and becomes graspable for analysis. After having revisited the major works of public-feeling scholarship, I will proceed by concentrating on one particular instance of public feeling, namely happiness, and work out the apparent and the hidden public and private dimensions of that particular desire and/or state. In the context of the US, the pursuit of happiness constitutes a foundational political claim laid down in the Declaration of Independence of 1776 as well as, arguably, a private fixation (as it does in much of the Western world); both are connected to the overarching myth of expressive individualism. The latter provides scripts for articulations of "affective states" (Gould 2010: 32) and guidelines on how to achieve the 'state' of happiness. Between a larger US national 'state fantasy' (cf. Pease 2009) of happiness and a highly individualistic creed of happiness, a particular and exclusive ideology of social organization on the basis of kinship – i.e., the heteronormative nuclear family – appears to be installed as the crucial site of re/production. It is the heteronormative nuclear family that articulates and supposedly mitigates the tension between the state fantasy and the harsh effects of economic competition; at the same time it also guarantees intimate fulfilment. In American culture, happiness ranges high as an indicator of successful self-realization. Now, if the family is seen as the preferred site of individual self-realization, it is also the affective site that as a primary social institution or Ideological State Apparatus (cf. Althusser 1971) is responsible for the individual's incorporation of ideology. This incorporated ideology can be described as tacit knowledge. The tacit dimension becomes obvious when we concede that "[t]o refer to happiness might suspend obligation to refer to anything else in making good an argument" (Ahmed 2012: 203). It is a 'killer argument,' so to speak, that does not have to be refined at all as no one would argue against happiness – or for unhappiness. I would like to show that we can discuss the presence and presentist forms of happiness as public feeling and as revealing a tacit knowledge that is culturally specific as well as normative and that needs to be historicized.

II. The Turn to Affect and Public-Feeling Scholarship

> Perhaps we truly encounter the political only when we *feel*.
> Janet Staiger, "Introduction: Political Emotions and Public Feelings" 4

> How does capitalism feel?
> Ann Cvetkovich, *Depression: A Public Feeling* 5

Over the last decade, academic discussions of affect, feeling, and emotion have been so extensive and intense that we have recently come to speak of an 'affective turn' and a 'turn to emotion' (cf. Clough/Halley 2007; Döring 2009; Gould 2010: 23). Philosophers, sociologists, literary critics, as well as cultural and media studies scholars have (re-)addressed the role of affects and emotions in multidisciplinary contexts ranging from trauma studies to queer theory, and affect theory has also developed new perspectives on knowledge production and acquisition. Frank Adloff has recently argued that in order to articulate personal experience individuals do not need to take recourse to prefabricated formulas and scripts (as, for instance, Eva Illouz suggests in her sociology of emotions [cf. 2007]), but struggle for a nuanced and adequate expression of their individual/personal/intimate feelings; drawing on Shawn Gallagher's concept of 'embodied cognition' (cf. 2005), Daniel Stern's notion of 'affect attunement' (cf. 1985), and John Dewey's pragmatist philosophy (cf. 2007), he argues for a social theory of emotional experience that takes into account effects of presence connected to bodily sensations and emotional response (cf. Adloff 2013: 103). The latter depend on implicit knowledge that is acquired intersubjectively and that is shaped by social and cultural constellations (cf. ibid. 113, 116). These specific constellations also condition/produce an individual's narratives of emotions (cf. ibid. 111), which are the singularly prominent form of expression once language has been acquired; these narratives are personal but also transpersonal (in the sense that they are culturally shaped and embedded). I want to suggest, however, that they have to be tied back to those very cultural scripts that are available to us (cf. Illouz 2007; Butler 1997; Appiah 1997) and that they can never exist solely as individual expressions. Public-feeling scholarship points to and analyzes this nexus between individual emotional narratives and (semi-normative) cultural scripts.[3] In order to develop new approaches to the nexus of the private and the political, a number of cultural studies scholars since the 1990s have

---

3 | From a structuralist-narratological perspective, the positions of Frank Adloff and Eva Illouz are not as far apart as Adloff's argument might suggest: both point to particular formulas and emplotments of emotions and both consider the narrativization of emotions as central. The difference between narratives (Adloff) and narrative formulas

taken their cue from Raymond Williams's (admittedly rather vague) concept of 'structure of feeling' (cf. 1977) and used it for addressing the public face of emotions as well as the privatization of publicly staged and circulating affects. Thus, public-feeling scholarship connects fruitfully to discussions of tacit knowledge and implicit understanding as it is interested in the circulation of affective energies and the available cultural forms of expression that are intelligible in and between intimate and public spheres. The term 'public feeling' was introduced first by a group of scholars, activists, and artists, among them Lauren Berlant, Vanalyne Green, Deborah Gould, Mary Patten, and Rebecca Zorach, that has founded and is collectively known as the Feel Tank Chicago. Most of these scholars connect their own work to Jürgen Habermas's 1962 analysis of the structural transformation of the public sphere, which was published in English for the first time only in 1989. Whereas the enlightenment public sphere is "imagined as a space of *knowledge*, a space of argument and counterargument" by Habermas (Soni 2010: 431), the public sphere in the second half of the 20th century has been running the risk of being "merely staged for manipulative purposes" (Habermas 1991: 31), and has taken on an affective rather than a "critical function" (ibid. 30).[4]

Lauren Berlant, whom I will single out here first, has devoted a trilogy to exploring what has crystallized as the construction of 'the intimate public sphere' (cf. 1997) in contemporary US culture and society: *The Anatomy of National Fantasy: Hawthorne, Utopia, and Everyday Life* (1991), *The Queen of America Goes to Washington City: Essays on Sex and Citizenship* (1997), and *The Female Complaint: The Unfinished Business of Sentimentality in American Culture* (2008). Whereas her analyses address phenomena of the 1980s and earlier

---

(Illouz) appears to be a gradual rather than a categorical distinction. For a discussion of the cultural coding of emotions, cf. Voss 2004: 33-38.

4 | It is somewhat surprising that there is little criticism in public-feeling scholarship of Habermas's 'blind spots' with regard to gender and subject formation. Feminist critic Nancy Fraser has recently "reconstruct[ed] the unthematized gender context of his material" (2013: 32) and has pointed out how Habermas "fails to focus on some dimensions of male dominance in modern societies" (ibid. 29) and how in his stabilization of the public-private dichotomy, his framework "is in important respects androcentric" (ibid. 32), particularly with regard to gendered power relations and to the gendered notion of citizenship: "[T]here are some major lacunae in Habermas's otherwise powerful and sophisticated model of the relations between public and private institutions in classical capitalism. [...] Habermas fails to understand precisely how the capitalist workplace is linked to the modern, restricted, male-headed, nuclear family" (ibid. 37). This is a critique that has yet to resonate in public-feeling work. Another blind spot certainly is the 'whiteness,' i.e. the racialized dimension of the bourgeois subject, which is absent from the work of both Habermas and Fraser.

historical periods, her diagnoses and claims have been even further substantiated by cultural developments in the US after 9/11 and the so-called 'domestic' and 'sentimental turn' following in its aftermath (cf. Faludi 2007; Werkmeister 2013). Berlant analyzes public spheres in the US as "affective spaces" (2008: 25) in which "intimate" themes such as "sexuality and reproduction, marriage, personal morality, and family values" (1997: 1) increasingly figure prominently in a public discourse on morals and are at the center of highly personalized ideological confrontations that ascertain the merit of politicians and political candidates in accordance with sentimental "character issues" rather than with their political aptitude (cf. ibid. 178). In fact, political discourse seems to be replaced with "anti-political politics" as the sentimentalist mode "develops *within political thought* a discourse of ethics that, paradoxically, denigrates the political and claims superiority to it" (Berlant 2008: 34). The resulting construction of an ideal citizenship by way of "sentimental cultural politics" (Berlant 1997: 4) radically transforms the notion of citizenship:

[T]he political public sphere has become an intimate public sphere [that] renders citizenship as a condition of social membership produced by personal acts and values, especially acts originating in or directed toward the family sphere. No longer valuing personhood as something directed toward public life, contemporary nationalist ideology recognizes a public good only in a particularly constricted nation of simultaneously lived private worlds. (Ibid. 3f.; cf. 177ff.)

This sentimental state fantasy invokes and reaffirms the "heterofamilial citizenship norm" (ibid. 21). All of this leads to a "denigration of the political sphere" (Berlant 2008: 10) as the state fantasy comes to bear on the political life of the nation and on its actors: "politics requires active antagonism, which threatens the *sense* in consensus: this is why [...] the political sphere is more often seen as a field of threat, chaos, degradation, or retraumatization than a condition of possibility" (ibid. 3, 11; cf. Wolfe 1991) against a sentimentalized intimate public sphere that is highly normative. Along those same lines, Lawrence Grossberg has argued that "the effect of transforming the terrain of ideological sites into affective epidemics is that it is no longer possible to treat them as the occasion for public debates" (1992: 292). Berlant's critique of sentimentalism ties in with a whole range of approaches that have investigated the cultural work of sentimentalism and its allegedly subversive potential;[5] in order to do its

---

5 | Jane Tompkins has most prominently argued in favor of appreciating the cultural work of sentimentalism (cf. 1985). Much earlier, James Baldwin (whom Berlant also draws upon) has noted the absence of genuine feeling in reaction to sentimental texts as they produce not sympathy but merely narcissistic pleasure that blocks political action and reform (cf. 1955). Glenn Hendler has extended the discussion of sentimentality

cultural work, sentimental politics – along the lines of 'structures of feeling' – has freed sentimentalism from a specific popular literary genre (namely that of the melodrama) and finds it to be in operation in all kinds of social, cultural, and political realms. Due to its ubiquity, we may add, it constantly conjures up, presentifies, and (re)affirms a culturally shared tacit knowledge.

Next to her voluminous work on sentimentalism, Berlant has scrutinized constructions of intimacy as public feeling in American culture which she links to both ideology and tacit knowledge. Of key interest in her analysis is how a sense of the 'normal' is produced and what constitutes a 'normal' affective economy or "normal intimacy" (Berlant/Warner 1998: 323), as they often rest on foundational claims that remain implicit:

[I]ntimacy reveals itself to be a relation associated with tacit fantasies, tacit rules, and tacit obligations to remain unproblematic. We notice it when something about it takes on a charge, so that the intimacy becomes something else, an "issue" – something that requires analytic eloquence. It becomes harder to see the presumption or even the desire for stable tacitness itself as a problem that reproduces panic in the intimate field. (Ibid. 7)

Thus, our notions of intimacy, which we do not have to address nor reflect since they rely (for the most part) on shared implicit understanding, are the effects of normative ideologies through which "certain 'expressive' relations are promoted across public and private domains – love, community, patriotism – while other relations [...] are discredited or simply neglected" (ibid. 5). In a queer reading of the parameters that shape our fantasies of the good life (and, by extension, the good state), Berlant and Warner find a hegemonic "constellation of practices that everywhere disperses heterosexual privilege as a tacit but central organizing index of social membership" (Berlant/Warner 1998: 319); the latter's very tacitness prevents any observation and discussion of the "constant failure of [those] heterosexual ideologies and institutions" (ibid. 320). By the exclusion of this failure from discourse, the heteronormative framework stays intact and continues to powerfully orchestrate intimacy in a (potentially) reproductive mode on a national level:

National heterosexuality is the mechanism by which a core national culture can be imagined as a sanitized space of sentimental feeling and immaculate behaviour, a space of pure citizenship. A familial model of society displaces the recognition of structural racism and other systemic inequalities. (Ibid. 313)

---

in American culture by including 'sentimental men' (cf. 2001). For a nuanced discussion of scholarship on sentimentalism in American culture, cf. Werkmeister 2013.

The evoked relation between individual feelings that 'go public' as collective feelings and – in turn – re-inscribe themselves in psyches and bodies hinges on the metaphor and the social unit of the family (and a particular kind of family at that). In the intimate public sphere, the citizen is interpellated as the member of a family (rather than as an individual). It is the implicit understanding of what it means to be a (good/proper/'happy') family member that circulates in the cultural and political imaginary and organizes affective states into emotional articulations, and hence produces public feeling. Again, with Louis Althusser we can say that the family as a primary Ideological State Apparatus renders it unnecessary for the Repressive State Apparatus to step in in order to stabilize the social order.

In a similar vein, Sara Ahmed has addressed the normative ideal of the nation as consisting of "happy families:"

Happy families: a card game, a title of a children's book, a government discourse; a promise, a hope, a dream, an aspiration. The happy family is both a myth of happiness, of where and how happiness takes place, and a powerful legislative device, a way of distributing time, energy, and resources. (2012: 45)

The relationship between the family and happiness is particularly interesting in an affective economy that "align[s] some subjects with some others and against other others" (Ahmed 2004: 117), meaning that we witness mechanisms of inclusion and exclusion along the lines of an affective/emotional investment in a particular societal norm. Overall, Sara Ahmed "challenges any assumption that emotions are a private matter, that they simply belong to individuals, or even that they come from within and *then* move outward toward others" (ibid. 117); rather, she contends that "emotions are not simply 'within' or 'without' but that they create the very effect of the surfaces or boundaries of bodies and worlds" (ibid.). Thus feelings are presentist, but also come in "sideways" and "backward" (ibid. 120). In the intersubjective realm, "the circulation of signs of affect shapes the materialization of collective bodies, for example the 'body of the nation'" (ibid. 121). Thus, happy families reiterate a culture of privatized "intensive nuclearity" (Lyubomirsky 2013: 103) that concomitantly creates the notion of the excluded (e.g. the "sad single"), and thereby invents a social pathology (ibid.). In Ahmed's study, the 'happy families' are reflected and refracted through the perspective of those excluded from it: "feminist killjoys, unhappy queers, and melancholic migrants" (2012: 49).

As a third important thinker on public-feeling complexes, Ann Cvetkovich in her work on public feeling initially addressed the melodrama as an affective genre that used "heightened feeling as a form of political expression" (qtd. in Staiger et al. 2010: 6); she counts melodrama among those genres "which have their origins in the cultural genres of early capitalism, to manage and contain cultural anxiety and dissent" (qtd. in ibid. 7), even as they may represent feelings in ways that "exceed the logic of management" (ibid.). In *Mixed Feelings* (1992), Cvetkovich problematizes readings of mass culture (in her case Victorian sensationalism) by Elaine Showalter – who addresses affective expression as subversive in the context of feminist politics and as the undoing of women's repression/oppression (cf. Cvetkovich 1992: 39) – and Fredric Jameson, who considers these texts merely as "affect management" (and thus containment) rather than as articulations of resistance (cf. ibid. 29). Cvetkovich herself in contrast has 'mixed feelings' about the political powers of affect; she shares with Deborah Gould the sense that "[a]ffect [...] greases the wheels of ideology, but it also gums them up" (Gould 2010: 33).

In *An Archive of Feelings* (2003), Cvetkovich works toward "the documentation and examination of the structures of affect that constitute cultural experience and serve as foundation for public cultures" (11). Here, she is particularly interested in a queer-theoretical perspective on affect in general and specifically in "affective forms of citizenship" (ibid.), as these often remain invisible (and implicit) and exist apart from institutional registers. Yet, the affective economies Cvetkovich seeks to describe do not merely gesture toward the inclusion and assimilation of gay citizens into established institutional practices (such as marriage) but identify "affective lives that counter the clichéd narratives of domestic contentment as well as anxiety, depression, and despair as the paradigmatic American national affects" (ibid. 12). Rather than following the worn-out path of a therapeutic discourse that often appears as a "substitute for political action" (ibid. 2) and that serves as a "privatized and personalized solution to problems that are ultimately social and collective" (ibid.), she envisions an archive of feelings on the basis of a reorganization of structures of feeling that brings about alternative ways of life. In this scenario, lesbian feelings, for example, thus may empower individuals and produce counterpublics (ibid. 285).

More recently, *Depression: A Public Feeling* (2012) reveals both formally and politically a more radical approach toward supposedly private economies of feeling (bad) by moving beyond the pathologization and medicalization of emotional suffering that may be considered a 'misreading' of its actual meanings: "What if depression, in the Americas at least, could be traced to histories of colonialism, genocide, slavery, legal exclusion, and everyday segregation and isolation that haunt all of our lives, rather than to biochemical imbalances?" (115). Part depression memoir, part cultural theory, Cvetkovich's *Depression* argues against the privatization and individualized 'treatment' of feeling, pain, and affect, and instead addresses depression, i.e. suffering, as a historical legacy of past trauma and identifies it as the potential grounds for solidarity and resistance; in fact, Cvetkovich's text insinuates that depression in its refusal to conform to a normalized affective state may actually be a practice of resistance in the face of capitalism's exploitative demands for flexibility, productivity, and resilience, and thus contains a severe critique of capitalism and its underlying myth of expressive individualism. Whereas Berlant and Ahmed seem to be engaged chiefly in exposing the ideological underpinnings of public feelings and their inherent normativity, Cvetkovich is also interested in how private and public affective worlds correlate: how one is transposed into the other or is reconfigured in interdependence with the other, and how these transformations can be put to use for the sake of political resistance.

The scholarship of public feeling extends far beyond the projects of those scholars I have singled out in my survey; it also includes many recent works in the realm of literary and cultural studies, cultural anthropology, and queer theory such as Glenn Hendler's historical work on 19th-century sentimental masculinity (cf. 2001), Kathleen Stewart's writings on 'ordinary affects' that I also draw on repeatedly in this essay (cf. 2007), Douglas Crimp's analyses of AIDS and mourning (cf. 2004), Michael Snediker's *Queer Optimism* (2008), David L. Eng's *The Feeling of Kinship* (2010), Erika Doss's work on memorial culture and public feeling (cf. 2010), Eva Illouz's *Cold Intimacies: The Making of Emotional Capitalism* (2007), as well as Catrin Gersdorf's work on coolness (cf. 2013).

These works all appear to identify a dimension of tacit knowledge that is partly revealed, i.e. presentified, in articulations of emotional states, practices, and narratives that in the process may also be removed from their original impulse (articulation as displacement), as these articulations of feeling take place in an already circumscribed and limited field of thinkable and intelligible (i.e. previously scripted) possibilities and are thus shaped or pre-figured by the social and cultural parameters of what can be 'felt' and explicated. Tacit knowledge resides "at the very edge/cusp of semantic availability" (Williams 1977: 134) and may be experienced as "an unease, a stress, a displacement, a latency" (ibid. 130) and as a variant, to phrase it in psychoanalytical diction, of the 'unthought known' (cf. Bollas 1987) which gets articulated in such a manner that it gestures beyond itself to some emotional, unspeakable yet 'recognizable' realm. The examination of public feeling thus involves analyzing explications and presentifications of individual and collectively shared forms of tacit knowing and tracing them back, so to speak, to subliminal and unconscious realms. These realms not only tell us something about the processes and histories of individual repression and displacement, but also grant us insight into a collectively shared 'political unconscious' (cf. Jameson 1981).

III. THE PURSUITS OF HAPPINESS

> Happiness is a warm gun.
> John Lennon

> Happiness is not around the corner. Happiness is the corner.
> BMW Z3 Advertising Slogan

> The American dream chants a mantra of ideals that are as serious as business itself and as thin as the talk at a supermarket.
> Kathleen Stewart, "Still Life": 406

Happiness, like any other emotion, "is not a private matter," but connects to political myths of the "body of the nation," as emotions such as happiness perform "the 'ordinary' work of reproducing the nation" (Ahmed 2004: 121-122). In fact, discourses of (earthly) happiness as public feeling are shaped by individual experience which in turn is determined by cultural scripts – quite literally in this case when we take the preamble of the Declaration of Independence as our point of departure – that, in turn, are incorporated and acted out by individual subjects. Happiness is explicitly addressed in the founding document of the nation, yet its exact meaning is not explicated;[6] we can speculate about its intended meaning in the historical context and its possible causes: Getting rid of the British king? Lower taxes? Property? Slaves? More property? More slaves? No taxes? As Jan Lewis notes when looking at the historical context, "the meaning of the concept was either so clear and commonly understood that no comment was required, or [...] its connotation was so vague and ambiguous that each could attach to it his own definition" (2000: 641). Both lines of reasoning presuppose tacit knowledge about the semantics of the term and about the notions of happiness. The 'happiness' of the Declaration of Independence seems to be very much linked to discourses of nation-building and to a hegemonic discourse of expressive individualism – note that the *pursuit* of happiness signals desire, deferral and quest, initiative and struggle. The meaning of happiness in

---

6 | Scholars offer a wide range of opinions on the semantics of happiness in the Declaration. Whereas Pauline Maier finds the rhetoric unspectacular (cf. 1998), Darrin McMahon has delved more into the possibility of different readings of that expression (cf. 2006: 314-19), and has pointed out that happiness also appears in other passages of the Declaration and in combination with "safety" (ibid. 314). 'Happiness' in the Declaration has furthermore been connected to the tradition of John Locke (happiness as property), Francis Hutcheson and the Scottish enlightenment, and to Jefferson's "synthesis" of both traditions (cf. von Eckardt 1959: 304).

this context encompasses a number of aspects and dimensions. First, it implies the notion of the manageability and perfectability of one's own life as evidenced in the boom of American self-help books that begins in the revolutionary era with Benjamin Franklin's autobiography – which actually *is* a self-help book – and in the belief that you can always *try again* to find happiness after all (hence the centrality of the 'pursuit'). Second, it stakes the normative claims of a particular (capitalist/Protestant) work ethic as a way (allegedly the only way) to get to happiness (as telos, so to speak) that sees happiness as a deserved reward for leading the right life; happiness thus becomes a way of measuring and qualifying lives, and is "used as a valid standard of conduct" (McMahon 2006: 349); but happiness is not only about success or failure, it is also about being 'normal' (not 'deviant,' 'pathological,' etc.), which concerns the work ethic but also other 'normal' institutions that may provide happiness (such as the family): "Happiness describes not only what we are inclined toward (to achieve happiness is to acquire our form or potential) but also what we should be inclined toward (as a principle that guides moral decisions about how to live well)" (Ahmed 2012: 199). Third, it includes the (rarely ever directly expressed) social-Darwinist notion of competition. Fourth, this presupposition, then, is manifested in the denial of US society's social stratification and the avoidance of a rhetoric of class (a diagnosis often formulated in Marxist readings of the Declaration) in the face of the tacitly accepted fact that "the promise of happiness depends upon the localization of suffering" *elsewhere* (Ahmed 2012: 195), a given that is played off against a highly sentimentalized affective state (one that James Baldwin, in fact, would call unfeeling and cruel; cf. 1955). All of these aspects are part of the myth of expressive individualism, which holds such a crucial place in US culture and its history of ideas that it may well be considered an American umbrella myth and a driving force in American civil society. Paradoxically, *expressive individualism* and the individual pursuit of happiness became foundational for constituting a new and meaningful *collective identity*. Whereas early US intellectual history assumed that self-interest fuels the greater common good and that public happiness is "more than the sum total of individual happinesses" (Lewis 2000: 643), this notion is increasingly in crisis in the second half of the 19th century with the radical and rapid "incorporation of America" (cf. Trachtenberg 2007 [1982]).[7] In the American exceptionalist logic, (worldly, economic) success, pleasure, and happiness have always been bedfellows in hegemonic myths of the nation and the national subject, and these myths rest on a discourse of an 'imagined happiness' which in turn pre-figures public

---

7 | This 'crisis' is certainly already inscribed in the document even as it remains largely submerged. In fact, we may speculate whether all those designated as "we, the people" can 'catch'/'catch up with' happiness and be happy at the same time – and what about those who do not yet belong to that 'we' in 1776?

feeling and its display in "moments of 'creedal passion'" (Kunow 2013: 53). Soni, however, finds that from the beginning, the individual 'pursuit of happiness' actually spells the absence of happiness as a *shared* political project, since it "does nothing to install a political horizon of happiness in the text" (2010: 457): "Happiness is assigned to the margins of politics; it is the private concern of the individual, sheltered from political interference" (ibid.). In a public-feeling framework, the Declaration's 'happiness' is so suggestive because it declares (the pursuit of) private happiness to be its unique political project, and thus is formative for happiness as a public feeling in the US.

Generally speaking, myths (including that of expressive individualism as/ and happiness in the US) are part of a discursive formation (and constitute a semiotic system) that claims intersubjective authority and undisputed validity. This prevalence, in my argument, works not only to establish the nation as an 'imagined community' (cf. Anderson 2006), but also extends to all those interpellated as its members, i.e. as citizens. The social function of myths is to respond to an affective desire for ontological (re)assurance, and myth operates in civil-religious forms that create within a group (i.e., the 'nation') a semi-conscious yet deeply affective bond (cf. Bellah 1967) which can be experienced and articulated as a kind of public feeling sitting at the intersection of individual experience and collectively intelligible explication. Often, familial constellations are invoked in order to do the work of mediating between the individual and the nation (cf. Althusser 1971). A similar function may be allotted to the routines of public feeling (as partial articulations of the tacit dimension of myth in its ideological function). 'Happiness' as an "American universality" (Claviez 1998: 16) appears to have been pursued relentlessly since 1776 (and possibly even longer) and has evolved into a central tenet of American civil religion (cf. McMahon 2006: 314) while making many people (nationally and on a global scale) very unhappy (and I am here not referring to the British king). In 1968, in the midst of the escalating war in Southeast Asia and in the wake of Martin Luther King's assassination, presidential candidate Hubert Humphrey still promised his voters a "politics of happiness" (Solberg 1984: 332); between 1776 and 1968 and beyond, happiness and its pursuits have remained key rhetorical concepts in US political culture and can be considered as constructing happiness as a public feeling in a national economy of affect and alleviation not least by tapping into a tacit reservoir of beliefs and practices.

IV. Engendering Public Feeling: The Case of Happy, Not So Happy, and Desperate Housewives

> [T]he only pursuit, the only goal a woman is permitted is the pursuit of a man.
> Betty Friedan, *The Feminine Mystique:* 36

> In our time, when intimacy saturates all aspects of the public sphere, from politics to culture to law, its regimes and temporalities are certainly as instrumental in pacifying the citizenry and securing social cohesion as were those of the workplace when work ruled the land. [...] [I]s reading *Capital* as a marriage manual really all that idiosyncratic?
> Laura Kipnis, "Adultery": 29

In order to bridge the chasm between self-interest and the common good and to camouflage the discrepancy between individual claim and national fantasy, the family functions as a primary institution that on the one hand mitigates the full force of expressive individualism and on the other poses an additional emotionally invested incentive for success. "The most powerful affective epidemic in the contemporary US is organized around and across the family" (Grossberg 1992: 285), which at times even "displaces the individual as the site of rights and liberties" (ibid. 287), a tendency that Grossberg identifies, similarly to Berlant, with the neo-conservatism of the Reagan years but sees by no means limited to that era: "In the name of the family, the space of individual rights can be sacrificed, even though it apparently violates Americans' supposed ideological commitment to individualism" (ibid.). The ideology of the family as a stand-in for the nation and as the social location of private fulfilment and rewarding long-term intimacy also conditions the specific emotional repertoire available to the family members depending on their position within this basic social unit. This ideology has always interpellated women as family members (and, by extension, citizens) of a particular kind: as wives and mothers with the affective needs for and specific access to the 'happy' states of romance and parenting. Historically, these interpellations have emphasized the private dimension of women's circumscribed lives (as 'angels in the house') as inverse to the public domain of men. Somewhat paradoxically, discourses on public feeling have thus insinuated that domesticity provides happiness in women's lives by making this private state of happiness available as public sentiment (naturalizing gender roles and rendering deviations from the model pathological) – a matter that has been addressed by a whole range of 19th- and 20th-century feminist scholars including, most prominently, Lydia Maria Child, Elizabeth Cady Stanton, Charlotte Perkins Gilman, Elaine Showalter, Nancy Chodorow, Annette Kolodny, Caroll Smith-Rosenberg, and Nina Baym.

In the wake of second-wave feminism in the 1960s and '70s, Betty Friedan's consciousness-raising text *The Feminine Mystique* (1963) addressed forms of female happiness and unhappiness by contrasting the dominant model of 1950s (happy) womanhood that included marriage, motherhood, and domesticity with empirical evidence showing that many women who were supposed to be happy because they 'had it all' – husbands, children, houses, cars, electric kitchen gadgets, etc. – were not at all the 'happy housewife heroines' (cf. ibid.) of 1950s patriarchal discourse. Friedan used the term 'mystique' to describe the ideological construction and effective policing of gender boundaries: "When a mystique is strong, it makes its own fiction of fact. It feeds on the very facts which might contradict it, and seeps into every corner of the culture, bemusing even the social critics" (ibid. 60). We can address this mystique as 'false consciousness' and/or as tacit knowledge: "Consciousness might be about how the social is arranged through the sharing of deceptions that precede the arrival of subjects" (Ahmed 2012: 165). From the perspective of tacit knowledge scholarship, this 'sharing of deceptions' is part of a collective tacit knowledge which is immunized against subversive interrogations by the simple fact that it is internalized and incorporated as tacit and cannot easily be reflectively addressed. Writing in a pre-feminist idiom, for Friedan, women's unhappiness is famously "the problem that has no name" (2013 [1963]: 9) as it is contained by way of an implicit understanding of ideologically produced gender difference that can hardly be explicated, let alone overcome. Friedan's critique addresses the 1950s 'Cold War' state's re-negotiation of the gendered conditions of happiness and of happy families, which marks single life as "causing unhappiness" and as "harrowing" (Carosso 2013: 73) and thus allocates a repertoire of negative feelings to the unmarried and the childless; the American nuclear family, of course, is in this fashion and in more or less subtle ways contrasted to its antithetical image of the dysfunctional family in socialism, which is purportedly bereft of all attachment and emotion and constitutes a field of the totalitarian state's intervention rather than the site of a privileged, God-ordained intimacy.[8] Beyond that dichotomous 'Cold War' model, it is intimated that the American family may be in crisis as well, as Deborah Weinstein has pointed out in her study *The Pathological Family: Postwar America and the Rise of Family Therapy* (2013). A number of scholars have addressed the obsession with normality, norm fulfilment, and deviance in these decades that appeared in conjunction

---

8 | The claimed superiority of one form of family/household over the other is also at the center of the so-called kitchen debate between Nixon and Khrushchev in a model kitchen space at the American National Exhibition in Moscow in July 1959 (cf. Kusmierz 2008).

with an affective economy of the 'Cold War' state which attached itself to every aspect of life and invited an open display of emotions that rendered the family and 'proper' family relations a matter of the state's survival and triumph, and labeled any political or ethical deviation 'un-American.' Here, the pursuit of happiness, again, figures as a patriotic act and becomes the 'pursuit of normality' (cf. Creadick 2010). "Deeply internizable," Creadick suggests, "normality became a way of talking about heterosexuality, middle-classness, whiteness, able-bodiedness without ever mentioning them" (ibid. 143). Thus, the majority defines normality according to their own 'average,' while the legitimacy of the normative claim of 'averageness' remains elusive and "foggy" (ibid. 142). This fogginess can well be described as a tacit dimension in Creadick's own argument and equally echoes in other recent studies about this period (e.g. Weinstein 2013; Carosso 2013); while most of these studies do not explicitly address tacit knowledge in the context of 'Cold War' culture, we can detect a tacit dimension in their insistence on the period's (partially implicit) normativity. At the same time, they point to what can be described as public-feeling choreographies of explications and presentifications in narratives and cultural practices. One platform of public-feeling discourses certainly is the booming self-help, self-management, and self-promotion literature ranging from Dale Carnegie's *How To Win Friends and Influence People* (1936) and Betty O'Connor's *Better Homes and Gardens Storybook* (1950) to *Dr. Spock's Baby and Childcare* (1946) (which contains a reference to tacit knowledge in its very first sentence: "You know more than you think you do"). Through this discourse, 'Cold War' ideology thus was tacitly instilled as knowledge of the 'American way of life' into (often female) American readers seeking advice on all matters of life. It is no coincidence that this self-help market and its promise of happiness by conformity were also targeted by Friedan's critique.

Notions of gendered happiness and normality in America are obviously not limited to the 1950s and '60s or the 1980s; they have become the object of renewed debates in post-9/11 US culture and its domestic (re)turn because "[t]he contemporary media environment is saturated by romantised, idealized, and indeed conservative images of selfless and satisfied 'good' mothers who conform to the ideology of intensive mothering" (Feasey 2012: 2) – and do so voluntarily and happily. The television series *Desperate Housewives* (2004-2012) has successfully dramatized stories involving 'heroic homemaking' and 'competitive parenting;' in repeated cycles of gradual success and complete failure, the series' lead characters are endlessly in pursuit of (mainly) domestic happiness and – a fresh ingredient lacking in earlier discourses – a proper work-life balance. When a friend of the four main characters commits suicide in the very first episode of the series, they wonder at her funeral "what could have made her so unhappy," since she "was healthy, had a great home, a nice family. Her life was [...] our life." The series (borrowing from the gothic mode) introduces the Freudian uncanny or, in Bhabha's term, the 'unhomely' (cf. 1992) into the seemingly perfect suburban homes and thereby asks whether the lifestyle it represents really is unequivocally worth pursuing and can provide happiness, while alternately displaying and shrouding what Laura Kipnis has called the "toxic levels of everyday unhappiness" (2000: 39) that are the cost of trying and failing to maintain a monogamous family life. The series has been controversially discussed as a postfeminist take on gender roles that reifies traditionally essentialized aspects of womanhood (also by 'quoting' 1950s and '60s aesthetics and visual styles) even as it pretends to critique them. Although the four protagonists at first glance appear to represent different types of femininity and different life choices in terms of career and family, a strong implicit normativity binds them together in their striving for a happiness that is ultimately based on and put in relation to *the* hegemonic structure of kinship: the nuclear family.

More recently, Mary Boyd Alley's *Meditations of a Happy Homemaker: Not a Desperate Housewife* (2006), an exemplary case of contemporary advice literature (originally written for a local church newsletter), once more affirms the ideology that Betty Friedan already took issue with in the early 1960s. Self-help and advice literature is a particularly resonant phenomenon for the investigation of tacit knowledge because it often claims to explicate implicit knowledge that allegedly was once shared but somehow got lost and now needs to be recuperated. Of course, this 'recuperation' includes the promise of a reward (often happiness) and clearly entails an ideologically conservative (if not reactionary) dimension. Alley's title presents the book as a critical intervention into both feminist and postfeminist discourses as it references and speaks back to Friedan as well as to the more recent television series. In a language of religious public feeling and anti-intellectualism, the author speaks – happily – with the authority of experience on matters of household management, child rearing, and celebrating the nation, all of which seem somehow intricately and 'logically' connected. The text reminds one of George Bush's often-ridiculed statement that "[w]e want to promote families in America. Families is where our nation finds hope, where wings take dream [sic]" (2000). Notwithstanding the grammatical errors and catachrestic imagery of this comment and the inadvertent self-parody it contains, its aim obviously is to tap into supposedly commonly held assumptions about the 'good life' and its perpetuation at the national level as well as on the level of the family.

It is against the backdrop of these kinds of descriptions and prescriptions of public feeling that Laura Kipnis develops her provocative thoughts on adultery as an anti-hegemonic variant of intimacy that (in a sentimental nation) may constitute a quasi-revolutionary act. Her argument is concerned with

> the public face of adultery in America at this moment in history, when adultery has become the favored metonym for all broken promises, intimate and national, a transpar-

ent sign for tawdriness and bad behavior. It's about adultery as a cover story. [...] It's about the fear that adultery *puts things at risk*: from the organization of daily life to the very moral fabric of the nation. (2000: 13-14)

As the family ideologically underpins the nation state, adultery (and the whole range of emotions connected to it) as the 'other' of familial normalcy and stability is perceived as a breach of the social contract, and the adulterer virtually becomes an enemy of the state to be hunted down – as for instance in "national adultery scandals" where every citizen can become a "detective" (Jameson qtd. in ibid. 35). In turn, marriage is reaffirmed as the only source of good citizenship and the proper framework for the 'pursuit of happiness' (which Kipnis would call 'regular unhappiness'):

But if adultery summons the shaming language of bad citizenship, this also indicates the extent to which marriage is meant to function as a boot camp for citizenship instruction, a training ground for resignation to the *a priori*. Anything short of a full salute to existing conditions will be named bad ethics. (Ibid. 14)

Kipnis's argument lends itself well to an exploration of public feelings that are embedded in non-reproductive, non-heteronormative forms of intimacy and have recently been discussed in queer-theoretical work on polyamory and kinship. Ann Cvetkovich has gathered an "archive of lesbian feelings" (2003: 239) such as mourning and shame (i.e. unhappiness), and Sara Ahmed, in the tradition of Betty Friedan, has employed the voice of the feminist killjoy in her blog against what Herbert Marcuse referred to as "a *happy consciousness* which facilitates acceptance of the misdeeds of this society" (qtd. in Ahmed 2012: 169). If affect is "articulated through the mediating effects of ideological narratives to produce different forms of emotional response and involvement" (Grossberg 1992: 81), the work of explicating the tacit dimension of public feelings is an archaeology of hidden knowledge that allows for identifying and tracing the relays through which this knowledge is both transmitted *and* contained in a wider circulation.

V. Conclusion: H Is for Happiness

> The American dream fights back from the womb of the middle class where forms of optimism, sentimentality, and a longing for interiority become tactile.
> Kathleen Stewart, "Still Life": 410

> Is this all?
> American housewife quoted in Betty Friedan, *The Feminine Mystique:* 15

Public feeling as conceptualized by Lauren Berlant, Sara Ahmed, Ann Cvetkovich, and others exemplarily reveals the interdependence of presence and tacit knowledge; it can indeed be thought of as a kind of nodal point that connects a shared implicit understanding to the explication and presentification of that understanding and thus reveals its origin and investment in hegemonic cultural scripts and cultural figurations. The available repertoire of public feeling is culture-specific, and in a US context, it is happiness that looms large as one particular foundational articulation of political emotion. Even if the pursuit of happiness as a political and private project does not begin and end with the Declaration of Independence, this document has cast a long civil-religious shadow over different kinds of primary institutions, among them the family. Whether we focus on US cultures of public feeling of the 1950s and '60s, the 1980s, or the post-9/11 decade, similar observations have been made by scholars about the display of public feeling in the context of a particular state fantasy that is maintained as an overtly gendered state of approximate private happiness – and vice versa. Public feelings organize how, why, and when we are 'happy' as private individuals and as members of a couple, group, team, or nation. Happiness has been singled out here in order to serve as a point of entry into current debates on public feeling and in order to trace affects, emotions, and their complex articulations to see 'where they take us' (cf. Ahmed 2012). In order to more fully explore the ways in which tacit knowledge helps us navigate affective economies but also forestalls the articulation, explication, and presentification of counter-hegemonic ones, one could envision an encyclopaedia of public feelings that begins with A as in angry,[9] annoyed, afraid, affectionate, anxious, alarmed, and aggravated, and ends with Z as in zany, zealous, and zen. We could think of thick descriptions of perceptions, 'ordinary affects' (cf. Stewart 2007), and emotional states and their function for political/state ideologies. Ann Cvetkovich has done such work in *An Archive of Feelings*

---

9 | Deborah Gould has, for example, analyzed the politics of representations of the so-called "angry AIDS activists" (2010: 25).

and, more recently, in her project "The Alphabet of Feeling Bad," which focuses on often excluded negative emotions. Thinking about the ensembles of public feelings and the protocols they follow and are embedded in sheds light on their tacit presences in everyday life as well as the latent workings of ideology. In a similar vein, Simon Thompson and Paul Hoggett offer a "typology of political feelings" (2012: 7) and analyze how these inform social relations and are used for political mobilization. In terms of practices of resistance, Sue Campbell has looked into the availability of non-normative feelings for expressing personal concerns (cf. 1997), and Ann Cvetkovich wonders whether melancholia and sadness can be read as a more "radical self-possession" (2012: 153) rather than as pathologies. Judith Butler has described a "tacit performativity" (1997: 159) that resignifies dominant cultural scripts of public feeling in the process of mimesis and re-enactment, "producing a scene of agency from ambivalence" and "a repetition in language that forces change" (ibid. 163). Thus we may also find a subversive element in the reiteration of public feelings that may call into question their straightforward categorization and containment: feelings "have conventionally accessible labels like 'happy' or 'sad'" yet "sometimes they are inchoate and slippery, suffusing or torquing our experience in ways that may be overwhelming and inexpressible" (Shotwell 2011: xii). Whereas in this essay I have developed a perhaps somewhat deterministic view on the pre-figuration and containment of affective economies in order to conceptualize the relationship between tacit knowledge and public feeling for critical purposes, in a next step we could engage more fully with the various degrees of identification and dis-identification at work in the performances and presences of public feeling that may appear to implicitly or explicitly refuse or deconstruct hegemonic cultural scripts. In Butler's work, it is the figure of Antigone who openly disobeys the protocols of public feeling and insists on the (public) mourning and burial of her brother, a declared enemy of the state, thus rejecting both the hegemonic affective economies of kinship and the tyrannical law of the state (cf. 2000). With Judith Butler and Alexis Shotwell, we can say that it is Antigone's claim that points us to the possibility of knowing, feeling, and acting 'otherwise.'

WORKS CITED

Adloff, Frank (2013): "Gefühle zwischen Präsenz und implizitem Wissen," in: Ernst/Paul, *Präsenz und implizites Wissen*, 97-124.
Ahmed, Sara (2004): "Affective Economies," in: Social Text 22.2, 117-39.
—. (2012): The Promise of Happiness, Durham: Duke UP.
Alley, Mary Boyd (2006): Mediations of a Happy Homemaker. Not a Desperate Housewife, Greensburg: Winters.

Althusser, Louis (1971): "Ideology and Ideological State Apparatuses. Notes Towards an Investigation," in: Louis Althusser, Lenin and Philosophy and Other Essays, https://www.marxists.org/reference/archive/althusser/1970/ideology.htm, accessed 10 March 2014.
Anderson, Benedict (2006): Imagined Communities. Reflections on the Origin and Spread of Nationalism, London: Verso.
Appiah, Kwame Anthony (1997): The Ethics of Identity, Princeton: Princeton UP.
Baldwin, James (1955): "Everybody's Protest Novel," in: James Baldwin, Notes of a Native Son, New York: Dial, 13-23.
Bellah, Robert (1967): "Civil Religion in America," http://www.robertbellah.com/articles_5.htm, accessed 25 Feb. 2014.
Berlant, Lauren (1991): The Anatomy of National Fantasy. Hawthorne, Utopia, and Everyday Life, Chicago: U of Chicago P.
—. (1997): The Queen of America Goes to Washington City. Essays on Sex and Citizenship, Durham: Duke UP.
—. (ed.) (2000): Intimacy, Chicago: U of Chicago P.
—. (2008): The Female Complaint. The Unfinished Business of Sentimentality in American Culture, Durham: Duke UP.
—. (2010): Cruel Optimism, Durham: Duke UP.
—. (2012): Desire/Love, Brooklyn: Punctum.
Berlant, Lauren/Warner, Michael (1998): "Sex in Public," in: Critical Inquiry 24.2, 547-66.
Bhabha, Homi K. (1992): "The World and the Home," in: Social Text 10.2-3, 141-53.
Bollas, Christopher (1987): The Shadow of the Object. Psychoanalysis of the Unthought Known, New York: Columbia UP.
Bourdieu, Pierre (1984): Distinction. A Social Critique of the Judgment of Taste, transl. Richard Nice, Cambridge: Harvard UP.
Bush, George (2000): "Where Wings Take Dream," in: Bushism Audio Gallery, http://politicalhumor.about.com/library/blbushism-wings.htm, accessed 19 June 2014.
Butler, Judith (1997): Excitable Speech. A Politics of the Performative, New York: Routledge.
—. (2000): Antigone's Claim. Kinship between Life and Death, New York: Columbia UP.
Campbell, Sue (1997): Interpreting the Personal. Expression and the Formation of Feelings, Ithaca: Cornell UP.
Carnegie, Dale (1981 [1936]): How to Win Friends and Influence People, New York: Simon and Schuster.
Carosso, Andrea (2013): Cold War Narratives. American Culture in the 1950s, Frankfurt: Lang.

Claviez, Thomas (1998): Grenzfälle. Mythos – Ideologie – American Studies, Trier: WVT.
Clough, Patricia Ticineto/Halley, Jean (eds.) (2007): The Affective Turn. Theorizing the Social, Durham: Duke UP.
Collins, Harry (2010): Tacit and Explicit Knowledge, Chicago: U of Chicago P.
Creadick, Anna G. (2010): Perfectly Average. The Pursuit of Normality in Postwar America, Amherst: U of Massachusetts P.
Crimp, Douglas (2004): Melancholia and Moralism. Essays on Aids and Queer Politics, Cambridge: MIT P.
Cvetkovich, Ann (1992): Mixed Feelings. Feminism, Mass Culture, and Victorian Sensationalism, New Brunswick: Rutgers UP.
—. (2003): An Archive of Feelings. Trauma, Sexuality, and Lesbian Public Cultures, Durham: Duke UP.
—. (2012): Depression. A Public Feeling, Durham: Duke UP.
Desperate Housewives (2004-12): USA, distr. Buena Vista Home Entertainment/Disney-ABC Domestic Television.
Dewey, John (2007): Erfahrung und Natur, Frankfurt/Main: Suhrkamp.
Döring, Sabine A. (2009): Philosophie der Gefühle, Frankfurt/Main: Suhrkamp.
Doss, Erika (2010): Memorial Mania. Public Feeling in America, Chicago: U of Chicago P.
Eng, David L. (2010): The Feeling of Kinship. Queer Liberalism and the Racialization of Intimacy, Durham: Duke UP.
Ernst, Christoph/Paul, Heike (2013a): "Einleitung," in: Ernst/Paul, *Präsenz und implizites Wissen*, 9-32.
—. (eds.) (2013b): *Präsenz und implizites Wissen. Zur Interdependenz zweier Schlüsselbegriffe der Kultur- und Sozialwissenschaften*, Bielefeld: transcript.
Faludi, Susan (2007): The Terror Dream. Fear and Fantasy in Post 9/11 America, New York: Metropolitan.
Feasey, Rebecca (2012): From Happy Homemaker to Desperate Housewives. Motherhood and Popular Television, London: Anthem.
Fraser, Nancy (2013): Fortunes of Feminism. From State-Managed Capitalism to Neoliberal Crisis, London: Verso.
Friedan, Betty (2013 [1963]): The Feminine Mystique, New York: Norton.
Gallagher, Shaun (2005): How the Body Shapes the Mind, Oxford: Oxford UP.
Gersdorf, Catrin (2013): "Kinds of Cool. Emotions and the Rhetoric of Nineteenth-Century American Abolitionism," in: Ulla Haselstein/Irmela Hijiya-Kirschnereit/Elena Giannoulis (eds.), The Cultural Career of Coolness. Discourses and Practices of Affect Control in European Antiquity, the United States, and Japan, New York: Lexington, 81-108.
Gould, Deborah (2009): Moving Politics. Emotion and ACT UP's Fight against AIDS, Chicago: U of Chicago P.

—. (2010): "On Affect and Protest," in: Staiger/Cvetkovich/Reynolds, Political Emotions, 18-44.
Grossberg, Lawrence (1992): We Gotta Get Out of This Place. Popular Conservatism and Postmodern Culture, New York: Routledge.
Habermas, Jürgen (1991): The Structural Transformation of the Public Sphere. An Inquiry into a Category of Bourgeois Society, transl. Thomas Burger/ Frederick Lawrence, Cambridge: MIT P.
Hendler, Glenn (2001): Public Sentiment. Structures of Feeling in Nineteenth-Century American Literature, Chapel Hill: U of North Carolina P.
Illouz, Eva (2007): Cold Intimacies. The Making of Emotional Capitalism, Cambridge: Polity.
Jameson, Fredric (1981): The Political Unconscious. Narrative as a Socially Symbolic Act, Ithaca: Cornell UP.
Jefferson, Thomas (1776): The Declaration of Independence, http://lcweb2.loc.gov/cgi-bin/ampage?collId=rbc3&fileName=rbc0001_2004pe76546page.db, accessed 19 June 2014.
Kipnis, Laura (2000): "Adultery," in: Berlant, Intimacy, 9-47.
Kunow, Rüdiger (2013): "'Watching One Another out of Fear.' Affective Communities and Medical Emergencies in the United States," in: Dirk Wiemann/Lars Eckstein (eds.), The Politics of Passion. Reframing Affect and Emotion in Global Modernity, Frankfurt: Lang, 51-68.
Kusmierz, Zoe (2008): "'The Glitter of Your Kitchen Pans.' The Kitchen, Home Appliances, and Politics at the American National Exhibition in Moscow, 1959," in: Sebastian Herrmann, et al. (eds.), Ambivalent Americanizations, Heidelberg: Winter, 253-72.
Lewis, Jan (2000): "Happiness," in: Jack P. Greene/J.R. Pole (eds.), A Companion to the American Revolution, Malden: Blackwell, 655-61.
Lyubomirsky, Sonja (2013): The Myths of Happiness, New York: Penguin.
Maier, Pauline (1998): American Scripture. Making the Declaration of Independence, New York: Knopf.
Massumi, Brian (2002): Parables for the Virtual. Movement, Affect, Sensation, Durham: Duke UP.
McMahon, Darrin M. (2006): Happiness. A History, New York: Grove.
O'Connor, Betty (1950): Better Homes and Gardens Story Book. Favorite Stories and Poems from Children's Literature, Des Moines: Meredith.
Pease, Donald (2009): The New American Exceptionalism, Minneapolis: U of Minnesota P.
Polanyi, Michael (1959): The Study of Man, London: Routledge and Kegan Paul.
—. (1969): Knowing and Being. Essays, ed. Marjorie Grene, Chicago: U of Chicago P.

Schmitz, Hermann (1993): "Gefühle als Atmosphären und das affektive Betroffensein von ihnen," in: Hinrich Fink-Eitel/Georg Lohmann (eds.), Zur Philosophie der Gefühle, Frankfurt/Main: Suhrkamp, 33-56.

Shotwell, Alexis (2011): Knowing Otherwise. Race, Gender, and Implicit Understanding, University Park: Pennsylvania State UP.

Snediker, Michael (2008): Queer Optimism. Lyric Personhood and Other Felicitous Persuasions, Minneapolis: U of Minnesota P.

Solberg, Carl (1984): Hubert Humphrey. A Biography, New York: Norton.

Soni, Vivasvan (2010): Mourning Happiness. Narrative and the Politics of Modernity, Ithaca: Cornell UP.

Spock, Benjamin (1946): Dr. Spock's Baby and Child Care. A Handbook for Parents of Developing Children from Birth through Adolescence, New York: Simon and Schuster.

Staiger, Janet et al. (2010): "Introduction. Political Emotions and Public Feelings," in: Staiger/Cvetkovich/Reynolds, Political Emotions, 1-17.

Staiger, Janet/Cvetkovich, Ann/Reynolds, Ann (eds.) (2010): Political Emotions. New Agendas in Communication, New York: Routledge.

Stern, Daniel (1985): The Interpersonal World of the Infant. A View from Psychoanalysis and Developmental Psychology, New York: Basic.

Stewart, Kathleen (2000): "Still Life," in: Berlant, Intimacy, 405-20.

—. (2007): Ordinary Affects, Durham: Duke UP.

Thompson, Simon, and Paul Hoggett, eds. (2012). Politics and the Emotions. The Affective Turn in Contemporary Political Studies, New York: Continuum.

Tompkins, Jane (1985): Sensational Designs. The Cultural Work of American Fiction, 1790-1860, New York, Oxford UP.

Trachtenberg, Alan (2007 [1982]): The Incorporation of America. Culture and Society in the Gilded Age, New York: Hill and Wang.

von Eckardt, Ursula M. (1959): The Pursuit of Happiness in the Democratic Creed, New York: Praeger.

Voss, Christiane (2004): Narrative Emotionen. Eine Untersuchung über Möglichkeiten und Grenzen philosophischer Emotionstheorien, Berlin: de Gruyter.

Waldenfels, Bernhard (2006): Grundmotive einer Phänomenologie des Fremden, Frankfurt/Main: Suhrkamp.

Weinstein, Deborah (2013): The Pathological Family. Postwar America and the Rise of FamilyTherapy, Ithaca: Cornell UP.

Werkmeister, Till (2013): Domestic Nation. Der sentimentale Diskurs US-amerikanischer Romane zum Elften September 2001, Berlin: LIT.

Williams, Raymond (1977): Marxism and Literature, London: Oxford UP.

Wolfe, Alan (1991): "Politics by Other Means," in: The New Republic 11 Nov., 39-41.

The End of Life and the Limits of Explication
Metaphors and Time in *Everyman* and *Tinkers*

Stephen Koetzing

> The neatly worked inner stretches of science are an open space in the tropical jungle, created by clearing tropes away.
> W.V. Quine, "A Postscript on Metaphor"

> Every metaphor is the tip of a submerged model.
> Max Black, *Perplexities*

> Old age isn't a battle, old age is a massacre.
> Philip Roth, *Everyman*

I. INTRODUCTION

In this article, I am interested in the ways figurative speech – and particularly metaphors – border on the limits of explication and may help to reveal what is commonly referred to as tacit or implicit knowledge. This kind of knowledge is usually said to be non-propositional and hence – at least within the realm of written language – inexplicable. However, theories of metaphor that extend the scope of metaphor beyond its existence as a rhetorical trope suggest a rethinking of the limits of language. I.A. Richards, for example, claims that "metaphor is the omnipresent principle of language" (1971: 92) and, as Manuel Bilsky observes, "asserts not only that all language is of [metaphorical] character but all thought is also" (Bilsky 1952: 131). Richards' ideas are shared by cognitive linguists like Petra Drewer, who speaks of metaphor as a bridge between language and cognition: "In cognitive linguistics metaphor finally overcomes its merely decorative past. It is no longer a trope which figuratively exemplifies an issue but part of the *knowledge* about this issue as well as part of its perspective assessment" (2003: 10, my transl.). The statements by Max Black and W.V. Quine quoted above in my view also are cases in point: Quine metaphorically plays with the notion of scientific, propositional, and supposedly metaphor-free knowledge as a clearing in the woods of human understanding, and Black suggests that metaphors are visible markers pointing to a 'deeper' insight. This brings to mind yet another term, which, as Heike Paul and Christoph Ernst argue, shares a relationship of mutual dependency with tacit knowledge: presence (cf. 2012a: 9). Metaphors, I claim, show this interdependency of presence and tacit knowledge in language. As visible markers in the text, they stick out and, at the same time, "invite [...] us to pass beyond the image" (Harries 1996: 77). The excess that metaphors create presentifies the limits of explication and thereby hints at insights that cannot be formulated within the limits of (propositional) language. Metaphors may thus be understood as carriers of tacit knowledge.

The test cases for the theoretical apparatus I develop here are Paul Harding's *Tinkers* (2009) and Philip Roth's *Everyman* (2006), which depict in great detail the troubles of aging by showcasing the frailness and dysfunctionality of their aged – and dying – protagonists. Knowledge about aging and dying is, I propose, to a high degree tacit knowledge, as it is social, corporeal, and emotional knowledge grounded in (individual) experience, which is non-propositional in nature (cf. Wieland 1999: 232). To flesh out how both novels presentify this knowledge, I will mainly focus on their temporal structures and on how they use time-related figurative speech to describe their protagonists. I suggest that in presenting knowledge about old age and dying to the reader, the texts create an "implicit understanding" (cf. Shotwell 2011) of or empathy for their protagonists. Taking into account the proliferation of such narratives in contemporary US literature and the fact that both novels tend to universalize their (white male) protagonists' individual experiences, I claim that these texts perform specific cultural work in that they allegorize the US and the crisis of the white male which has been declared in western societies in general and the US in particular at the beginning of the twenty-first century.

II. Presence and (Tacit) Knowledge

In the (re-)emerging discourse on presence, Hans Ulrich Gumbrecht's recent studies play a leading role, even though his central idea is hardly new. The loss of presence he diagnoses modern western societies with, which he attributes to a shift from "presence culture" to "meaning culture" roughly at the end of the sixteenth century (cf. 2012), is basically a reformulation of arguments put forward by Michel Foucault, Mikhail Bakhtin, and arguably even Sigmund Freud.

Presence in Gumbrecht's sense in fact resembles the all-encompassing feeling which Freud discusses as "oceanic feeling:"[1]

> Originally the ego includes everything, later it detaches from itself the external world. The ego-feeling we are aware of now is thus only a shrunken vestige of a far more extensive feeling – a feeling which embraced the universe and expressed an inseparable connection of the ego with the external world. If we may suppose that this primary ego-feeling has been preserved in the minds of many people – to a greater or lesser extent – it would co-exist like a sort of counterpart with the narrower and more sharply outlined ego-feeling of maturity, and the ideational content belonging to it would be precisely the notion of limitless extension and oneness with the universe – the same feeling as that described by my friend as "oceanic." (1949: 14-15)

While it is certainly the individual development of a human being that Freud has in mind, his description of the ego differentiating itself from its environment nevertheless can be set into relation with Bakhtin's elaborations on a historical shift in the perception of the human body. Bakhtin points out that the modern conception of the human body differs significantly from the conception of the grotesque body predominant in medieval times; he claims that while "the grotesque body is cosmic and universal" and is thus perceived as transcending its own boundaries (1984: 318), "[t]he body of the new canon is merely one body" and is essentially limited to "the individual, closed sphere" (ibid. 321).[2] The differentiation between cosmos/universe on the one hand and the individual on the other is also of concern to Erich Meuthen, who states that at the end of the sixteenth century, "the 'starry heaven above us' and the scope of 'moral law in us' do not yet appear to be incompatible spheres which can only be accommodated in the sublime experience" (2011: 29, my transl.). As Meuthen draws on Foucault's elaborations on an epistemic shift occurring in western thought at that time, his observations likewise pertain to the Cartesian mind/body dualism rather than to individual development. Coincidentally, it is Cartesianism that Gumbrecht delineates as a "scapegoat" (2004: xiv) by claiming that it is precisely this worldview that led to an exclusion of presence in western cultures:

---

1 | Cf. also Klaus Lösch and Heike Paul 2012: 154.
2 | Bakhtin too employs an oceanic metaphor when he describes the relationship between the old and new body canon. He calls the new canon, "the canon of art, belles lettres, and polite conversation," "a tiny island" in the middle of the "boundless ocean of grotesque imagery." For him, "[t]his limited canon never prevailed in antique literature. In the official literature of European people it has existed only for the last four hundred years" (1984: 319).

> The predominance and eventually the institutional exclusivity granted to consciousness and its role in human self-perception can be regarded as the essential innovation in the history of thought and ideas, which gradually turned the "medieval" world into a "modern" one. This development meant an increasing exclusion of everything corporeal and present that had undeniably been part of human self-reference throughout the Middle Ages. (Gumbrecht 2012: xxxi, my transl.)

The claims Gumbrecht makes about the transition from medieval to modern times is very similar to ideas by Foucault, who speaks about a shift from the episteme of resemblance to the episteme of representation at the end of the sixteenth century. Foucault writes:

> Up to the end of the sixteenth century, resemblance played a constructive role in the knowledge of Western culture. It was resemblance that largely guided exegesis and the interpretation of texts; it was resemblance that organized the play of symbols, made possible knowledge of things visible and invisible, and controlled the art of representing them. [...] And representation – whether in the service of pleasure or of knowledge – was posited as a form of repetition: the theatre of life or the mirror of nature, that was the claim made by all language, its manner of declaring its existence and of formulating its right of speech. (1994: 17)

In the episteme of resemblance, all knowledge, in other words, relies on an endless play of resemblances between the microcosmic and macrocosmic structures of the world and their interpretation. It is important here to notice the central role Foucault attributes to language: During that time language has its end in resemblance rather than in "its representative content, which was to have such importance for grammarians of the seventeenth and eighteenth centuries" (ibid. 35). The epistemic shift Foucault points out for the end of the sixteenth century is essentially a shift in the relation between signs and their meaning. Whereas in the episteme of resemblance, language is organized in a ternary and rather complex system which "requires the formal domain of marks, the content indicated by them, and the similitudes that link the marks to the things designated by them," the unity of which is guaranteed by the fact that "resemblance is the form of the signs as well as their content," language becomes organized in a denotative binary system of arbitrarily connected signifiers and signifieds in the episteme of representation (ibid. 42). Taking resemblance out of the equation causes a shift in human understanding: If "in the sixteenth century, one asked oneself how it was possible to know that a sign did in fact designate what it signified; from the seventeenth century, one began to ask how a sign could be linked to what it signified" (ibid. 43). For Foucault, "it is the Classical age that separates us from a culture in which the signification of signs did not exist," as at that time, the "profound kinship of language with the world" is starting to dissolve (ibid.). The question is whether this epistemic shift, which according to Gumbrecht caused a loss of presence, also caused knowledge which could be explicated in the language of resemblance to become (at least partially) inexplicable, that is to say tacit knowledge. If so, then a residue of this knowledge should be accessible via the figures of resemblance. Foucault explicitly negates the possibility to forgo "the signifying function of language" and return "to this raw being that had been forgotten since the sixteenth century" (ibid. 44). For him, there is only one exception to this rule: literature.

This assertion is far from surprising, as Foucault focuses on western scientific discourse, which – throughout the centuries and in contrast to literature – has been concerned with using 'pure' and propositional language, that is to say language that is (supposedly) denotative rather than connotative, and unequivocal rather than allusive. In this logic, tropes such as metaphors indeed are like Quine's tropical jungle, and have to be cleared away. This, however, is not to say that propositional language is truly metaphor-free – rather, readers tend to pay less attention to them in texts they deem 'non-literary,' as Gerard Steen's description of a set of tests designed to measure the "effects of discourse context" shows (1994: 63). The test subjects were given 'journalistic' ('non-literary') as well as 'literary' texts, and were asked to first "underline stretches of the text for their discourse-typical nature," and later to "explain in a few words why they had underlined the stretches in the two texts as typically literary and journalistic" (ibid. 67). Steen's findings suggest a relation between metaphors and reader expectations, because when given a text marked as 'literary,' subjects tended to underline metaphorical passages and explicitly refer to the metaphoricity of these passages in their explanations, whereas they never did this for the texts marked as 'journalistic' (cf. ibid. 73). In other words, it seems evident that when reading literature, readers are prone to pay special attention to metaphors whereas they tend to ignore them in texts they perceive to be 'non-literary.' Even if the perceived absence of metaphors in 'non-literary' texts thus is in part caused by reader expectation, the claim that propositional language is metaphor-free is still pervasive and might well be connected to the claim that non-propositional knowledge cannot be expressed in (written) language. My own understanding of this kind of knowledge by contrast is largely influenced by Alexis Shotwell, who develops her idea of what she terms "implicit understanding" from the observation that human knowledge comprises more than just verifiable claims and relies on more than just language. She writes:

We are intricately and intimately connected with others and with the world, and most of these connections happen alongside, beneath, and in other spheres than the words we say and the propositions we formulate. [P]ropositional knowledge [...] has been often understood as the only form of knowledge worth thinking about. We also know otherwise [...]. (2011: ix)

For this "implicit understanding," Shotwell delineates four categories, namely (1) "skill-based 'know-how' developed through practice," (2) "somatic knowledge" that "people have at the intersection of their bodily and conceptual systems," (3) "potentially propositional knowledge [...] that could be put into words but is not, now, in that form," and (4) "the category of affect and feeling" which "is not fully or generally propositional or considered a kind of knowledge." Furthermore, she emphasizes that "these four facets of implicit understanding are always experienced in co-constituting relation with one another" (ibid. xi-xii). Tacit knowledge is usually understood as knowledge that cannot (fully) be expressed in words, and Shotwell is a case in point, as she doubly marks this inexplicability: first, by explicitly differentiating between the terms 'propositional' and 'implicit,' and second, by using the term 'understanding' instead of 'knowledge,' which further highlights the radical difference of this 'other knowledge.' Furthermore, only two of her four categories suggest that (partially) explicating tacit knowledge through language is possible. If that is the case, the question arises as to if and how tacit knowledge can be conveyed in novels. Shotwell metaphorically suggests that "it is often at points of transition that the work of implicit understanding is most palpable" (ibid. ix): "[T]he implicit may be visible primarily at sites of a certain rupture in habitual activity, or points of breakdown in our conception of ourselves" (ibid. xvi). Therefore, my tentative answer is to take a look at metaphors as transitory figures of speech.

III. Metaphor and Context

The connection between metaphors and tacit knowledge is tangible in many theories of metaphor. Quine, for example, suggests that metaphors allow to formulate what "resists literal communication" (1996: 160), Paul Ricœur speaks of the "capacity of metaphor to provide untranslatable information" (1996: 141), and Michael Polanyi's famous dictum *"we can know more than we can tell"* (1967: 4) is echoed with a difference in Karsten Harries' claim that "metaphor transcends what can be captured by language" (1996: 72). In other words, the use of metaphors paradoxically seems to allow us to tell more than we can tell, which is more than obvious in the theories of metaphor themselves, as most (if not all) of them heavily rely on metaphors as carriers of meaning. This, of course, does not go unnoticed by their authors, who tend to point out the tautological structure of their own arguments and often revert to strategically and purposefully employing metaphors in their attempts to explain how metaphors work.[3] The apparent necessity to use metaphors for explaining their function

---

3 | This paper is no exception to the rule; as a matter of fact, it is this self-reflexivity that ties theories of metaphor, presence, and tacit knowledge together: all three border

demonstrates the power of metaphorical language. Metaphors are, as Harries puts it, "instruments to break the referentiality of language" (ibid. 78), and are therefore carriers of tacit knowledge. What is more, since their function can only be explained metaphorically, knowledge about metaphors themselves in part seems to be tacit knowledge.

In the following, I do not focus on metaphor in the strict sense, as is done in rhetorical metaphor theory, but instead use a broader approach that includes insights from cognitive metaphor theory and regards metaphor as overlapping with other figures of speech, such as simile, allegory, and metonymy. The difference between these two basic conceptualizations of metaphor can be understood as a difference in function: Whereas rhetorical metaphor theory foregrounds the psychological effects of metaphors, cognitive theory is more concerned with their cognitive function (cf. Kohl 2007: 65). George Lakoff and Mark Johnson underline the importance of cognitive metaphors: "Metaphors [...] are among our principal vehicles for understanding. And they play a central role in the construction of social and political reality" (2003: 159). Lakoff and Johnson argue that we constantly use what they call "unconscious" or "conceptual metaphors" in our everyday language and that we tend to employ them unconsciously for fundamental philosophical concepts such as morals, the mind, or time (1999: 155). Yet, the psychological and the conceptual dimensions of metaphor are by no means mutually exclusive, as Lakoff and Johnson's use of the term 'unconscious' already suggests – instead, they can be regarded as complementarily making up a continuum of metaphor usage in language. This is also one of the insights of Richards' theory of metaphor, who loosely divides metaphors into three categories, the first consisting of virtually all language, the second of "what we would ordinarily call 'dead' or 'sleeping' metaphors," and the third "refer[ring] to what are commonly called 'live' metaphors" (Bilsky 1952: 131-32). When Richards claims that metaphor is the "omnipresent principle of language," he has in mind a model of language in which "live" metaphors creatively combine hitherto separate aspects of thought and thus create new insights. Over time, these metaphors become conventionalized, that is to say "dormant" or "dead" metaphors (1971: 90-91).

Black picks up on Richards' ideas and explicitly posits an "interaction view" on metaphor as opposed to a "substitution view" or "comparison view," both of which he regards to be "the blind alley taken by those innumerable followers of Aristotle who have supposed metaphors to be replaceable by a literal translation" (1990: 51). Instead of understanding metaphors simply as elliptic similes, he is interested in "their power to present in a distinctive and irreplaceable way,

---

on the limits of explication as they try to explain in (written) language that which cannot (fully) be grasped by language. For a discussion of this connection cf. also Christoph Ernst's contribution in this volume.

insight into 'how things are'" (ibid. 50). For Black, metaphors clearly exceed the literal meaning of words on a page, and he suggests that this excess is negotiated in the reader's interpretation of tenor and vehicle (which he calls primary and secondary subject):

> In the context of a particular metaphorical statement, the two subjects "interact" in the following ways: (a) the presence of the primary subject incites the hearer to select some of the secondary subject's properties; and (b) invites him to construct a parallel implication-complex that can fit the primary subject; and (c) reciprocally induces parallel changes in the secondary subject. (ibid. 60)

It is important to notice that Black particularly emphasizes the interactive quality of metaphors. In his view, a metaphor neither is nor can it be replaced by a proposition with a 'clear' and stable meaning. Instead, it is to be considered "as a verbal action essentially demanding *uptake*, a creative response from a competent reader" (ibid.). The presence of a metaphor in other words requires readers to negotiate the knowledge it conveys. But how is one to conceive of Black's "uptake"? I think that Ralph Weber's almost Derridean approach to comparison may provide an answer to this question. In Weber's comparative model, two compared terms do not necessarily have to share a *tertium comparationis*, but instead are compared due to a perceived similarity between a *tertium* and a *quartum*, which also do not have to share a commonality, and so on:

> The question is whether "similarity in a similar respect" can be conceptualized without a point of commonality. An obvious objection is that the similarity between the *tertium* and the *quartum* [...] seems to rely again on a common respect. But that need not be so, for that similarity again could be one in a similar respect and so on ad infinitum. (2014: 157)

Besides Derrida, one is also easily reminded of Foucault's description of the episteme of resemblance as "an *episteme* in which signs and similitudes were wrapped around one another in an endless spiral" (1994: 32). What is more, the idea of a possibly endless interpretive process also accounts for the ambiguity of metaphor pointed out by Black (cf. 1990: 62): If a metaphor presents its reader with a virtually unlimited play of resemblances, then it is up to her to decide where this play may lead and when it may cease. Consequently, any metaphor requires a complex process of interpretation which intensifies the reading experience, as Wayne Booth claims when he argues that

> the receiver's process of interpretation is itself part of what is communicated; the activity of interpretation, performed at the speaker's command, produces a "bonding" which is part of the "meaning." Thus the act of interpreting metaphor will always be

more intense ("other things being equal") than engagement with whatever we take to be non-metaphoric (for some, what is *literal*; for others, what is *normal*). (1996:173)

Metaphors and the "uptake" they demand create a special bond with their readers, who in trying to make sense of them will inevitably have to refer to context, which in my view is at least threefold: 1) the context of the text's production, 2) the reader's own socio-cultural context, and 3) the context within which the metaphor is embedded in the text itself. While I would argue that for understanding a metaphor in a text the first of these three contexts matters only insofar as it is being reconstructed in the second, I would like to think of the second – metaphorically speaking – as Roland Barthes' *"already read"* (1977: 160).[4] The third type is concerned with context in the narrow sense of the term. Drawing on Gérard Genette, Ernesto Laclau points out the role of metonymy for the function of metaphor in narrative texts; with regard to the two axes of language, he locates metaphor on the paradigmatic and metonymy on the syntagmatic axis and defines their central working mechanism as analogy and contiguity, respectively. He also insists that the two tropes mutually imply each other and that it is this relationship which grants narrative unity and textual coherence (cf. 2008: 62-64). Furthermore, Laclau follows Genette in arguing that metaphor and metonymy are two poles of a continuum:

The main conclusion is that the notions of "analogy" and "contiguity" that are, respectively, the defining grounds of the two tropes, far from being entirely different in nature, tend, on the contrary to shade one into the other. [...] In one sense it can be said that metaphor is the *telos* of metonymy, the moment in which transgression of the rules of combination has reached its point of no return: a new entity has come into existence that makes us forget the transgressive practices on which it is grounded. But without those transgressive practices that are essentially metonymic, the new metaphoric entity could not have emerged.[5] (Ibid. 68-69)

---

4 | I am aware that phrases such as 'already read' and 'final vocabulary' (see below) because of their supposedly close relation to explicable, propositional knowledge may seem to be an odd choice when writing about tacit knowledge. However, I define 'text' broadly to include anything that can be 'read' rather than only written communication. After all, the term 'text' itself is a metaphor.

5 | Laclau's description strikingly resembles Foucault's elaborations on the four essential resemblances. For the latter, analogy is a combination of *aemulatio* and *convenientia* (cf. Foucault 1994: 17-23). Considering that convenience can be regarded as synonymous with contiguity and emulation a process of (paradigmatic) substitution, then Foucault, too, hints at the interdependence of metaphor and metonymy.

Therefore, it is not only the metaphors themselves that matter but also their situatedness in the text. Genette's metaphorical "first explosion" followed by a metonymical "chain reaction" (ibid. 63), however, would not occur without the reader's uptake. In my view, it is hence the continuous negotiation and reconciliation of the second and third types of context by the reader that are vital for 'grasping' metaphors. My idea of this process is similar to and informed by what Richard Rorty calls "redescription:" For him, every person has a contingent "final vocabulary" used for describing and understanding the world, which may change or expand when confronted with the alterity of a different vocabulary (cf. Frazier 2006: 21-22). Rorty argues that the process of redescription works particularly well in the reception of literary texts (and especially novels) because they help us exceptionally well to imagine the lives of others and to identify and sympathize with their suffering (cf. 2010: 393-94). He is thus interested in the world-making qualities of novels and their potential to help readers redescribe their own life-world via empathy.[6] The creation of empathy for their dying protagonists is central in both *Tinkers* and *Everyman*, as I will show in the following.

IV. *Tinkers*

Paul Harding's Pulitzer Prize-winning *Tinkers* tells the life story of George Washington Crosby – an old, bedridden, well-to-do horologist dying of cancer and Parkinson's disease – by switching back and forth between the last days of his life and memories of his childhood in rural Maine and his father's life as a tinker. Interspersed into this narrative are entries from the unfinished manuscript of an esoteric encyclopedia (supposedly written by the protagonist himself) and passages from a fictitious book called *The Reasonable Horologist*.

The novel loses no time to establish time as a central theme. The very first sentence informs the reader that "George Washington Crosby began to hallucinate eight days before he died" (Harding 2011: 7), and in doing so already draws attention to the passing of time and its relation to death. As Crosby hallucinates that his house is collapsing and burying him in the memorabilia of a lifetime, among them "boxes of forgotten board games and puzzles," "bags of family pictures – some so old they were exposed on tin plates," "newspaper clippings" from various stages of his life, "rusted tools," and "mangled brass works of

---

[6] | Drawing on the works of Wilhelm Dilthey and Theodor Lipps, Michael Polanyi remarks that empathy, or more precisely "indwelling," is "a striking form of tacit knowing" when it comes to "the understanding of man and of works of art" (1967: 17). For him, "it is not by looking at things, but by dwelling in them, that we understand their joint meaning" (ibid. 18).

clocks he had been repairing" (ibid. 9-10), the relation of these items to time passed is immediately pointed out: the games and puzzles are so old they are "forgotten," some of the photographs were recorded using an obsolete technology, the clippings have been cut out from dated newspapers, the tools are rusty, and the clockworks – besides obviously being instruments to measure time – allude to the protagonist's career as a horologist and thereby connect the aged Crosby thematically to time. This connection is further developed in a passage that informs the reader about how Crosby acquired his first broken clock together with an old repair manual at a tag sale and subsequently changed his career from working as a machinist to repairing and trading clocks and watches. In the middle of this passage, a shift in perspective takes place. It starts with a heterodiegetic narrator telling the reader about how "[a]s a machinist, he knew gear ratios, pistons, and pinions," and how he combined this knowledge with his "Yankee" insight into "where the old money lay [...]. He found that bankers paid well to keep their balky heirlooms telling time" (ibid. 14-15); the narration then suddenly switches to the imperative style of an instruction manual explaining how to clean a clock:

Lay the clock facedown. Unscrew the screws [...]. Examine the dark brass. See the pinions gummed up with dirt and oil. [...] Poke your finger into the clock; fiddle the escape wheel [...]. Stick your nose closer; the metal smells tannic. [...] Lift the darkened works from the case. Lower them into ammonia. Lift them out, nose burning, eyes watering, and see them shine and star through your tears. (Ibid. 15)

This switch from external focalization to Crosby as the focalizer strips the narration of its distancing mediation and allows for an empathic experience of the protagonist's life-world. The passage presents the reader with knowledge about Crosby's profession by appealing to several human senses: the touch of the escape wheel, the smell of the clock's metal, the biting sensation of the ammonia, and the sight of the dirty and cleaned brass works. The detailed description makes the task of cleaning and repairing clocks – and by extension the novel's protagonist – palpable. Only a few pages later, the intimate connection between the horologist and his clocks is taken to extremes. In one of his lucid moments, the dying Crosby realizes that the many clocks set up in the living room have all stopped and he links this realization immediately to his own situation: "When he imagined inside the case of [the Stevenson grandfather's] clock, dark dry and hollow, and the still pendulum hanging down its length, he felt the inside of his own chest and had a sudden panic that it, too, had wound down" (ibid. 33-34). The analogy drawn between Crosby and clocks is further emphasized in this passage when the narrator informs the reader that after his death the protagonist's wife kept a dozen of the finest pieces from his collection running and arranged around her living room in such a way that they seemed, in their precise alignment, with which she fussed and fine-tuned for months, to strike a chord that nearly conjured her dead husband, almost invoked him in the room [...]. (ibid. 34)

The clocks are metaphors for Crosby; their mechanics represent his guts, and their winding down his dying. While it is not at all uncommon to use time-related metaphors when referring to the dying of a human being – metaphors such as 'her time has come' or 'his time is running out' would be cases in point – it is the novel's over-emphasis of the time motif that makes the difference here. "Time is one of the assumed yet irreducible terms of all discourse, knowledge, and social practice," Elisabeth Grosz writes,

[y]et it is rarely analyzed or self-consciously discussed in its own terms. [...] It has an evanescence, a fleeting or shimmering, highly precarious "identity" that resists concretization, indication or direct representation. Time is more tangible than any other "thing," less able to be grasped, conceptually or psychically. (1999: 1)

The understanding of time, in other words, largely relies on tacit knowledge; and the novel tinkers with this notion. In the interspersed passages from *The Reasonable Horologist*, *Tinkers* makes several attempts to concretize time. These passages present the reader with detailed descriptions of marvelous antique clocks, one of which, for example,

supposedly seen in eastern Bohemia [...] had the likeness of a great oak tree wrought in iron and brass around its dial. As the seasons of its homeland changed, the branches of the tree turned a thousand tiny copper leaves, each threaded on a hair-thin spindle, from enameled green to metallic red. Then, by astounding mechanisms within the case (fashioned to look like one of the mythical pillars once believed to hold up the earth) the branches released the leaves to spiral down their threads and strew themselves about the lower part of the clock-face. (Harding 2011: 18)

The passing of time is here exemplified metaphorically by the seasonally changing appearance of a tree. The microcosmic man-made contraption mimics macrocosmic processes to presentify (tacit) knowledge, but the play of resemblances does not stop here, if one considers that the image drawn upon – the tree – is itself a commonly used metaphor for human life (and lineage). In this sense, the tree is a two-sided image that plays with and connects conceptualizations of time and life through the clock's appearance. This connection is picked up again in another passage from *The Reasonable Horologist* towards the end of the novel, which makes an effort to liken the universe to a clock: "For is it not true that our universe is a mechanism consisting of celestial gears, spinning ball bearings, solar furnaces, all cooperating to return man [...] to that chosen hour we know of from the Bible as Before the Fall?" (ibid. 179). Here, the universe and the meaning of life are explained by referring to the working mechanism of a clock, the circular dial of which continuously lets the clock hands revisit the hours as time passes. Considering that in this analogy, human beings are both the makers of clocks and "ignorant insect[s] crawling across the surface of that [universal] clock" (ibid.), the play of resemblances can be seen to fold in on itself virtually endlessly. Altogether, the excessive usage of time-related imagery throughout the novel presentifies time and – via the metaphoric connection between (broken) clocks and its (dying) protagonist – superimposes time-related (tacit) knowledge and (tacit) knowledge about aging and dying. In doing so, the text defamiliarizes the reader from her own understanding of time, old age, and death and thus demands a renegotiation of this knowledge and these concepts.

Tinkers also draws attention to the fact that clocks are themselves metaphors, as the vocabulary used to describe them shows: Terms such as 'clock face' or 'clock hands' suggest that we conceptualize clocks in metaphorical relation to the human body and tend to conceive of time in spatial dimensions. Therefore, the passages from *The Reasonable Horologist* bring to mind that clocks themselves can be understood as metaphors used to conceptualize and structure (the passing of) time. In this vein, *Tinkers'* several meticulous descriptions of clocks and clockworks also draw attention to the fact that the text is temporally structured like a countdown: The novel's first sentence reveals that its protagonist has eight days to live,[7] and every time the text returns to and refocuses on the old man lying on his deathbed, it is by mentioning the time left until his death. The novel thus forecasts and frequently reiterates the outcome of the story – Crosby's death. It also immobilizes the old man by confining his body to a hospital bed. Lakoff and Johnson explain that we tend to conceptualize time metaphorically in terms of motion (cf. 1999: 140). They point out two basic and antidromic metaphors: the "moving time" and the "moving observer" metaphor. For the former, the observer is considered to be fixed and time to be moving, for the latter, it is the other way round (cf. ibid. 140-147). In confining Crosby's body to the bed, the novel employs the moving time metaphor. By counting down to his death, his end is portrayed as inevitable, and his time as running out. In contrast, in the passages where Crosby hallucinates and remembers episodes of his life, time is fixed as Crosby's wandering mind renders him mobile (again) in his memories. The frequent oppositions of moving time and moving observer metaphors thus underline the transitions between the immobilized old protagonist and the younger mobile selves of his memories. In this conflict of selves, the protagonist's inevitable death clearly shifts the weight towards the

---

7 | Eight days is about the time span a fully wound clock will run.

dying Crosby, for whose depiction his younger, retrospective selves serve as the backdrop; the frail old man's medical condition is rendered in visceral detail:

George was dehydrated ninety-six hours before he died. The younger of his two daughters, Betsy, sat by the side of his bed, trying to give him water. The hospital had provided dozens of small, individually wrapped pink sponges on paper sticks. The sponges were meant to be dipped into water and then sucked on by patients too ill to drink from a cup. [...] He was dying from renal failure. His actual death was going to be from poisoning by uric acid. Whatever food or water he managed to consume never came back out of his body. (Harding 2011:57-58)

Passages like this one stage the old man's increasing alienation from life. Crosby's body is failing to perform basic life-sustaining functions and the medical devices provided to aid him further distance him from the living. Not only do the individually-wrapped sponges allude to the sterile environment of a hospital, but they are also mounted on paper sticks which essentially create a distance between the terminally ill man and his daughter caring for him. At the end of the novel, Crosby's alienation from mankind is complete:

Human consideration was no longer to be his, for that consideration could be expressed now only by providing physical comfort, and physical comfort was as meaningless to him (to it; what lay before his family now – the it formerly he [...]), was as meaningless to him now as it would have been to one of his clocks, laid out in his place to be dusted and soothed with linseed oil, fussed over and mourned even before it was was (because that is how the living prepare, or attempt to prepare, for the unknowable was – by imagining was as it is still approaching; perhaps that is more true, that they mourn because of the inevitability of was and apply their own, human, terrors about their wases to the it, which is so nearly was that it will not or simply cannot any longer accept their human grief) as its broken springs wound down or its lead weights lowered for the last, irreparable time. (ibid. 184)

The narrator clearly emphasizes the change of the personal pronoun referring to Crosby from "he" to "it." In this sense, the novel attests to the insight of Masculinity Studies that "'old men' are not men at all," as conceptualizations of masculinity usually (and implicitly) imagine men as young, active, and virile agents (Thompson 1994: 13). Moreover, the transformation from a living person to a dead thing is described in an almost Heideggerian fashion as a process which cannot be fully grasped by the bystanders who are caught in the emotional conflict of not wanting to let go and having to witness the terror of Crosby's death. In this light, the 'dead' metaphor of a dismantled clock on his workbench, which is used to describe Crosby's condition, demands renewed attention and scrutiny because the likening of the protagonist to a clock – the person to a thing – constitutes an act of seemingly inhumane and unjustifiable violence. In other words, the novel calls upon the reader's empathy for its feeble and dying protagonist.

Tinkers clearly holds an excessively introspective and empathy-demanding view on its protagonist's plight, and, by doing so, ideologically implicates its readers. Considering that the novel is titled *Tinkers* and tells the American Dream story of a tinker's son, the text can be interpreted as a comment on the US-American national character, as the US have often been referred to as a nation of tinkerers (a term that is semantically close to the noun 'tinker'); this stereotype has also quite recently been employed by Barack Obama, who at a science fair held at the White House in 2012 praised the US as "a nation of tinkerers and dreamers" (2012: n.p.). The fact that Crosby is described as a man who built his own house and – before falling terminally ill – could perform all the workmanship necessary to maintain it makes him a quintessential tinkerer (cf. Harding 2011: 12). Moreover, his full name, George Washington Crosby, alludes to the first US president and thereby metonymically connects the protagonist to the US. His building and maintaining his own house and raising a family can thus be interpreted as a metaphor for taking care of the nation, a task that he is no longer able to perform as he is dying. His family, in contrast, does not seem to share his skills or work ethic, as they cannot even perform the simplest tasks – Crosby's daughter spills the water when she tries to make him drink from a cup, and one of his grandsons cuts the old man with a razor while shaving him. What is more, in his death throes, Crosby imagines cracks in the ceiling of his house which nobody cares to fix. The crisis he faces in death is therefore double: not only is he losing control but his offspring is also unfit to take over his responsibilities. Crosby's death, therefore, becomes equivalent to the loss of the US national character imagined along the lines of WASP ideology. A similar case can also be made for *Everyman*.

V. *Everyman*

Much of what I have said about *Tinkers* also holds true for Philip Roth's *Everyman*, which also focuses on the life and death of an upwardly mobile man who rises from humble origins to become a well-to-do and respected art director of an advertising agency in New York City. Starting with the unnamed protagonist's funeral at which family members and a few friends have gathered to mourn his death, the text recounts his life in retrospective as a series of illnesses and attempts to surgically treat them, the last of which eventually fails.

Although *Everyman* does not draw upon the time motif as excessively as *Tinkers*, its exposition still draws on watches as a theme rather heavily. In his eulogy, the deceased's older brother Howard mentions that their father owned a small jewelry store and would run the same newspaper ad every month asking customers to trade in their watches. "All these watches that he accumulated – most of them beyond repair," Howard recalls,

> were dumped in a drawer in the back of the store. My little brother could sit there for hours, spinning the hands and listening to the watches tick, if they still did, and studying what each face and what each case looked like. That's what made that *boy* tick. [...] He used to take them and wear them – he always had a watch that was out of that drawer. One of the ones that worked. And the ones he tried to make work, whose looks he liked, he'd fiddle around with but to no avail – generally he'd only make them worse. (Roth 2007: 7-8)

In this passage, the text draws an analogy between watches and the protagonist, whose many illnesses and treatments – which will eventually lead to his death – can metaphorically be related to his attempts at repairing broken watches as a young boy; when he finally dies of cardiac arrest during his last surgery he, too, is "beyond repair" – just like the broken watches from the drawer in his father's jewelry store. The illnesses from which he suffers and his death further underscore this analogy in that most of his ailments are related to the cardiovascular system, which like a watch is essentially a circular system driven by a pacemaker. This circular analogy is also carried out on the structural level of the text. Georgiana Banita points out that *Everyman* "gives a spare stylistically minimalist overview of an ordinary man's life, [...] a life that comprises ten illnesses and ten operations with brief spans of good health in-between" (2009: 102); adding the two anthropological constants – birth and death – to these ten illnesses and operations yields twelve events which structure the protagonist's life. His life cycle thus structurally resembles the dial of a clock, which is further emphasized by the fact that the novel starts with his funeral and ends with his death – in other words, the narrative comes full circle, just like a clock hand after a full revolution. And while in contrast to *Tinkers*, *Everyman*'s story is narrated mostly in chronological order, there is a similar alteration of mobility/immobility in that the protagonist's life itself is structured by alternating phases of good health and illness/hospitalization. Similar to the deteriorating health of *Tinkers*' Crosby, these frequent illnesses are depicted as a reason for the protagonist's alienation from his surroundings after his retirement. The narrator points out that

> [a]ll these procedures and hospitalizations had made [the protagonist] a decidedly lonelier, less confident man than he'd been during the first year of retirement. Even his cherished peace and quiet seemed to have been turned into a self-generated form of solitary confinement, and he was hounded by the sense that he was headed for the end. (Roth 2007: 79)

This passage is once again reminiscent of a Masculinity Studies intervention into Age Studies. Against the gain in prestige and status usually attributed to aging (white) men, Stephen Whitehead argues that "the years from fifty onwards may signal a deep and lasting existential crisis, compounded by insecure work conditions, health problems, crisis of confidence over sexuality and relationships, and deepening recognition of their own mortality" (2002: 199-200). For Roth's protagonist, this crisis becomes palpable through an increasing estrangement, which can be observed on an intracultural as well as inter- and intrapersonal level.[8] Intrapersonally, his aging and continuously decaying body as well as his innumerable bypasses and stents and especially the defibrillator "lodged beneath the skin of his upper chest [...] with its wire leads attached to his vulnerable heart" (Roth 2007: 75) cause him to feel a "sense of estrangement brought on by his bodily failings" (ibid. 79). Interpersonally, his defibrillator stigmatizes him in the eyes of his daughter. When he shows her the bulge on his chest under which the defibrillator rests, "she ha[s] to turn away" because the feeble old man he has turned into no longer is the man "he was when she was ten and eleven and twelve and thirteen, without impediment or incapacity" (ibid. 75-76). Intraculturally, his estrangement takes the form of a self-imposed exile. *Everyman*'s protagonist decides to leave New York City in the aftermath of 9/11 to live at a retirement village at the Jersey Shore (cf. ibid. 63). His choice of a beach resort for elderly people over New York – one of *the* US-American cultural hubs – is a step towards self-marginalization at the end of the protagonist's life. At the resort, he is more and more frequently confronted with the deaths or serious illnesses of old friends and former colleagues, which cause a shift in his perception of himself, as he suddenly sees the inevitability of death and even considers committing suicide. In an "attempt to revive the old spirit by reviving memories of his colleagues' lives," the protagonist calls the widow of his former boss and two hospitalized former colleagues (ibid. 155). The futility and hopelessness of this attempt is summed up by the narrator with the often-quoted phrase "[o]ld age isn't a battle, old age is a massacre" (ibid. 156). In the context of the novel, the term 'massacre' of course also alludes to the events of 9/11 – just like in the case of Crosby in *Tinkers*, the personal crisis of *Everyman*'s protagonist thus can also be related to a national one, as it is around the time of the so-called terrorist attacks that his ailments, which had previously afflicted virtually all of his body, start to concentrate on his heart. His decision to leave "attackable Manhattan" (ibid. 63), the 'heart' of New York City, can thus be seen as a futile attempt to flee the vulnerability of his own heart. Considering that 9/11 has commonly been interpreted as an attack on core US-American values, the direction of this comparison, however, can also

---

8 | Here I draw on Klaus Lösch and Heike Paul's typology of strangeness (cf. 2012: 154-155).

be reversed. The namelessness of Roth's protagonist universalizes the old man, who furthermore at one point in the text ponders that "[s]hould he ever write an autobiography, he'd call it *The Life and Death of a Male Body*" (ibid. 52); and the novel's title further adds to the picture: the old white man is the (American) Everyman, and therefore – similar to Harding's George Washington Crosby – metonymically refers to the US as a nation and its core values. In this vein, his demise can once again be understood as a comment on the national character. The empathy the text creates for its protagonist-in-crisis, in other words, subliminally also mediates the idea of the US as a nation-in-crisis at the end of the so-called American Century.

VI. Conclusion

When it comes to the limits of explication in propositional language, metaphors are powerful cognitive tools because of their capacity to convey tacit knowledge. Understood as a continuum that ranges from conceptual and 'dead' metaphors to 'live' metaphors, they moreover exemplify the interdependency of tacit knowledge and presence. As visible markers in the text, they presentify tacit knowledge by demanding interaction in the sense of contextualization, (re)negotiation, and interpretation from the reader. Fiction proves to be an extraordinarily good medium for conveying knowledge through metaphors because of the special attention paid to tropes in literary texts. This allows for a reanimation of 'dormant' metaphors through defamiliarization, and hence a recontextualization and reinterpretation of tacit knowledge.

The two novels analyzed in this essay are cases in point: Both draw on metaphors from the donor field of clocks and watches to point out the frailty and feebleness of their aged and dying protagonists. And while it is not at all uncommon to conceptualize aging and dying metaphorically in relation to time, it is the emphasis both texts lay on time and its relation to old age and death on the structural level as well as the level of content that draws attention to these 'dead' metaphors and asks the reader to renegotiate her (tacit) knowledge about old age and death. To this end, both novels offer very similar images of loss and estrangement: The loss of control of both the body and the mind, the death of friends and companions, social alienation as well as the estrangement from family and one's own former self all evoke empathy for their protagonists, which is furthered by the tendency of both texts to universalize the plight and suffering of their respective protagonists. And it is this empathy that demands redescription and thus may lead to a new (implicit) understanding of what it means to grow old and die.

Regarding the contemporary proliferation of US fiction that focuses on aged and dying white men, the novels are two examples of a literary phenomenon whose extensive scholarly analysis remains a desideratum at this point. However, given the very similar mechanisms employed by both *Everyman* and *Tinkers*, a tentative claim can be made regarding the cultural work these novels perform. With their tendency to universalize and showcase in visceral detail the sufferings of aged white male protagonists, these texts comment on the nation. The crises of their protagonists allude to a nation-in-crisis, and their demise becomes a lament for the loss of the 'national character' and core US-American 'values.'

Works Cited

Bakhtin, Mikhail (1984): Rabelais and His World, Bloomington: Indiana UP.
Banita, Georgiana (2009): "Philip Roth's Fictions of Intimacy and the Aging of America," in: Roberta Maierhofer/Heike Hartung (eds.), Narratives of Life. Mediating Age, Münster: LIT, 91-112.
Barthes, Roland (1977): "From Work to Text," in: Roland Barthes, Image, Music, Text, London: Fontana, 155-164.
Bilsky, Manuel (1952): "I.A. Richards' Theory of Metaphor," in: Modern Philology 50.2, 130-137.
Black, Max (1990): Perplexities. Rational Choice, the Prisoner's Dilemma, Metaphor, Poetic Ambiguity, and Other Puzzles, Ithaca: Cornell UP.
Booth, Wayne C. (1996): "Ten Literal 'Theses,'" in: Sacks, On Metaphor, 173-174.
Drewer, Petra (2003): Die kognitive Metapher als Werkzeug des Denkens. Zur Rolle der Analogie bei der Gewinnung und Vermittlung wissenschaftlicher Erkenntnisse, Tübingen: Narr.
Ernst, Christoph/Paul, Heike (2012a): "Präsenz und implizites Wissen. Zur Interdependenz zweier Schlüsselbegriffe der Kultur- und Sozialwissenschaften," in: Ernst/Paul, Präsenz und implizites Wissen, 9-32.
—. (eds.) (2012b): Präsenz und implizites Wissen. Zur Interdependenz zweier Schlüsselbegriffe der Kultur- und Sozialwissenschaften, Bielefeld: transcript.
Foucault, Michel (1994): The Order of Things. An Archeology of the Human Sciences, New York: Vintage.
Frazier, Brad (2006): Rorty and Kierkegaard on Irony and Moral Commitment. Philosophical and Theological Connections, New York: Palgrave Macmillan.
Freud, Sigmund (1949): Civilization and Its Discontents, London: Hogarth.
Grosz, Elisabeth (1999): "Becoming... An Introduction," in: Elisabeth Grosz (ed.), Becomings. Explorations in Time, Memory, and Futures, Ithaca: Cornell UP, 1-11.

Gumbrecht, Hans Ulrich (2004): Production of Presence. What Meaning Cannot Convey, Stanford: Stanford UP.

—. (2012): "Etwas klarer sehen. Reaktionen auf ermutigende Einwände," in: Sonja Fielitz (ed.), Präsenz interdisziplinär. Kritik und Entfaltung einer Institution, Heidelberg: Winter, xxvii-xxxv.

Harding, Paul (2011): Tinkers, London: Windmill.

Harries, Karsten (1996): "Metaphor and Transcendence," in: Sacks, On Metaphor, 71-88.

Kohl, Katrin (2007): Metapher, Stuttgart: Metzler.

Laclau, Ernesto (2008): "Articulations and the Limits of Metaphor," in: James J. Bono/Tim Dean/Ewa Plonowska Ziarek (eds.), A Time for the Humanities. Futurity and the Limits of Autonomy, New York: Fordham UP, 61-83.

Lakoff, George/Johnson, Mark (1999): Philosophy in the Flesh. The Embodied Mind and Its Challenge to Western Thought, New York: Basic.

—. (2003): Metaphors We Live By, Chicago: U of Chicago P.

Lösch, Klaus/Paul, Heike (2012): "Präsenz, implizites Wissen und Fremdheit aus kulturwissenschaftlicher Perspektive," in: Ernst/Paul, Präsenz und implizites Wissen, 151-183.

Obama, Barack (2012): "Remarks by the President at the White House Science Fair," http://www.whitehouse.gov/the-press-office/2012/02/07/remarks-president-white-house-science-fair, accessed 7 Feb. 2012.

Meuthen, Erich (2011): Sprachkraft. Versuch über Ironie und Allegorie, München: Fink.

Polanyi, Michael (1967): The Tacit Dimension, Garden City: Anchor.

Quine, W.V. (1996): "A Postscript on Metaphor," in: Sacks, On Metaphor, 159-160.

Richards, I.A. (1971): The Philosophy of Rhetoric, Oxford: Oxford UP.

Ricœur, Paul (1996): "The Metaphorical Process as Cognition, Imagination, and Feeling," in: Sacks, On Metaphor, 141-157.

Rorty, Richard (2010): "Redemption from Egotism. James and Proust as Spiritual Exercises," in: Christopher J. Voparil/Richard J. Bernstein (eds.), The Rorty Reader, Malden: Wiley-Blackwell, 389-406.

Roth, Philip (2007): Everyman, New York: Vintage.

Sacks, Sheldon (ed.) (1996): On Metaphor, Chicago: U of Chicago P.

Shotwell, Alexis (2011): Knowing Otherwise. Race, Gender, and Implicit Understanding, University Park: Pennsylvania State UP.

Steen, Gerard (1994): Understanding Metaphor in Literature. An Empirical Approach, London: Longman.

Thompson, Edward H. (1994): "Older Men as Invisible Men in Contemporary Society," in: Edward H. Thompson (ed.), Older Men's Lives, Thousand Oaks: Sage, 1-21.

Weber, Ralph (2014): "Comparative Philosophy and the Tertium. Comparing What with What, and in What Respect?" in: Dao. A Journal of Comparative Philosophy 13.2, 151-171.
Whitehead, Stephen M. (2002): Men and Masculinities. Key Themes and New Directions, Cambridge: Polity.
Wieland, Wolfgang (1999): Platon und die Formen des Wissens, Göttingen: Vandenhoeck und Ruprecht.

Moving Images of Thought
Notes on the Diagrammatic Dimension of Film Metaphor

Christoph Ernst

For film studies, one of the most promising theoretical frameworks to discuss the relevance of tacit knowledge can be established by bringing together cognitive semantics and semiotics. Drawing on George Lakoff and Mark Johnson's cognitive theory of metaphor and Charles S. Peirce's notion of diagrammatic thinking, I propose that the diagrammatic structure of film metaphor is a semiotic relation which can be read as a visualization of tacit knowledge. This theoretical argument will be illustrated by an analysis of a short and highly conventionalized metaphorical sequence from Steven Soderbergh's *Solaris* (2002).[1]

I. A Theory of Film Metaphor?

The question whether such a thing as film metaphor exists is in itself subject to metaphorical drift. Is it possible to apply a linguistic term like metaphor to film, or is film metaphor nothing more than a metaphor *for* metaphor? The paradox of having to define metaphor itself by means of metaphors has led some critics to dismiss the linguistic concept of metaphor as irrelevant to film (cf. Arnheim 2002: 247f.). This, of course, is problematic at best. There have been numerous attempts to use metaphor for theorizing film, or even to define a specific 'cinematic' or 'film' metaphor.[2]

---

[1] | This work presents parts of the findings from my research project 'Diagrammatische Denkbilder – Grundzüge einer Medien- und Filmtheorie der Diagrammatik im Anschluss an Charles S. Peirce and Gilles Deleuze' funded by the German Research Foundation (DFG) from July 2011 to January 2013. A broader and more detailed study of diagrammatic media and film theory can be found in Ernst 2015 (forthcoming). For help with this paper I would like to thank Katharina Gerund and Sebastian Schneider.

[2] | For a historical overview cf. Thiele 2006.

Discussions of film metaphor have always depended on contemporaneous linguistic and rhetorical theories of metaphor. Film theory until the 1950s had an understanding of metaphor as a literary trope or poetic concept in the tradition of Aristotle, Cicero, and Quintilian (cf. Clifton 1983), i.e. as an explicit comparison. In the 1930s, Eisenstein proposed to define metaphor as the semantic tension between two contrasting shots connected by montage (cf. Eisenstein 2006: 9ff., 15ff., 58ff., 88ff.; Whittock 1990: 70ff.). Film theory from the 1960s onward adopted a semiological understanding of metaphor from structuralists like Jakobson and Lacan, who provided a new conceptualization of metaphor based on the differentiation between paradigma (metaphor) and syntagma (metonymy). Metz considered metaphor to be a syntactic relation between two possible alternative shots primarily on the paradigmatic axis of the 'text' of the film (cf. Metz 2000: 148ff., 205ff.). With the rise of cognitive film theory in the 1980s came an understanding of metaphor derived from cognitive semantics, which led to 'cognitive semiotics' approaches (cf. Buckland 2007). Carroll regarded metaphor to be the inferential decoding of a paradoxical semantic co-presence of two ontological entities in one shot (cf. Carroll 1994, 1996; Whittock 1990: 97ff.).

These approaches focus on different levels of communication and meaning (pragmatic, syntactic, semantic), but all of them discuss issues relevant to film. Considering metaphor to be irrelevant to film theory thus does justice neither to film theory nor to the theory of metaphor. But it is necessary to keep in mind that metaphor is not an exclusively linguistic fact, as cognitive theories of metaphor have provided empirical evidence that metaphor is a phenomenon within perception itself. Following this notion, one has to assume that linguistic metaphor is only one of several types of metaphor. Pictorial metaphor would be another type, and audiovisual and dynamic forms of film metaphor a third one. Especially the different ways in which media like language and film adapt configurations that realize a metaphorical relation are of great interest (cf. e.g. Forceville 2005). But what is a metaphorical relation? Lakoff and Johnson give a simple answer:

The heart of metaphor is inference. Conceptual metaphor allows inferences in sensory-motor domains [...] to be used to draw inferences about other domains [...]. Because we reason in terms of metaphor, the metaphors we use determine a great deal about how we live our lives. (2003: 244)

In other words, a metaphor is a mode of thinking which involves perceptual inferences. A cognitive theory of metaphor thus is in fact a *perceptual* theory of metaphor. While a perceptual notion of metaphor accounts for all kinds of semiotic representations of metaphor (linguistic, pictorial, cinematic, etc.), it is of special importance in (audio-)visual and dynamic representations like film images.

II. Experiential Realism and Conceptual Metaphor

In their cognitive approach to metaphor, developed in *Metaphors We Live By*, "The Contemporary Theory of Metaphor," and *Philosophy in the Flesh*, Lakoff and Johnson (cf. Lakoff/Johnson 1999, 2003; Lakoff 2011) seemingly establish a sharp contrast between 'internal' and 'external' metaphors, with 'internal' metaphors referring to 'conceptual' metaphors rooted in the embodied mind, and 'external' metaphors to the rhetorical trope commonly used in language and other media. This distinction could be criticized as the manifestation of a dualistic universalism,[3] but one has to take into account that Lakoff and Johnson's theory of metaphor is situated within two larger projects: *cognitive semantics*, i.e. the linguistic effort to describe the cognitive aspects of natural language semantics (cf. Evans/Green 2009), and *experiential realism* or *experientialism*, which is positioned against the 'objectivism' or '*a priori* philosophy' found in the traditional philosophy of language (cf. Johnson 1987: 194ff.; Lakoff 1987: 260ff.; Lakoff/Johnson 1999: 74ff, 94ff.; 2003: 185ff.).[4] Experiential realism relies on the notion of an embodied mind, for which the dimension of tacit (or implicit) and non-propositional knowledge of the body is crucial (cf. Johnson 1987). Lakoff and Johnson call tacit knowledge the "cognitive unconscious" and define it as knowledge that "operates beneath the level of cognitive awareness, inaccessible to consciousness and operating too quickly to be focused on" (Lakoff/Johnson 1999: 10). For them, the 'cognitive' encompasses not only propositional and explicit knowledge but also tacit and non-propositional knowledge: "The cognitive unconscious is vast and intricately structured. It includes not only all our automatic cognitive operations, but also all our implicit knowledge" (ibid. 13; cf. 11f.). This broad notion of the 'cognitive' implies two types of tacit knowledge: first, the realm of *cognitive-automatized faculties* consisting of the basic operations of the nervous system and perception, which are autonomous bodily functions; second, the realm of *implicit sociocultural knowledge*, i.e. knowledge consisting of learned and archived faculties which have become 'tacit' through embodiment and have been automatized by practice. Lakoff and Johnson assume that it is the second type of tacit knowledge which structures cognitive concepts and call it the "'hidden hand' that shapes how we conceptualize all aspects of our experience" (ibid. 13).

---

3 | Certainly a statement like the following may sound provocative to anyone defending an *a priori* of culture: "In short, metaphor is a natural phenomenon. Conceptual metaphor is a natural part of human thought, and linguistic metaphor is a natural part of human language" (Lakoff/Johnson 2003: 247).

4 | For a critique of Lakoff and Johnson's philosophical approach cf. Haser 2005.

Despite the fact that they are primarily interested in tacit knowledge as it is generated by basic operations of the body, this 'corporeal *a priori*' is by no means ignorant toward cultural differences. Not only rhetorical linguistic metaphor but also its cognitive basis – conceptual metaphor – is susceptible to sociocultural differences. Yet, Lakoff and Johnson are certainly not cultural relativists. One has to keep in mind the *relation* between highly culturally specific *semiotic structures* and far less culturally dependent *cognitive structures* as represented in the distinction between linguistic and conceptual metaphor. Even if Lakoff and Johnson speak of the 'cognitive,' they are by no means naive proponents of an *a priori* of neural structures. This is most evident in their theory of metaphor.

III. THE BASIC STRUCTURE OF METAPHORICAL MAPPINGS

Lakoff and Johnson's theory of conceptual metaphor is widely accepted as a framework of metaphorical relations (cf. e.g. Gibbs 2008). For the purpose of this paper, we can break this framework down to five basic premises:

i. Metaphor is a relational mapping between a source domain A and a target domain B.
ii. In metaphor, source domain A and target domain B do not coalesce but are co-present.
iii. Metaphor is a mode of seeing A *as* B under the assumption that A *is* B.
iv. The process of seeing A *as* B under the assumption that A *is* B is a perceptual inference.
v. As a perceptual inference, metaphor relies on embodied tacit knowledge.

The first premise argues that metaphor is a phenomenon within the human cognitive apparatus. Metaphor thus is not only a phenomenon on the 'surface' of cultural representations, as Lakoff and Johnson famously proposed that "[t]*he essence of metaphor is understanding and experiencing one kind of thing in terms of another*" (2003: 5). Metaphor thus is understood to rely on intellectual inference ('understanding') and sensorimotor perception ('experiencing'). The process of metaphor is furthermore specified as a relation between two semantic domains, one of which is used to understand and experience the other. Like many others, Lakoff and Johnson call this 'mapping' (cf. Johnson 1987: 69ff.).

The operation of 'mapping' (which is a metaphor itself) is explained by the second premise. Korzybski famously stated that "[a] map is not the territory it represents, but, if correct, it has a similar structure to the territory which accounts for its usefulness" (1948: 58). In 'cartographic' relations, the target domain ('territory') and the source domain ('map') are co-present but do not converge. Metaphor similarly does not simply project a source domain onto a target domain – the source domain is treated as a map and then projected onto the target domain. This leads Lakoff and Johnson to the hypothesis that common source domains are based on embodied semantics. Lakoff and Johnson posit a *tertium comparationis* for metaphorical mappings, which operates as a second 'map' *within* the relation 'A as B' and can be described as an 'image-schema' (cf. Johnson 1987). Image-schemas are kinesthetic schemas that are generated from basic body movements and constrain the mapping of metaphor: "To say that image-schemata 'constrain' our meaning and understanding [...] is to say that they establish a range of possible patterns of understanding and reasoning" (Johnson 1987: 137).

The third premise is a consequence of the second. If the metaphor of 'mapping' holds, metaphor is inferential in a specific way. In order to see the epistemological advantage provided by the operation of considering something (the map) as something else (the territory), one has to know that there is a difference between the two, but at the same time one has to suspend this awareness and treat the map *as if* it actually were the territory in an operation that seems to be a mode of parallel seeing. When Lakoff (2011: 269) proposes TARGET-DOMAIN AS SOURCE-DOMAIN and TARGET-DOMAIN IS SOURCE-DOMAIN as the metaphors to define metaphor, the connection between 'as' and 'is' implies that A is regarded as B under the assumption that A is B.

The fourth premise relates to the inferential nature of conceptual metaphor. Metaphor is not isolated from perception but appears in various forms of cultural representations (language, pictures, moving images, sound, etc.) that are connected to modes of perception. The aesthetics of metaphor thus is rooted in embodied *aisthesis*.[5] The inferential nature of metaphor is best illustrated by conclusions drawn from analogical reasoning, an example of which is provided by Johnson's description of a sexist argument (cf. 1987: 10f.):

'A woman is responsible for her physical appearance
Physical appearance is a physical force (exerted on other people)
Therefore a woman is responsible for the force she exerts on men'

The form of inference is:

$F(A)$
$A=B$
$\therefore F(B)$

---

5 | For a discussion of the famous metaphor of 'seeing,' which is a metaphor for the process of gaining an insight ('KNOWING IS SEEING'), cf. Lakoff/Johnson 2003 and Blumenberg 1999.

The equation A=B relies on the metaphor Physical Appearance Is A Physical Force. Such metaphors trigger an analogical generalization based on the coherent complex of meaning established by a conceptual metaphor. Generalizations can become mindsets that influence perception and eventually result in practical and often hurtful consequences.

Given that metaphors are perceptual inferences, the fifth premise accounts for the role of tacit knowledge in those inferences. The inner working of a metaphorical mapping is expressed by two principles: the principle of highlighting and hiding, and the invariance principle. Highlighting and hiding indicates that metaphor does not refer to existing similarities but rather creates similarities. This is achieved by hiding incoherent (non-similar) features and highlighting coherent (similar) features of a domain (cf. Lakoff/Johnson 2003: 10ff.). Even more important is the invariance principle, which states that the basic schematic structure of a domain cannot be transformed by mappings – the source domain and the target domain are co-present but do not converge. Image-schemas then serve to organize the mapping between the two domains: "[…] the invariance principle blocks the mapping of knowledge that is not coherent with the schematic or skeletal structure of the target concept" (Kövecses 2010: 131; cf. Lakoff 1990). The invariance principle can be considered to be the crux of metaphorical inference: "Metaphorical mappings preserve the cognitive topology (that is, the image-schema structure) of the source domain, in a way consistent with the inherent structure of the target domain" (Lakoff 2011: 278). Lakoff continues: "The Invariance Principle hypothesizes that image-schema structure is always preserved by metaphor" (ibid.). A metaphorical mapping reduces the complexity of a domain's content by creating an image of two skeletal structures in order to generate and regulate the highlighted and hidden similarities. This indicates the significance of image-schemas as a *tertium comparationis* in metaphorical mappings.

IV. Image-Schemas and Tacit Knowledge

The essence of Lakoff and Johnson's theory of tacit knowledge is contained in the notion of image-schemas, which are particularly important in the process of exemplifying and visualizing concepts of abstract thought (cf. Johnson 2007: 141). Constituting structural couplings between the body and its surrounding environment, image-schemas are "structures of sensorimotor experience by which we encounter a world that we can understand and act within" (ibid. 136). Relevant in "meaning-making, abstraction, reasoning, and symbolic interaction" (ibid. 135f.), image-schemas are *spatial, dynamic,* and *logical* (cf. Johnson 1987: 25). They are located within the modes of everyday 'basic-level categorizations"⁶ of perception: *"A schema is a recurrent pattern, shape, and regularity in, or of, these ongoing ordering activities"* (ibid. 29f.). Johnson explains their logic by using the CONTAINER schema as an example:

> [...] consider what follows if your car keys are *in* your hand and you then place your hand *in* your pocket. Via the transitive logic of Containment, the car keys end up *in* your pocket. Such apparently trivial spatial logic is *not* trivial. On the contrary, it is just such spatial and bodily logic that makes it possible for us to make sense of, and to act intelligently within, our ordinary experience. (2005: 22)

The transitivity of CONTAINER comes from everyday bodily actions which are generalized into basic principles of categorization and categorical identity. In consequence, for Lakoff und Johnson there is no basic contradiction between the body-based logic of tacit knowledge and the logic of abstract symbolic (conventionalized) systems:

> The central idea is that image schemas, which arise recurrently in our perception and bodily movement, have their own logic, which can be applied to abstract conceptual domains via primary and higher-level conceptual metaphors. Image-schematic logic then serves as the basis for inferences about abstract entities and operations. [...] There is no disembodied logic at all. Instead, we recruit body-based, image-schematic logic to perform abstract reasoning. (Johnson 2007: 181)

Drawing on Johnson's notion of image-schemas, Lakoff in *Women, Fire, and Dangerous Things* identifies five basic image-schemas: CONTAINER, PART-WHOLE, LINK, CENTER-PERIPHERY, and SOURCE-PATH-GOAL (cf. 1987; for further discussion cf. Hampe 2005). Most research has been done on the CONTAINER schema (cf. Lakoff 1988: 141ff., 2011: 274ff.), whose structural elements, basic logic, and sample metaphors are the following (cf. Lakoff 1987: 272f.):

Structural elements of CONTAINER: Interior, Boundary, Exterior.

---

6 | Derived from Rosch's prototype theory (cf. Lakoff/Johnson 1999: 26ff.; Lakoff 1988: 132ff.; 1987: 31ff., 46ff.), basic-level categorizations are the 'typical' way of categorizing objects on a 'basic level' of abstraction. The prototype of a 'chair' for example is a schema which is neither specific nor abstract; the idealized prototypical domain of a 'chair' features "mental images, gestalt perception, motor programs, and knowledge structure" (Lakoff/Johnson 1999: 27) which all come together in a perceptual inference. Prototypical knowledge of a 'chair' thus is defined by 'knowing that' as well as 'knowing how.'

Basic logic of CONTAINER: Everything is either inside or outside a container (P or not P). Transitivity: If A is in a Container B and X is in Container A, then X is in Container B.

Sample metaphors based on CONTAINER: Metaphors of the visual field (something comes 'into sight' or goes 'out of sight'), metaphors of the mind ('to have something in mind,' 'to get something out of one's head').

These features offer an illustration of CONTAINER as a spatial and proto-logical schema but they do not account for the notion of image-schemas as *dynamic* patterns. However, in his paper "Cognitive Semantics" Lakoff also provides a diagram of CONTAINER as a dynamic form of an inference (cf. 1988: 142) in which CONTAINER is depicted as the movement of an inference. It presents itself as the transitive sequence 'if X is in Container A and A is in Container B, then X is in Container B.' Lakoff and Johnson understand image-schemas as 'moving images' in the sense of a moving sequence of inference. They identify basic dynamic image-schema operations such as SUPERIMPOSITION, by which schemas are transformed and thus create a gestalt of the schema as a 'moving image of thought.'

According to the convention of using small caps for conceptual metaphors, SUPERIMPOSITION is also represented in this way because it belongs to a special category of basic 'image-schema operations' (cf. Johnson 1987: 25f.). Image-schema operations are transformations of image-schemas that allow for categories to fit into metaphorical mappings. In SUPERIMPOSITION, this is achieved through a basic diagrammatic thought experiment: "Imagine a larger sphere and a small cube. Increase the size of the cube until the sphere can fit inside it. Now reduce the size of the cube and put it within the sphere" (ibid. 26). A second image-schema operation is called MULTIPLEX TO MASS (or MASS TO MULTIPLEX). MULTIPLEX TO MASS operations describe the process of 'zooming in' or 'zooming out' when perceiving a multitude of objects as a multitude of different entities ('Multiplex') up to the point when the multitude of entities is perceived as a single entity with an individual gestalt as a group ('Mass') (cf. ibid.).

Following Kant's notion of schema (cf. 2002: B 176/A 137-B 187/A 147), an image-schema has the character of a rule.[7] However, for Johnson image-schemas are not simply regular patterns: The schema is the whole form of a moving sequence of inference. As Johnson points out, the form of an image-schema has gestalt-like qualities – the whole is greater than the sum of its parts. Johnson claims that those gestalts are non-propositional (cf. 1987: 27). The gestalt of a schema – its 'inherent meaning' – is dynamic (cf. ibid. 42ff., 62ff.). As a mov-

---

7 | Similarities and differences between Kant's notion of schema and the notion of image-schemas are discussed in Johnson 1987: 147ff.

ing image of thought, the gestalt is described as an analogical form for a holistic experience, which is why the whole of the gestalt of an image-schema like CONTAINER can only be explained through the dynamics of a whole sequence of transformations via image-schema operations. These transformational image-schema operations are at work in metaphorical mappings: Image-schemas operate as schematic *tertia* in mapping source domains onto target domains while preserving the relational structure of a domain.

But how can this process be observed? An answer can be found in Lakoff and Johnson's notion of 'complex' conceptual metaphors, which are figurations of conceptual metaphors in semiotic representations such as film metaphors. Culturally specific representations of metaphors consist of different types of conceptual metaphors. In *Metaphors We Live By*, Lakoff and Johnson (heuristically) distinguish between three basic types of conceptual metaphor, all of which are based on the body-schema (cf. 2003: 264):

(i) The most basic metaphorical relation is called *orientational metaphor*. Orientational structures act as a target domain by using deictic relations of the body, as e.g. in MIND IS UP, EMOTION IS DOWN (cf. ibid. 7ff.). Orientational metaphors are very simple metaphors of limited semantic complexity.

(ii) *Ontological metaphors* are more complex relations that operate on the basis of mappings between an abstract target domain and an object-like source domain, as e.g. in TIME IS MONEY. Personifications like WAR IS A MACHINE also count as ontological metaphors.

(iii) The most complex metaphorical relations are *structural metaphors*, which are complex mappings between an abstract target domain and a concrete source domain. Unlike ontological metaphors, the concrete source domain is not an object but a 'knowledge-scenario' about a type of action, e.g. the notion of 'Journey' in LIFE IS A JOURNEY. Structural metaphors require to be thought through on the basis of their proposed structural resemblance.

Tacit knowledge, as represented in image-schemas, is essential for understanding each of these three types of metaphor: For understanding an orientational metaphor, one needs a body as well as knowledge of the basic relations of that body; for understanding an ontological metaphor, one needs 'know-how' about an object; for understanding a structural metaphor, one needs complex knowledge of what is and is not possible in a situation, i.e. implicit knowledge of the 'rules' of a situation. In short: Lakoff and Johnson's notion of image-schemas is concerned with the effect of tacit knowledge on metaphorical mappings. Tacit knowledge in the form of image-schemas is crucial especially when it comes to creating structural resemblances between target and source domains.

V. Career is a Journey – Metaphor and Image-Schemas

Let us examine an example which demonstrates how image-schemas are at work in conventionalized everyday conceptual metaphors: CAREER IS A JOURNEY. The source domain 'Journey' relies on image-schemas of movement, as in statements like 'my new job is not really a step forward but sideways' or 'she really made her way up the ladder.' One image-schema for describing movement in this metaphor is FORCE. Johnson considers FORCE to be an image-schema which reveals something about the *"internal structure"* of image-schemas as "experiential schemata" (1987: 41). According to Johnson, FORCE can be divided into seven basic types, one of which is FORCE-BLOCKAGE (as in making a step 'sideways'), and another is FORCE-ENABLEMENT (as in making it 'up the ladder'). The metaphor CAREER IS A JOURNEY generally describes an upwards movement, as e.g. in TO HAVE A CAREER IS MOVING UP THE LADDER (going 'up the ladder' also means climbing 'higher').

Lakoff and Johnson call this metaphorical coherence 'entailment' (cf. 2003: 87ff.). While mapping describes the basic operation of metaphor, entailments take cultural configurations of conceptual metaphors into account. Entailments are semantic implications between two conceptual metaphors; e.g. in CAREER IS A JOURNEY, the SOURCE-PATH-GOAL schema is implied as the schematic structure. Relying on image-schemas, entailments show certain logical features: "the grounding of the whole is the grounding of its parts" (Lakoff/Johnson 1999: 63). If there is A there is also B, and if there is no B there is no A. The fact that one domain can be explained by different metaphors increases the complexity of entailments. For Lakoff and Johnson, a semantic domain can itself be a metaphor (cf. 2003: 97ff.; Kövecses 2010: 121ff.).[8]

Depending on the complexity and type of metaphor, image-schemas may interact. If the metaphor HAVING A CAREER IS MOVING UP THE LADDER leads to an inference like 'in a high position it is difficult to breathe because the air is getting thin,' then two additional image-schemas are at work, namely PATH, which underlies the application of FORCE to movement ('movement is a FORCE on a PATH'); and SCALE, which underlies PATH in HAVING A CAREER IS MOVING UP THE LADDER.

Let us focus on the relation between the image-schemas PATH and SCALE (cf. Johnson 1987: 113ff., 123ff.), which share many features but are also characterized by a variety of differences. PATH is horizontal, progressive (if you have earned an MA you may move on to earn a PhD), and closed; SCALE is vertical and open, implies quantity and intensity, relates to numbers, and is cumulative (if you hold a PhD you are a postdoc and can become a professor – at least if

---

8 | This accounts for the fact that metaphors themselves can become conventionalized schemas.

there is no obstacle that limits your force). Finally, in contrast to PATH, SCALE can be measured (the 'track record' which reflects the 'path' of your career). While horizontal directions evoke linear movement, vertical directions are associated with growing quantities and qualities ('the air is getting thin,' 'the pressure is rising') (cf. Johnson 1987: 123ff.).

Such operations of image-schemas within complex metaphors constitute a very interesting problem. They can be regarded as being equivalent to connotation in semiotic (or, to be precise, 'semiological') theory (cf. Barthes 1977). Entailments and the influence of image-schemas describe how connotations are organized *logically* but not necessarily logically *consistent*. For semiotics and semiology, this leads to the hypothesis that the rhetorical effect of semantic connotations that are inherent in linguistic metaphors of various kinds seems to be connected to tacit knowledge. For this hypothesis, the creativity of image-schemas in mappings and entailments is significant (cf. Lakoff/Johnson 2003: 96). In order to understand how tacit knowledge translates into semiotic representations, it is necessary to focus on image-schemas and image-schema operations which structure connotations of complex metaphors. These operations can be observed by examining the interactions between conceptual metaphors in complex rhetorical figurations of metaphor such as film metaphors. Analyzing metaphorical mappings reveals how tacit knowledge is 'at work' in semiotic representations, and therefore in culture at large. But is it really possible to comprehend image-schemas and image-schematic operations within metaphors, and how do they translate into a semiotic theory of the inherent logic of connotations? The answer, as I will illustrate, can be found in pragmatist semiotics, particularly in Peirce's concept of diagrammatic reasoning.

VI. Semiotics and Second-Level Diagrammatic Reasoning

It is no coincidence that Lakoff employs a diagrammatic form of representation for the logic of CONTAINER. Diagrams are able to depict spatial logic and dynamic patterns (cf. Lakoff 1987: 273; Evans/Green 2009: 180). Nevertheless, Johnson holds that "schemas are not diagrams on a page" (1987: 79): As entities of tacit knowledge, image-schemas are not to be confused with their semiotic representations in diagrams. Similarly, conceptual metaphors are not the same as linguistic metaphors; the latter instead are structured through conceptual metaphors and image-schemas. To what extent then do tacit structures 'motivate' externalized semiotic representations?

While researchers in many disciplines have adopted Lakoff and Johnson's thesis of intrinsically spatial, dynamic, and logic image-schemas, there is one particularly controversial issue. Semioticians (e.g. May 1995, 1999; Pietarinen

2011) have argued that Lakoff and Johnson propose image-schemas as self-evident internal logical structures and thus ignore the fact that schemas are culture-specific.[9] These critics fail to understand the idea of image-schemas as embodied tacit knowledge, because as semioticians, they have no concept of embodiment and tacit knowledge; they can describe how concepts of the 'body' are culturally 'constructed,' yet they cannot account for embodiment in cognition. What is problematic in Lakoff and Johnson however is not their category of image-schemas but rather their idea of an *iconic resemblance* between gestalt-structures of embodied tacit knowledge and conventionalized semiotic forms such as algebra (cf. Lakoff/Núñez 2000), which relates to the discussion of whether mathematical/symbolic systems are motivated through embodied perception. Given that tacit knowledge undergoes a transformation when it is explicated and that there are also forms of tacit knowledge which always remain 'tacit' and cannot be explicated at all ('strong' notion of tacit knowledge) (cf. Renn 2004; Loenhoff 2012), Lakoff and Johnson's theory seems to be inconsistent. However, at least to some degree this assessment turns out to be unjustified if we take into account Peirce's notion of diagrammatic reasoning.

From ca. 1896 onward, Peirce tried to find a semiotic justification for pragmatism (cf. Meyer-Krahmer/Halawa 2012) by developing the visual logic of his existential graphs (cf. Pietarinen 2003). Diagrammatic thinking should provide a paradigmatic 'scene' of everyday analytical thinking (cf. Peirce 1906, 1976/IV: 313ff.). Peirce considered reasoning with diagrams to be an ideal-typical situation within the continuum of perception, belief, and action. The famous doubt-belief schema of 'habit-taking' and 'habit-breaking' in diagrammatic reasoning provides a way to reflect on everyday analytical reasoning as described in pragmatism (cf. Peirce 1973). Of particular interest are situations in which a formerly unquestioned belief is thrown into doubt ('habit-breaking') and it becomes necessary to explicitly *think* in light of a failing automatism about how to deal with these situations. Such critical situations also include intrinsically 'creative' moments. It is this pragmatic situation of thinking analytically in the face of a crisis which Peirce's diagrammatic reasoning sought to reconstruct. To understand this reasoning, it is essential to take into account, first, that Peirce considered thinking in signs itself to be a diagrammatic process; and second, that moments of crisis which precede 'habit-breaking' can be studied paradigmatically in moments of mistaken perceptual judgments. For Peirce, perception is an unconscious, continuous, and abductive reasoning in signs[10] which is transformed into a conscious thought process when a percept no longer fits into established schemata and categories of perception, and

---

9 | This argument is not in the least new; Peirce already used it in his critique of Kant's notion of schema (cf. Eco 2000).

10 | For an extensive discussion of Peirce's theory of perception cf. Roesler 1999.

subsequently into the schemata of action (what Peirce calls 'habits'). Peirce's concept of diagrammatic reasoning is a mode of diagrammatically making explicit a problematic hypothesis about a percept, i.e., a percept that cannot be explained by the habits of perception is made explicit and externalized as a diagram ('diagrammatization').

The world of the visible provides privileged examples for examining everyday pragmatism in light of diagrammatic reasoning (cf. Eco 2000; Pape 1995, 1997). By means of structural resemblance, a diagram serves as a medium for externalizing the implicit explanatory rule of the abductive mode of perception. Peirce calls this 'hypothesis.' It is the hypothesis that is being externalized and transformed into a diagram in a process that can be considered as *second-level* diagrammatic reasoning, which works on the basis of an externalized and conventionalized diagram. To clarify the notion of diagram in second-level diagrammatic reasoning, May and Stjernfelt's (2008: 67f.) categorization of diagrams is useful. They differentiate between image diagrams (e.g. a transit map), diagrams proper (e.g. a tree diagram), and symbolic diagrams (e.g. an algebraic expression). Through externalization, such a diagram is transformed and becomes a medium upon which deductive experiments may be performed (cf. May 1999: 186; Stjernfelt 2007: 104).

For Peirce, the most important thing about a diagram is that it constitutes a logical space for the eye to perceive logical connections not present (or hidden) in the original percept. The diagram can offer an innovative and creative solution to a problem because it shows possibilities which are not present in the premises of the construction of the diagram. According to Peirce, this situation is analogous to the process of redefining beliefs in light of explicit thinking. By thinking with the help of a materialized diagram (e.g. a map), conclusions can be reached in two ways: either the diagram 'automatically' provides the conclusion ('corrolarial deduction'), or the diagram has to be transformed ('theorematic deduction') (cf. Peirce 1998: 298). The major feature of diagrams is their ability to create evidence that is *structurally similar* to perceptual evidence in the continuum of perception, belief, and action:

> It is, therefore, a very extraordinary feature of Diagrams that they *show*, – as literally *show* as a Percept shows the Perceptual Judgment to be true, – that a consequence does follow, and more marvelous yet, that it *would* follow under all varieties of circumstances accompanying the premises. [...] Meantime, the Diagram remains in the field of perception or imagination; and so the Iconic Diagram and its Initial Symbolic Interpretant taken together constitute what we shall not too much wrench Kant's term in calling a *Schema*, which is on the one side an object capable of being observed while on the other side it is General. (Peirce 1976/IV: 318)

As Eco has argued (cf. 2000), Peirce modifies the Kantian notion of empirical schemas in order to uncover their creative potential as well as the conventionality of schema-based thinking. For Peirce, a perceptual schema, for instance of a dog, cannot be created internally, as it depends on codified sociocultural, semiotic knowledge. A diagram-like perceptual schema is projected onto culturally archived knowledge and provides a regular 'type' for classifying the percept of a dog. Therefore the diagram is a medium for explicitly reasoning with schemas of visual perception. Regarding this point, Peirce's theory has a similar problem as Lakoff and Johnson's. How can diagrams create a similarity with the actual dynamics of a perception? Can such an automatized and implicit operation be reflected in an explicit and externalized, highly codified and conventionalized practice like diagrammatic reasoning, which is regulated by rules of explicit logical discourse and geometry? Can such a semiotic practice be a model for pragmatism? It clearly cannot. Yet, for Peirce, the border between implicit automatisms of everyday practices and their explicit, externalized, and codified modes of reflection like language – or diagrammatic reasoning – is not completely impermeable. If this assumption holds true, then second-level diagrammatic reasoning may resemble a process of *first-level* diagrammatic thinking. Peirce assumes modes of diagrammatic thinking without actually relying on an externalized diagram. First-level diagrammatic thinking does not stand for the process of thinking *with* an externalized diagram but for perceiving conflicting perceptual information represented in a sign, for example in an image, *as* a diagram. Stjernfelt (2007: 101) uses the following example to describe this diagrammatic dimension within the structure of visual perception:

Take a photograph of a tree – it is an icon in so far as not previously explicit information may be gathered from it – say, e.g. the fact that the crown of the tree amounts to two thirds of its overall height. This fact was remarked nowhere earlier, neither by the photographer nor the camera nor the developer – and by noticing it you performed a small experiment of diagrammatic nature: you took the trunk of the tree and moved upward for your inner gaze in order to see it cover the height of the crown twice, doing a bit of spontaneous metric geometry, complete with the implicit use of axioms like the invariance of translation. Of course, this is an ordinary icon in so far as nobody constructed it with diagrammatic intention. Nevertheless, you used it – *in actu* – that way. This continuum between diagrams proper (be it pure or empirically) and diagrammatic use of ordinary icons show the centrality of the diagram for the icon category as such.

This example hints at what Hoel calls the "diagrammatic conception of the perceptual process" (2012: 263) in the works of Peirce, which has been adopted by different theorists of diagrammatic reasoning (cf. e.g. Bauer/Ernst 2010) even if it is highly problematic.¹¹ On the one hand, Peirce clearly favors second-level diagrammatic reasoning for methodological reasons (e.g. in his existential graphs); on the other hand, he clings to the notion of a diagrammatic process which supposedly underlies those externalized inferences that operate with the help of materialized diagrams. This tension in his theory is created by the influence of *tacit* schematic operations in perception, which are also diagrammatic in nature and can be labeled diagrammatic *thinking*,¹² and *explicit* diagrammatic operations as in second-level diagrammatic *reasoning*. Stjernfelt considers this differentiation when he differentiates between the use of 'diagrams proper' (second-level diagrammatic reasoning) and a 'diagrammatic use of ordinary icons' (first-level diagrammatic thinking). Many theories struggle with the distinction between second-level and first-level diagrammatic operations (the problem remains unsolved e.g. in Bauer/Ernst 2010). Overemphasizing one or the other type of operation leads to further problems. First-level diagrammatic thinking tends to overstretch the diagram category and leads to a kind of 'pan-diagrammatism.' In addition, it lacks the plausibility of second-level diagrammatic reasoning. Vice versa, second-level diagrammatic reasoning cannot be limited to explicit reasoning with externalized diagrams – as its proponents in the philosophy of mathematics tend to believe (cf. Wöpking 2010, 2012) – because it cannot account for the obvious ability of perception and cultural practices to regard a sign, e.g. an iconic sign, *as* a diagram.

I think theories of metaphor can be of help in order to escape this dilemma. If first-level diagrammatic thinking is accepted as an implicit inferential mode of perception that operates upon schematic tacit knowledge, then metaphor – taken as a perceptual inference – can be considered as a process of *perceptive diagrammatization* and regarded as a blueprint for first-level diagrammatic thinking *without* overstretching the diagram category. Structural mapping in metaphor, as outlined above, can be considered as a conflicting relation that leads to diagrammatic thinking as a reflection on schematic structure. Bringing together Lakoff and Johnson's theory with Peirce's pragmatist approach, we can assume that conceptual metaphor relies on diagrammatic signs to realize structural mappings. Especially visual types of metaphor like film metaphor

---

11 | Hoel (2012: 266) indirectly reflects on those problems when she writes: "The broad take on the diagrammatic as a general theory of mediation raises questions concerning the status of diagrams proper, to which Peirce assigns a very specific, epistemic task: Diagrams are the sort of sign that are capable of communicating evidence, which is certainly not the case with just any human sign or tool."

12 | See Ernst 2015 (forthcoming) for a more precise description of this process which includes a distinction between 'perceptive diagrammatization' as an automatized operation and 'first-level diagrammatic thinking' as an intentional mode of seeing.

seem to have a relation to first-level diagrammatic thinking, as they translate conceptual metaphors into sociocultural representations.

VII. Perceptive Diagrammatization and Metaphor

In order to exactly determine the relation between perceptive diagrammatization as a part of first-level diagrammatic thinking and metaphor, there are basically two general approaches: we can either focus on metaphor in diagrams, or we can discuss the diagrammatic nature of metaphor. The first approach is concerned with second-level diagrammatic reasoning, the second deals with first-level diagrammatic thinking. There are many controversial theories about metaphor in diagrams. While representationalist theories are skeptical of the idea that second-level diagrammatic reasoning is influenced by metaphor (cf. Blackwell 1998), information theory, which provides empirical evidence for the influence of metaphor on diagrams, comes to the opposite conclusion (cf. Ziemkiewicz 2010; Ziemkiewicz/Kosara 2008). Media theory generally also supports the latter position, but whether second-level diagrammatic reasoning is influenced by metaphor or not is not the main question of this paper; rather I want to explore whether there is evidence for metaphor to be inherently structured by a process of perceptive diagrammatization as a part of first-level diagrammatic thinking.

Stjernfelt mentions as an example for this process the discovery of the stereochemical arrangement of carbon atoms in Benzene by August Kekulé, who when sitting before a fire and observing the flames forming a ring was reminded of the Ouroboros, a symbol of a serpent eating its own tail, which inspired him to think of Benzene not as a linear chain but as a ring (cf. 2007: 102).[13] As Stjernfelt explains:

That discovery thus formed a spontaneous case of diagrammatical reasoning, realized in the shape of metaphors. The flame was taken as a metaphor of the snake which, in turn, was taken as a metaphor of the carbon chain – a structure of metaphors held together by the common diagram of a piece of line, able to bend. The spontaneous diagram experiment argued that the Carbon chain, just like a snake, was able to form a ring, and subsequent chemical analysis corroborated the idea, leading to a major breakthrough in organic chemistry. (ibid.)[14]

---

13 | For a detailed account of this incident see Rocke 2010: 293ff., 312ff.

14 | Drawing on Peirce, Stjernfelt uses the term 'diagrammatic reasoning' in a broad sense, which of course is not incorrect. However, for heuristic reasons I differentiate between first-level diagrammatic thinking and second-level diagrammatic reasoning.

A process of perceptive diagrammatization within first-level diagrammatic thinking seems to be a fundamentally important concept for metaphor. *Seeing* the flames as the Ouroboros triggers a diagrammatical insight because the process is rooted in diagrammatic thinking. Kekulé had to see the analogy on the level of a creative variation of conventionalized perceptive schemata. The image of the Ouroboros in the fire enables the metaphor by the implied schema of the circle. Thus metaphorical seeing can itself be described as a diagrammatic operation which provides a perceptual theory of first-level diagrammatic thinking. Furthermore Kekulé had to know how to manipulate the conventionalized system of notation in order to translate the metaphor into the specific form of notation of the Benzene ring. Thus he was able to combine knowledge generated by first-level diagrammatic thinking with knowledge on the second level of diagrammatic reasoning.

Peirce's theory of metaphor supports this idea because it categorizes both diagrams and metaphors as icons. Following Peirce, an iconic sign always appears in sociocultural contexts as a complex configuration ('hypoicons') of different iconic aspects, which means that diagrams can be part of metaphors. In his *Syllabus of Certain Topics of Logic* of 1903, Peirce elaborates:

Hypoicons may roughly /be/ divided according to the mode of Firstness of which they partake. Those which partake of the simple qualities, or First Firstness, are *images*; those which represent the relations, mainly dyadic, or so regarded, of the parts of one thing by analogous relations in their own parts, are *diagrams*; those which represent the representative character of a representamen by representing a parallelism in something else, are *metaphors*. (Peirce 1998: 274)

Peirce identifies structural resemblance as the main characteristic of diagrams, and the more complex representation of 'parallelism in something else' as the main characteristic of metaphor. Peirce also held that "[m]any diagrams resemble their objects not at all in looks; it is only in respect to the relations of their parts that their likeness consists" (ibid. 13). Structural resemblance does not represent the elements of an object but the relations between elements, and is not limited to mimetically copying the visible features of an object. It is possible that it resembles invisible features, because to 'visualize the invisible' (e.g. relations) is a characteristic feature of diagrams. Diagrams thus are a structural element in metaphors which *are* inferential relations based on structural resemblance.

As mentioned above, metaphor for Peirce "represent[s] the representative character of a representamen by representing a parallelism in something else" (ibid. 274). As a form of iconicity, metaphor is designed to explore something new about an object (cf. Anderson 1984: 462ff.). This is called the 'operational' notion of iconicity (cf. Stjernfelt 2007: 90ff.). Icons are used to create and explore similarities in order to generate new insights about an object. Peirce's notion of metaphor is cryptic at best, but two aspects of his definition are of interest here, both of which illustrate the diagrammatic nature of metaphor: First, the parallelism in metaphor is creative; second, this creativity is diagrammatic. This is already implied in the term 'parallelism.' As Anderson (1984) and Hausman (1994: 205ff.) demonstrate, 'parallelism' is an operation through which structural resemblances between two representamens and their respective objects can be seen.[15] This process of 'stereoscopic' seeing needs a *tertium* which is based not on an *analogical* but *structural* isomorphism. Take for example the linguistic metaphor 'the field smiles.' According to Anderson's reading of Peirce, the iconicity

[...] of metaphor lies neither in field nor in smile, but in the unity of the two: a third thing, which they somehow constitute. Thus, the ground of a metaphor is an 'isosensism' between a metaphor and its icon [...]. Moreover, what resemblance obtains between the constituents of metaphor is created in the articulation of the metaphor. Unlike logi-

---

15 | At this point I would like to give a speculative interpretation of Peirce's differentiation between the 'representation of a representative character of a representamen' on the one hand and the 'representation of a parallelism in something else' on the other. According to Peirce, the first operation depends on the second. First there is *structural resemblance in the signans*. The representamen is the part of the sign in which something is represented, e.g. a phonetic sequence in language (i.e., the 'signans'). Therefore the form of metaphor itself, the way it represents something, is part of the metaphor. Metaphor is not only present in the content of language but also in the form of the signs used to express metaphor. Jakobson uses the example of Caesar's *veni, vidi, vici*; the form of the sentence reflects the sequence of events, as there is a structural resemblance between the linearity of the sentence and the content expressed. Jakobson, drawing on Peirce, saw this as a case in which the syntactic structure of sentence becomes a diagram of events (cf. Jakobson 1988: 85; Lakoff and Johnson discuss the same issue, cf. 2003: 136ff.). But in metaphor, this form of structural resemblance depends upon *structural resemblance in the signatum*. To understand what *veni, vidi, vici* means is to catch the representation of the sequence of events on the level of syntax. The same goes for metaphor: If one does not understand the metaphor on the level of the signatum, its resemblance on the level of the signans (representamen) cannot be understood. This interpretation could provide an answer to the problem of different representations of metaphor in different media (linguistic, pictorial, cinematic). As media have different forms, the 'representation of a representative character of a representamen' is expressed in them in different ways. Media like language or film vary in their potentiality to realize metaphorical form. Nonetheless one has to understand the metaphor on the level of content, which is provided by the inventory of linguistic and conceptual metaphor of a sociocultural context, to 'get' the metaphor.

cal isomorphisms, metaphorical resemblances are not traceable to antecedent links. (1984: 458f.)

Strub further explains: "The interpreter of metaphor has to try to relate the two structures of meaning, or, to put it in Peircean terms, has to let one structure become the diagram of the other structure" (1994: 231; my transl.). Farias and Queiroz, who focus on metaphor as a rule of inference, come to the same conclusion: "We can assume, therefore, that metaphors [...] shall depend on a certain internal diagrammatic coherence in order to assume their status of instantiated icons of laws" (2006: 294). If 'field' or 'smile' are deleted in 'the field smiles,' the metaphor is lost (cf. Anderson 1984: 462). For Peirce, metaphor is a form of inferential relation, but this relation is already realized in perception. Thus metaphor is, as Strub points out, "stereoscopical seeing, in which two objects or situations are superimposed" (1998: 270; my transl.). Obviously, there is a diagrammatic relation within the inner workings of metaphorical operations.

According to Lakoff and Johnson's theory, image-schemas and image-schema operations draw attention to the necessity of considering structural resemblance between domains in metaphorical inferences. Diagrammatic signs seem to be the semiotic correlates of this image-schematic process and appear in Peirce's theory of metaphor as the 'parallelism' of metaphor. Image-schemas and image-schema operations can be regarded as relevant for perceptual processes of 'visual thinking.' As a semiotic operation, diagrammatic thinking is based on sociocultural schemas and knowledge; image-schemas on the other hand are located in bodily tacit knowledge. Therefore we can assume that image-schemas and image-schema operations represent the influence of embodied cognition in semiotic processes of diagrammatic thinking. First-level diagrammatic thinking and its various forms are implicitly informed by image-schemas and image-schema operations which can only be observed indirectly in sociocultural contexts through iconic relations like perceptive diagrammatization in first-level diagrammatic thinking.

If we accept this relation between first, image-schemas and perceptive diagrammatization in practices of first-level diagrammatic thinking, and second, iconic resemblance between tacit knowledge (image-schemas) and semiotic representations (diagrams), then it is possible to overcome the dilemma of having invisible 'tacit' cognitive operations on the one hand, and socially 'visible' semiotic operations on the other without any connection between them. Lakoff and Johnson describe the influence of tacit cognitive knowledge as structurally coupled with semiotic diagrammatic operations in culture and communication.[16] Certain forms of metaphor – and I propose that film metaphor is one

---

16 | The relevance of the notion of 'structural couplings' as developed in Luhmann's systems theory for tacit knowledge is discussed in Ernst 2013.

of them – then are not 'reflexive' but 'performative' ways of operating with tacit knowledge through the medium of metaphor and of representing it in diagrammatic configurations.

VIII. COMMUNICATION AS CREATION IN SODERBERGH'S *SOLARIS*

I would like to give a simple example for this process.[17] Steven Soderbergh's 2002 remake of Andrei Tarkovsky's science fiction classic *Solaris* (1972) features a significant change in the visual depiction of the planet Solaris, which the scientists in the film assume to possess an alien form of intelligence. While Tarkovsky shows Solaris as an oceanic planet, in Soderbergh's version, Solaris appears as a hybrid between a gas planet and the human brain.

Figure 1: *The planet in Soderbergh's Solaris (2002)*[18]

Figure 2: *Kelvin sleeping*

---

17 | For a more detailled discussion of this example see Ernst 2015 (forthcoming).
18 | All screenshots taken from *Solaris* (2002).

When Chris Kelvin (George Clooney) goes to sleep for the first time on the space station (TC 00:20:12), in a brief sequence, the process of falling asleep is shown as an unconscious communication between Kelvin's mind and the mind of the planet. Soderbergh uses montage and shot size to actualize the semiotic equivalent of the image-schema operation of MULTIPLEX TO MASS when zooming in on the planet.

(i) Lying on his bed, Kelvin closes his eyes. Soderbergh contrasts a medium shot of the sleeping Kelvin with a long shot of the planet (TC 00:20:21). The starting point of the MULTIPLEX TO MASS type of zooming in is MASS. As viewers, we see the planet as a whole within the frame of the long shot. We know about the sleeping Kelvin in the space station and about the existence of this strange planet. From the moment Kelvin lies down to rest, ambient, somnambulistic music plays and marks his falling asleep on the diegetic level of sound.

(ii) Next is another medium shot of Kelvin, this time from a slightly different camera angle, which Soderbergh contrasts with a medium shot of Solaris. The planet now exceeds the frame and transgresses the image field of the cadrage (TC 00:20:32). The medium shot still depicts the planet as such, but in contrast to the long shot, we can see more details of its surface. The focus on MASS is destabilized; MULTIPLEX, as represented by the details of the planet's surface, is established as a second, yet latent visual focus.

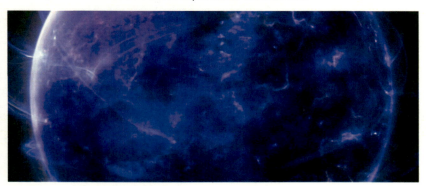

Figure 3: Zooming in on the planet

(iii) The next logical step is a contrast between a close-up of Kelvin and a close-up of details of the planet's surface (TC 00:20:36), which completes the shift from MASS to MULTIPLEX; the planet is no longer discernible as a whole. The focus is now on the swirling energy on the surface, which is depicted as lightning bolts. These swirls, which resemble the popular image of 'firing' neurons, establish an analogy to neural activity while the rhythm of the montage is accelerated: The time between contrasting shots is halved per pair of shots. The contrast between the switching shot sizes of the planet on the one hand and the increasing shot size of Kelvin's head on the other evokes the process of falling asleep as a process of 'sinking in.' The increased frequency of the montage rhythm furthermore implies the idea of a more associative state of mind. A connection is established between the process of sinking into Kelvin's mental subjectivity (his 'dream-consciousness') and the zooming in on the planet by going from long shots of Solaris as a whole to close-ups of the surface, which suggests a form of 'communication' and 'connection' between Kelvin's mind and the 'mind' of the planet.

Figure 4: Arriving at MULTIPLEX: *Swirls of neural energy*

(iv) At this point, Soderbergh cuts away from the planet. A brief flash indicates a third image (TC 00:20:41). We see a medium close-up of two female hands holding a round artifact. This opens up a second diegetic layer which supplements the interplay between Kelvin and the planet. The medium close-up of the hands is not cut back to the swirls of energy on the planet's surface; instead, we see the sleeping Kelvin, which indicates that we are inside his dream. This is followed by a second interplay between Kelvin and the ensuing dream sequence. In an analepsis, a series of decreasing shot sizes (from close-up back to medium close-up) shows that Kelvin is staring at a woman and thereby reveals the female hands as Kelvin's perception-image (point of view shot). Kelvin and the woman sit opposite each other on a train. Because we know Kelvin is sleeping, this second diegetic layer is established as a diegesis-within-the-diegesis ('internal diegesis').

Figure 5: Inside the CONTAINER *of Kelvin's mind: Rheya in Kelvin's memories*

(v) Now we are in Kelvin's mind (internal view of Kelvin). We can assume that the woman is part of Kelvin's memory. In one of the close-ups of Kelvin's face (external view of Kelvin) that are contrasted with the interior of Kelvin's dream, for a brief moment one can see a twitching of his face: While it was without expression in all of the preceding shots, it now shows reaction and movement (TC 00:21:21).

(vi) The montage cuts back to the planet. An extreme close-up of the planet's surface shows swirls of energy moving towards and connecting with each other, which references Michelangelo's *The Creation of Adam* (ca. 1512). At this point the implied viewer anticipates the woman to be a memory of Kelvin's dead wife Rheya (Natascha McElhone). When Kelvin wakes up later in the sequence she lies right next to him and has turned into a corporeal, living entity – the 'mind' of Solaris is able to materialize human memories. There is a moment not only of communication but also of connection between Kelvin's mind and the mind of Solaris, and the moment of connection between the two swirls of energy is an instance of physical creation.

Figure 6: LINKING *up minds: The moment of creation*

Figure 7: Michelangelo's The Creation of Adam (ca. 1512)[19]

IX. IMPLICIT DIAGRAMS AND MOVING IMAGES OF THOUGHT

Based on this analysis, I want to propose some ideas on the interplay between image-schemas and conceptual metaphors as belonging to tacit knowledge of the 'cognitive unconscious' on the one hand and their semiotic representation in form of film metaphors read as diagrams on the other. In his study on film metaphor, Whittock (1990: 50) develops a basic schema of metaphorical operations in film. On the level of montage, the metaphorical mapping of the sequence in *Solaris* is a metaphorical relation termed 'parallelism' (A/pqr) / (B/pqr) (cf. ibid. 66f.). As Eisenstein has shown, the cinematic form of contrasting montage aims at a 'third' image *not* visible in film that constitutes a *tertium comparationis* used to understand the meaning of the sequence (cf. 2006: 161). Contrasting montage was used to *create* similarities between different objects with little iconic resemblance, and established analogies between unrelated objects based on structural resemblance. The 'third image' was considered to be a 'thinking image' inside the cognitive processes of the viewer, who has to mobilize conceptual metaphors as inferential operations to 'understand and experience' these images. Film semiotics and its philosophical versions, e.g. Deleuze's film philosophy (cf. 1983, 1985), conceptualize the process of thinking as an autonomous operation of film (cf. Deleuze 1985: 203ff.). The 'thinking' of a 'subject' is not only a cognitive activity but also an activity that adheres to the laws of mediatized semiotic relations: "all thought is dialogical, and is embodied in signs" (Peirce 1976/IV: 316ff.). Not only does one think with signs,

---

19 | Image source: http://en.wikipedia.org/wiki/File:Creación_de_Adán_(Miguel_Ángel).jpg.

but also vice versa. The problem that results from bringing semiotics and cognitive theory together is of particular importance to theories of diagrammatic thinking, because diagrams can be regarded as 'inferential machines' that actually let you think something – they are "formal machines for Gedankenexperimente" (Stjernfelt 2007: 99).

Peirce and others have invested a considerable amount of effort in describing how diagrams create information through their spatial relations, e.g. in a phenomenon called 'free ride' (cf. Shimojima 1996: 17ff.; Wöpking 2010). Diagrams deliver certain inferences 'for free,' and thus do the 'thinking' for their users. Nonetheless these theories discuss diagrams in very specialized discourses like logic (e.g. Peirce's existential graphs) and geometry, which have seemingly clear criteria for what is true and what is false. In such a discourse it is possible to describe how a diagram can automatize the creation of information. In other words: theories of automatized creation of information in diagrams focus on special cases of second-level diagrammatic reasoning. The problem of a cinematic form of thinking with the viewer points to diagrammatic signs playing a prominent role; in this case second-level theories of diagrammatic reasoning are not helpful, because they focus on diagrams proper.

First-level diagrammatic thinking is based on the operation of perceptually 'diagrammatizing' an already existing sign as a diagram (e.g. a picture) and conducting an experiment on that picture, which generates knowledge about the picture that is not explicit in its surface structure. To clarify this point: first-level diagrammatic thinking is a way of seeing things in order to see structural resemblances and experiment with them (perceptual diagrammatization). While it would be futile to speculate on the mental states of a spectator performing such an experiment upon the moving images of a film, it is reasonable to consider film metaphor as a cinematic form designed to use the semiotic possibility of producing a diagrammatic relation *within* an iconic configuration for the narrative purpose of visualizing the transition into the mind of Kelvin. In the film metaphor as a semiotic configuration, an implicit diagrammatic icon is created which represents the invisible and implicit structural resemblances expressed in the metaphorical parallelism, and is not visible as a 'diagram proper' in the sense of second-level diagrammatic reasoning.

Working as a *tertium comparationis* for realizing the structural mapping of film metaphor, this implicit diagram comprises the whole of the relational semiotic arrangement as it unfolds in time and is thus consistent with the unfolding of an image-schema like CONTAINER as an inferential sequence. We cannot isolate particular shots of the film metaphor as 'diagrammatic' – the sequence has to be seen as a whole, as a relational configuration that implies an inference based on an implicit diagram. While the individual pictures of the sequence from *Solaris* are not 'diagrammatic' themselves, the relation (sic!) between the pictures unfolding in time as a film metaphor is. The sequence certainly is not an 'image diagram' (like a map), a 'diagram proper' (like a graph), or a 'symbolic diagram' (like a chemical formula), but taken as a whole sequence of unfolding relations the metaphorical parallelism operates due to an implicit diagram, providing orientation (like a map), abstracting from the iconic object-level (like a graph or sketch), establishing a pattern from which logical conclusions can be drawn (like a logical formula), and arranging 'valency' of the shots (like in chemistry, which was one of Peirce's prime analogies to explain diagrammatic icons). And it is interesting to note that film seems to rely on this process especially in visualizations of the mind.

In his theory of existential graphs, Peirce suggests different names for this implicit type of diagram. He calls it the "moving picture of thought," "a portraiture of thought," "a moving picture of action of the mind and thought," or "a moving picture of the action and thought" (qtd. in Pietarinen 2003: 2). This 'picture' is not a picture in the literal sense but a semiotic effect created in cognition when a second-level diagrammatic experiment is performed. 'A moving picture of thought,' for example, is the configuration seen *in* a map when one thinks *with* the map, which leads to Peirce's theory of deduction and especially his theory of 'hypostatic abstraction' (cf. Peirce 1906: 522; Hoffmann 2005: 180f.). In second-level diagrammatic reasoning, a 'moving picture of thought' or 'thought-image' is created that by deduction leads to new beliefs and action. I think it is plausible to describe the diagrammatic effect inherent in the metaphorical parallelism with Peirce's ideas on diagrammatic reasoning; however, there are also very important differences. In second-level diagrammatic reasoning, 'moving pictures of thought' are created as an *explicit* gestalt by an externalized image diagram, diagram proper, or symbolic diagram, whereas in film metaphor, we do not find such an explicit gestalt. While a diagram is present in the semiotic configuration, it remains implicit in the relation of pictures. The 'thought-image' of second-level diagrammatic reasoning is explicit and reflexive, but through film metaphor we gain a *connotational* 'thought-image' which *implicitly and performatively* lays out semantic implications of the story by functioning as a visual medium for metaphorical inferences of conceptual metaphors, image-schemas, and image-schema operations.

X. Linking Up Minds

A brief interpretation of the connotations created by the diagram present in the full sequence of 'linking up' the planet with Kelvin's mind supports this theoretical claim. By zooming in on the planet, the sequence visualizes the orientational metaphor CONSCIOUSNESS IS UP, SLEEPING IS DOWN by means of MASS TO MULTIPLEX image-schema operations. Movement from top to bottom (from Solaris in a long shot to Solaris in a close-up) is paralleled with the process of 'sinking' into Kelvin's dream. This parallelization is realized through montage; the metaphorical operation here is typical of cinema. The illusion of moving into Kelvin's mind is created by the variation of shot sizes of the planet and their parallelization with static images of Kelvin's head. Similar to Eisenstein's theory (cf. 2006 158ff.), a metaphorical message is realized not by means of camera movements but rather through the montage of contrasting shots and thus through creating structural resemblance. The impression of moving 'downwards' – as performed in MASS TO MULTIPLEX – 'into' the planet or 'into' Kelvin's head is enhanced by the acceleration of the frequency of cuts and by the increase of the shot size of the contrasting shots. The sequence culminates when the diegesis-within-diegesis of Kelvin's dream is established. Once the implied spectator has moved 'into' Kelvin's head, the transgression of the boundary into the CONTAINER of Kelvin's mind is complete.

This is supported by the depiction of Solaris as a fluid, gaseous planet, which is reminiscent of imagery of human brain activity. The orientational process of 'sinking' into sleep is established by zooming in onto the fluid surface of the planet. As an orientational metaphor, CONSCIOUSNESS IS UP, SLEEPING IS DOWN provides a framework for structural metaphors as COMMUNICATION IS PHYSICAL CONTACT (she really 'touched' me). This metaphor is structural in nature, but it has a strong ontological connotation when it comes to the moment of creation. In the fictional world, the mind of the planet is able to physically ('ontologically') manifest ('fluid') memories. The moment of creation is marked as a moment of physical contact between two entities and is represented here by the connection of the two swirls of energy. Ontologically, the communication between Solaris and Kelvin is a moment of creation as depicted by the ontological metaphor MEMORIES ARE PHYSICAL SWIRLS OF ENERGY.

Like the monolith in Stanley Kubrick's *2001: A Space Odyssey* (1968), the alien intelligence in *Solaris* is *too* alien for humans to understand. Solaris' intelligence is capable of connecting to the human psyche, literally 'reflecting' or 'mirroring' unconscious states of mind. The human psyche breaks down, as it cannot break 'through' the mirror and understand the alien intelligence. This interpretation is supported on the level of language-based narration. Kelvin watches the video diary of the late scientist Gibarian (Ulrich Tukur), who says about the endeavor of human space exploration: "But when you think about it, our enthusiasm is a sham. We don't want other worlds, we want mirrors" (TC 00:19:46). The connection with the alien planet thus is a connection with a radically *other* form of intelligence. Maybe this intelligence could be proven to be 'superior' if there were a scale to measure it, but it definitely provides humanity with a mirror, as Gibarian notes.

The metaphor COMMUNICATION IS PHYSICAL CREATION imposes a set of connotations on the motif of otherness. Being ontologically confronted with manifestations of the human psyche, otherness is depicted as a *medial* form of otherness. Solaris is unintelligible not only because it is an alien intelligence but also because it mirrors latent content of the human psyche, and thus thwarts every attempt to understand it. Soderbergh's film introduces the planet as a medium that manifests psychic content. As a medium, the planet evades being objectivized by creating memories. Whether there is something 'behind' the medium remains unclear, because any human who attempts to understand the planet only looks at his or her own mirror-image. Reading the planet as a medium is even more plausible when we take the image-schematic structure of the COMMUNICATION IS PHYSICAL CREATION metaphor into account.

COMMUNICATION IS PHYSICAL CREATION is based here on the image-schema LINK. To create something through communication means to connect something, to bring something together. According to Lakoff, a LINK is logically symmetric: if A is connected with B then B is connected with A – which is exactly the logical consequence of the plot structure of the sequence. Nevertheless there can be a hierarchy within the schema: "If *A* is linked to *B*, then *A* is constrained by, and dependent upon, *B*" (Lakoff 1987: 274). This hierarchy is also represented in the story, and is coherent with the connotations of the sequence: Kelvin's mind 'links up' with Solaris but is also dependent on the planet.

The main image-schematic operation the LINK schema is transformed into is MASS TO MULTIPLEX, which is realized by zooming in on the planet through increasing shot sizes. MASS TO MULTIPLEX is used to depict moving into the 'container' of Kelvin's mind. While LINK implies physical contact, we need to transgress the boundary of the CONTAINER schema to get into Kelvin's mind. In contrast to Tarkovsky's version, Soderbergh uses mental subjectivity to motivate the ontological manifestation of Rheya, and shows what is actually 'created' by the structural metaphor COMMUNICATION IS PHYSICAL CREATION. Of course this is neither subtle nor in any way innovative, but precisely because (!) the sequence is so conventional it is interesting how much it relies on metaphor – especially when it comes to visualizing mental subjectivity and the transgression 'into' mental subjectivity.

To sum up the connotations of the example: we see Solaris (A) with certain features that evoke an analogy to the human brain, and we see Kelvin sleeping (B), which matches the connotations of the brain via the orientational metaphor CONSCIOUSNESS IS UP, SLEEPING IS DOWN. The metaphorical parallelism unfolds through the dynamics of the visual narration. The increasing shot size of Solaris and the depiction of Kelvin as motionless parallels A (Solaris) and B (Kelvin). The metaphor of COMMUNICATION IS PHYSICAL CREATION is visually framed by the LINK schema. The connotation of LINK is a connection between the alien intelligence of Solaris and Kelvin's memories. The image-schema operation MASS TO MULTIPLEX operates on the LINK schema in order to move into the CONTAINER of Kelvin's mind. By 'zooming in' on the planet we transgress the boundary of the CONTAINER. Once we are inside the CONTAINER and learn about Rheya, the metaphor COMMUNICATION IS PHYSICAL CREATION unfolds through the LINK schema. Hence the ontological aspect of this metaphorical configuration is inherent in the motif of Solaris and Kelvin 'touching.'

In this example the semiotic representation of film metaphor is located on the connotative level of story. If one fails to understand the analepsis that motivates the appearance of Rheya as a living being, one cannot understand the story; the diagram in the parallelism of film metaphor acts as a 'cue' (cf. Bordwell 1992, 1995) in the form of a 'map' enabling one to catch the story's philosophical implications.[20]

XI. CONCLUSION: *SEEING* TACIT KNOWLEDGE

It is impossible to 'see' tacit knowledge, but certain semiotic forms and especially diagrammatic forms provide scripts that enable us to recognize how tacit knowledge constitutes meaning, e.g. in connotations of film metaphor. Lakoff and Johnson's concept of image-schemas is of special interest when it comes to visual semantics (cf. Buckland 2007: 26ff.), which can be illustrated by considering an implicit diagram in film metaphor that is designed to create structural resemblances on the basis of diagrammatic icons. Film metaphors produce relational images in the semiotic configuration (diagrams) which act as implicit 'thought images.' These implicit diagrams *in* the semiotic form of film metaphor are the focal point of tacit inferences, structure connotative layers of meaning in film, and thus allow us indirectly to *see* tacit knowledge in the form of a tacit 'moving image of thought.' They constitute an implicit but nonetheless diagrammatic way of 'thinking' with film.

---

20 | I would like to point out once again that the image-schemas and metaphors mentioned in the analysis above are *not* to be confused with the implicit diagram which acts as a *tertium* in the semiotic configuration of the sequence. Image-schemas and image-schema operations are performed within the constraints of the implicit diagram or 'thought image' implied in film metaphor as a semiotic parallelism. With good reason we can assume that the point of contact between the 'conceptual' layer and the 'semiotic' layer of a complex metaphorical configuration can be found in image-schema operations like SUPERIMPOSITION or MULTIPLEX TO MASS. And we should be careful not to confuse SUPERIMPOSITION as an image-schematic operation with superimpositions in film: Superimpositions are semiotic forms; SUPERIMPOSITION is a mode of inferential thinking on a latent level of perception.

Works Cited

Anderson, Douglas (1984): "Peirce on Metaphors," in: Transactions of the Charles S. Peirce Society 20.4, 453-468.

Arnheim, Rudolf (2002): Film als Kunst, Frankfurt/Main: Suhrkamp.

Barthes, Roland (1977): "Rhetoric of the Image," in: Roland Barthes, Image, Music, Text, ed. and transl. Stephen Heath, New York: Hill and Wang, 32-51.

Bauer, Matthias/Ernst, Christoph (2010): Diagrammatik. Einführung in ein kultur- und medienwissenschaftliches Forschungsfeld, Bielefeld: transcript.

Blackwell, Alan F. (1998): Metaphor in Diagrams, Cambridge: Diss. Cambridge U.

Blumenberg, Hans (1999): Paradigmen zu einer Metaphorologie, Frankfurt/Main: Suhrkamp.

Bordwell, David (1992): "Kognition und Verstehen. Sehen und Vergessen in Mildred Pierce," in: Montage/AV 1.1, 5–24.

—. (1995): Narration in the Fiction Film, London: Routledge.

Buckland, Warren (2007): The Cognitive Semiotics of Film, Cambridge: Cambridge UP.

Carroll, Noel (1994): "Visual Metaphor," in: Jaakko Hintikka (ed.), Aspects of Metaphor, Dordrecht: Kluwer, 189-218.

—. (1996): "A Note on Film Metaphor," in: Noel Carroll, Theorizing the Moving Image, Cambridge: Cambridge UP, 212-223.

Clifton, N. Roy (1983): The Figure in Film, East Brunswick: Associated UP.

Deleuze, Gilles (1983): Cinéma 1. L'Image-Mouvement, Paris: Les Èditions de Minuit.

—. (1985): Cinéma 2. L'Image-Temps, Paris: Les Èditions de Minuit.

Eco, Umberto (2000): Kant and the Platypus. Essay on Language and Cognition, New York: Harcourt Brace.

Eisenstein, Sergej M. (2006): Jenseits der Einstellung. Schriften zur Filmtheorie, Frankfurt/Main: Suhrkamp.

Engel, Franz/Queisner, Moritz/Viola, Tullio (eds.) (2012): Das bildnerische Denken. Charles S. Peirce, Berlin: Akademie.

Ernst, Christoph (2013): "Präsenz als Form einer Differenz. Medientheoretische Implikationen des Zusammenhangs zwischen Präsenz und implizitem Wissen," in: Christoph Ernst/Heike Paul (eds.), Präsenz und implizites Wissen. Zur Interdependenz zweier Schlüsselbegriffe der Kultur- und Sozialwissenschaften, with Katharina Gerund/David Kaldewey, Bielefeld: transcript, 49-76.

—. (2015): Diagrammatische Denkbilder. Theoretische Studien zur Medien- und Filmästhetik der Diagrammatik. forthcoming.

Evans, Vyvyan/Green, Melanie (2009): Cognitive Linguistics. An Introduction, Edinburgh: Edinburgh UP.

Farias, Priscila/Queiroz, Joao (2006): "Images, Diagrams, and Metaphors. Hypoicons in the Context of Peirce's Sixty-six-fold Classification of Signs," in: Semiotica 162.1, 287-307.
Forceville, Charles (2005): "Cognitive Linguistics and Multimodal Metaphor," in: Klaus Sachs-Hombach (ed.), Bildwissenschaft zwischen Reflexion und Anwendung, Köln: Halem, 264-284.
Gibbs, Raymond W., Jr. (ed.) (2008): The Cambridge Handbook of Metaphor and Thought, Cambridge: Cambridge UP.
Hampe, Beate (ed.) (2005): From Perception to Meaning. Image Schemas in Cognitive Linguistics, Berlin: de Gruyter.
Haser, Verena (2005): Metaphor, Metonymy, and Experientialist Philosophy. Challenging Cognitive Semantics, Berlin: de Gruyter.
Hausman, Carl (1994): "Metaphorische Ikons und telelogischer Zufall," in: Uwe Wirth (ed.), Kreativität und Logik. Charles S. Peirce und das philosophische Problem des Neuen, Frankfurt/Main: Suhrkamp, 195-208.
Hoel, Aud Sisel (2012): "Lines of Sight. Peirce on Diagrammatic Abstraction," in: Engel/Queisner/Viola, Das bildnerische Denken, 253-271.
Hoffmann, Michael H.G. (2005): Erkenntnisentwicklung. Ein semiotisch-pragmatischer Ansatz, Frankfurt/Main: Klostermann.
Jakobson, Roman (1988): "Die Suche nach dem Wesen der Sprache," in: Roman Jakobson, Semiotik. Ausgewählte Texte 1919-1982, ed. Elmar Holenstein, Frankfurt/Main: Suhrkamp, 77-98.
Johnson, Mark (1987): The Body in the Mind. The Bodily Basis of Meaning, Imagination, and Reason, Chicago: Chicago UP.
—. (2005): "The Philosophical Significance of Image Schemas," in: Hampe, From Perception to Meaning, 15-34.
—. (2007): The Meaning of the Body. Aesthetics of Human Understanding, Chicago: Chicago UP.
Kant, Immanuel (2002): Kritik der reinen Vernunft, Stuttgart: Reclam.
Korzybski, Alfred (1948): Science and Sanity. An Introduction to Non-Aristotelian Systems and General Semantics, Lakeville: Inst. of General Semantics.
Kövecses, Zoltan (2010): Metaphor. A Practical Introduction, New York: Oxford UP.
Lakoff, George (1987): Women, Fire, and Dangerous Things. What Categories Reveal About the Mind, Chicago: U of Chicago P.
—. (1988): "Cognitive Semantics," in: Umberto Eco/Marco Santambrogio/Patrizia Violi (eds.), Meaning and Mental Representation, Bloomington: Indiana UP, 119-154.
—. (1990): "The Invariance Hypothesis. Is Abstract Reason Based on Image-Schemas?," in: Cognitive Linguistics 1.1, 39-74.
—. (2011): "The Contemporary Theory of Metaphor," in: Frederik Stjernfelt/Peer F. Bundgaard (eds.), Semiotics. Critical Concepts in Language Studies, Vol. II: Linguistics, London: Routledge, 264-311.

Lakoff, George/Johnson, Mark (1999): Philosophy in the Flesh. The Embodied Mind and Its Challenge to Western Thought, New York: Basic.

—. (2003): Metaphors We Live By, with a new afterword, Chicago: Chicago UP.

Lakoff, George/Núñez, Rafael E. (2000): Where Mathematics Comes From. How the Embodied Mind Brings Mathematics into Being, New York: Basic.

Loenhoff, Jens (2012): "Einleitung," in: Jens Loenhoff (ed.), Implizites Wissen. Epistemologische und handlungstheoretische Perspektiven, Weilerswist: Velbrück, 7-30.

May, Michael (1995): "Diagrammatisches Denken. Zur Deutung logischer Diagramme als Vorstellungsschemata bei Lakoff und Peirce," in: Zeitschrift für Semiotik 17.3/4, 285-305.

—. (1999): "Diagrammatic Reasoning and Levels of Schematization," in: Troels Degn Johannson/Martin Skov/Berit Brogaard (eds.), Iconicity. A Fundamental Problem in Semiotics, Kopenhagen: Nordic Summer UP, 175-194.

May, Michael/Stjernfelt, Frederik (2008): "Measurement, Diagram, Art. Reflections on the Role of the Icon in Science and Aesthetics," in: Morten Søndergaard/Peter Weibel (eds.), Magnet. Thorbjørn Lausten's Visual System, Heidelberg: Kehrer, 53-73.

Metz, Christian (2000): Der imaginäre Signifikant. Psychoanalyse und Kino, Münster: Nodus.

Meyer-Krahmer, Benjamin/Halawa, Mark (2012): "Pragmatismus auf dem Papier. Über den Zusammenhang von Peirce' graphischer Praxis und pragmatischem Denken," in: Engel/Queisner/Viola, Das bildnerische Denken, 273-302.

Pape, Helmut (1995): "Der Gedanke als Überblendung in der Folge der Bilder. Peirce' visuelles Modell geistiger Prozesse," in: Deutsche Zeitschrift für Philosophie 43.3, 479-496.

—. (1997): Die Unsichtbarkeit der Welt. Eine visuelle Kritik neuzeitlicher Ontologie, Frankfurt/Main: Suhrkamp.

Peirce, Charles S. (1906): "Prolegomena to an Apology for Pragmatism," in: The Monist 16.4, 492-546. http://www.jstor.org/stable/27899680, accessed 12 Dec. 2013.

—. (1973): Lectures on Pragmatism. Vorlesungen über Pragmatismus, ed. Elisabeth Walther, Hamburg: Meiner.

—. (1976): The New Elements of Mathematics by Charles S. Peirce, IV vols., ed. Carolyn Eisele, Atlantic Highlands: Mouton Humanities P.

—. (1998): The Essential Peirce. Selected Philosophical Writings, Vol. 2 (1893-1913), ed. Peirce Edition Project, Bloomington: Indiana UP.

Pietarinen, Ahti-Veikko (2003): Peirce's Magic Lantern of Logic. Moving Pictures of Thought, http://www.helsinki.fi/science/commens/papers/magiclantern.pdf, accessed 17 Aug. 2013.

—. (2011): "An Iconic Logic of Metaphors," http://www.helsinki.fi/~pietarin/publications/Iconic%20Logic%20of%20Metaphors-Pietarinen-2011.pdf, accessed 17 Aug. 2013.

Renn, Joachim (2004): "Wissen und Explikation. Zum kognitiven Geltungsanspruch der 'Kulturen,'" in: Friedrich Jaeger/Burkhardt Liebsch (eds.), Handbuch der Kulturwissenschaften, Vol. 1: Grundlegung und Schlüsselbegriffe, Stuttgart: Metzler, 232-251.

Rocke, Alan (2010): Image and Reality. Kekulé, Kopp, and the Scientific Imagination, Chicago: Chicago UP.

Roesler, Alexander (1999): Illusion und Relativismus. Zu einer Semiotik der Wahrnehmung im Anschluss an Charles S. Peirce, Paderborn: Schöningh.

Shimojima, Atsuhi (1996): On the Efficacy of Representation, Indiana: Diss. Indiana U.

Solaris (1972): USSR, dir. Andrei Tarkovsky.

Solaris (2002): USA, dir. Steven Soderbergh.

Stjernfelt, Frederik (2007): Diagrammatology. An Investigation on the Borderlines of Phenomenology, Ontology, and Semiotics, Dordrecht: Springer.

Strub, Christian (1994): "Peirce über Metaphern. Zur Interpretation von CP 2.277," in: Helmut Pape (ed.), Kreativität und Logik. Charles S. Peirce und das philosophische Problem des Neuen, Frankfurt/Main: Suhrkamp, 209-232.

—. (1998): "Spiegel-Bilder. Zum Verhältnis von metaphorischer Reflexivität und Ikonizität," in: Johann Kreuzer/Tilman Borsche/Christian Strub (eds.), Blick und Bild im Spannungsfeld von Sehen, Metaphern und Verstehen, München: Fink, 265-277.

Thiele, Ansgar (2006): "Schuss und Gegenschuss ist Krieg – Teil I: Überlegungen zu metaphorischen Prozessen im Film," in: Metaphorik.de 10, 133-160.

2001. A Space Odyssey (1968): USA/UK, dir. Stanley Kubrick.

Whittock, Trevor (1990): Metaphor and Film, Cambridge: Cambridge UP.

Wöpking, Jan (2010): "Space, Structure, and Similarity. On Representationalist Theories of Diagrams," in: Olga Pombo/Alexander Gerner (eds.), Studies in Diagrammatology and Diagram Praxis, London: College Publications, 39-56.

—. (2012): Raum und Erkenntnis. Elemente einer Theorie epistemischen Diagrammgebrauchs, Berlin: Diss. Free U. (unpublished)

Ziemkiewicz, Caroline (2010): Understanding the Structure of Information Visualization Through Visual Metaphor, Charlotte: Diss. U of North Carolina. http://cs.brown.edu/people/cziemki/documents/ziemkiewicz-caroline-2010-phd.pdf, accessed 1. Aug. 2013.

Ziemkiewicz, Caroline/Kosara, Robert (2008): "The Shaping of Information by Visual Metaphors," in: IEEE TVCG 14.6, 1269-1276. http://cs.brown.edu/people/cziemki/documents/ziemkiewicz10_implied-dynamics.pdf, accessed 1 Aug. 2013.

Improvising Faith

An Essay on Implicit Knowledge and Living within God's Story

Wolfgang Schoberth

I. INTRODUCTION

What does it mean to be a believer? What is faith? Faith is commonly understood, first, as a set of propositions which the believer accepts; second, as a system of moral rules which the believer tries to observe; and third, as a doctrine that includes religious duties the believer has to fulfill. Each of these three aspects is obviously explicit and refers to an intentional act, whether intellectual or moral, and thus presupposes the idea of a rational and moral subject which adheres to or disregards explicit religious commandments. This popular interpretation of faith is also broadly accepted in academic discourse, where it provides guidelines for theorizing religion as well as for qualitative and quantitative research in the field of religion.

Although these three aspects are obviously important in Christian religion, to focus on them exclusively is often misleading and impedes understanding the true nature of faith; it also leads to theological impasses and to misperceptions in cultural studies. I want to show that focusing on the implicit moments in Christian life instead is more productive. Explicit articulations of faith are of course not to be neglected, but the implicit side of Christian faith is not merely an antecedent to explicit faith, nor is it a matter of decline; to the contrary, faith can only be understood by considering the interdependency of both its implicit and explicit dimensions, which I would like to do in this paper by taking a closer look at the practices of faith. One promising model or metaphor for describing these practices is musical improvisation, especially as it occurs in Modern and Free Jazz; this will be discussed at the end of my paper. Christian life takes place in the dialectic between the implicit and explicit dimensions of faith; what Christians do is to perform Christian faith under the very specific circumstances in which they find themselves, and they do so by improvising with the materials provided by Christian tradition.

II. Faith and the Implicit

While the verb 'believe' is a common term used in many different contexts, 'faith' obviously is connected to a person's identity: a person may have lots of different beliefs, but not different faiths.[1] Therefore, the verb 'believe' when referring to 'faith' is a source of misconceptions, especially when used transitively. Faith thus is not an action but rather marks a person's specific status or even character. To believe this or that does not make one a believer – and faith is not the sum total of one's beliefs.

The role of implicitness in faith is apparent in the fact that becoming a Christian is neither the result of accepting dogmas or convictions, nor of a personal decision, nor of studying the Bible. In terms of religious socialization, it is clear that becoming a Christian means to be gradually socialized into a certain kind of practice: becoming a Christian means to become acquainted with and adopt the practices and forms of life of Christians. Before being able to evaluate or even understand the doctrines of faith, a person will already have participated in and performed practices such as hymns, prayers, gestures, and rites.

But is this faith 'implicit'? Scholastic theology developed the concept of *fides implicita* as a counterweight to the intellectualization of faith: If faith were merely a complex system of assertions, then everybody in error about a theological tenet would be a heretic; since even a theological expert can hardly be expected to follow the increasingly difficult debates in every detail, it would be completely unreasonable to demand full understanding and acceptance from the layman and from the uneducated (cf. Wüstenberg 2007: 77ff.). *Fides implicita* therefore means that a Christian has only to believe the necessary and basic truths of faith – the extent of those truths has never been defined (cf. ibid. 78) – but on the whole adopt the belief of the church without examination or engagement. In this conception, faith is implicit in the sense that the average believer trusts in the faith of the church; the teaching office of the church, executed by the bishops, cares for the explication and pureness of faith. The Reformers and Protestant Orthodoxy sharply rejected the concept of implicit faith (cf. Sparn 1990), because it contradicts the principles of Reformation theology on at least two crucial points: First, faith cannot be separated from the person; nobody can believe in my stead. Second, the concept of *fides implicita* insinuates that the church is the subject of belief, thus the individual Christian is, in this conception, restricted to an indirect access to faith – hence, from a Reformation-based perspective, what at first glance appears to lighten the burden of the individual believer is in reality a form of disenfranchisement. Reformation theology finds

---

[1] Somebody who is attracted to different religions does not have multiple religions, but instead combines elements from different traditions into one faith.

both of these aspects completely unacceptable because they undermine the very core of faith. If faith is, as Protestant theologians emphasize, essentially the personal relation to God in Jesus Christ, then it cannot be separated from personal identity. Since they define faith essentially as *fiducia* (trust), any delegation of faith must obviously be considered an absurd idea: nobody can trust on somebody else's behalf.

The idea of implicit faith implies that faith does not relate to the whole person, but is just one province in human life beside others.[2] Reformation theology disapproves of any division of faith; because faith is not a human activity but a gift from the Holy Spirit, it can neither be divided into parts or grades nor assigned for duty. And because the subject of faith is not the church but the Spirit, there is no hierarchy in faith between clergy and laity. The Reformation concept of faith is complex and easy to misunderstand if the foundation of faith in the potency of the Holy Spirit is ignored. As soon as it is reduced to human capacities this concept seems to lead into a dilemma: From the common priesthood of all believers seems to follow that every Christian must understand the same complex system of beliefs as the professional theologians on the one hand – with unacceptable consequences not only with regard to small children[3] and mentally disabled persons. On the other hand, if faith is detached from the traditions of the church its content and its source get lost: the story of God in Israel and Jesus Christ.

In order to recover the Reformation-based perception of faith, it is necessary to reflect the genuine passivity of Christian life (cf. Link 1984), which is the anthropologic correlate of justification and the basic insight that God's acting is the beginning and the substance of faith. It is impossible to trace these relations in detail here, instead of which I will focus on one essential aspect which can be identified as the genuine dialectic of the implicit and explicit dimensions of faith: Because faith is grounded in God's story, being a Christian means to know about this story, becoming better acquainted with it and letting it become one's own story. Faith on the other hand is not at human disposal but latent, and comes, so to speak, from outside. There are two important and correlating approaches in recent theology which elucidate this dialectic: George Lindbeck's proposal to understand doctrines in analogy to the rules of gram-

---

2 | In this respect, there is an astonishing parallel between scholastic theology and modern Protestant theology as inaugurated by Schleiermacher in opposition to the theology of the Reformation.

3 | Infant baptism may be the best test case for Luther's understanding of faith. His thoughts on the *fides infantium* (faith of the infants) are unreasonable for most modern theologians who interconnect belief and subjectivity, but are a direct consequence of his theological premises and probably a significant approach for overcoming theological reductionism which results from the confusion of faith with explicit convictions.

mar and Dietrich Ritschl's concept of implicit axioms, both of which, instead of understanding the implicit and explicit dimensions of faith, antithetically show how they interact. After my discussion of Lindbeck and Ritschl, I will turn to Nicholas Lash's reflections on the performance of the Scriptures, which shed light on the role of implicitness in living with the Bible.

III. Doctrine and Implicit Knowledge

In his influential study *The Nature of Doctrine*, George A. Lindbeck outlined a theory of religion and doctrine which was intended to give a new impulse to ecumenical discussions (cf. 1984). Lindbeck, who had been involved in Catholic-Lutheran dialogue for decades, clearly saw that on the explicit level of doctrine there were few chances of overcoming the long-standing disagreements between the Catholic and Lutheran churches: because each tradition has doctrines which are in distinct contradiction to doctrines of the other tradition, any doctrinal unification would mean one of the two parties having to give up fundamental convictions – since the Mariological dogmas and the dogma of the infallibility of the Pope, for instance, are simply unacceptable to Protestants, conciliation on the level of explicit assertions is impossible.

Lindbeck's basic idea is to take doctrinal formulations neither as ontological propositions, as is done in so-called orthodox traditions of all denominations, nor as symbolic (and therefore replaceable) expressions of an underlying truth, as is the understanding of doctrine in liberal traditions. As the orthodox or propositional view is binary – the doctrine of the immaculate conception for example is either true or false, with Protestants and Catholics holding opposing views as to its validity – there is no room for discussion. Because this situation is intolerable for Lindbeck, he questions the underlying model. The liberal or symbolic view in contrast can cope with this situation by referring to a postulated truth behind the explicit statements of doctrine; according to this perspective, what really matters is not the explicit formulation, but the hidden truth which is expressed in it. Though popular in contemporary theology, this answer is dissatisfying as well, because it insinuates that the doctrinal truth is generally not visible in explicit religious manifestations and becomes visible only to those interpreters who break through the veil of ecclesial tradition. Because of its disregard for the actual practice of Christian life and because of its vagueness, Lindbeck rejects this model as well. He approaches and proposes a model instead that is not only ecumenically helpful but is also firmly grounded in epistemology, and is more realistic than the 'cognitive-propositional' or 'experiential-expressive' model of religion. Referring to Wittgenstein's philosophy as well as to Clifford Geertz' cultural anthropology, he calls this model "cultural-linguistic" (Lindbeck 1984: 32ff.). I cannot discuss this model broadly here;[4] for the purpose of this essay I will concentrate on Lindbeck's conception of the relation between explicit and implicit dimensions of faith. His theory acknowledges the importance of explicit doctrines, traditional creeds, and established denominational communities, but also the basic importance of implicit knowledge in faith: believers know more than they can tell, as Christian practices and forms of life contain dimensions of the truth of faith that cannot be explicitly expressed, and faith moreover refers to dimensions beyond the predictable.

To illustrate this relation, Lindbeck compares the role of doctrines in faith to the role of grammar in spoken and written language. Ordinary speakers do not have to be grammarians and may even be unable to name the rules of grammar, yet their ability to communicate with others nevertheless relies on the existence of such rules. The implicit rules of grammar thus are the (necessary but not sufficient) condition for meaningful utterances. This model can be applied to faith and doctrine: Most believers lack the theological and historical knowledge to fully understand traditional dogmatic assertions, which however does not mean that they are not 'competent Christian speakers.' Their language is not the language of theology, but the language of faith: "Technical theology and official doctrine [...] are second-order discourse about the first-intentional users of religious language" (Lindbeck 1984: 69). Thus doctrines can be compared to the rules of grammar, and theologians to grammarians. Doctrinal assertions are, in this model, the explicit verbalization of the rules which ensure that religious language and religious practice can achieve their purpose. Christian language and practice need the accompaniment of explicit doctrine and critical theological reflection because they are always in danger of losing their destination and their hope, which arises from the gospel. They are endangered, just because they are flexible, creative and individual – if it is *living* language and *living* faith –, just because they are situated and grounded in present life. And they need the solid foundation in the gospel to persist as *Christian* language and faith.

Lindbeck's model shows that the implicit and explicit dimensions refer to each other. Explication is neither 'better' (as implied by an intellectualist conception) nor 'lifeless' or 'rigid' (as claimed by an expressive conception): either criticism results from a misunderstanding of the purpose and nature of doctrine and theological statements, which neither replace the first-order language of faith nor sublimate unelaborated speech and practices but instead require the reality of a Christian community, serve as the medium that makes faith communicable, and allow the critical reflection of religious reality. Because Christian faith is truth-oriented, it requires an authority that allows examining and if necessary correcting its practices and statements. So faith itself demands

---

4 | For a broader discussion cf. W. Schoberth 2009.

explication in doctrines and theological reflection, although these explications are secondary to the life of faith. This function can again be compared to the relation of a spoken natural language to its grammar: even though language needs the rules of grammar and speech needs critical examination, explicit grammatical rules are descriptive, not prescriptive, and do not exist on their own but are *ex post facto* conceptualizations of spoken and written language. School grammar itself needs examination and correction, because its *ex-post* conceptualizations may turn out to be insufficient or inadequate for describing an ever-changing language. Rules of grammar can only be 'right' if they not only adequately describe a language, but also actually regulate the way it is used by speakers.

IV. Implicit Axioms and the Language of Faith

The clarification of the mechanisms that actually steer speaking and acting is the focus of Dietrich Ritschl's work on "implicit axioms."[5] Ritschl is not only a systematic theologian who shares Lindbeck's interest in ecumenical questions but also worked in the field of medical ethics and was active for many years as a psychoanalyst. It is most likely his background in psychoanalysis that redirected his view from the explicit statements to the unarticulated devices that steer persons' actions, feelings, perceptions, and speech. These devices are called "axioms" because they are not only true for the specific person – although they can of course be doubted by other persons –, but function as the basis for a person's orientation in the world, as a necessary condition for acting and speaking; they are "implicit" because they usually can't be articulated and because their effect is independent of the explicit knowledge of actors/speakers. Psychoanalysis can be understood as a long process of discovering the devices that really steer a person's life, some of which may even never come to light. Nevertheless, it is worth exploring these implicit orientations, especially when it is suspected that those presently governing the conduct of a person (or a community) may not be helpful or even harmful – the therapeutic task is in Ritschl's eyes one main purpose of theology (cf. 2008: 123).

As long as we are considering only theological discourse (and not other non-conceptual forms of Christian practice), it is safe to assume that such steering devices can be reconstructed with the help of articulated theological concepts. Because theology has its medium and its life in concepts and arguments – otherwise it could not fulfill its critical and therapeutic function –, the 'steering devices' of theology are presumably never principally implicit: they

---

5 | For an exposition of Ritschl's thoughts on "implicit axioms" cf. I. Schoberth 1992, ch. 1.4.2.

can be given explicit formulation, thus they can be seen as implicit knowledge in a weak sense. Theological axioms therefore coincide with "regulative statements;" they "ensure thought and speech which can be examined, and ordered action" (Ritschl 1986: xxi). Ritschl's reflections are in this respect very close to Lindbeck's concept of explicit theology as the grammar of faith.

Similar to Lindbeck, Ritschl emphasizes that "theology is not identical with the totality of the thought and language of believers," but is "only a small part of that, the part that claims to regulate, to examine and to stimulate this thought and language, and also the action of believers" (1986: 1).[6] In contrast to regulative sentences – "Dogmas, indeed, are the best examples for explicit steering devices" (2008: 111f.) – implicit axioms lie "behind such explicit articulations" (ibid. 111). Ritschl is fully aware of the epistemological problems of his reference to "the field of pre-linguistic steering devices" (ibid.), which is one reason why he hesitated to develop an elaborated theory of implicit axioms; but here lies the importance of his ideas as well: limiting faith to explicit statements, much less to dogmas, is a source of misinterpretations not only in theology.[7]

In the following I would like to concentrate on the junction between the implicit and the explicit, which is extremely important for understanding the life of believers. This junction is most easily grasped as the transition from pre-linguistic faith (in theological concepts: the presence of the Holy Spirit) to regulative sentences, for which the traditional expressions of faith – dogmas and theological statements, but even more importantly hymns and religious songs, prayers and benedictions, and above all the stories and the language of the Bible – are essential. Therefore I want to focus on the question of how the explicit expressions of Christian tradition flow into the reality of the lives of the believers. This reality is not a series of intentional and deliberate acts but predominantly a stream of sensations and manifestations of one's character,

---

6 | Empirical research in the field of religion must be aware of this difference. Non-professional speakers may not be able to articulate the regulative sentences they follow in their lives as Christians, and may have to rely on conventional terms and definitions regardless of whether they are adequate for describing their lives and faith. Researchers using established methods such as questionnaires or narrative interviews depend on an approach to language which is common in academic milieus, but unusual for others, so the interviewer might see a mirroring of his own categories. There is no direct path from the informant's repeating or rejecting of (theological and other) categories to their actual orientations and the reality of their faith.

7 | For the purpose of this paper it is not necessary to further discuss the questions which arise from the problem that those pre-linguistic dimensions must be communicated with language or else will be excluded from reflection and even communication: it is the challenge of speaking at the boundaries of language. Theology works on these questions in the self-reflection of its constitution and its method.

which is why implicit and explicit expressions do not follow one upon the other but irreducibly interpenetrate each other. Doctrines emerge from and then flow back again into the implicit axioms of faith which steer the believer's speaking, thinking, and acting.

Ritschl's concept of implicit axioms can be understood as relating to the deep structure of human life in general: Implicit axioms are present not only in Christian life, they are a general feature of the life of every individual; however, the difference between believers and non-believers lies in the quality of the axioms that steer their lives: in contrast to the implicit axioms governing the actions, perceptions, and reflections of nonbelievers, those of a believer are formed by faith. The operative axioms in a Christian's life are not identical with doctrine or biblical norms but they are *shaped* by the Christian tradition. Collectively valid axioms and those which are valid in an individual's life are always interdependent. Faith always includes both the axioms which hold my story within the whole story of the community of believers and so finally within the story of God, and axioms which actualize this story in *my* life.[8] These two basic moments of faith elucidate, first, that faith is not a province in life among others, but governs life as a whole; and, second, that faith is at the same time individual and based on the community of believers. The implicit dimension of faith is irreducible because it is the precondition for the realization of faith in a person's life. On the other hand, this realization is only possible as the realization of a tradition. The identity of faith, within the community as well as in a person's life, lies in the connection with the *ecumene* of all Christians across time and space; therefore, individual axioms can and sometimes must be criticized by the historically established regulative sentences as well as by those generated by present-day theology. The reality of faith, within the community as well as individuals, relies on the ability to find authentic expressions and relevant actualizations of the Christian tradition.

V. Performing the Scriptures

The relation between individual faith and the Christian tradition should therefore not be reduced to the categories of application or interpretation. Christian tradition is not a fixed system; the misinterpretation of the Bible as a collection of standards, norms, and pieces of advice may have resulted from wrongly equating the exegesis of the Bible by professional theologians in academic

---

8 | This largely coincides with Ritschl's analytical distinction between themes of lasting importance and such of momentary concern; it would be a pathological development if one would be overestimated at the expense of the other (cf. Ritschl 1986: xxi et passim).

contexts with the reading practices and lived experience of Christians. Even professional theologians approach the Bible differently in liturgical or pastoral compared to academic contexts. Nicholas Lash suggests that a performance rather than a hermeneutical model[9] is more helpful for understanding how Christians use the Scriptures, as Christians perform rather than interpret the Scriptures or apply biblical norms. It is not by accident that Lash uses an aesthetic category, as practicing the arts has much in common with the life of faith – not least the importance in both of implicit dimensions and their location at the boundaries of language.

It is an advantage of the performance model that it is neither textualist nor intentionalist. The authority of the Scriptures cannot be separated from the life of the community, as Lash points out: "We talk of 'holy' scripture, and for good reason. And yet it is not, in fact, the *script* that is 'holy,' but the people: the company who perform the script" (1986: 42). But it would also be wrong to say that the community 'makes' the authority of the Scriptures: a performance of any text has its quality in the genuine faithfulness to the given script. A performance must be faithful in both directions, faithful to the tradition and faithful to present reality. It demands a responsibility of the performers which consists not only in a careful reading, but also in an openness to the present. Being overly meticulous may not benefit a performance, as Lash illustrates with the example of one of Beethoven's late string quartets:

> Consider four people playing the quartet. What are they doing? They are interpreting the text. Even if the performance is technically faultless (and is, in that sense, a "correct" interpretation) we might judge it to be lifeless, unimaginative. There is a creativity in interpretation which, far from being arbitrary (the players cannot do whatever they like with the score) is connected in some way with the fidelity, the "truthfulness" of their performance. (1986: 40)

This example demonstrates the interdependency of score and performance: The musicians not only reproduce the piece, but also produce a unique performance which is not a rendition of the work's intrinsic meaning, as the work means only insofar as that it is being performed anew time and again, and each performance is inimitable.

One of the advantages of Lash's performance model is that it accentuates both sides equally: the present experiences and needs of Christians as well as the Christian tradition and its foundation in the story testified in the Bible. Merely repeating traditional formulas or biblical quotations would not only

---

9 | There is good reason to assume that this model of interpretation is not of theological but rather juridical origin, which would connect to the fallacy of conceptualizing God as a kind of legal authority and the Bible as a *corpus juris*.

mean to deceive the present life of the Christian community but also violate the spirit of the Scriptures and tradition, which under new conditions require new performances to unfold their stimulating power. The Scriptures for a very special reason definitely belong to those "texts that only begin to deliver their meaning in so far as they are 'brought into play' through interpretative performance" (Lash 1986: 41f.): While written by human writers the Biblical texts claim to point to God's own acting – the intentions of their authors are secondary; the authors rather step back behind the story they tell. It is therefore quite appropriate to call the biblical authors 'witnesses:' Witnesses themselves are not interesting but the subject instead to which they testify, yet they are indispensable because the subject would be inaccessible without their testimony. So it is the specific character of this story which needs to be performed and which gives the performances their strength. It is again the unique topic of the story which embraces the present life of the believers across time:

> To put it very simply: as the history of the meaning of the text continues, we can and must tell the story differently. But we do so under constraint: what we may *not* do, if it is *this* text which we are to continue to perform, is to tell a different story. (ibid. 44)

Christians read the Bible because the story transforms their own reality through the performance of the story. Precisely for present reality's sake the performers must be faithful to Scripture, and the academic discourse on biblical texts serves to ensure that the same story is performed and not the performer's ideas: "The academics have an indispensable but subordinate part to play in contributing to the quality and appreciation of the performance" (ibid. 41).[10] The decisive factor remains the presence of the Spirit, who connects the past with the present:

> It follows that, for the practice of Christianity, the performance of the biblical text, to be true, it must be not only "true to life," but "true to *his* life:" and not only "true to his life," but "true to God." That it is so, and may be made so, is at once our responsibility, our hope and our prayer. (ibid. 45)

Of course, the model of performance has its limitations, just as any model: It is not easy to define who the artists are and who the audience is – and maybe it should not be defined, and for Christians there is no time when they do not perform.[11] But the advantages prevail: 'Performing the Scriptures' shows the crucial relevance of being faithful to the Biblical tradition and as well to the

---

10 | Sometimes academic theology itself plays a part in telling a different story.

11 | Cf. Lash (1986: 46): "But, for each Christian actor the performance of the biblical text ends only at death. The stage on which we enact our performance is that wider

present life; it makes clear that the Christian community as a whole is responsible for the quality of the performance – this implies that there is no authority which can secure the one and only truth but an ongoing dialogue within the people whose lives are shaped by performing the story –; it illustrates that every believer has to dare to perform in communion with the performances of others. But I would propose to go one step further: Living as a Christian does not only mean "Performing the Scriptures," because this performance has no score – it is an improvisation.

VI. THE ARTISTRY OF IMPLICIT KNOWLEDGE: IMPROVISATION

Christians do not enact biblical episodes for an audience; rather, their performance of the Scriptures and their acquaintance with the Bible helps them to live their lives: Christians perform the Scriptures in an unpredictable drama. Samuel Wells is right when he questions "the assumption that the Bible is a script that the church performs;" he suggests instead "that it is more like a training manual that forms what Christians take for granted" (2004: 214).[12] There is no script because the preconditions and the circumstances of the performance are all new in the life of any Christian; Christians are continually confronted with and have to find solutions for problems that nobody has previously solved because these problems are irreducibly linked to a particular life story. Improvising music exemplifies well the challenges and the promises that are connected with individuality and the openness of life. Improvisation should not be considered as strictly antithetical to musical composition, for there is evidence, as Jeremy Begbie emphasizes,

> that not only is there an element of improvisation in virtually all music of all cultures, but that there is scarcely a musical technique or form of composition that did not originate in improvisation or was not essentially influenced by it. This suggests that instead of regarding music which is strictly notated and largely planned as the norm and improvisation as an unfortunate distortion or epiphenomenon, it might be more illuminating to invert that and ask whether improvisation reveals to us fundamental aspects of musical creativity easily forgotten in traditions bound predominantly to the practices of rigorous rehearsal and notation. (2005: 730)

---

human history in which the church exists as the 'sacrament,' or dramatic enactment, of history's ultimate meaning and hope."

12 | Wells' book is in its intention and in its theological direction close to the proposal which is given in this paper, the difference being that Wells follows the paradigm of a dramatic improvisation while I concentrate on improvisation in music, especially in jazz.

In other words, improvised music is both a magnifier of essential features of music and an example of coping with and rejoicing in the unpredictable. Therefore, it can also provide a parable for living the faith, which can be illustrated on the basis of five aspects:

(1) *Time and moment*: Music is the art of the moment. This is evident most intensively in improvisation, where music comes from this specific moment and vanishes when the musicians stop playing. On Eric Dolphy's last record *Last Date*, Dolphy can be heard saying: "When you hear music, after it's over, it's gone, in the air. You can never capture it again" (1964). This pertains even to recorded music: Dolphy speaks about *hearing* music. If the record is replayed, a new moment happens. Hearing music and playing music always happen in a brief moment, when musicians and their audience come together within the space opened by the music, and thus give the experience of time itself. In this respect, there is no fundamental difference between improvised and composed music: Hearing music means to confide in the stream of time. Dolphy's statement even points to the beauty of the fleetingness of time, which is the precondition for the musical moment; reciprocally music brings to light that this fleetingness is not only reason for lamentation, as Jeremy Begbie states:

> Put more positively and theologically, music can serve as a means of discovering afresh and articulating the theological truth that limited duration can be beneficial, and as such, an expression of divine generosity. (2000: 93)

Music can foreshadow the touch of time and eternity. This exposition to the moment and this irreproducibility of an improvisation (and of performing a score) doesn't mean that one has to sit in on the magic event – this common opinion is little more than an attenuation of the romantic idea of the aura of an artwork.[13] Recorded music – whether of improvisations or different interpretations of a Beethoven quartet – still is the presentation of a fleeting moment.

Improvisation is even more the art of the moment than music in general: Musicians and listeners must come together in *this* moment – otherwise there is no performance. What a musician plays *now* is decisive – a tone once played cannot be retracted. Improvising means to follow what emerges *now* – what has been learned or played before does not count. Improvisation depends on the ability to play as simple or as complex, as loud or as soft as the moment demands.

(2) *Interplay and the respect for the other*: Improvisation has to expect the unexpected because the musicians never know what their fellow musicians are going to play in the next moment. Many times it is even impossible to deter-

---

13 | Walter Benjamin's classic criticism of this idea hasn't become less important (cf. 2005).

mine whether a dissonant note or a shriek is a fault or an intensive expression – only the ongoing music will decide what it is. Miles Davis' famous advice for improvisers is first to be heard as the wisdom of interplay: "Do not fear mistakes. There are none." Accept what the others play; what at first may appear to be wrong or inappropriate may turn out to be a new idea, a thrilling plot twist or a breach of settled habits. It should not be concealed that wrong notes may turn out as wrong and simply as mistakes; that is the risk of improvisation. But it is worth assuming the opposite: unpredictability is essential for jazz. As the saxophone player Archie Shepp puts it: "That's jazz, man – you never know..." (qtd. in *Jazz à Porquerolles*).

Respecting my co-musicians, then, is the beginning of a certain form of charitableness towards myself. *I* know that I played an unintended note; the others don't. As soon as I hear what my fellow musicians made from my wrong note I may realize that the allegedly 'wrong' note was probably the best I could do. The respect for the other is the root of self-respect, especially when different traditions and preferences come together. Willie Jennings emphasizes that such interplay can be exemplary:

Churches could learn much from reflecting on a jazz band. Here are a group of people who work very hard at listening, yet give up nothing of themselves in that process, but in fact only gain a true sense of themselves in the common task of making music, producing sound that makes a central statement that exists only through the constitutive performances of each musician. (2011: 15)

(3) *Accepting, testing, and breaking the rules*: Even jazz has its rules, of course, and it would be a mystification to ascribe the capability to improvise (or to swing and to play the blues) to a natural disposition, even if under the guise of glorifying the native and the natural. These rules can be written down and taught; they are the basis of jazz education. At their best, these rules are derived from the improvisations of the jazz masters. But the masters themselves did not play by applying rules, and students' improvisations which follow the rules perfectly, while being technically correct, may sound predictable and boring.

Musical rules are not natural laws but conventions and clichés: A dominant seventh chord need not always resolve in the tonic – in Blues a dominant seventh may even be the tonic – nor is the indeed common resolution of a dissonance compulsory; and the II-V-I-progression, while being the most common harmonic sequence in jazz from swing to hard bop, likewise is not obligatory. Laws of music are nothing but conventional, and most of them have been broken or ignored at some point in the history of music and in different musical cultures: Hence, nobody has to avoid 'Avoid Notes.' The alleged necessity to resolve a dissonance or to intone 'correctly' etc. are clichés that articulate the conventions of a certain style or culture. But nobody can talk without clichés, otherwise he or she wouldn't be understood. Reciprocally there would be no dialogue if one of the partners only used clichés and common phrases. If a musician wants to sound in a certain manner, it is necessary to use the formulas which are typical for the style and genre, but a bare aggregation of correct formulas leads to an improvisation that will be totally meaningless.

The characteristics and the established rules of a certain style thus are the outward form of an artwork but not the artistic event itself. Ornette Coleman's often-cited maxim, "Let's play the music and not its background!" makes this manifest: Despite the fact that his music neglected the rhythmic, harmonic, and structural conventions of the jazz tradition which were regarded as essential and obligatory, it was not only obviously jazz music but indeed a vital innovation and – from today's perspective – a necessary contribution to the jazz tradition. Music does not depend on received formulas, and for a musician it is only logical to test this by giving up the traditional guidelines. An analogous experience was made in painting with the discovery that the artistic moment is completely independent from the sujet: The impressionists raised ordinary life scenes to artistic spheres, and abstract painters demonstrated that a painting does not even need subject matter in the traditional sense at all. The great masters regularly broke with the artistic conventions of their time and have been criticized for doing so: By exposing themselves to be chastised as bunglers or charlatans, innovative individuals revitalize the arts.

Jeremy Begbie emphasizes that "[a]rtists are attracted to novelty" (2011: 5), and adds that this attraction can be exemplary for believers and the church.[14] While the church – just as any other institution – tends to hold the established perspective, and while many people turn to religion in search for stability, the gospel is oriented towards God's future and is therefore the source of hope. The church is an extraordinary institution because its only *raison d'être* lies outside itself; it would stop being the church if it failed its foundation and life in the gospel – and the gospel is in its core promise. This is why the church and Christian believers need the impulse which comes from the transgression of the existing order, which can be exemplarily learned from the arts. Willie Jennings states that "[j]azz musicians expose a messianic secret, that deliverance from one-dimensional visions of life has come to us in the elegant act of performing" (2011: 15). Because from their concentration on the music, on the moment and the interplay – with other musicians, the audience and, as many jazz musicians assert, a transcendent presence –, there arises a unique openness: "Jazz musicians in the midst of playing often gesture toward new possibilities, making visible the reality of hope" (ibid.).

---

14 | Cf. Begbie (2011: 6): "For those of us who have been in the church for some time, we can easily forget that newness is built into the gospel. The aroma of novelty is on every page of the New Testament."

(4) *Preparation and spontaneity*: Innovation is not obligatory for each improviser, but jazz improvisation is exemplary here, too, because the personal authenticity of the musicians is crucial: technical perfection is subordinate to having one's own voice. Innovation is an ambiguous term, first, because it cannot be planned: If one tries too hard to play innovatively, failure is predictable; innovation is a problematic concept, second, because it can only be identified by comparing an artistic event to a given set of regulations, and this comparison is bound to intellectual concepts, not to aesthetic means; and third, innovation is impossible without its foundation in tradition. While breaking the conventional rules of jazz, Ornette Coleman's music is undoubtedly jazz: It swings without the ride on the cymbal and the walking bass, and its harmonic flavor tastes like jazz even without jazz's conventional progressions, etc. It sounds like jazz because it is rooted in jazz and speaks in the tongues of jazz: The underlying continuity is the 'sound' of jazz, or, to put it another way, the implicit knowledge of how to play jazz. It is this implicit knowledge which shapes improvisation and makes improvisation possible at all. Improvisation is no sorcery and is not restricted to miraculous geniuses but rather is the outcome of long-term preparation. Breaking the rules and playing with the rules does not end in arbitrariness because improvisers immersed in the stream of music have learned to play their own music by selecting from, actualizing, and transforming tradition. Therefore improvisation is based on a reservoir of implicit knowledge: Reacting within one moment is not possible as an act of reflecting and weighing up. It is the advantage of writing music to have the time to generate good ideas and to discard bad ones. But improvising means to rely completely on one's implicit knowledge, which is comprised of music once heard, influences incorporated from previous performances, life experiences, etc. Breaking the rules does not produce chaos if it is based on wisdom and the implicit knowledge of an underlying continuity: "music demonstrates that there can be ordered change, that change need not imply chaos" (Begbie 2000: 85).

Learning to improvise is a genuine form of preparation: An improviser has of course to learn his or her instrument, has to study the masters, will from time to time copy them, and adopt standard phrases. But learning to improvise is essentially to prepare oneself for the unpredictable; it is learning to speak with one's own voice without being obsessed with one's own ideas. Improvisation can only succeed when the musicians do not force their preconceived ideas upon the music: Improvisers prepare themselves for years to be able to encounter the unexpected and to cultivate the venture of the presence. Lester Bowie, longtime trumpet player of the Art Ensemble of Chicago, puts it this way:

We don't go on stage with one person trying to put a will on the music. We prime ourselves to follow the will of the music. See, when you play music, all you do is to prepare yourselves to accept the spirit. Like, when you practiced (sic!) your instrument you don't go on the stage to play what you practiced. You just prepare yourselves to be overwhelmed by the music, to let it put you in a spiritual state. And *then* you express yourself without regard to where it's coming from. *You just do it!* (qtd. in Solothurnmann 1977: 52)

(5) *Transcendence*: It is significant that Bowie refers to the spirit, although this reference should not be too easily identified as the Holy Spirit: Christian faith is grounded in the story of Jesus Christ,[15] which cannot be articulated by improvising music, although it may reference or quote from church music, etc. But in a wider sense there can be discerned affinities in that both are based on trust in what will emerge, the acceptance of what the other players articulate, and the courage to go ways into the unknown. These features might be referred to as 'religious,' because they are rooted in a general habitus of existence which is characterized by the openness to transcendence.[16] This may be proven by the fact that many (US-American) free improvising musicians see themselves as religious individuals yet often avoid referring explicitly to Christianity[17] and instead prefer to speak of 'spirituality,' a label for forms of religiosity which refuse being bound to an established religion. John Coltrane's statement in the liner notes of his record *Meditations* (1965), "I believe in all religions," is frequently cited in this context. The reluctance towards explicit Christian references may remind theology, on the one hand, of the dark side of the history of Christianity in America, and on the other hand, of the necessity to refute legalistic misconceptions of Christian life.

VII. Living as a Christian

The characteristics of improvisation are shared and realized also by non-believing musicians, the religious content of whose work has to be rediscovered

---

15 | In biblical terms, there is the need of the charisma of distinguishing between spirits (cf. 1 Cor 12:10), as this spirit is obviously implicit and, at the moment, anonymous. But theology should not be too anxious: "Quench not the Spirit" (1 Thess 5:19).

16 | 'Religion' is used here in a broad sense and without expanding on the problem that it is, as Joachim Matthes has insisted, a Eurocentric concept (cf. 2005). The term is used here without insinuating the existence of something like 'religion in itself' as a basis or general class for different historical realizations. I speak of religion from a Christian point of view to mark those dimensions of faith which are less articulated and distinguished and for those who do not, or not yet identify themselves with explicit Christianity, but seek their way in the Halo of the gospel.

17 | It would be worthwhile to analyze the fact that religion and spirituality are common topics in the statements of American jazz musicians but almost invisible among European colleagues.

by those who are familiar with God's story. The titles of improvisations and records, for instance, by the American saxophone player and pianist Charles Gayle often reference Christianity explicitly: "Redemption," *Daily Bread*, "Jesus Christ and Scripture," to name a few (cf. 1992, 1993, 1995). But the listener who does not know about the titles would probably not guess that Gayle's music contains a Christian message,[18] and it is likely that Gayle's titles are given *ex post*: The Christian musician recognizes the dimension of faith in his playing, because he knows about the grace and the beauty, and maybe he remembers religious perceptions while playing; and he wants to give his listeners a clue to his experience. Precisely because he avoids proselytizing, his music can be a strong witness.

This may shed light on the relation between the explicit and implicit dimensions of faith: Without explication, critical discussion and self-examination would be impossible. But the explicit theological argument and statement proceed from the lived faith, and they have their meaning in their impact on the lives of the believers and the community of believers. Within the life of faith, explicit statements appear on rare occasions; even the traditional doctrines, e.g. in the spoken Creeds, are liturgical and not immediate arguments; they are learned as traditional formulas and not as an immediate personal expression. But this does not diminish their role in the individual life of a believer and their present relevance for the Christian community. The liturgical use of traditional formulas is no simple repetition but is each and every time a new performance, as David F. Ford points out:

> The character of the Jewish and Christian worshipper is inextricable from communal testimony to God in narrative and other genres. But worship is a present activity which constantly improvises on the past in new situations. (1999: 100)

Explicit statements and codified tradition need to be performed by the community of believers; and this performance is again steered by the implicit knowledge of the believers. The formulas themselves guide in a certain respect the growth and the transfer of this implicit knowledge which has its center in the disclosure of present life in the light of the Gospel. This implicit knowledge is in permanent transition; it integrates and repels multiple influences and forms a specific constellation in the life of each believer, as Ford points out: "It is intrinsic to Christian faith that it is true to itself only by becoming freshly embod-

---

18 | This is true even more in Europe where the biographical and musical backgrounds are different: European listeners and musicians are rarely rooted in worship music, and European church music is based on quite different implicit knowledge, so that European jazz improvisers become familiar with the sound of gospel music at a later period in their lives, if ever.

ied in different contexts" (1999: 144). Ford in this context also cites Bourdieu's term 'necessary improvisation' to describe this way of life (cf. ibid.). Christian faith has one of its core moments in the certitude that this process is possible neither by the sole activity of the subject nor by accident or determination but by the guidance of the Holy Spirit. Reciprocally, confidence in the Spirit is no anxious adherence to past expressions but the openness to the fresh and faithful presence.

A believer is a person who accepts that his or her implicit axioms should be congruent with God's story; this congruence is the opposite of uniformity and instead is the actual shape of a life lived in the presence of God. The uniqueness of a Christian life is grounded in being shaped by Christian tradition as the tradition of God's story, and equally in the improvisations of the individual believer who adopts, selects from, and transforms tradition in order to react to and live in his or her world in the presence of God.

Works Cited

Begbie, Jeremy (2000): Theology, Music, and Time, Cambridge: Cambridge UP.
—. (2005): "Theology and Music," in: David Ford/Rachel Muers (eds.), The Modern Theologians. An Introduction to Christian Theology Since 1918, 3rd ed., Malden: Blackwell, 719-735.
—. (2011): "Faithful Novelty. Why Artists and Pastors Need Each Other to Enrich the Life of the Church," in: Divinity Magazine (Fall), 5-9.
Benjamin, Walter (2005 [1936]): "The Work of Art in the Age of Mechanical Reproduction," in: Andrew Utterson (ed.), Technology and Culture. The Film Reader, London: Routledge, 105-26.
Coltrane, John (1965): Meditations. Impulse! Records.
Dolphy, Eric (1964): Last Date. Limelight Records.
Ford, David (1999): Self and Salvation. Being Transformed, Cambridge: Cambridge UP.
Gayle, Charles (1992): Repent. Knitting Factory Records.
—. (1993): Consecration. Black Saint.
—. (1995): Daily Bread. Black Saint.
Jazz à Porquerolles (2003): FRA, dir. Frank Cassenti.
Jennings, Willie James (2011): "Seeing God in Jazz. The Music of Jazz and the Art It Inspires Points to the Incarnation of God," in: Divinity Magazine (Fall), 13-15.
Lash, Nicholas (1986): "Performing the Scriptures," in: Nicholas Lash, Theology on the Way to Emmaus, London: SCM, 37-46.

Lindbeck, George A. (1984): The Nature of Doctrine. Religion and Theology in a Postliberal Age, Philadelphia: Westminster.

Link, Christian (1984): "Vita passiva. Rechtfertigung als Lebensvorgang," in: Evangelische Theologie 44, 315-351.

Matthes, Joachim (2005): Das Eigene und das Fremde. Gesammelte Aufsätze zu Gesellschaft, Kultur und Religion, Würzburg: Ergon.

Ritschl, Dietrich (1986): The Logic of Theology. A Brief Account of the Relationship between Basic Concepts in Theology, London: SCM.

—. (2008): "The Search for Implicit Axioms behind Doctrinal Texts," in: Dietrich Ritschl, Bildersprache und Argumente. Theologische Aufsätze, Neukirchen-Vluyn: Neukirchener, 111-123.

Schoberth, Ingrid (1992): Erinnerung als Praxis des Glaubens, München: Kaiser.

Schoberth, Wolfgang (2009): "Kulturhermeneutik und Religionsforschung. George A. Lindbecks Religionstheorie und das Verstehen christlicher Lehre," in: Gabriele Cappai/Shingo Shimada/Jürgen Straub (eds.), Interpretative Sozialforschung und Kulturanalyse. Hermeneutik und die komparative Analyse kulturellen Handelns, 1st ed., Bielefeld: transcript, 227-347.

Solothurnmann, Jürg (1977): "Zur Ästhetik der afro-amerikanischen Musik. Timbre – Geräusch – Emotion," in: Jazz-Forschung 9, 49-68.

Sparn, Walter (1990): "Implizite Axiome und impliziter Glaube. Eine Erinnerung und eine Nachfrage," in: Wolfgang Huber (ed.), Implizite Axiome. Tiefenstrukturen des Denkens und Handelns, München: Kaiser, 326-337.

Wells, Samuel (2004): Improvisation. The Drama of Christian Ethics, London: SPCK.

Wüstenberg, Ralf K. (2007): "Fides implicita 'revisited' – Versuch eines evangelischen Zugangs," in: Neue Zeitschrift für Systematische Theologie und Religionsphilosophie 49.1, 71-85.

Questions to Mark Johnson

In your work, you have constantly challenged the mind/body dichotomy and the philosophical conception of the relationship between feeling and thinking/knowledge. How exactly does bodily knowledge structure and influence how we make meaning and sense of the world?

I'm going to reverse the priorities within your question, because I think that experiencing meaning is prior to any acts of knowing. So, let's start with embodied meaning first. A good deal of my research has been devoted to exploring the way structures and processes of our embodied experience play a crucial role in how things stand forth and have meaning for us. Both phenomenological and cognitive science approaches have helped us appreciate the role of sensory-motor processes – which include qualitative and emotional dimensions, as well as image schematic structure – in shaping our conceptual systems. Meaning, therefore, cannot be limited to language, but rather reaches down into the visceral depths of our bodily interactions with our environment. As the American pragmatist philosopher John Dewey argued, we must stop over-intellectualizing experience and meaning, and we need to recognize the severe limitations of any philosophy that sees meaning as entirely linguistic, conceptual, and propositional. Instead, we need a theory of embodied meaning, thought, and language. Our capacities to conceptualize and reason presuppose prior processes of meaning making that emerge from our bodily engagements with our various structured environments. We take the measure of our world as much through body movements, felt qualities, and emotions, as we do through conceptual discriminations. Moreover, cognitive science research has revealed that most of our meaning-making goes on beneath our conscious awareness and involves structures of bodily experience that we acquire automatically and non-consciously just by living and acting in our surroundings.

We can now ask how embodied meaning becomes the basis for all our modes of knowing. Once you understand that meaning is grounded in our bodily experience and interpersonal interactions, you have to abandon any notion of a "God's Eye" or disembodied conception of knowledge. Rather than thinking of *knowledge* as a body of allegedly absolute and objective truths about reality, we need to focus, instead, on the acts and processes of *knowing*, which emerge from embodied and embedded communal inquiry. If we start with the fact that we are, first and foremost, meaning seekers and meaning makers, acting through our ongoing interactions with our environments, then knowledge takes on a different character than it has been thought to have. Instead of emphasizing knowledge as a body of propositional claims about the world, we should think of knowing as being able to function well in our world. William James and John Dewey proposed that we can claim to know something only insofar as we can operate on that understanding of our world in such a way that it continues to allow us to function, more or less successfully. *Knowing* is a way of being in and transforming our world that helps us develop a richer and more satisfactory relation to our world and other people. Therefore, knowing is a doing, an action, rather than a body of propositions that supposedly map onto a fixed and static world. Knowing doesn't just *describe* a pre-existing world, but rather *transforms* our relations to our world by giving us a different understanding of, and active relation to, our surroundings.

Therefore, from the perspective of our embodied minds, knowledge becomes a term of achievement. To say that our current understanding of our situation constitutes knowledge, amounts to saying that seeing our situation in a certain light helps us function more or less successfully, for now. If environmental conditions change, or if our interests and purposes as inquirers change, so too will what we think constitutes appropriate knowledge. However, one must always remember that there can never be anything absolute or complete and finished about any knowledge claims.

What role do our individual bodies play, i.e. to what degree is bodily knowledge and tacit knowledge gender specific and determined by cultural, social, and historical contexts?

Most of the research on embodied cognition assumes a more or less generic embodiment. It is assumed that there are some universal characteristics of human bodies that play a crucial role in how we experience and make sense of our world. If so, then our shared embodiment would provide supposedly universal structures of meaning and thought. There is *some* truth to this view. For example, our visual processing systems, our ability to experience sounds and to feel textures, our upright posture, our bodily symmetry, our use of our hands, our capacities for locomotion, our emotional processes – to name just a few – are capacities shared by most, but not all, humans. Consequently, it is no surprise that structures of our mundane sensory and motor experience play a huge role in how we experience meaning and how we understand our surroundings and other people. That is why natural languages around the world typically tend to have ways to indicate verticality, motion through space, spatial location, emotional valence, temporal change, and so forth that derive from our shared bodily perceptions, feelings, and actions.

However – and this is the crucial point – much embodied cognition research suffers from what Robin Zebrowski calls "the Myth of the Standard Body," which leads us to assume that our conceptual structures are grounded in the universal features of all human bodies. Zebrowski argues, to the contrary, that there are actually a wide variety of forms of human embodiment, and that any "standard body" is just a statistically determined norm that lies within a wide continuum of various forms of human embodiment. To state the obvious, different human bodies have different anatomical features that support different functions (e.g., insemination vs. egg production, giving birth, nursing an infant).

In addition to these anatomical/functional differences, there are also bound to be culturally different interpretations of even the most apparently universal image schemas, such as verticality, containment, and balance. To cite just one possible example, it is my experience that, although American, Japanese, and Chinese cultures all value balance, Japanese and Chinese cultures place far more emphasis on balance and emotional/psychological constraint and evenness than Americans tend to. There is a more fine-textured vocabulary related to various experiences of balance in those cultural traditions than one finds in America. Consequently, we tend to find universal bodily structures and processes that are, nevertheless, differently articulated in culturally different meaning complexes, institutions, and practices. Another example is that, while we would expect every culture and language to mark gender differences (at least partially tied to alleged sex differences), the vast range of differing interpretations and value judgments about gender distinctions across cultures is obvious and pervasive.

How do intermediary concepts like metaphors help us access or describe tacit knowledge? How can we approach this methodologically?

An analysis of conventional conceptual metaphors in a culture can provide profound insight into what constitutes knowledge within a given community of inquirers. Conceptual metaphors involve a cross-domain mapping of structures and relations from a body- and experience-based source domain to shape our understanding of a target domain. For example, the common and widespread KNOWING IS SEEING metaphor uses the objects, relations, and knowledge we have of a source domain (here, vision) to structure our conception of the target domain (here, the acquisition and growth of knowledge). We thus understand and talk about knowing in terms relevant to our experience of seeing, as in "I *see* what you mean," "That was an *illuminating* argument," "Descartes based knowledge on *clear and distinct* ideas," and "Those experiments *shed new light on quantum theory.*"

Now, the point I want to make is that we can therefore gain considerable insight into our tacit knowledge by analyzing the source domains of the conceptual metaphors we have for knowledge practices. Since these source domains provide the conceptual and inferential structure for our grasp of the target domain (here, a form of knowing), metaphor analysis allows us to discover the logic and inference structures operative in our deepest and most unconscious conceptions of knowledge and acts of knowing. In *Philosophy in the Flesh*, George Lakoff and I gave the detailed conceptual mappings for some of our most basic metaphors for mind and thought, and it turns out, as you would expect, that each of these metaphors carries with it its own distinct conception of knowing. Thus, visual metaphors will lead us to understand knowing as *seeing clearly and unmistakingly* some idea-object or relation of idea-objects. Tactile metaphors for knowing will treat knowledge as *touching and manipulating* idea-objects. The conception of thinking as metaphorical motion along a path leads to knowing as moving directly from one idea-location to an adjacent one. The metaphor of IDEAS AS FOOD leads to knowing as the cultivating, preparing, tasting, swallowing, and digesting of ideas (as food). In short, analysis of conceptual metaphors is an important source of understanding of our tacit modes of knowing and what a culture counts as knowledge.

You argue in The Meaning of the Body *that "an aesthetics of human understanding should become the basis for all philosophy, including metaphysics, theory of knowledge, logic, philosophy of mind and language, and value theory" (2007: x). How will such an aesthetics change theories of knowledge and how does it help us to understand tacit knowledge? How do you conceive of the role of literature, the arts, or music for research on tacit knowledge?*

This is a really big and complicated question, but I perhaps can make a few suggestions about what it means to take aesthetics seriously. In *The Meaning of the Body* I argued that aesthetics should not be construed, as it traditionally has been, as pertaining only to our creation, experience, and judging of art and beauty. Instead, we should follow pragmatist philosophy and contemporary cognitive neuroscience in realizing that aesthetic dimensions (such as qualities, images, image schemas, feelings, and emotions) should be seen as integral to our ability to have any sort of meaningful experience, appraisals, and thought. In other words, aesthetics pervades all aspects of human experience – art, science, politics, morality, economics, religion, technology – and covers all of the structures and processes by which anything can be meaningful and valuable to us.

One major implication of this recognition of the primacy of the aesthetic is the understanding that thinking and knowing are as much matters of feeling and emotional response as they are matters of conceptual and propositional inference. Another important implication is that there can be no absolute "fact-value" split, because all modes of knowing involve processes of evaluation and appraisal. To cite just one example of this significant observation, any form of knowing requires that we first decide which aspects of our environment should count as phenomena, data, and significant results. This requires valuation. Some of these values are selected automatically and unconsciously for us by the needs and demands of our bodily survival and maintenance. Other values will come from what our culture considers it important to explain, and what they will allow to count as a form of explanation or justification.

We can no longer sustain the illusions that thought and reason have nothing to do with feelings and emotions, that there are value-free modes of cognition, or that methods of inquiry can ignore the qualitative dimensions of experience. My preferred way to express this is to say that aesthetics reaches down into the depths of human meaning making, thinking, valuing, acting, and knowing. This is bound to be unsettling to those who want to retain traditional objectivist views of thought, knowledge, and reason, but such views are incompatible with what the cognitive sciences are learning about how humans constitute knowledge practices. The work of neuroscientists like Antonio Damasio is finally giving us new directions and tools for exploring the aesthetic dimensions of our tacit (and explicit) knowing, but we are only just beginning to explore the vast depths of our processes of knowing.

You have also raised the very big question of the role of the arts in how we know our world. What I've said in response to your earlier question about embodiment and tacit knowing should make it clear that the arts can give us a more expansive, rich, and deep understanding of our lives and our world than is possible through the selective abstractions that underlie the different sciences. You know that I am a big fan of the importance of the sciences for expanding and deepening our understanding of ourselves and our world, but there are limitations and partialities of every method of inquiry we have fashioned. Dewey argued that works of art do a better, less selective and abstractive, job than the various sciences when it comes to enacting for us concrete, lived situations with all their specificity, qualitative unity, and depths of meaning. It is well known that through fictional narratives, for example, we are imaginatively immersed in the concrete complexity of human life, in a way that makes it possible for us to encounter more of what is important and relevant to, say, moral considerations. Artworks don't merely *re-present* life situations; rather, they *enact* situations with all their detail in a way that enriches our grasp of meaning.

According to your theory, also spirituality and faith have to be viewed as embodied: How would you describe the nexus between embodiment, tacit knowledge, and faith?

I have to confess that I can find no evidence, either experientially or scientifically, for the traditional theological view of humans as consisting of a transcendent, disembodied mind or soul that is somehow temporarily yoked to a finite material, passionate body. We are inescapably bodily creatures, but this does not mean that we are merely animate lumps of matter, for we are not just physical, biological organisms, but rather are also constituted by our interpersonal relations and cultural embeddedness. However, rejecting a dualistic view of the self does not mean that we can have no experience and sense of spirituality. On the contrary, there are various traditions of spirituality that do not presuppose a dualistic metaphysics, but rather see humans as complex embodied cultural creatures in ongoing interaction with their multi-layered (material, interpersonal, gendered, racialized, and cultural) environments. There are traditions of embodied spirituality to be found within Buddhism, Quakerism, pragmatism, and body-work practices that locate our spiritual home within *this* world, rather than in some transcendent or eternal realm. In these traditions spirituality is tied to our experience of ourselves as part of, and contributory to, a more comprehensive creative process that is always at risk and always changing.

I am partial to John Dewey's notion of faith as directed toward the possibilities of human intelligence and imagination to continuously transform our world for the better. Instead of faith in some otherworldly ideal realm, Dewey's faith and hope lies in the fact that humans are part of an ongoing creative temporal process in a way that human contributions, when intelligently guided, can actually help make the world better. Perhaps the most appropriate metaphors for this transformative process would be built around source domains pertaining to artful making and imaginative creation. Living well and rightly would be a project of ongoing aesthetic creation and enhancement of experience through growth of meaning and value.

In the last decades, the diagnosis of a theory deficit has led scholars from different disciplines (including sociology, philosophy, and cultural studies) to introduce new terms and to proclaim several theoretical "turns;" for example, issues such as space, performativity, materiality, or affect have been programmatically included into theoretical and methodological discourse. Does the current proliferation of theories about tacit knowledge or implicit understanding – in your opinion – constitute another "turn" or even "paradigm shift," and how does the debate about tacit knowledge relate to emerging fields and proclaimed turns including, for example, the "affect turn" or current research on "public feeling"?

I regard all of these "turns" as most welcome contributions to a very much enriched conception of human mind, thought, language, and value. All of the emphases you mention are finally opening up hitherto neglected or under-appreciated aspects of human mind and experience that promise to dramatically expand our understanding of what it means to be human. We haven't yet been able to overcome the deeply entrenched dualist and disembodied conceptions of mind, but there is a growing chorus of voices, from different perspectives and approaches, showing that we have to recognize the central role of the body in how we experience and make meaning, how we think, and what we count as knowledge. Different approaches critique different parts of the traditional disembodied view, but together they are opening new horizons that have to be pursued in order to get an adequate understanding of humanity. I see each of these approaches as focusing our attention on one or more of the previously overlooked or denigrated aspects of our embodiment. I happen to be particularly interested right now in the affective turn, as you name it, because it reveals how emotional response patterns and feelings operate to determine what matters to us and how we interact with and transform our surroundings, both physical and cultural. So, from my perspective, these are all major advances toward the recognition of our embodied, embedded, and enactive engagement with our environment.

It seems fair to call this series of changes in perspective an emerging paradigm shift, of sorts, but we have to remember that there is no monolithic core of methods, perspectives, and practices here, but rather a diverse set of loosely related, and sometimes not entirely consistent, orientations and views. This increasing attention to the embodiment of meaning, knowledge, and value is salutary, but we must not think that dualistic, disembodied views are simply going to fade away. We need to keep striving for a deeper, more comprehensive, and more coherent understanding of what it means for humans to be embodied enactive creatures in a changing world.

Questions by Katharina Gerund

List of Contributors

Frank Adloff is professor of sociological theory and cultural sociology at FAU Erlangen-Nürnberg.

Alexander Antony is a doctoral candidate in sociology and a fellow of the interdisciplinary doctoral program "Presence and Tacit Knowledge" at FAU Erlangen-Nürnberg.

Christoph Ernst is assistant professor ("Wissenschaftlicher Mitarbeiter") of media studies at FAU Erlangen-Nürnberg.

Katharina Gerund is coordinator of the interdisciplinary doctoral program "Presence and Tacit Knowledge" at FAU Erlangen-Nürnberg.

Michael Hubrich is a doctoral candidate in sociology and a fellow of the interdisciplinary doctoral program "Presence and Tacit Knowledge" at FAU Erlangen-Nürnberg.

Mark L. Johnson is Philip K. Knight professor of liberal arts and sciences in the department of philosophy at the University of Oregon.

David Kaldewey is junior professor for science studies and sociological theory at the "Forum Internationale Wissenschaft", University of Bonn.

Stephen Koetzing is a doctoral candidate in American studies and a fellow of the interdisciplinary doctoral program "Presence and Tacit Knowledge" at FAU Erlangen-Nürnberg.

Jens Loenhoff is professor of communication studies at the University of Duisburg-Essen.

Heike Paul is professor and chair of American studies at FAU Erlangen-Nürnberg.

Joachim Renn is professor of sociological theory at the University of Münster.

Theodore R. Schatzki is professor of philosophy and geography and senior associate dean in the College of Arts & Sciences at the University of Kentucky.

Wolfgang Schoberth is professor of systematic theology at FAU Erlangen-Nürnberg.

Rainer Schützeichel is professor of sociology at the University of Bielefeld.

Alexis Shotwell is an associate professor in the department of sociology and anthopology at Carleton University in Ottawa.

Loïc Wacquant is professor of sociology at the University of California, Berkeley, and researcher at the Centre européen de sociologie et de science politique, Paris.